THE SPRINGTIME OF FREEDOM

P.

Ironside M

b

Alu

Miss Linc

PRINTED IN U.S.A.

THE SPRINGTIME
OF FREEDOM

Evolution of Developing Societies

WILLIAM McCORD

NEW YORK OXFORD UNIVERSITY PRESS 1965

25481

For my Grand-father, who fought to free the slaves in America's Civil War . . .

For my brother, who died in the fight against fascism . . .

For my friends, who today struggle to extend the realm of freedom from Mississippi to New Delhi . . .

For my sons, who, I trust, will continue in their tradition and combat oppression wherever it may exist in the world.

CONTENTS

FOREWORD

When Professor William McCord asked me to write a foreword to his book *The Springtime of Freedom*, I gladly accepted for various reasons. The first of them was sentimental and personal. McCord's work impressed me as an achievement which I myself would have loved to realize—and would have been proud to have realized—if I were today in my thirties and not in my seventies. For when I was in my thirties I was concerned with the "springtime of freedom" at a time when its coming was hardly discerned by anyone. Then I wrote a number of books, now long out of print and outdated by the unexpectedly rapid march of events, from *A History of Nationalism in the East* (meaning by the word "East," of course, Asia, not Eastern Europe), which I started to write in London in 1923, to *Western Civilization in the Near East*, which was completed in Jerusalem in 1932 under its original title *Die Europäisierung des Orients*.

Now thirty years later the "springtime of freedom" which I then foresaw has come. It started in 1946-47 when the United States set the Philippine Islands free and when, on a much broader basis, England, the motherland of modern liberty, did the same in India, Pakistan, Burma, and Ceylon. Ten years later this process reached its second stage: In 1956 the last old-fashioned imperialist aggression against Egypt not only came to naught, but, a predictable result, fortified the native regime; one year later Britain granted independence to Ghana; and in 1962, after eight years of the most oppressive struggle which, at least temporarily, darkened democracy in France, Algeria achieved independence. But the granting of independence or the achievement of nationhood did not solve the problems, as some had hoped, any more than it did in Europe, where a similar process took place between the 1860's and the 1920's.

Freedom, as understood in the English-speaking countries of modern times, is a difficult growth, especially in a soil unprepared for it by past history. The difficulty is today increased by the all-inclusive revolution in political thought and social structure, in ideas and in ways of life, which is going on everywhere. I have tried lately to outline its roots and its fundamental issues in a short book *The Age of Nationalism. The First Era of Global History* (1962) and to relate the observations of my lifetime to this process in a brief autobiography which I called *Living in a World Revolution* (1964). Such a transformation, unique in its dizzying speed and all-encompassing universality, produces unprecedented crises and profound unrest and arouses exaggerated hopes and fears. We may not have the answers to all its challenges; many of its complex problems will admit only of very imperfect solutions and some of none, at least in any foreseeable future; but the task is to try to understand and to ask some of the right questions.

Better than any other single book of which I know, McCord's work achieves this goal. In spite of his youth—he is in his early thirties—Professor McCord has published a great number of books and articles in empirical sociology and the other social sciences. Brought up in the methods of contemporary American social science, he has also gained the ability of seeing broad human issues in all their complexity and has become conscious of the need for "value-laden statements." Such statements may be out of place in the natural sciences but are inevitable—though they may be hidden—in a work of scholarship which deals with people, their activities, aspirations, and predicaments. It is this refreshing element of personal involvement which makes the book that I was asked to introduce not only informative, but thought-stimulating and even exciting reading. The problems of the global revolution which has emerged from the period of the world wars, which started half a century ago, are brought to life with the warmth and immediacy of an observer who, trained as a scholar and well versed in the scholarly literature of the social sciences, knows of the transitional character of his observations and the limitations of his, and anyone's, judgments.

When I came to the United States in 1931, I found among college youth and their teachers little understanding for the growing interdependence of peoples everywhere and for the demands of freedom, equality, and dignity, which, due to the spread of modern Western ideas, were then agitating Chinese and Indians, Arabs and Africans.

(This happened at a time when many people on the European continent turned to an excessive, aggressive, and self-centered nationalism and when their scholars rejected with scorn and derision the modern Western ideas and the heritage of the Enlightenment.) Professor McCord's book exemplifies the revolutionary change which has taken place in the American consciousness in the last three decades and the regained vitality of modern Western civilization. This civilization has been called a civilization of dialogue, of an open mind and of an open society. To its continuing dialogue Professor McCord's book which, as he remarks, will arouse controversy has made an important and refreshing contribution.

Hans Kohn

Center for Advanced Studies
Wesleyan University
Middletown, Connecticut

PART ONE

Portrait of Transitional Man

Introduction

BREAD OR FREEDOM

> The history of the world is none other than the progress of the
> consciousness of freedom.
>
> FRIEDRICH HEGEL

With a passion unequaled in past centuries, the peoples of the underdeveloped world today demand freedom and bread. They want bread
in the most fundamental of ways: food, shelter, clothes, and health.
The Indian peasant desires more than his two bowls of rice a day. The
Egyptian father wants his newborn child to avoid, somehow, the
trachoma which has afflicted 80 per cent of the population, and he
thinks that this is now possible. The Nigerian mother is desperately
eager for her children to read. She believes, for the first time, that they
have a *right* to education. And the more ambitious may dream of shirts
and shoes, radios and bicycles, a bed and a table. All are simple wants,
yet immensely difficult to satisfy on a per capita income of $120 in
Egypt, $70 in Nigeria, and $55 a year in India.

They want "freedom," too—perhaps not always the "Western" freedom to vote for competitive political parties—but certainly, universally,
they wish to be free of colonial rule, of the arbitrary power of landlords, of the unjust decisions of corrupt judges, of the insidious threat
of political informers. The Ghanaian journalist wants the power to
criticize the government without fear of imprisonment; the Arab peasant desires redress against the petty harassments of local police officials;

3

the Indian farmer wants to rescue his land from its usurpation by absentee moneylenders.

Increasingly, politicians and generals, intellectuals and new "redeemers" proclaim to their peoples that freedom—at least the "corrupt" formal freedoms of the West—must be sacrificed in the drive for economic abundance. They claim that only an authoritarian government,* master of a centralized economy and unified society, can provide the bread so ardently desired.

This argument, that only an authoritarian regime can flourish, was forcefully presented to me one day in 1961 by several members of Ghana's parliament. Resting after a tour of government buildings, we sat in the impressive hall of parliament, before the great mace (a symbol, ironic in that context, of parliament's power). Outside stood a more than life-sized statue of Nkrumah, draped in realistic clothes which fluttered in the wind. Inscribed on its base was Nkrumah's proclamation: "Seek ye first the political kingdom and all other things will be added unto it." Ghana's political kingdom of that era was one in which all power rested with the "saviour." The free press and an

---

* At the risk of being pedantic, I should define "authoritarian," a term which will recur throughout the book. I conceive political societies as arranged on a spectrum stretching between a "liberal" polity and an "authoritarian" one. At its most extreme, an authoritarian society exhibits definite institutional characteristics: (1) a small elite makes all political decisions without any institutionalized means of recourse to the people's will; (2) the government refuses to recognize a rule of law superior to its whims; (3) the government treats all organizations as ultimately members of the same political body and as subject to the government's directions; (4) the government forbids criticism in the press, pulpit, or open assembly; (5) the government does not allow any right to privacy, for in theory, a man's work, home, and family should be in its service. As for a "liberal" society, I can think of no better criteria than Jefferson's: "Equal and exact justice to all men of whatever state or persuasion, religious or political . . . freedom of religion, freedom of the press, freedom of the person under habeas corpus; and trial by juries impartially selected—these principles form the bright constellation which has gone before us, and guided our steps through an age of revolution and reformation." Scandinavian countries approach most closely to this ideal.

Two qualifications should be added: In the underdeveloped world, no nation fully conforms to either of these ideal types. Even China, which most closely adheres to the authoritarian model, does allow "people's assemblies" that reflect popular will and partially influence the elite's decisions. And Mexico, normally considered a liberal democracy, actually functions as a one-party state whose jails house many a political prisoner. It should also be added that centralized state control over an economy does not necessarily make a nation *politically* authoritarian (although, as I shall argue, economic collectivism often melds into political authoritarianism).

independent judiciary had been crushed, opposition leaders languished in jail, and only an occasional bomb disturbed the monolith.

When I prodded my guides about the desirability of such repression, one replied: "We must govern an uneducated, superstitious, violent people, a nation divided by tribal, religious, and economic conflicts. Democracy, in your Western sense, requires a literate, sophisticated, united people, well practiced in self government. This we lack. Further, the opposition has resorted to violence and we must, of course, reply with violence. Above all, we wish to modernize our society and end poverty, disease, and ignorance for all time. How could we possibly do this if every bush farmer were given the power to decide whether to build the Volta Dam or accept an increase in taxes, or agree to a reduction in consumer imports?"

Many Western intellectuals, probably a majority, subscribe to a similar pessimism. Thus, Sidney Lens, a writer and labor leader widely traveled in the developing nations, has concluded that the social-economic revolution so universally desired in these countries simply cannot be reconciled with democracy:

> *Grant full political democracy in any of the harassed new lands and the government soon would be overthrown by reactionary elements . . . the fact is that fully advanced democracy, of the type we have established in the West, is possible only if Castro were to abandon the revolution itself. The same can be said of Nkrumah, Nasser, Sékou Touré, the Nigerians, and many others.*[1]

Those who adhere to this opinion cling to the tattered hope that a new form of freedom—an "African" democracy, an "Arab Socialism," an Indonesian middle way will emerge. After years of African study, Smith Hempstone has argued:

> *All that can be said at this juncture is that Western Democracy is not going to work in Africa. . . . A new synthesis is in the making and something new in political organization is about to emerge, an "Afrocratic" system which utilizes the form but not the substance of democracy and draws much of its inspiration from indigenous institutions.*[2]

Everywhere I journeyed I heard the same refrain, most resoundingly in those nations which had best managed to construct a liberal democracy. Harried British civil servants, deserting Nigeria after years of work, trembled over the divisive tribal conflicts which threatened to tear apart that nation's fragile federalism. Certain Indian businessmen bitterly complained that every M.P. could be "bought" by private interests and that democracy was merely a façade hiding corruption. Many Philippine intellectuals decried the gulf between the poverty of the peasants and the glamorous opulence of Manila's elite. How long, they asked, would the people tolerate a political system which allowed such suffering amidst such luxury?

Can one wonder, then, that Robert Heilbroner, one of our most perceptive social commentators, has contended, "Taking the long perspective of the decades ahead it is difficult to ignore the relative 'efficiency' of authoritarian over parliamentary regimes as a means of inaugurating growth." [3] With good reason, he fears that the stirrings of change throughout the underdeveloped world mark "the commencement of a chapter of tragedy and sorrow." [4]

Here I wish to inquire about the validity of these views. Can the emerging nations end the tyranny of the stomach without resorting to the tyranny of the slave camp? Can political freedoms survive while a people drives itself from economic stagnation to growth? Can a self-sustaining economic advance even begin within the framework of freedoms which we loosely call "liberal democracy"?

It is immodesty of the highest order to suggest that one has discovered some set of policies which might assure freedom from want as well as freedom from tyranny. And it would be even greater folly to presume that the same formula could fit an Ashanti tribal order and the patron system in Brazil, the overstuffed island of Java and the nomadic peoples lightly sprinkled over northern Nigeria.

Yet, no one who has visited the new nations can fail to notice a fundamental, discouraging sameness to their basic problems: devastating poverty plus social obscurantism plus the lure (or reality) of political despotism. Nor can one deny the immense appeal of an elitist, authoritarian ideology to the intellectuals of these countries. The midcentury history of the emerging nations would seem to proclaim, as did events in the Europe of the 1930's and 1940's, that authoritarianism is the wave of the future. Few in the West, and even fewer in the developing nations can foresee the means by which economic growth can occur without recourse to a Mao, Castro, or Nkrumah.

Is this the whole story? I think not. This book is an attempt to demonstrate that political tyranny and economic centralization are *not* the only paths for the developing nations. Another alternative exists, an approach which might justly be called "pluralism"—a policy which would diffuse both economic and political power as widely as possible throughout the society.

While such a pluralistic program offers substantial hope that freedom can grow in the new nations, the whole drift of modern history, it is well to remember, has been leading toward authoritarianism in the new nations. The last two decades have marked an exchange of one dictatorship for another in China, the collapse of effete, decadent parliaments in the Middle East and Asia, the ascent of charismatic figures, and the assumption of power by generals and bureaucrats throughout the world.

I differ from the prophets of doom, however, in two important respects. I believe neither that these developments were unavoidable nor that they must continue in the future. The drift to authoritarianism is, in large part, the result of a "self-fulfilling prophecy" promulgated by intellectuals. In the developing nations, in the absence of an informed public opinion, the beliefs of a small intellectual elite exert paramount influence. Too often, the elite's opinion that tyranny must facilitate and accompany a drive to economic abundance has drawn its sustenance from a misreading of history. The belief rests on questionable generalizations about the "preconditions" of economic improvement and the "prerequisites" of liberal democracy. It is predicated upon an unarticulated or, at best, utopian vision of the good society.

In the following pages I will address myself to an examination of these generalizations, most particularly to the basic premise of the authoritarians: the belief that the underdeveloped masses cannot rule themselves but must be herded by benevolent dictators who will guide them to economic affluence and will then, ultimately, relinquish power. I believe that this view both contradicts history and libels the capacities of the "new peoples." As a Ghanaian correspondent recently wrote me:

> . . . *abettors of Nkrumah's regime implicitly tell us that we are incapable of appreciating . . . values based on the belief in the sanctity of human life and personal freedom. They do not realize what an insult this is to some of us, who have not only had the benefit of Western education, but who have had personal experience of the values which informed our most primitive governmental arrangements, before the white man set foot in Ghana, values which went into the evolution of central government from the beginning of this century, values which fostered the move for independence in the late forties and early fifties, values caricatured and betrayed by Nkrumah's regime.*
>
> *In short, values derived from the belief that above everything else, men matter.*

There is, indeed, a reservoir of freedom in many of the emerging nations: a concern for individual rights and personal dignity derived not only from the West but from Ashoka and Ibn Khaldun, Buddhistic as well as Ibo traditions. Whether this urge to freedom can prevail against the lure of authoritarianism is, today, in doubt. How the issue will be resolved depends on the effectiveness with which the developing countries confront their social, economic, and political challenges.

The Social Challenge

> As a man casts off worn-out garments and takes others that are new, even so the embodied one casts off worn-out bodies and passes on to others new.
>
> BHAGAVAD-GITA, 500 B.C.

In the summer of 1962 I visited a village, set in the great alluvial plain which surrounds New Delhi. The head man—a mustached, grave person, dressed in shorts, undershirt, and a hand-spun shawl—greeted me with the delightful graciousness so characteristic of Indian villagers. He proudly displayed a bare school room, a council hall which doubled as a clinic, and a small factory where the people manufactured tools and furniture.

Several of his aides pulled some chairs together, and we sat in the middle of the workshop, perhaps the coolest spot in the small town. While the women covered their faces and hid, a knot of children and young men gathered at a respectful distance to watch the curious visitation of a live American.

The leader's village had been one of the first participants in a "block" development plan and had, for ten years, received the ministrations of agricultural advisers, technicians from the Small Industries Board and a team from the Ford Foundation which had unsuccessfully attempted to build an electric generator powered by bullocks. Ten per cent of its 1500 people could read newspapers; some of the younger men worked in the city; and posters of Nehru interspersed with DDT signs covered the mud walls.

At the center of this development stood the head man, "Mr. Krishna." As the elected leader of the village *panchayat* (town council), he formed a critical link in the political chain joining the village with the district, regional, and national centers of influence. As the head of the local co-operative, he led his neighbors in initiating economic improvement. In several important ways, then, the hopes for political and economic modernization of the village rested with Mr. Krishna.

Yet, while an agent of innovation, he still lived in a traditional social universe, little affected by modern life. In significant ways, this traditional culture blocked his effective participation either in economic development or in India's liberal democracy.

I asked him about politics, for example, and posed that universal question in the India of 1962: "What will happen after Nehru?" The passing of Nehru from the political scene would not distress him, he responded, for Nehru's successor would govern the nation with ability. His guess as to the successor? There could be no question about that, he felt, for Nehru, as a good father, must have raised fine sons. And, in Mr. Krishna's view of politics, the deserving son always inherited his father's power. The introduction of an election system had little changed his belief that political influence flowed naturally through channels of inheritance.

The strenuous government efforts to alter the caste system had also failed to change his traditional attitudes. He noted that no intermarriage had occurred in his village and that the untouchables still drew their water from separate, "impure" wells. "Perhaps this will change," he commented, "especially if they get more money. But for now, they know their place, we know ours . . . they are happy doing their proper job, rather than longing to take over that of another."

I inquired, too, about the birth-control campaign, a massive propaganda effort to halt the population growth which erodes India's economic advances. Trucks had visited the village, bearing placards which pleaded "Choice, not chance!" Mr. Krishna knew and approved of the government's intentions. He demonstrated a surprisingly sophisticated knowledge of the economic havoc wrought by uncontrolled breeding. When I asked him about the success of the plan, however, he responded that the village produced as many children as ever. He attributed the failure of birth control to a government policy restricting the making of *ghee*. When I looked dubious, he added, "Didn't you know? The man who eats *ghee* has fewer children—if we don't get *ghee*, we keep on having babies."

Like so many in the underdeveloped world, Mr. Krishna was a transitional man, a strange mixture of the new and the old. He lives in a society which is aware of the modern world, of elections and tractors and newspapers. But it is also one which tenaciously preserves traditional attitudes and superstitions, traditional social relationships and world views.

As we parted, he told me that the brightest boy in the village had been sent to an American university to complete his education. The villagers had pooled their resources to furnish the money to supplement the boy's fellowship. After four years, the student had not returned but had settled comfortably in Boston. "He even bought a car," Mr. Krishna added ruefully, but with a wry smile, "I guess he wanted to live like the natives."

Increasingly, for good or ill, the emerging peoples desire to live in their homes like the "American native" does in his. Yet so much in their traditional culture and social structure inhibits the achievement of this goal. One cannot have a real democracy in India unless Mr. Krishna comes to understand the meaning of elections; one cannot create "equal opportunity" if Mr. Krishna continues to believe that fate has ordained the *harijans*' (untouchables') suffering; one cannot construct a modern economy unless Mr. Krishna realizes that contraceptives and not *ghee* influence birth rates.

This does not mean that traditional society must be utterly destroyed. A peasant society provides a base of co-operation and security which cannot easily be replaced in the modern world. It offers, above all, a framework of meaning and significance to the individual. To destroy deliberately these virtues in an unthinking drive for modernity would be regrettable. Nevertheless, certain social changes—put in motion by education, persuasion, the law, or simply economic evolution itself—must accompany the creation of a politically free, economically vigorous society.

This is the first challenge: to construct a society receptive to modernization without utterly destroying traditional civilizations.

The Economic Challenge

> Hundreds of millions of people, whose forebears patiently accepted lives of misery are involved in . . . "the revolution of rising expectations." What had been a distant dream has now become a passionate demand.
>
> PAUL HOFFMAN

The money spent on advertising alone in America each year could sustain all of the people in tropical Africa. So, too, could the income expended on American women's cosmetics.

America's defense budget is 60 per cent greater than India's entire national income, although India's population is two and one-half times that of America.

Parents in the developing nations can anticipate that half of their children will die before the age of ten.

Each night in Calcutta, 250,000 people sleep on the streets.

Latin America, at its current rate of development, will require 352 years to achieve one-third of the present level of wealth in the United States.

The impact of such poverty can hardly be imagined by the Westerner; it must be seen to be comprehended. Before grasping the scope of suffering in the developing nations, one must have the shattering experience of watching urban workers in Mexico City seeking food in the garbage pails of the rich, or of visiting African villages where everyone had malaria, or of seeing Middle Eastern workshops where small children work fourteen hours a day, their eyes almost blinded with flies.

The scale of poverty in these nations was illustrated for me, most directly and personally, while visiting a village in the Uttar Pradesh region of India. An untouchable, clad in rags and covered with open sores, knelt over a pile of raw cow dung, fingering it meticulously. He stopped every so often to drop a piece of it in a little bag. I asked the young doctor by my side, a recent graduate who had altruistically volunteered for a tour of duty in the village, what the *harijan* was doing. He replied rather apologetically that the man collected dung for the village fires, but before burning it, he picked out pieces of grain which the cows did not entirely digest. "He and his family eat it," the doctor said, and then coloring, added, "But come, let me show you the new building for our school and clinic." We passed into a small hospital where the doctor proudly exhibited sterilizing equipment, a modern operating room, and a storehouse of drugs furnished by American aid.

This contrast symbolizes the contradictions which exist throughout the underdeveloped world: a peasant, carrying out a traditional, degrading task as his ancestors had done for centuries, and a sophisticated physician attempting to bring the village into twentieth-century life. Almost universally, the leaders of the emerging nations have announced their dedication to the goal of ending this curse of poverty. Many have created impressive five-year plans devoted to changing drastically the nature of their economies.

Nigeria, for example, is a huge country blessed with unused land, impressive mineral reserves, and untapped sources of energy. An ambitious plan adopted in 1962 will attempt to expend over a billion dollars in a massive attempt, the largest in Africa, to provide the framework of economic advance. The problems that faced Nigeria's economic planners ranged from the minuscule to the gigantic. I visited the

planning ministry, for example, on the day before the new plan was
to be submitted to the National Planning Council. An assistant rushed
into the office of Wolfgang Stopler, the brilliant American economist
and temporary adviser to the government. Stopler asked for some basic
statistics on capital investment. "We just don't have them," his young
aide replied, "perhaps we might call the regional offices." (Nigeria, at
the time, was divided into several, semi-autonomous regions, each with
its own economic planning ministry, guarding its prerogatives jealously.) "We might find out how much each of them has spent—if they
would release the information," the aide suggested apologetically. On
this shaky scaffolding, Nigeria's economic fate for the next ten years
had to be projected.

At every stage, Nigeria's planners grappled with critical problems.
Where to find the money? In an economy already squeezed to the subsistence level, where could one discover the capital necessary for any
type of economic growth? For every dollar of improvement in production, three or four dollars of capital must be invested. Without stepping up the process of capital formation, this rather grim requirement
could not be met.

Even assuming that money could be pumped into the economy,
where would be the men to run it? Modest estimates indicated that
Nigeria would need at least 20,000 new managers, technicians, and
scientists. But where was a largely illiterate nation to find such men?

How should the nation allocate its limited resources? Do you begin
with schools, health facilities, and improved farming, following eminent economist Jacob Viner's belief that, "The first requirements for
high labour productivity under modern conditions are that the masses
of the population shall be literate, healthy, and sufficiently well fed to
be strong and energetic. In many countries, if this were achieved, all
else necessary for rapid economic development would come readily and
easily of itself." [5] Should you, in contrast, concentrate on activities
more directly productive to the nation's economic capacity? And, if so,
what type of production—heavy industry or consumer industry? Factories or a Niger River Project? Commodity production for export or
improvements in domestic agriculture?

In the long run, of course, investments complement each other, but
the basic problem is that the vicious circle of poverty must somehow be
breeched immediately, not in some far-off future. The people will not
tolerate indefinite delays. Assume, for example, that economists decide
that Nigeria could make reasonable use of a tin smelter. Such an industry could produce goods (including the ubiquitous tin roofs of

Nigeria), it could provide work, and it could aid in solving the balance of payments problem by replacing imports with domestic products. Then assume that some money has been laid away for investment. Where should it go? To building the smelter itself? Or, first, to training the workers and engineers who will be required? Or, perhaps, to extending the road system, since somehow the new goods must be transported to market? Or should agricultural development precede all else, since the tin workers, teachers, engineers, and road workers must be fed? A choice has to be made, since there is not money available for every plan: each dollar spent on a school means that much less for agriculture, or smelters, or roads.

Further, in a democratic nation such as Nigeria was in 1961, political and social factors greatly complicate economic decisions. If the North gets a new tin smelter, the West feels slighted unless it can share in the development. If the Western region builds a new technical institute, the East demands one, too. Parents riot in the East when the regional government, down to its last penny, must impose a school tuition fee. Political orators demand the abolition of private industry and foreign investments, although these may be the only instruments available for creating a new industry. Even the simplest of economic decisions involves counterbalancing a number of social and political pressures.

Herein lies the basic economic appeal of authoritarianism. An authoritarian government can prosecute its plan of development with a ruthlessness eschewed by democratic states. It promises to avoid the compromises, inefficiencies, and hesitations supposedly inherent in liberal democracy. And while this claim has often been demonstrably false, it holds out a promise of salvation.

This represents the second challenge: how to make the bitter choices involved in economic growth without recourse to political tyranny.

The Political Challenge

> My legacy to India? Hopefully, it is 400,000,000 people capable of governing themselves.
>
> JAWAHARLAL NEHRU

By whatever method, leaders in the developing nations must assure the legitimacy of the state. As Seymour Martin Lipset has ably argued, the system has "to engender and maintain the belief that the existing political institutions are the most appropriate ones for the society." [6] Too often in the new nations, national borders conform to the accidents of colonial history rather than to linguistic, ethnic, religious, or economic groupings. Somehow, the people's allegiance has to be transferred, at least partially, from the subgroup to the national state; somehow, ways have to be found to envelop the laws, policies, and actions of the national government in the mantle of legitimacy. The linguistic riots in India, the tribal conflicts of Africa, the armed revolts in South-East Asia reveal the enormity of this problem.

Both traditional and new social groups must also be integrated into a workable political system. In a period of rapid social change, this represents a formidable political problem, for as Tocqueville pointed out, ". . . epochs sometimes occur in the life of a nation when the old customs of a people are changed, public morality is destroyed, religious belief shaken and the spell of tradition broken." In such a time, "neither the instinctive patriotism of a monarchy nor the reflecting patriotism of a republic" can prevail.[7] For political leaders who desire economic and social change, a battle must be mounted on two fronts. On the one hand, the resistance of traditional groups to economic change must be overcome, without totally alienating them from the state. On the other hand, the claims of new social groups (Westernized intellectuals, trade unions, or newly founded peasant associations) must be juggled in a way that such groups, too, will refrain from revolution.

And of course, in any state, public order and stability have to be maintained. In Africa, where some parliaments collapse in fist fights; in India, where students burn streetcars in protest against higher fares; in Venezuela, where the President carries scars from numerous assassination attempts—in these restless countries, the sheer maintenance of public order assumes high priority. While economically advanced nations such as France have not totally solved the problem, the situation in the newer countries seems even more precarious.

Again, on the political level, authoritarianism exerts a forceful appeal to statesmen faced with such problems. For it appears far easier to crush traditional groups than to contend with them peacefully; Cuba's forceful confiscation of land is a quicker method of rural change than Venezuela's gradual plan of compensated land reform. It seems simpler to transform all trade unions and co-operatives into instruments of a single party, as Nkrumah has done, than to attempt to meet all the conflicting claims of such groups, as Nehru has attempted. To bestow legitimacy on the state through means of irrational indoctrination and an intolerant nationalism (à la Sukarno) has more appeal than slowly building national unity through education, as some Nigerian leaders have tried. Throughout the developing world, coercion, not persuasion, seems to offer the surest path to political stability.

Thus, for the liberal or social democrats of developing nations, the difficulties would, indeed, seem formidable. They must strive to conquer the social and economic challenges while simultaneously sustaining the rule of law, preserving personal liberties, and offering the people the widest possible role in governing themselves. There are few precedents for such an ambitious undertaking. In the West's evolution, liberal democracy generally came as the culmination of a long process of social and economic change—a capstone to the alterations wrought by the Renaissance and Reformation, by the Enlightenment and the Industrial Revolution. As Aneurin Bevan has commented, "It is highly doubtful whether the achievements of the Industrial Revolution would have been permitted if the franchise had been universal. It is very doubtful because a great deal of the capital aggregations that we are at present enjoying are the results of the wages that our fathers went without." [8]

Launched on an enterprise never before attempted, as the men of the developing countries are, even the strongest of nerves may falter. "Can we imagine a sequence of events that might lead eventually to industrialization of all peoples of the world?" Harrison Brown has asked, "Can we further imagine political, economic, and social structures that would permit the resultant society to maintain a long-range stability? When we enumerate all the difficulties in which the human species can become embroiled, it would appear a priori that the probability of successful transition along any path would be extremely small." [9]

Yet, as even Marx conceded, men make their own history. Committed to liberty, clear in their understanding of the issues, willing to bear certain sacrifices, the men of the emerging nations can forge a history which will offer them both bread and freedom. This book is an attempt to aid such men of good will as they navigate the treacherous passages of development.

Transition

> Their culture is "in transition," meaning that it is going to hell
> in a handbasket before the onslaught of the Age of Technology.
> OLIVER LaFARGE, describing
> contemporary Mexicans

Carolina Maria de Jesus tried to raise her illegitimate children in one
of the slums which disfigure São Paulo's opulence. Like many of her
neighbors, she lived in a cardboard shack, earned a few cruzeiros a day
collecting waste paper, and found her most succulent meals in the
bones discarded by a nearby butcher. Unlike her fellow victims, Carolina wanted to write. When she composed poems or novels, she was
"in a golden place, with crystal windows and silver chandeliers. My
dress was finest satin and diamonds set shining in my black hair. Then
I put away my book and the smells came in through the rotting walls
and rats ran over my feet. My satin turned to rags and the only thing
shining in my hair were lice." [10]

She kept a daily journal which tersely recorded her misery. During
election campaigns, she wrote in *Child of the Dark*, the politicians
condescended to visit her *favela* (slum). They distributed bread and
promises, heady words and optimism. After election, they hastily re-
treated to the city's healthier quarters, leaving the suffering *favelados*
unchanged. In her despair, she cried out, "Brazil needs to be led by
a person who has known hunger. Hunger is also a teacher. . . . Those
who govern our country are those who have money, who don't know
what hunger is, or pain or poverty." [11] And again, when a kindly police
officer advised her that the slum was an "unfortunate" environment
for her children, she exclaimed, ". . . if he knows this why doesn't he
make a report and send it to the politicians? To Janio Quadros, Ku-
bitschek, and Dr. Adhemar de Barros? Now he tells me this, I a poor
garbage collector. I can't even solve my own problems." [12]

Although seldom so eloquently, this plea echoes throughout the
underdeveloped lands. The *favelados* of the world demand more than
gestures, more than ineffective pity, more than the entrancing oratory
of either corrupt "democrats" or dictators. They want action which is
predicated on a deep comprehension of their most immediate, pressing
needs.

The beginning of wisdom in dealing with the problems of development lies in understanding individuals such as Carolina de Jesus. Be-

fore we can intelligently examine the abstract issues of political liberty and economic change, we must divorce ourselves from our own affluent world. We must eschew, equally, the optimism which views man as infinitely adaptable, the romanticism which longs for the virtues of an unrecapturable past, and the scorn for "native" capacities which so often blinded colonial rulers. And we must give up that supposedly realistic opinion, so much in fashion today, that the *favelados* neither understand nor care about protections for individual liberty, self-government, and individualism.* When transitional men have the capacity to articulate their beliefs, as did Carolina de Jesus, they often voice an inherent democratic desire which lies deep in their traditions, however easily they are forgotten by the old elite or the new tyrants.

With all the realism at our disposal, we must try to grasp the nature of transitional man—the actual motives, and values, and social milieu of those caught midway between traditional and modern modes of life.

Too often, economic or political plans have foundered for lack of such understanding. Because its leader was a health-food faddist, Burma has squandered millions on yeast plants when no one wished to buy the product. Certain African factories failed to produce at capacity until the seating arrangements for workers had been changed; the managers had failed to realize that laborers, traditionally accustomed to squatting during work, could not accommodate themselves easily to the Western sitting position. Liberal, progressive political parties, such as Ghana's United party, have gone down in defeat because of their inability to respond to the people's most basic desires or because of their inability to integrate traditional tribal symbols into their political appeals. Ambitious relocation schemes, such as those in Nigeria and Indonesia, have collapsed because leaders did not recognize the degree to which peasants would cling to their land in the belief that their ancestors had made it sacred. It is evident that many (although by no means all) of the obstacles to progress in the newer nations are essentially social in nature.

Any assessment of the chance for democratic development should properly begin, therefore, with an examination of human nature as it is revealed in the emerging nations. In particular, two of the most

---

* These Western terms have, of course, a different meaning in each cultural context. An Egyptian professor may chafe under restrictions upon his freedom of speech, while his peasant comrade may care about freeing himself solely from the irritating tyrannies of local bureaucrats or landholders. Slavery may mean different things to different people, but I have met few men anywhere who desire to be under the arbitrary, unrestricted power of another.

prominent clichés about transitional man require careful consideration. These beliefs serve, sometimes innocently, as buttresses in the argument of those who desire an authoritarian solution to the problems of development. First, the almost trite opinion that a "revolution of expectations" has swept the new nations deserves re-evaluation. Exactly what are those new aspirations? Is the desire for the appurtenances of modern life so compelling, as the authoritarians argue, that men will eagerly sacrifice everything else for its achievement? Secondly, we must reflect on the argument that the traditional order—the land-tenure pattern, the religious or political systems—must be tossed into the wastebasket of history. Is traditional society so inimical to progress that it must be violently transformed? Is it correct, as one of the most brilliant analysts has concluded, that progress requires ". . . nothing short of a pervasive social transformation . . . a wholesale metamorphosis of habits, a wrenching reorientation of values concerning time, status, money, work; an unweaving and reweaving of the fabric of daily existence itself"? [13]

To answer these questions, we must look closely at village life, for it is in the village that 70 per cent of transitional men live. The political and economic battles of development may not always be initiated in the village, but here they will be fought.

I

THE TRANSITIONAL VILLAGE

A bold peasantry, their country's pride,
When once destroyed, can never be supplied.

OLIVER GOLDSMITH

If one strolls down a village street in India or Egypt, Java, or Ghana, one sees immediately certain differences in dress, food, skin color, and religious symbols. Below the surface differences, however, rest fundamental similarities, resemblances that come from the way of life which bare subsistence enforces upon man. Everywhere, the great majority of villagers work in the fields, raising their own food and, increasingly, crops for exchange in the market. Their homes, huddled together for protection, often have only a single room as shelter for each family. On the walls, one might find a pan or two, perhaps calendars or religious icons as decorations. Floor mats serve as beds. For their meals, the peasants would normally eat a single dish each day, one which typically had less than the minimum number of calories that the U.N. has specified as nutritionally necessary. Open sores on the children's faces and their thin, crippled bodies testify to the illness which debilitates the village. The battle to survive (which, on the average, the peasant wins until he is twenty-eight) occupies everyone.

The sameness of village life can be seen throughout the underdeveloped world, in South America, Africa, and Asia. In Latin America, villages are the backbone of society. In Mexico alone there are thou-

19

sands of villages, seldom exceeding 400 inhabitants each. These typical communities, as Frank Tannenbaum has described them, are almost totally isolated from each other. Normally, they consist of a few
rude houses enclosed upon themselves, surrounding a small square.
The church and a jail dominate the town. The food is grown locally.
The town is "peaceful, quiet, self-conscious, and proud." [1] Above all,
it is poor. Some 60 per cent of the villages have no potable water, and
throughout Latin America, 1000 children die each day for lack of
water. Fifty-two per cent of the population eat less than 500 calories
a day (Americans consume 3100). And, of course, the villages lack
heat, light, sewage, or garbage disposal systems. Seventy per cent of
the people cannot read. In 1961, one million Latin Americans died of
starvation or the lack of properly nutritious food. [2]

Although more plentifully supplied with food, African villagers
hardly fare better. As George Kimble has drawn the classic picture of
a tropical African village, one finds similar destitution. The villages
exist in primitive isolation, producing pitifully small yields from their
infertile lands. Shelter, clothes, medicine are all in short supply.
Schooling, while it has grown splendidly in Africa, still does not reach
out far into the "bush." Almost every villager is habitually unwell from
smallpox or malaria, sleeping sickness or sheer malnutrition. Medical
care is usually far distant from the village; throughout Africa, there is
an average of only one hospital bed for every 1300 people (as compared
to one for every 100 persons in America). Kimble's conclusions about
the tropical African village apply with equal strength to other areas:

> In the African social drama sickness has a strong claim to being the
> arch-villain. It is bad enough that a man should be ignorant, for this
> cuts him off from the commerce of other men's minds. It is perhaps
> worse that a man should be poor, for this condemns him to a life of
> stint and scheming. . . . But what surely is worst is that a man
> should be unwell, for this prevents his doing anything much about
> either his poverty or his ignorance. [3]

To take a specific example of village life from another area, let us
examine Khampur in Uttar Pradesh as an illustration of the general
pattern in India. In Khampur, 1500 people subsist in a handful of
mud huts, with seven people sleeping in each room. All but the very
young and old, a carpenter, soap maker, and shoe repairer, work on the
land, growing "English" vegetables, cotton, and dates. That is, they
work when they can, for some 30 per cent of the men can find employ-

ment only eight days a month. In Khampur, as in all underdeveloped villages, a surplus of idle labor exists, begging for productive work. *This enforced idleness constitutes the greatest waste in developing countries.*

Several large landholders and their families control 50 per cent of the land. Long ago, these absentee owners had deserted the village for the pleasures of city life. The rest of the land is held by the villagers, each family cultivating an average of somewhat less than an acre.

In Khampur, as in the other transitional villages, agricultural productivity is shockingly low. The average hectare in India, for example, yields about one-third the amount of rice of that in America, one-fourth that of Australia. Part of this difference comes from the extraordinarily small size of landholdings. A significant portion of Khampur's individually owned fields are less than one-quarter acre in size, thus prohibiting efficient cultivation.

This rigorous existence has reduced the amenities of life in Khampur to a minimum. Only the richest of homes possesses a chair or table. Only the most prosperous peasant can boast of shoes or more than two well-worn robes. To leave one's dinner, fully satiated, occurs no more than a few times each year. Toys do not exist, of course, and the children turn to their pets, the ponderous bullocks (each accompanied by a little bird perched on its back), for amusement.

For recreation, the adult males attend frequent religious festivals in honor of gods which capriciously govern their harvests. In the evenings they gather around the radio, that ubiquitous intrusion into the village's tranquility, listening intently to the oracle of modern life. Sometimes, one of the few village literates reads and interprets the day's newspapers. In times of wealth, the men splurge by buying tobacco for the village's five bubble-pipes or, perhaps, they journey to the next town where a coffee shop offers its luxurious wares. The women seldom share even those petty pleasures. Shrouded in veils, their single diversion comes from gossiping at the village well, the "women's club" of Khampur.

Modern civilization invades Khampur only incidentally: in the radio, in the public health nurse who visits occasionally, in the political symbols scratched on mud walls, in the trucks that carry a few workers to the city. Most importantly, modern life intrudes in the person of the village teacher, a young man who himself has passed only the lowest of educational hurdles. The teacher imparts his knowledge in a totally bare classroom, devoid of everything except the primitive slates which his students use. But this does not deter the children, for every child in Khampur seems to desire ardently the knowledge that literacy will open to him. Aside from these influences from the outer, different world, Khampur lives enclosed upon itself.

How long one can live is the primary preoccupation of every villager. For in Khampur, where half of the children die before they are ten and rats carry the bubonic plague and every adult has at times experienced malarial fever, death cannot be hidden.

In its physical essentials, therefore, the transitional village, whether in India, Latin America or Africa, suffers from extreme poverty, hunger, pervasive ignorance, and disease. Economically, villagers draw the barest subsistence from their lands. The potential of the village—most significantly, the latent resources of "hidden" unemployed labor—goes unfulfilled.

In its seclusion and suffering, its servitude to nature's will, the village creates a structure of human relationships which helps it to carry out the precarious business of life. This social milieu of peasant life has been classically described by anthropologists. Robert Redfield has searched for the essence of peasant culture, a set of values and social relationships which characterize all rural societies, by comparing Hesiod's description of Greek peasantry, a nineteenth-century English village, and contemporary Mexico.[4] Other investigations, by Oscar Handlin on East Europeans, S. R. Srinivas on Indians, and Oscar Lewis on Latin Americans, have further delineated a common portrait of village social structure and values.

From the results of these disparate investigations, one can begin to perceive the social fabric of village life, to detect an almost universal pattern of relationships and values which reappears in Togo as well as Thailand, Guinea as well as Mexico. The important fundamental characteristics of village society are, first, its social isolation and cohesion; second, the predominance of hierarchical ("traditional," "ascriptive") relationships; and, third, the prevalence of fatalism.

Above all, the village is *socially isolated*, convoluted upon itself, preoccupied with parochial concerns. It is a self-sufficient, independent entity. Sir Charles Metcalf's comments on India in 1832 apply with little qualification today:

The village communities are little republics, having nearly everything they want within themselves, and almost independent of any foreign relations. They seem to last where nothing else lasts. Dynasty after dynasty tumbles down; revolution succeeds revolution . . . , but the village community remains the same. . . .[5]

Enforced by physical and geographical factors, this isolation has several social and political consequences. Each villager becomes closely involved with his neighbors, he is truly their "brother," even though symbolically they may be divided by caste or religious differences. Everyone knows the other members of the village, their vices, virtues, and eccentricities. Regardless of his temperament, even the most misanthropic villager must engage in co-operative enterprises with his fellows, for the preservation of them all depends upon mutual aid. The contacts of the villager rarely extend beyond the town limits, except perhaps for the rather vague linkage of tribal, caste, or religious ties. Only the exceptional peasant in India, for example, visits areas farther than twenty miles from his home or chooses his wife from a group that lives more than eight miles away. The family becomes all-important in such an environment, for personal survival depends upon aid from one's relatives, all of whom, from grandfather to second cousin, live close by. The reproduction of children, as a source of protection and prestige, naturally takes on unusual significance. Thus, one traditionally greets the Indian bride with the incantation, "May you be blessed with sixteen children."

As its own "republic," the village often feels little in common with the political "center" and indeed may be only casually aware of the state's existence. Kussum Nair has reported questioning Indian villagers on their political attitudes. In Bhoola, a Bhil village in Sirohi district, she asked them about the ruling Congress party. One villager responded:

"Yes, we have heard of the Congress. We have heard of the Congress; yes. Everyone talks of it.

"But," pauses Kania, gravely puckering his bushy eyebrows, "but now that you mention it, we do not know whether Congress is a man or a woman." [6]

In Indonesia, anthropologists have tried to test the depth of political awareness by circulating pictures of national leaders and requesting peasants to identify them. Typically, villagers might recognize Sukarno but would fail to know any other political figure on the national scene. Invariably, however, they could identify the local party boss, for only this political personage has immediate importance to them.

In Africa, parochialism appears in its most pronounced form. Colin Turnbull, in his superlative account, *The Lonely African*, quotes the bewilderment of one Congolese peasant in the face of governmental attempts to forge unity:

"They [the government] say these lands are not foreign, because they are next to ours—but they must be foreign, because their beliefs are different. The circumcised can not live with the uncircumcised. Let the circumcised live by themselves, for them that is the right thing to do, and we have no quarrel with them for that—it is merely not our way. But let us live our way, because for us that is right." [7]

Such detachment and disunity create obvious difficulties for leaders wishing to patch together a unified nation. One other political result of the village's isolated cohesion is that it impedes the implementation of any governmental measure that threatens the village's basic unity. The Indian government, for example, has passed a number of admirable laws aimed at land reform. Local officials have found it hard to carry out land redistribution since the landlords are not, as one might expect, a hated, distinct group within the village. Separate "interest groups," in the Western sense, do not always exist. Rather, landlords form part of integrated village life. Sometimes they, and quite often their agents who collect rent, come from the same extended family as the villagers themselves. Laws which implicitly demand that the peasants set themselves apart from (or against) the landlords do not fare well in the face of such cohesion.[8]

The village's tight cohesion has, in Metcalf's words, "contributed more than any other cause to the preservation of the people . . . and to the enjoyment of a great portion of freedom and independence." [9] At the same time, the villager's intense identification with his local community separates him from the broader purposes of the national state. And in former colonial areas, the state may be viewed not only as strange and distant but as actively malevolent.

A second paramount characteristic of the village is the *hierarchical* nature of social relations. For the villager, social life takes place within a set of rigidly ordained relationships, defined by tradition, handed down from one's ancestors. Each man knows his proper place from childhood on; his vocation, rights, and duties are ascribed at birth. Women remain at the bottom of the ladder, the religious leader or nobleman at the top. Progress in life does not consist in altering one's position by individual effort but rather in passing from one prescribed state to another, from (an often pampered) childhood to productive manhood to the elder's responsibilities and respect. The pressures of a subsistence economy enforce hierarchism, for if each person could question at will his duty to fulfill a particular job, the village might not produce that small amount of food which barely sustains it. The imprimatur of the ancestors is on the traditional modes of human interaction. Since it worked for one's forefathers, why change it?

The Western observer, seeing the rigidity and traditionalism of the usual village hierarchy, normally reacts only to the baleful effects of the system. Admittedly, from the economic point of view, the typical village often condemns the potential innovator to frustration. Women almost never receive the education or opportunities that would fit their capacities. Any economic change must first receive the elders' sanction, and often, to the village's detriment, they refuse to alter traditional ways.

Politically, too, the typical village environment can lead liberal democrats to despair, for it sometimes seems to spawn only authoritarianism. Walking through villages in Egypt, for example, one cannot help seeing the pervasive, humiliating deference of the "lower classes" to their superiors. The peasants still kiss the hand of their landlord (although officially, the revolution has made them equal), and they do not quarrel when he swings open the door of their huts without invitation or warning. In such a hierarchical structure, one can hardly expect villagers to develop a political stance other than that adopted by the village "masters."

A further effect is that villagers often tend to portray politics as primarily a matter of personal relationships and "pull." Thus, the Latin American peasant looks first to his *patrón* as the source of political guidance. In return for subservience (and graft), the peasant receives protection and can benefit from the *patrón's* exercise of influence.

One can seldom uncover in village life an ideology that treats the individual as separate from his group and as possessing rights that transcend the group. Elders, using the power bestowed by ancestors and gods, reign as supreme authorities; such supremacy does not provide fertile ground for some of the Western concepts of freedom. As Millikan and Blackmer have pointed out, "To an individual who has absorbed with his mother's milk the attitude that it is wrong to speak or even think freely until the duly honored elders and persons in superior positions have expressed their opinions, the concept of freedom of thought and expression may be an impossible one to accept." [10]

In their quickness to condemn the authoritarian aspects of the village hierarchy, however, social scientists may all too easily overlook its indigenous democratic elements and its protections for individual liberty. The rights of the elders are usually closely circumscribed by tradition. The petty tyrant who oversteps these limits is overthrown. In many villages, discussion of issues can proceed openly and vigorously—at least until the chief or the village council reaches a decision. As Matungi, an old African chief, has described the process in his village:

We believe it is better for disputes to be settled as simply as possible, and by the people themselves. It would be easy for the chief to settle all disputes simply by commanding, but this would merely stop the fight, it would not cure the wound. So we discuss our grievances, and all members of the family take a part because blame is seldom on one side alone.[11]

In reaching legal decisions, the tribunal listens to all opinions on the case, since its purpose, as Turnbull puts it about Congo practices, "is to establish justice, not simply to apply the law." [12]

Colin Rosser's description of the political process in a Kulu village could just as easily fit transitional villages in other areas:

All discussions and decisions take place in full public hearing of the community. The public listens to the arguments . . . and hears how a decision has been reached. As soon as the council has come to a decision, one of the permanent members and one of the elders leave the platform and squat before the assembled villagers. They announce the decision and call for opinions. That is, each council decision is followed by an immediate referendum to the general public.[13]

In Nigeria, Chief H. O. Davies has proved, village traditions laid down a similar equalitarian base for "direct democracy." [14] Before colonization, the Yorubas developed a constitutional monarchy and the Egbas had a democratic polity, governed by elected city fathers. Western concepts of limited power were by no means alien to children of this tradition.

While hierarchical in nature, the village polity derives its sovereignty from a direct appeal to the wishes of the people. As Rosser concludes in his investigation of a fairly representative Indian village: "The most striking fact about the political and judicial organization of the village appears to be the extent to which it rests on public sentiment. . . . The village is intensely egalitarian and has a well-developed sense of justice as an abstract concept." [15]

We should not romanticize "village democracy," for, after all, power does flow in authoritarian channels. The same equalitarianism that serves as a brake on authority can also lead to a tyranny of the majority. The "outsider" in a village can be most cruelly treated, and one is reminded of Ibsen's observation that "the most dangerous enemy to freedom amongst us is the compact majority."

Nevertheless, it would be equally unwise to dismiss the village as a potential base for liberal democracy. The village "republics" may not exhibit all the virtues which Jefferson found in the independent farmer's life, but they do provide essential protections of the villager's life and liberty. Moreover, they offer an opportunity (which is seldom equaled in the more "advanced" nations), for direct participation in the political process. Western concepts of the social contract are, in fact, natural to many villagers. One may say that Rousseau and Locke probably have a more spontaneous appeal than Lenin or Stalin, for their doctrines correspond to village reality.

A third aspect of the village atmosphere, its profound *fatalism*, requires comment, for it is this element in the village ethic which leads many scholars to believe that progress is impossible. Indeed, no one who has experienced village life can overlook the way in which fatalism reinforces the village's inertia. The attitude toward change of one 96-year-old leader of an Indian village typifies the beliefs one finds throughout the peasant environment. I had asked him what had changed most in his lifetime. Objectively, of course, he had witnessed national independence, land reform struggles, the infiltration of roads, machines, medicine, schools, and new methods of agriculture into his area. Yet, after he had ruminated for several minutes, he replied, "Why, nothing has really changed. Prices are a little higher now than in earlier years. After all, what could possibly change?"

This conviction that existence cannot be altered by passing events has a foundation in the hard realities of village existence. If one is always under the command of fickle nature, life may seem to change superficially, but actually one cannot escape the round of seasons, the cycle of drought and flood, the threat of locusts or plague.

The implacability of fate was poignantly illustrated for me in another Indian village where the peasants and government advisers had striven for a decade to improve conditions. The peasants had learned to use new implements and fertilizers, to produce profitable crops for market, and to contour plow their lands. They had laboriously built by hand a dirt barrier to keep out the flood from an adjoining river. One year, exceptional rains caused the river to rise. The government had not yet found the money to build concrete dams up-river which would have diverted the flow. The village's dirt dams collapsed before an onslaught of water. Because of the river's chemical content, the land was all but permanently ruined. A decade's effort went for nothing.

Confronted with nature's will in its unmasked brutality, it is hardly surprising that the peasant resigns himself to fate. In his despair, he turns to religion in the hope that by placating the supernatural he can save himself from the gods' anger. He shrouds his life in ritual and reverence. "The entire community . . . regards the earth as Mother Earth, a deity, and the crops and manure are regarded as Lahksmi, the Goddess of Wealth," anthropologist M. N. Srinivas has commented about a Mysore village, "The domestic lamp, granary, a heap of grain, grain measure, etc., are all objects of ritual respect." [16] Even new developments, obviously initiated by man's will, become enveloped in mystical respect. When a new irrigation canal is driven through an Indian field, it is not at all uncommon for the villagers to gather around and worship the innovation, as if God had put it there by magic.

Similarly, in Latin America, the Church's emphasis on resignation to God's will colors all social relations. Every town has its chapel, every person his special saint. The priest attends all public affairs, comforts the people in disaster, and lends God's sanction to every major event in life.

The life of the family and of the individual is greatly and continuously involved with the Church [one historian has said], . . . *it gives life a certain quality and adds something to the meaning of daily activities which is lacking in the United States.*[17]

Much more than in a secular civilization, religion in the developing countries gives life a meaning in an all too meaningless world. It provides a weapon, however fragile, with which to dispel mystery. At the same time, the inherent conservatism of religion in the developing nations has served as a powerful, independent obstacle to change. In South America, where the Church has been one of the greatest landholders, it was customary (until recently) for the priest to stand beside the *patrón* in fighting land reform. In India, religion sanctified a caste system which could hardly be reconciled with contemporary equalitarian ideals. In Africa, religious beliefs concerning ancestral ownership of the land have hindered individual initiative in rural improvement.

Ordained by religion, the conservative fatalism of the village has caused some social scientists to give up hope that economic stagnation can end without shaking the whole village structure to its foundation.

Psychologist David McClelland has produced convincing evidence that men must possess a strong drive for achievement, an "other-directed" market orientation, before a modern economy can emerge. His comparative research suggests that the ethic of traditional, inert, fatalistic villages discourages the development of such attitudes. The values of the village, he argues, must in some degree be jettisoned: "If people want the benefits of the advanced material culture of modern civilization—which they do whenever they come in contact with it, and such contact is inevitable—then they must accept many of the values and other culture patterns which support such a civilization." [18] Kussum Nair, in her consideration of the human element in Indian development, concluded that a majority of Indian villages, "in spite of the efforts of extension agencies and the inducements offered by them, seem inert and indifferent. They pass up repeated opportunities to increase production and income, even when opportunity knocks at their very door." [19] Such studies might lead to the belief that the village ethic is an almost insurmountable barrier to economic advance.

Yet, other analysts have argued that the explanation for village inertia should not be traced to an "innate" conservatism. Rather, they contend, the peasants' hesitancy to adopt innovations comes from a quite rational calculation of the risks involved. From his wide experience in problems of development, Paul Hoffman, for example, has described how Ceylonese fishermen carefully watched a demonstration of outboard motors. For weeks, they weighed and debated the utility of the new machinery. When they saw, however, that the motor-equipped boats were hauling in double-size catches, they quickly made up their minds. "The 'stubborn native,' " Hoffman found, "simply wants proof." [20] And English economists Peter Bauer and Basil Yamey have amassed evidence which demonstrates that village values may define the direction of economic activity but that the institutional framework does not prohibit adjustments in the economy.[21] They cite, as illustrations, the flexibility of Malayan farms in trying new methods of rubber production, of African peasants in switching to cocoa cultivation, and of Guatamalan "penny capitalists" in calculating their costs of production.

Indubitably, certain specific aspects of village culture may drastically curtail economic improvement. The Indian villagers' support of 240 million cows, while men starve, is a sad case in point; in some areas, the maintenance of old-age homes for cows takes precedence over all other types of economic activity. And certainly, the typical villager is not wholly an "economic man" in the Manchester tradition. He often does not exhibit the same eagerness for profit or for extended exertion as the classic figure of laissez-faire tradition. Indeed, the original colonizers of Africa generally found the African totally satisfied with his economic way of life. The simple inducements of pay could not lure him away from the village, and various coercions (such as the imposition of taxes which could be paid only in cash) had to be introduced.

Yet, on balance, the evidence leads to the conclusion that the village can tolerate, or even welcome, economic innovations if two conditions are fulfilled: The villagers must be convinced that the change is worth the risk, that the introduction of a new technique will not destroy the small surplus which saves them from extinction. And the villager must possess the capital, the skills, and knowledge of the market required for the particular innovation.

I have been discussing the village as if it were a static entity, as if its politico-economic structure, its isolation, hierarchism, and fatalism were unchanging elements in an eternal bucolic scene. While traditional society has, in fact, been remarkably stable, the forces of modernity in the past century have stirred it in profound ways. Exposure to the modern world's abundance, the infiltration of new ideas, the influence of colonial rule, and, often, the colonialist's contempt for peasant culture has set in force processes which cannot be reversed.

The specific impetus for change—we will not necessarily call it progress—comes from many sources: the blandishments of mass media, the spread of education, the benefits of medicine, the promise of proselytizing religions, the lure of profit in a new market-oriented economy, and, even, as in Nigeria, from odd-looking helicopters which descend precipitously on remote villages, bearing campaigning politicians. Large and small, these forces converge in a frontal attack on customary village isolation, practices, and values.

Their effect has been to subvert the traditional village order, to initiate changes which could not have been envisioned by the typical peasant described by Robert Redfield. The peasant's reverence for land, his deep belief that the farmer close to the earth has more value than the prettified city merchant, has been challenged by the glittering appeals of new cities. In consequence, the peasants' self-respect has often given way to a sense of servitude and inferiority unexperienced by their fathers. Few young men wish to continue as peasants, unless they must. Even in Israel, the idealistic Kibbutzim movement may die out as a younger generation succumbs to the materialism of Tel Aviv.

Religion, too, has suffered. The peasant woman saying her prayer beads is still the norm in most villages, but the young girl who believes nothing has become increasingly common. The old religions appear to have less and less relevance to manipulation of a new machine world. The traditional structure of social and political power has also begun to crack, for the fledgling tractor mechanic may well have more prestige than an ancient leader. And for the first time the most depressed groups (such as India's untouchables) have begun to question seriously the justice of their situation.

The demonstrative power of modern medicine has gone far in undermining village fatalism, for the peasant has now seen in this most supremely important way that nature's tyranny can be overthrown. Familiarity with medical knowledge has seeped down to the most isolated village. In one of the most remote Indian areas, for example, I recall approaching a group of old men who smoked a common pipe, passing the stem from mouth to mouth. They asked me to sit with them and offered the end of the pipe for me to smoke. I hesitated, thinking of the diseases which could be contracted. But feeling the guilt of the over-hygienic Westerner, I grasped the pipe and plunged it into my mouth. Everyone laughed. "Dear sir," one of them said, "don't you know how to smoke? If you stick the pipe in your mouth, you might get sick—infested with germs, you understand? Cup your fist around the stem, like we do." This knowledge that a few simple precautions can avoid death has done more than anything else to change many peasants' view of a malevolent universe.

The villager today stands in midstream between two styles of life; he is wrenchingly in transition, between a traditional peasant culture and the new ethic of modernity. The gradual erosion of the old order has left many peasants with a gnawing feeling of purposelessness. Masoudi, a Congolese who attempted to adopt Belgian ways, speaks for many transitional villagers:

I died the day I left this village and went to Matadi [a city]—there is no point going back there. I am an old man . . . and I have only one worry. I believed in your world at one time, even if I did not understand it, and I tried to follow your ways. But in doing this I lost my spirit. It left me somewhere . . . and I am empty.[22]

Some villagers, such as Matungi, a fellow townsman of Masoudi, have self-consciously clung to the old traditions:

I have tried to keep my dignity. I have tried to remain a man in the eyes of my father. Whatever I may have done with my body, I have never betrayed my beliefs with my mind. But for my children it is different. They do not know good and bad as I know it. . . . After I am dead there will be no one left, unless somewhere I have planted a seed that has yet to grow and provide nourishment for those who live on.[23]

Most often, as Matungi realized, strivings to retain traditional culture are unsuccessful. Ranged against the tradition are all the lures of modern life, particularly as these are invitingly displayed in cities. The movement toward the city, with its supposed amusements, jobs, and comforts, is perhaps the most important social trend in the developing nations. In many countries, urbanization is literally depopulating the countryside of the better-educated men, the more skilled artisans, and those with the most ambition. In some areas, such as Mexico City (which mushroomed from 1.5 million to 4 million in 17 years), the pace has been so rapid that the nation will soon become predominantly urban rather than rural.

The cities create an "urban man," imbued with attitudes quite different from those of the traditional peasantry. The world of these new transitional people deserves attention for, in the view of many, these are the men of the future.

II

THE TRANSITIONAL CITY

Our world is the outer edge of civilization. Do you know where I
sleep? Under bridges. I'm going crazy. I want to die.

An anonymous *favelado* in
Child of the Dark

"Why should I stay in my village? It's dreary, dark, and dirty," the
Egyptian youth responded, typical of high-school students whom I
interviewed in 1962. His father had been pleading with him to continue on the land, but to no avail, for the boy replied, "There is nothing to do in the village, no movies, no night clubs, no dancing! Any-
way, the land could not support both me and my brothers."

In this lies the city's promise: the push of escaping rural poverty and
the pull of excitement and luxury. The city's magnetism extends
throughout the developing world to the most primitive areas. Even in
rural Africa, public opinion polls show that only 8 per cent of schooled
boys wish to continue in their father's farming occupation. In the
more developed nations such as India, the move to the cities has become a torrent.

A few statistics from India illustrate the scope of urbanization: Indian cities are growing at a steady rate of 50 per cent per decade, and
some centers even outdistanced this pace. New Delhi, in the single
decade of 1941-51, increased in size by 107 per cent. The most
conservative demographers estimate that Indian cities will somehow
have to absorb 140 million new immigrants before the end of the cen-

33

tury. In a city such as Calcutta—where carts circulate each morning to pick up the dead from the sidewalk—the extent of this growth can barely be comprehended. By the year 2000, unless the pattern of growth is reversed, Calcutta's population will have expanded from 2.5 million in 1962 to a possible 66 million. Some experts, noting that industrialization and urbanization have been historical bedfellows, believe that this trend is inevitable. "To put it succinctly," sociologist Kingsley Davis, one of the most cautious of generalizers, has said, "60 per cent of its population must move from the countryside to the cities. This is a problem so formidable that few governments seem willing to face it realistically: yet, if *rapid* economic development is to be achieved, the territorial shift must also take place *rapidly*." [1]

If the ambitions and policies of developing nations are not changed, few would question the prediction that this human flood will occur (although one can legitimately quarrel with the belief that urbanization is necessary for economic growth). Regardless of the future, it seems beyond dispute that the developing nations are already heavily overurbanized, burdened with festering cities beyond their capacity to support.

Arthur Lewis, a distinguished contributor to the dialogue of economic development, has demonstrated that in every new nation one or two towns have developed far beyond the ability of the municipality to provide houses, jobs, transportation, or schools. Part of this excessively rapid growth takes place for sheer economic reasons: new industries naturally tend to locate in areas where industry is already concentrated. Another reason lies in the tendency of some governments simply to spend more on one or two "prestige" cities and ignore others. As Lewis recalls:

> *Once when I pointed out to a Prime Minister that he was proposing to spend 50% of his development program on his capital city, which had only 5% of the population, he was quite surprised. "But why not?", he asked. "Surely, when you think of England you think of London, when you think of France you think of Paris . . ." "No," I replied, "when I think of England, I think not of London, but of Manchester, and this is precisely why I oppose spending half your money beautifying the capital."* [2]

However false the tinsel of these cities, their image of luxury continues to inveigle the peasant into immigration. At first, when the ex-villager enters the city, he must be overwhelmed by the glory of New Delhi's Secretariat, Mexico's Reforma Boulevard, Accra's government buildings, or by the Paris-like magnificence of Cairo along the Nile. But soon, he has to face the physical realities of city life—the *barriada*, or *favela*, or *bidonville* which are the rotten cores within the apple. Unless he has unusual training, he quickly discovers that no one wants his labor. The curious fact about the city is that its unemployment problem exceeds even that of stagnant villages. In Madras, as an illustration, only 25 per cent of the working people can engage in directly productive activity; the rest sell shoestrings, beg, sleep, find odd jobs now and then, or earn a few pennies running errands. Paradoxically, as the typical city grows and develops, greater amounts of men go out of work. As Lewis describes Kingston, Jamaica, "The more jobs you create in Kingston, the more unemployment you have in Kingston." [3] Attracted by the promise of lucrative employment, the migrant leaves his village and its system of natural social security, only to find that nothing awaits him in the city.

The first shock which cities administer to the migrant, therefore, is a tangible demonstration that he is neither wanted nor needed.* The new urbanite discovers in other ways, too, that he has traded his peasant heritage for a mess of pottage. Typically, his housing (if he finds any at all) is greatly inferior to that of the village. In India, to cite one case, 34 per cent of rural families live in one room, but in Calcutta 79 per cent must crowd into a single chamber. Further, while only 14 per cent of Indian peasant families must somehow squeeze into a floor area of less than fifty square feet (something less than the size of an average American bathroom), the majority of urbanites (70 per cent) can find nothing better as their home. In some Indian cities, an unlucky 20 per cent must sleep in the gutters.

The city dweller normally cannot scrape together enough food to maintain his health. Richard Meir has shown that an average subsistence budget in an Indian city—one which would provide sufficient food and clothing, but little else—requires some $250 a year. Yet, the typical city resident can earn only $60 a year. In consequence, the crude death rate in Indian cities often markedly surpasses that of villages, even though the city is more liberally supplied with medical facilities.

Objectively, then, the city migrant often discovers himself deprived

---

* This shock is perhaps greatest for the "early leavers," those who have received some primary education and then quit school in the anticipation of economic rewards. Bereft of specific skills, they can find no place in an urban economy. For this reason, among others, the popular policy concentrating resources on primary education must be viewed with some caution.

of a job, housing, sufficient food, or adequate medical protection. Rather than offering salvation, the move to the city only deepens frustration.

How does the new environment affect the urbanite's character? What happens, in the city, to traditional attitudes, values, and social relationships? Exposure to a city's wiles, its contrasts and strange experiences, opens new vistas to the ex-villager. He learns that other styles of life exist, other religions, political authorities other than that of his village. Because he must, he learns to tolerate attitudes and habits which clash with his own. In some ways, this broadening of horizons is useful, for the urbanite may begin to feel sympathy for forms of behavior utterly different from his old ways. Daniel Lerner, in his extensive research on the Middle East, has nicely demonstrated the correlation between urbanization, literacy, exposure to the mass media, and empathy—the ability to put oneself in the situation of others.[4] He reports that the typical Turkish villager is at a loss to respond to such a question as: "What would you do if you were President or Turkey?" The villager cannot conceive of a situation in which he would have anything in common with such an exalted figure. The city dweller, in contrast, can visualize the President's role and problems. He can vicariously participate in a world beyond his immediate experience. Ultimately, such empathy leads to attitudes of tolerance, so necessary for a liberal society.

Other vistas, however, are also opened to the urbanite, and these result more in jealousy than tolerance, a rage at injustice rather than a willingness to accept varied ways of life. Perhaps most significantly, the urbanite sees new levels of wealth of which he was previously only dimly aware. The villager to some degree, knows about economic inequality, of the lucky few's wealth. But the urban resident sees evidence of it at every hand. He cannot avoid the glaring contrast between, say, the magnificent apartments which line Rio's beaches and the slums clutching its hills. Even in those countries which have striven to avoid such obvious differences, distinct inequalities still exist. The few skilled oil workers in Venezuela or the Middle East earn many times the salary of the average laborer. The schoolteacher in Ghana or Nigeria earns from five to seven times the per capita urban income. Because of the shortage of trained people, these differentials in income are built into the nature of developing economies. Often as development proceeds, the gap in income gets wider rather than narrower. Thus, in Mexico, despite great economic progress, one per cent of the population received 66 per cent of national income in 1955, whereas in 1940 they had taken only 34 per cent.[5]

Inevitably, the discords of inequality infect the city person with discontent. Formal public opinion polls give some signs, however inadequate, of the depth of the urbanite's alienation. Indian polls, for example, have revealed that 78 per cent of Calcutta residents believed that "a change in the present social system is necessary." [6] Similar interviews in Santiago, Chile, indicated that 89 per cent of the people demanded important social changes. [7]

This discontent can seldom be assuaged by the balm of traditional religions, for a further impact of the city is its implacable pressure toward secularization. Confronted with a society where machines have replaced the gods, where traditional incantations have no bearing on whether people find jobs, where movie stars displace village idols, the urbanite abandons his faith in the old religion. In the Middle East, polls indicate that 50 per cent of young urban migrants give up their Islamic beliefs, and in Africa, as one anthropologist has observed, the conflict between Westernized, city values and traditional religion "results either in the abandonment of all belief, which is perhaps the most logical solution, or else in the adoption of the outer form of Western belief without any inner conviction." [8]

While losing the metaphysics which gave his life significance, the typical urban person learns that traditional modes of social intercourse are either irrelevant or harmful in the city. In trying to adjust to a commercially oriented economy, for example, the city dweller is judged by "achievement" standards, by what he can produce, not who he is. The old village pattern where each person was automatically responsible to his neighbors and each knew his traditional role in life gives way to more individualistic criteria. Ideals of economic co-operation do not fit well with the standards of a competitive economy. The extended family system tends to disintegrate in an urban society with its new standards, higher costs, and greater mobility. Also the traditional hierarchical relationships of the village undergo systematic attack: the chief, or brahmin, or *patrón* loses his influence, and new authorities, frequently charismatic political figures, attempt to replace them. In every way, the urbanite becomes socially isolated. His religious, political, and familial universe crumbles in contact with the demands of an urban environment.* He stands alone and unprotected.

* Because of the simple fact that the city is a male-dominated area (more men than women enter the city seeking jobs), this isolation extends to the sexual area. As Shanti Tangri has observed on Indian cities, isolation chokes off "the traditionally accepted avenues for sex gratification, while extramarital sex . . . is severely limited. Sexual frustration is . . . very high. In addition, there are neither sufficient opportunities to participate in sports nor to attend sports

In response to this "culture of poverty," as Oscar Lewis has aptly termed it, the typical city person can cope with his frustration in several ways. A few can adjust themselves successfully to the city: they adopt the clothes and customs, learn new skills, find jobs, and shed their village background. The "adjusted elite" of civil servants, intellectuals, army officers, entrepreneurs, and some industrial workers win the city's rewards of economic and political power, but they constitute only a small minority of urbanites. Much more in evidence is the large group of "urban villagers," people who attempt to retain peasant culture, to re-create village life while existing in a city.

A UNESCO study of Stanleyville, the Congo, illustrates the way urban villagers deal with their new situation.[10] In 1956, two-thirds of Stanleyville's Africans, who had been born in the country, had migrated to the city less than five years earlier. Few had received any sort of education which qualified them for technical work. While earning relatively good salaries (from $17 a month for unskilled workers to $35 a month for white-collar employees), most of the city dwellers still returned to the bush periodically, often in fulfillment of tribal obligations. Many participated in voluntary organizations (financial societies, veterans groups, new religions) created to replace tribal bonds. The majority, however, preserved many of their traditional tribal ways. Most belonged to tribal organizations, practiced traditional *rites de passage*, paid a bride price, adhered to traditional brotherhoods, and, with the usual hospitality, welcomed indigent relatives who came to live with them in the city. They tried, in other words, to maintain traditional values while simultaneously responding to an urban culture.

The reaction of the urban villager is usually, though not always, unstable, for the man who wishes to live in two worlds cannot feel at home in either. The majority of urban residents are in a transitional, anomic state, moving steadily away from peasant values. This "anomic urbanite" is a hollow man who can no longer subscribe to the old values but has found nothing to replace them. As numerous studies have remarked, profound disillusionment poisons every urban center, regardless of geographical area.[11] In São Paulo, Carolina de Jesus exclaimed, "There is no meaning to my life . . . the day is sad as my soul . . . I think that my insipid life was too long." [12] In Mexico, Oliver La Farge noted (in commenting on Oscar Lewis's profound study, *Five Families*):

---

spectacles, where, on weekends, like their American counterparts, they may work off their steam by yelling some team to victory." [9] It does not seem totally unlikely that this sexual isolation plays a role in the rowdy indiscipline of student, labor, and unemployed groups.

"The most striking things about these families are their general malaise, the rarity among them of happiness or contentment, the rarity of affection. . . . Above all, where hunger and discomfort rule, there is little spare energy for the gentler, warmer, less utilitarian emotions and little chance for active happiness. . . . These broken cultures no longer give satisfaction, no longer 'make life worth living.' " [13] And in Africa, as anthropologist Colin Turnbull has concluded about urban people, ". . . there is a common theme apparent in their attitudes and in their actions, every one of them. The theme is a sense of a lack of something in their lives. The new world they have embraced, with various feelings, leaves them with an emptiness, a void that they all recognize and all want to fill." [14]

The anomic person seeks solace in crime, alcohol or magic. He may search for a new community, a secret society, or a new religion to replace the old order.* Or he may turn to politics in the hope that some new authority can both provide meaning in his life and relieve his economic frustration. The anomic urban person is remarkably amenable to authoritarian appeals, for once he has lost the comforting security of traditional order, he strives to regain his stability with frantic intensity. He who has seen the collapse of a worshiped authority wants to create a new one.

The cities become centers of modern, dynamic authoritarian movements. It is the city where the mobs rush into the streets and the demagogue's rantings find their most pulsing response. There the "true believer" flourishes and, in consequence, the politics of irresponsibility and passion. It hardly matters what the leader says, for many anomic persons respond to authoritarianism in a curiously undiscriminating fashion. In India, an urban district enthusiastically supported S. P. Mukerji, the leader of the Jan Singh, the most authoritarian of rightwing movements. When Mukerji died, the same constituency swung with equal fanaticism to the support of a Communist candidate. Politically, the anomic person simply wants someone to tell him what to do, someone who promises the sky, someone to fill the emptiness of his existence.

For the average urbanite, therefore, the city is truly the outer edge

---

* Social patterns in transitional cities today tend to reproduce eighteenth- and nineteenth-century European history: the urban man flocks to new salvationist religions, as the new industrial worker in London took to Methodism in droves. Thomas Hodgkin, in comparing new African churches to Methodism, has pointed out: "Both movements have offered a connection within which brotherly relations can be restored and human dignity can be rediscovered." [15]

of civilization, not the utopia of his dreams. Having experienced the desperate emptiness of urban existence, many of them long for a return to the village. Indian polls, as one indication, showed that 61 per cent of urban residents would prefer to go back to their villages, if economic opportunities were available.[16] This point is worth some emphasis: the urbanite who has lived in both worlds would generally choose the village.* The migrant, after all, usually succeeds only in trading a spartan rural life for the even harder ways of the city, the warmth of close personal relations for urban anonymity, the restricted authority of a village tribunal for the urban dictator's false promises of security. In the city, the transitional man loses his bread, his soul, and his freedom. An observation about urban Africans would serve well to summarize the state of impoverished urban man throughout the transitional societies: ". . . They are sad, because when they say that their old ways had many things to offer that western civilization has lost, they know with bitter certainty that they are right, and they know that these are the things that have made life worth living, and living well." [17]

Implications

> An acre in Middlesex is better than a principality in Utopia.
>
> THOMAS MACAULAY

With the tableau of developing societies spread before us, we are now in a better position to understand the human meaning of the "revolution in expectations." From the radio or movies, the colonial district officer or missionary, the city schoolteacher or politician, transitional men have been enthralled by a new set of ideas. Whether in the village or the city, they have begun to discard certain basic premises concerning the nature of man, society, and the physical universe.

Most important, they have come to an appreciation, however cautious, that man's own efforts can change his destiny, that progress is possible, if not probable. This new awareness leads only too often to a more profound discouragement, for progress does not come cheaply.

One might expect the discontent which bubbles within transitional

---

* Even more impressive is the fact that this particular sample was drawn from university graduates, the group presumably least likely to be attracted back to a village. Naturally, if these men could fulfill their highest aspirations in the city, the vote might well be different, but they have learned that the economic situation has foreclosed this option.

men to boil into utopian aspirations, into hopes that someone will usher in a kingdom of God which will immediately end their suffering. Indeed, in the cities, authoritarian movements encourage this sentiment and draw to their ranks many who seek an all-embracing salvation. Yet, one of the most encouraging facts about developing nations is that the majority of people have not yet succumbed to utopian unrealizable visions.

The aspirations of most transitional men, particularly in villages, are realistic and quite specific. Surveys in Calcutta, Travancore-Cochin, and New Delhi have shown that the people regarded the rise in food prices and unemployment as the two most urgent problems requiring governmental attention.[18] And in an African study, E. T. Sherwood revealed that the peasant's greatest aspiration was to have his own farm, simply "to be a free man." [19] Ninety-eight per cent of the African sample mentioned poverty and hunger as their greatest fears; 60 per cent cited the apprehension that their children might have to steal, "take to crime or commit murder" in order to live. Transitional men, in other words, have the most reasonable of aspirations: a hope that their immediate, limited economic needs can be satisfied, and a desire that their children may escape the compulsions of poverty.

In specific terms, the essential meaning of the revolution in expectations is that a vision of progress has tempted transitional men. They will welcome change as long as it can bring a tangible improvement in their personal economic situation. Greater freedom, land of their own, cheaper food, a job—these are the limited aspirations of the majority.[20]

The fact that their expectations are so reasonable, so confined to particular goals, has major significance. Politically, it suggests that governments which give their people only Asian Games and nationalism, nebulous visions of Pan-Africanism or social justice cannot long hold their allegiance. The people want bread not circuses. Economically, it weakens one of the major premises of planners in both authoritarian and democratic nations: the presumption that transitional men will sacrifice all other goods in the search for an ever-increasing standard of material abundance. After her investigation of Indian villages, Kussum Nair concluded:

From what I have seen and experienced . . . it would seem that a great majority of the rural communities do not share in a concept of an ever-rising standard of living. The upper level they are prepared to strive for is limited and it is the floor generally that is bottomless. . . . If my observation is correct, it largely invalidates one of the prin-

cipal assumptions on which present planning for economic develop-
ment in the rural sector is based. For in a situation of limited and
static aspirations, if a man should feel that his requirements are just
two bags of paddy per year, he works for two bags but not for more. If
he looks up to the stars, it is only to worship them, not to pluck
them.[21]

Thus, for those fully aware of the choice involved, they do not wish
to sacrifice the freedom, warmth, security, and even leisure provided
by traditional life simply in a scramble for riches. Yet, is it possible
for even the best-intentioned government to preserve the virtues of
traditional order and simultaneously to create an economy which will
satisfy even the limited aspirations of transitional men? The consensus
today seems to be that even the most minor of economic advances requires a fundamental social transformation; a "social cost" must be
paid. From the Marxist point of view, economic development ". . .
implies the crude but crucial fact—often, if not always, overlooked—that
development has historically always meant a far-reaching transformation of society's economic, social, and political structure. . . ." [22]
Equally, experts from M.I.T.'s Center for International Studies (as
Keynesian a bastion of Western policies as one can find) reach similar
conclusions: "The face-to-face relations and warm powerful family ties
of a traditional society must give way to more impersonal systems.
. . . There must be a radical shift in balance to urban life . . . the
paramount requirement for the modernization of any society is that
the people themselves must change." [23]

Here, we begin to enter that morass of arguments about the "social
prerequisites" of progress. It is impossible to deal with the issue sum-
marily, and we shall return to it when we have surveyed the relevant
historical, economic, and psychological data. At this point, however,
we can at least raise some questions about the sociological generalizations which underpin the position of those who advocate a politically
authoritarian solution to the dilemmas of development:

1. Transitional man, particularly the peasant, is not simply a newly
aroused animal who will trade his heritage to anyone who promises him
luxury.

2. The peasant is not just a dull clod requiring centralized direction
from above. Village development need not be "an exercise in advanced
animal husbandry," as one Ghanaian official described it to me.
Rather, the peasant appears to be a rational man whose caution springs
from experience, not "stubbornness." He certainly requires advice,

guidance, and help from outside sources, but he can well do without dictation and compulsion.

3. Traditional peasant culture is not one which lends itself easily to the unrestrained demands of modern authoritarian governments. Although hierarchical in nature, the village has developed ancient concepts of justice, limited power, and democratic participation in government which will not die easily.

4. There is little reason to believe that traditional culture must inevitably be torn up by the roots for development to proceed. Obviously, there are specific social obstacles to economic growth: religious taboos in India, retrograde land-tenure patterns in Latin America and, everywhere, the pall of ignorance. But it must also be recognized that village culture can be a base for innovation. It is not the social quagmire of stagnant attitudes and customs so often portrayed.[24]

5. Rather than being a "necessary" aid to economic growth, urbanization in developing nations appears, at this point in history, to have worsened the masses' welfare.

While some of the generalizations of authoritarians about transitional man cannot be entertained as universally valid, they do have a single, central perception which gives weight to their position: the recognition that man in the developing nations is miserable and, most importantly, is newly aware of his misery.[25] To a greater or lesser degree, men of all nations have accepted the originally Western convictions that there is progress and that all men should share in it.[26] Can one really wonder, then, that authoritarianism has seduced so many transitional men, particularly among city dwellers? The authoritarian promise of abundance and social justice inevitably appeals to those who have subscribed to the "subversive" ideals first propagated during the European Enlightenment. The authoritarian claims that no other method can as successfully overcome the economic challenge, that the human condition can be changed in no more efficacious way. Is the propaganda believable? Here, as in all important affairs, we must first turn to history, for the authoritarian appeal rests essentially upon supposed historical facts.

PART TWO

The Quest for Bread

III

HISTORY'S MODELS

> Most of the great positive evils of the world are in themselves removable, and will, if human affairs continue to improve, be in the end reduced within narrow limits. Poverty in any sense implying suffering may be completely extinguished by the wisdom of society. . . .
>
> JOHN STUART MILL

Stirred from their slumber by Rousseau and Mill and Lenin, by colonialism and American films, the developing nations have emerged from the chrysalis of tradition. A new awareness of their poverty has gripped the people of the world and even an Ethiopian Lion of Judah or an Imam of Yemen can ill afford to ignore it. Demands for a new order surge in the cities and have disturbed the remotest village. The desires are simple. Developing peoples want bicycles, not Cadillacs; seeds not combines; school teachers not nuclear scientists. And the potential resources are surprisingly available: Unused land in Africa and Latin America, unexploited minerals in Asia, and everywhere a large pool of unemployed labor.

Radical reorganization of the economy is necessary if even these rudimentary needs are to be met. Most developing nations invest productively not more than 5 per cent of their incomes. The growth in national product often does not reach 2 per cent a year, a rate insufficient to keep pace with increases in population. In other words, many of the underdeveloped economies are not just stagnant, or simply failing to fulfill their potential; they are actually retrogressing.

In all of the transitional societies, the people demand a rise in real per capita income. This need not involve a spectacular leap into the luxuries of Westchester County, or even of Moscow. The improvement must, nevertheless, mean a tangible increment in the goods and services available to the average man.

In Rostow's felicitous phrase, the task lies in stimulating these economies to the point of "take-off," much like lifting a rickety old plane off the runway. They must reach a stage where productivity begins to exceed population growth in a steady and substantial way. To achieve this goal, as we have already noted, requires the resolution of immensely difficult problems in the most rational way possible.

The intent of the next chapters is to detail the nature of these hard choices and to outline alternative solutions to the economic problem. In one important sense, the emerging peoples can claim a better fortune than the men of the West. When the entrepreneurs, farmers, and workers of seventeenth-century Europe started on the road which culminated in economic abundance, they had no inkling where it might lead. They stumbled into affluence. Today, history presents us with a number of models which reveal the several ways that "take-off" has already occurred, the tasks entailed, and the results achieved. Leaders of the developing nations may legitimately conclude that none of these past experiences pertains to their unique situation, but at least such a judgment may now be taken consciously and after reflection on the evidence.

For the emerging nations, the most important by far of these case studies are the records of Europe in the eighteenth and nineteenth centuries, Russia after the Bolshevik Revolution, and Japan in the late nineteenth century. The significance of Europe derives from the fact that it represents the first, classic economic revolution. It serves as the negative model for many ideologists in the underdeveloped countries, for they wish to avoid at all costs the pitfalls supposedly inherent in capitalist development.

Communist claims of transforming a peasant society into the world's second-greatest industrial power within the space of 35 years lend a special aura to Russia's experience in the eyes of the developing nations. It acts as the pre-eminent example for those who equate steel factories and sputniks with utopia. So pervasive is Russia's appeal that economist Alec Nove has concluded, "Perhaps the biggest service that Western economists and sociologists could render [the developing nations] . . . is to show more imagination in devising practical alternatives to the Communist model." [1]

Japan's history has regrettably not won the same attention as Russia's, even though the Meiji regime's "guided capitalism" made an equally impressive breakthrough from stagnation to growth. Indeed, hampered as it was by numerous burdens shared by the new nations today, Japan's advance may well prove to be directly pertinent to contemporary problems.

We shall examine each of these examples, but not in the conviction that history will repeat itself. Too much has changed, too many new problems have appeared for one to believe that the policies of an earlier era can be adopted unaltered into a program of our time. People have indeed learned from history; it is exactly this which reduces the direct relevance of history's lessons. As Eugene Staley has said, contrasting nineteenth-century Europe with the developing nations, ". . . people who know what has happened *since* 1850 have a different understanding of and reaction to events than the people who had to react in 1850."[2]

Europe's Drive to Abundance

> Modern civilization which originated in seventeenth-century England and Holland represents the greatest all-encompassing revolution in the conditions of human life. . . . Science acquired social significance; it became the most powerful instrument for raising the dignity and establishing the equality of all individuals.
>
> HANS KOHN

An economic revolution which had been gathering force imperceptibly for hundreds of years swept Western Europe in the eighteenth and nineteenth centuries. Rural, traditional societies, not totally unlike those of today, found themselves by 1900 in the spectacularly different world of cities and factories and ever-burgeoning wealth. It was a world in which men applied science and technology increasingly to every aspect of existence. The machine, rather than man himself, became the primary source of productive energy. While technological change had begun early—between the twelfth and fifteenth centuries, craftsmen invented textile machines, brick kilns, and even sophisticated means for smelting iron—the Newtonian synthesis provided the essential stimulus for innumerable advances. By the nineteenth century, every economic activity came under the aegis of science. Technology had created the machine tool, that epitome of industrialism—an instrument which could make copies of itself.

This unleashing of productive forces created a degree of wealth previously unimagined. World trade doubled every twenty years in nine-teenth-century Europe, and the pile of goods mounted with startling rapidity. Textile production in England, to take one illustration, increased by three thousand per cent during this period, although the industry had already reached a highly advanced level by 1800. Europeans responded with a boom in human productivity. Population went up by three-quarters of a per cent each year, the highest rate then known. In England and the Lowlands, Northern Europe and, more falteringly, in France, a take-off into affluence had been achieved by 1900.

What forces prompted this first transformation from economic stagnation to astounding growth? Bacon, Newton and their works deserve the primary credit. Yet clearly this new science could not have been pressed into such diversified service if Western Europe had not also undergone a commercial, colonial, agricultural, and social revolution.

The commercial revolution of earlier centuries produced a new economic environment which, to Marx's critical eye, "left no other nexus between man and man then naked self-interest, than callous cash payment." If it did that, it also created a new set of freedoms: freedom to buy and sell, freedom to move, a freer choice of occupation. Responding to various influences, large sections of Western Europe had abandoned the barter system and had become "market societies," in which cash transactions assumed a central role in the economy. With the advent of a new commercial life, a series of changes followed in train. Feudal landholders, anxious for cash to buy the exotic goods brought from newly explored lands, sought to raise money from their serfs by charging a cash fee (instead of the traditional "payment in kind" of agricultural produce). As a result, labor became increasingly a "commodity" and increasingly mobile. A paid laboring class, able to move more freely from area to area, slowly evolved. Merchants, standing at the core of a market society, found both their numbers and power greatly augmented. Cities assumed greater importance, as urban activities of a commercial nature multiplied.

Perhaps the most significant of these changes lay, simply, in the great extension of credit as an important financial institution. As Joseph Schumpeter, in his classic theory of economic growth, described the function of credit, ". . . the structure of modern industry could not have been erected without it . . . talent in economic life 'rides to success on its debts.' " [3] As the market economy spread, so too did opportunities for cash investment in new, productive activities. A class of entrepreneurs, using the joint stock company and other instruments of credit, jumped to take advantage of these opportunities. Capital investment moved far ahead of the level characteristic of stagnant societies and soon greatly exceeded 5 per cent of national income.

The surplus capital which these new entrepreneurs dispersed into industry came partially from funds accumulated in Europe itself. In no minor measure, however, it issued from the colonies opened by exploration. Spanish accumulation of gold, Dutch exploitation of the Indies, English colonization of India brought immense wealth to the home countries—the latter described with asperity by economist Paul Baran, as "an elaborate, ruthless, systematic despoliation. . . ." [4] There can be little question that the colonies contributed significantly to the enlargement of capitalism. William Digby has estimated that between £500 million and £1 billion were transferred from India to Britain during the period between Plassey and Waterloo. K. T. Shah and K. F. Khambata have suggested that over 10 per cent of India's national income during the early part of the nineteenth century was sent to England.[5] In essence, therefore, the developing nations of today subsidized Europe as it began its economic advance. Surely, this fact alone indicates that Western aid today should be regarded not as a sentimental gift, but as a just return on investments.

Radical changes in agriculture facilitated the deployment of this fund of capital into industrial activities. The agricultural revolution of the eighteenth and nineteenth centuries brought about both an intensification of production and major alterations in the countryside's social organization. New methods of cultivation and fertilization resulted in a steadily mounting production of food. Thus, in France between 1789 and 1848, the amount of wheat doubled, wine production went up threefold, and potatoes by fifty times. The availability of unused land benefited rural growth. In France at the beginning of the nineteenth century, 66 per cent of land lay fallow, but by 1850, half of this had been brought under the plow. Not wholly facetiously, one might even trace this transformation to the introduction of the humble beet. Faced by blockade during the Napoleonic wars, the governments of continental Europe promoted the cultivation of beetroots as a source of sugar. They did not fully anticipate that this would bring better rotation of other crops, more intensive methods, and more nutritious forage for cattle. While the causes differed (and sometimes depended on "accidents"), the nineteenth century did witness an unprecedented upsurge in food production, one impossible to match in many of the contemporary developing regions. Without this increase, the shift of workers from the farm to industry would not have been possible.

An equally important change took place in the organization of agriculture. The first stage in this evolution, accomplished in England as early as the sixteenth century, marked the end of serfdom and the creation of a free peasantry, a new class guided by motives of personal profit. In some European nations, a second trend occurred: the movement toward enclosure and the consequent push of the peasant from the land to the city. In England, feudal lords began to cultivate as private domains land which had formerly served as the common property of the peasantry. Land used for cattle grazing by an entire village was confiscated by the lords as sheepwalks for their own flocks. By the end of the nineteenth century, ten million acres (half of England's arable land) had been enclosed. Dispossessed peasants, unable to earn a living, flooded the cities and formed a new destitute labor force.

Other social changes accompanied the advance of industrialism. Taken together, they amounted to a true social revolution. The first profound changes, as Adam Smith noted, were reflected in an increasing specialization and division of labor. This greater differentiation manifested itself not only in the economy but also in such matters as the collapse of the guild system (with its manifold social functions), the assumption by several groups of the family's traditional activities, and the separation of religion from other sectors of social life, such as education.[6] This pluralization of society also brought in its wake a greater interdependence of man on man. While the eighteenth-century peasant could survive quite easily on his independent plot of land, his urban brother in the nineteenth century had become almost totally dependent on the services of other people.

In addition, the balance of political power shifted as the economic realm altered. Industrialization entailed a direct attack on the feudal nobility; gradually, privileges, power, and rights devolved upon the new classes produced by the economic revolution, but this only occurred after the process had been well advanced. Finally, as writers such as Dickens and Hugo have poignantly described, industrialism brought mass suffering. Wrenched from traditional society and thrust into a world which they did not desire, the new man of the nineteenth century sought relief in the gin mill or Methodism, the Chartist movement or the Paris Commune.

Over centuries, therefore, the men of Western Europe accumulated capital and invented a new technology, transformed agriculture and revolutionized their social structure in the creation of an industrial civilization. New men and machines, more money and food—these constituted the essential factors in Europe's rise from poverty. During its most critical period, this revamping of the economy usually took

place not in the context of a democratic order but within a fundamentally authoritarian structure, a polity which did not allow the impoverished industrial worker or peasant any immediate political recourse for their discontent.

Few would dare contend that the emerging countries could or should
duplicate this process. Among other attributes, the new nations lack
colonies as a source of capital, immigration outlets for the population
boom, and the fertile, unused lands which served so vital a part in
Western Europe's evolution. Further, as Simon Kuznets has shown,
Europe greatly exceeded the emerging nations simply in the amount
of wealth available. Most European countries had about double the
per capita income in 1800 of many contemporary underdeveloped nations.[7] Above all, the developing nations simply do not have the time;
the example of Europe's abundance lends an urgency to the economic
challenge which cannot be ignored. In their search for a quicker road
to growth, many in the developing nations not unnaturally turn away
from the nineteenth century and look to Russia for guidance.

The Soviet Example

> Without freedom, heavy industry can be perfected, but not justice
> or truth.
>
> ALBERT CAMUS

Russia, in 1917, presented a strangely varied economic landscape. Observers legitimately portrayed it as an underdeveloped, peasant, feudal
society. Some 80 per cent of the people lived in villages and 75 per
cent were engaged in agriculture. Most Russians scratched out their
subsistence in a fashion quite similar to contemporary peasants in the
underdeveloped lands. The Russian economy nevertheless had advanced far beyond the level of Western Europe in 1700 or even 1800.
Emancipation of the serfs in the 1860's and, more significantly, the
Stolypin reforms of 1906 inaugurated an agricultural revolution which
brought about an explosion in food production. And from 1880 on-
wards, Russia had undergone a great spurt in industrialization. The
government encouraged construction of railways as well as large industries in textile production, iron, coal, and oil. The banking system
was well developed, and large sums of foreign capital had been invested
in the economy.[8] In addition, the nation had developed an elite of
technicians, engineers, and skilled labor, which had been unavailable
to Western Europe during its development period.

By 1917, Russia could be described as a largely traditional economy, but one deeply infused with modernity. The very fact that Russia had lagged behind the West allowed it to construct the most modern steel plants and textile factories of the period. Russia could purchase the most advanced machinery from the West in a time when most European capitalists found it uneconomical to attempt such investments. When Lenin assumed power, therefore, he hardly confronted the same perplexing problems which face leaders of today's underdeveloped nations. He had at his disposal an economy much more modern than those of contemporary developing nations, even though its foundation had been ravaged by war and it was under attack by capitalist states.

The scope of this advantage can best be seen by comparing Russia in 1913 with India in 1956, as economist Oleg Hoeffding has done.[9] In industry, Russia exceeded India's economy by 200 per cent in coal production, 600 per cent in sewing machines, and 700 per cent in steel, —and this, despite the fact that India is the most industrialized of the developing nations and is actually the seventh-greatest industrial power in the contemporary world. In agriculture, Russia produced some 30 per cent more grain per capita in 1913 than did India in 1956. By any criteria, the Soviet experiment began at a much higher standard of economic development than that reached today by the emerging countries. This, in itself, should caution those who generalize indiscriminately about the relevance of communist "forced-draft" techniques.

Nevertheless, the Soviet achievement cannot be treated with disdain. The communist acceleration of the economy, later reflected in an astounding rate of growth, began in a faltering way. Between 1917 and 1921, Lenin introduced a program of "war communism." The government nationalized banks, factories, and railways and turned them over to workers' control. Cooks became managers, as Marx had hoped. The party abolished differential salaries and the profit system; small craftsmen and retail traders, living off profits, were hounded out of existence. Having destroyed the market, Lenin attempted to run the economy by requisitioning food from the country to feed urban workers. He tried also to direct from above the production goals of the factories. These initial policies, coupled with the war's effects, had a disastrous impact on the nation. By 1921, industrial production had fallen to 21 per cent of the prewar level and agriculture to less than half of its former productivity. The peasants ate the available food, and stubbornly resisted orders to trade it for nonexistent consumer goods.

The economy's disintegration forced Lenin to initiate the New Economic Policy, the famous "two steps backward, one step forward."

Between 1921 and 1926, the government allowed small traders to function, private industry commenced limited production again, and experiments in workers' rule over industry gave way to a more traditional managerial approach. Wage differentials reappeared, and remain strongly in force today. Farms could again operate for profit, and so food reappeared in city markets. By 1926, this partial retreat to capitalism allowed both industry and agriculture to achieve prewar quotas of production.

With a bit of fat on the economy once again, the party felt better prepared to push Russia further on the path of industrialization. Everyone in the Communist ranks desired industrialization, but the party heatedly debated the pace and methods of the process. The basic issue revolved around the question of how to stimulate the agricultural sector to produce enough food to support an expanding industry. The party's "right wing" defended a gradual approach. They wished to sacrifice temporarily the production of capital goods for that of consumer items which could be used to induce the peasantry to send food to market. As agricultural production increased, they hoped to skim off the peasant profits through taxation and devote the surplus to building industry—primarily, at first, by importing machinery from capitalist nations. The "left wing," in contrast, distrusted dependence on the West, argued that the agricultural sector would not produce sufficient capital for industrial expansion, and contended that the peasants would not co-operate unless prodded by stricter compulsions.

In 1928 Stalin settled the dispute with a series of simple, if brutal, decisions. Heavy industry, he declared, would take precedence over all else, and thus the government centralized industrial control and invested heavily in major capital goods. Trade unions, which had in a minor but inconvenient way pressed for higher wages, were abolished. Stalin collectivized farms into "artels" where the peasants received a wage, and the planners assumed power not only over the distribution of produce but also over whatever profits derived from the communes. Industrial workers received identity cards which effectively controlled their job mobility. Those who protested met death or imprisonment. Six million kulaks died in battle against the government's exploitation of their lands; other millions disappeared into slave labor camps; and the purges destroyed all who could have possibly challenged Stalin's power.

These horrors accomplished the dictator's goal of industrialization. By Russian claims, national production between 1928 and 1937 grew at a rate of 15.7 per cent a year, and between 1945 and 1950 at the even faster pace of 20 per cent annually. Western social scientists have partially discounted these estimates, but even the lowest calculation shows that the Russian economy had advanced by 5 per cent a year.[10] Most analysts agree that a reasonable estimate would fall around 7 per cent annually.[11] This represents an almost magical leap into the future and far outstrips the West's rate of growth, except during very short, exceptional periods. Today, Russia has emerged as the second-greatest industrial power. Her heavy industry produces at about half the American level and in some sectors exceeds America. By the turn of the century, not a few economists wager, Russia will have outdistanced all of her rivals.

What elements in Stalin's policy brought about this triumph? Perhaps most importantly, Russia (unlike the West) accumulated huge sums of capital by the elementary, drastic device of severely *reducing* the people's consumption. While money poured into heavy industry, the real wages of workers in Russia declined substantially between 1928 and 1952.[12] Supplies of food fell sharply: grain production, affected by collectivization, decreased by 50 per cent, and meat consumption was actually lower in 1952 than in 1915. Housing also suffered. While America, during her period of industrialization in the 1880's, invested 30 per cent of capital allocations in housing, Russia devoted only 9 per cent of its budget to building houses. As the standard of living retrogressed, the government extracted capital from the people's hides in the most systematic exploitation ever undertaken.

The so-called "turnover tax" served as perhaps the basic instrument for capital accumulation. The government would buy commodities at a fixed price, impose a turnover tax, and then sell the goods in the retail market at an artificially inflated price. Thus, for example, in 1936 the government purchased wheat from farmers at a compulsory price of 15 rubles per ton. It was then sold on the market at 107 rubles per ton. The government pocketed the surplus and invested in industry.

Backed by this massive fund of capital (some 16 to 25 per cent of national income), the government directed investment to the single overriding goal of producing a heavy industrial base. Through its absolute command over the market, the government could cut down on all other investments which conflicted with its primary aims. Average investment in factories, dams, and utilities amounted to 45 per cent of all investments, about twice the usual level. Stalin also assigned an exceptionally high priority to investments in technical education, schooling designed to produce the engineers and mechanics for servicing the new industry. By directing investment in ways substantially different from Europe's, the Communists created an unbalanced economy in which agriculture, service, consumption goods, and housing suffered but heavy industry boomed. Indeed, Russia today is surfeited with heavy industry. Its planners find great difficulty in shifting to the creation of light industries and better agriculture, as the government has now ordered.

The success of the Russian experiment can reasonably be traced to two factors: a high rate of capital accumulation, achieved by bleeding the people, and an unusual capacity to direct investment into a single channel. Backed by organs of terror, a ruthless repression of dissent, and total, if often ineffective, planning, Russia operated as a closely centralized "war economy" molded to the fulfillment of Stalin's will.[13] Many who advocate the adoption of the Soviet system by the developing nations fail to realize that this approach, while admittedly capable of achieving its paramount aim, was extraordinarily inefficient by objective standards. In forcing industrialization down the throats of the Russian people, Stalin extravagantly wasted national resources.[14] Agriculture, as we have noted, suffered a startling drop in production. Even today, America produces twice as much cotton and potatoes, and triple the sum of grain per acre as does Russia. This was, however, only the first and most apparent of many wastes. Russia required much more electricity to run its factories and a great deal more metal in its products, for each item produced, than did Western Europe or America. In labor productivity, the average American worker produced twice as much cement, five times the coal, and sevenfold more sugar than his Russian counterpart. Analysts can explain these striking differences partially in terms of natural factors (e.g., the relative infertility of Russian land) and partially in terms of conscious Soviet policy (e.g., Russia's labor surplus made it economically rational to squander human energy). These variables alone, however, cannot explain the marked differentials in productivity between certain American and Russian industries, equally well designed and equipped with modern machinery.

Much of the inefficiency has to be attributed to the atmosphere of terror, which could do a great deal to discourage initiative, and to centralized planning which sometimes committed errors on a colossal scale. When the government demanded an increase in tin roofs, to cite one illustration, the roofing industry did not have the proper capacity to fulfill the order. The roofing factories did, however, manage to gobble up all of the extra tons of tin arbitrarily allocated by the planning powers by the simple, if costly, expedient of making each roof heavier. Since the government measured fulfillment of its plan by the number of tons of tin consumed, the planners were happy, even though vast amounts of metal had been wasted.

To summarize, Russia like Europe had enormous sums of capital at its disposal, a food surplus, and virtually unlimited amounts of land and resources at the time it began its rapid development. Few developing nations can claim these boons. Russia's advance was by no means the bootstrap operation glowingly pictured by its defenders, rather it was a forced maturation of a quite modern nation which had already attained the status of a major industrial power by 1917.* Emerging nations today cannot afford to waste their more meager resources in the grandiose fashion which Russia did. Most importantly, they are unable to accumulate capital by reducing consumption, for this would mean starvation and revolt. Russia, with a food surplus, could neglect agriculture in a quest for Dnieper dams; the newer nations cannot.

In considering the pertinence of Soviet history to emerging nations, a rational man must reject the Russian model, in its pristine form, solely on economic grounds. And for those who long for liberty as well as bread, reflection on the somber happenings in twentieth-century Russia can lead only to Camus' conclusion that the perfection of heavy industry has little to do with creating a humane, just society.

The Japanese Model

> By external circumstances and by the ambitious temperament of her own people, Japan has been obliged . . . to compress into a few decades an economic development which most other industrialized nations have spread over at least a century.
>
> M. D. KENNEDY

Only one non-Western society, Japan, has succeeded in making the "great ascent." It did so while handicapped by burdens which far exceeded those of the West or Russia. In 1868, when the pulse of growth began to beat faster, Japan lacked an industrial base comparable to that possessed by Europe in 1800 or Russia in 1900. She had only tiny amounts of arable land which could be brought under cultivation. She was critically deficient in the basic mineral resources, a supposed pre-

---

* Russia's recovery after World War II can more legitimately be described as an economic miracle. Perhaps 50 per cent of its capital capacity had been destroyed, yet the economy blossomed once again. By this point, however, Russia could use German reparations and the economic resources of its newly acquired satellites.

requisite for industrialization. Because of the international situation, she could neither impose protective tariffs (which played a significant role in aiding continental Europe's infant industries) nor could she depend upon colonies as a source of capital, resources, and markets. The nation could not boast of a cadre of trained personnel such as that which carried out Lenin's and Stalin's ambitions. Japan's per capita income rested at a much lower level than Europe's or Russia's at the beginning of their expansion and, thus, capital did not lie ready at hand.

Despite unpropitious circumstances (which resemble closely the situation in today's new nations), Japan underwent an economic transformation which surpassed Europe's and rivaled Russia's in its scope and pace. From almost nothing in 1868, Japan built 4600 industrial concerns by 1896. Between 1878 and 1887, a critical decade of expansion, the total national product increased by 42 per cent. From the end of the nineteenth century through World War I, the amount of food approximately doubled. Each decade until the 1930's, national production increased by almost 50 per cent.

A poor peasant society, almost devoid of resources, actually created a modern economy. The transition began with a deliberate decision taken by a small elite. Until 1868, the Tokugawa clans ruled Japan as a typically feudal regime, consciously secluded from Western contact. The West intruded on this isolation intermittently, but most devastatingly in 1863 and 1864 when European ships bombarded Sotsuma and Choshu. This undeniable demonstration of modern technology's superiority convinced a dissident group of samurai—the "outer clans" already alienated from the ruling clique—that Japan had to abandon its traditionalist policies. Under the Meiji rulers who succeeded to power in a relatively bloodless manner, these nobles vigorously pursued a program of modernization.

The tasks of the Meiji were eased by the fact that, while Japan was a rural, traditional society in 1868, it had not been utterly stagnant under Tokugawa rule. To some degree, Japan had already experienced a commercial revolution, similar to that in the West. Money had circulated since 1690; a small merchant class receptive to modern innovations had developed; and urban concentrations had begun to grow. In consequence, a pool of mobile labor existed, and a base had been laid for "market-oriented" attitudes. Further, like the West and Russia, Japan enjoyed an agricultural surplus. As Thomas Smith has made clear, Japan under the Tokugawa had shifted from a communal to an individual system of farming.[15] When the introduction of new fertilizers and techniques, the substitution of rice for unirrigated crops, and the cultivation of new products for urban markets supplemented this change, the result was an upswing in production. Under the Meiji, total farm output increased markedly. Japan could, therefore, easily accommodate the population expansion which accompanied her initial economic growth. Until the 1890's, Japan actually exported food.

While fortunate in possessing a food surplus, the Meiji rulers faced formidable obstacles in their desire to transform the economy. Stung by humiliations at the hands of the West, they sought to create a nation which could recoup its military glory. Certainly, Japan's military adventures worked to her temporary advantage in providing resources and markets. Further, the nationalism cultivated by the Meiji may well have provided a psychological framework which eased the burdens of economic growth. On the other hand, the leaders squandered money on the military. The army budget alone increased from one million yen in 1868 to 107 million yen by 1908. For good or ill, the drive to modernization got its impetus from an urge to make Japan into a major military power, a nationalist goal apparently shared by the people.

To assure the foundation for military power, the nobles had to construct a modern, growing technical base. They succeeded in doing this with extraordinary rapidity by following a series of policies which differed in basic ways from the Western model and also in certain significant features from that of Russia. These differences deserve the closest attention, for they represent the first response of a non-Western nation to problems fundamentally similar to those of the contemporary developing countries.

First, unlike the West even in its mercantilist era, the government assumed paramount importance as the stimulant to growth. The state took a hand not only in creating the "social overhead" of railroads, irrigation canals, and roads but also as the initiator of directly productive enterprises. Throughout the nineteenth century, some 50 per cent of all investment came from government coffers. The policy could be termed one of "guided capitalism." The rulers established model factories, producing silk and cement, cotton and soap. After the enterprise had demonstrated its utility, private entrepreneurs, often drawn from the same noble class as the government bureaucracy, took over control. This pattern of economic change differed markedly from that of the West, for the propellers of change were in no sense bourgeois enterpreneurs but rather members of the ruling nobility. As Robert Bellah has argued in his stimulating analysis of Japanese values:

Only one class was in a position to lead the nation in breaking new ground: the samurai class. From the nature of its situation, its locus of strength was the polity, not the economy. I am insistent on this point because the tendency to regard economic developments as "basic" and political developments as "superstructure" is by no means confined to Marxist circles but permeates most current thinking on such matters.[16]

The Meiji rulers accumulated their investment capital essentially by squeezing it from the peasantry.[17] Agricultural production mounted steadily under the new government, but taxation held down the farmers' consumption and skimmed off the new profits for further investment. A land tax, imposed in 1873, forced farmers to pay a fixed charge on the value of their land amounting to about 25 per cent of the yield. As production climbed, so did tax returns.* In consequence, by 1875, revenue from the land tax accounted for 85 per cent of government income. Paul Baran has underlined the immense significance of this measure: "It is . . . no exaggeration to say that the main source of primary accumulation of capital in Japan was the village which, in the course of its entire modern history, played for Japanese capitalism the role of an internal colony." [18]

The pattern and type of industrialization undertaken also contrasted with that of the West and Russia. In those regions heavy industrial complexes formed the base of economic development. Japan, in contrast, emphasized light, cottage industries, widely decentralized throughout the country. These small workshops produced handmade consumer goods or components which were later assembled in the cities. In 1878, 81 per cent of all production in the textile industry came from light or cottage units; by 1930, the proportion was still 59 per cent, and even today it remains at 35 per cent. In a nation possessing an overabundant supply of labor, this policy had much in its favor. Since human energy could replace expensive imported machines in the productive process, capital could be conserved while, simultaneously, the talents of unemployed men could be released.

Such a program allowed Japan to grow very quickly, without the investment of enormous sums of capital. During similar periods, Japan

---

* A moderate inflationary spiral of some 8 per cent a year accompanied the process of capital accumulation and economic growth. Indeed, a "controlled" inflation was also characteristic of the Russian and European patterns of growth. As some of the "tougher-minded" fiscal experts fail to realize, moderate inflation may create a set of optimistic expectations which can serve to facilitate rather than impede economic growth in developing areas.

and England invested approximately the same, relatively small amounts of capital, but Japan's growth in per capita product outraced England's by more than two to one. The program also meant that economic change came gradually; rather than being ripped unceremoniously from their lands and placed in the alien environment of a factory, the Japanese integrated new productive processes into their old ways of earning a living. One might say, too, that economic growth in Japan was "family-centered"; even today 30 per cent of Japan's labor force works in their own homes with their families, as compared to only 2 per cent in America and 0.2 per cent in Britain. The Japanese policy, therefore, demonstrated for the first time in history that "labor-intensive" light industry could serve as the vehicle for economic advance.

The nature of social change also differed in Japan. Radical alterations in the fabric of social life accompanied Europe's march into industrialization and occurred largely in a spontaneous, unplanned fashion. In Russia, the Bolsheviks precipitously and often unsuccessfully tried to destroy the traditional social order. The Meiji regime also set itself the task of initiating pervasive social reforms, aimed at facilitating economic growth. Yet many reform measures were also designed to buttress tradition, rather than to dismantle it.

In the attempt to modernize their society, the Meiji rulers attacked on several fronts. They undermined feudalism by breaking up landed estates and by encouraging the growth of small, individually-owned farms. This dismemberment of feudalism took place with remarkable ease; some former Tokugawa lords even voluntarily surrendered their land, perhaps because land in Japan did not have the supreme importance as a mark of noble status which it did in Europe. Indeed, in the whole process of feudal reform, the only serious rebellion was not triggered over the land issue, but rather occurred when the Meiji demanded that some traditionally oriented samurai should surrender their ritual swords. Antagonism arose, in other words, when the new government tampered with the symbols not the substance of the feudal order—a phenomenon which contemporary modernizers might do well to remember. New symbols were also created to ensure the people's allegiance. In particular, the rulers sought to create a cult of reverence for the Meiji emperor.

The Meiji also endeavored to "westernize" significant segments (although not all sectors) of their society. The government encouraged students to travel abroad for technical education. They opened their ports to trade and to European advisers who soon flooded every ministry. They abolished certain feudal practices such as the torture of criminals, and they even ordered civil servants to wear European clothes. They poured effort into the creation of a modern educational system, particularly technical schools. The rulers spent a very high proportion of the national budget on education, especially in contrast to Europe of the time. Within an astonishingly short period, these various measures produced a core of Japanese equipped with modern skills and attitudes.

While the Meiji desired the human resources to staff their expanding industry, they did not by any means wish to disband traditional society. In fact, they deliberately tried to cement the ties which linked a person to his family, his community, his traditional values, and to the Meiji emperor. Among other undertakings, the government legally defined the individual's responsibilities to his family and local village. The law made children responsible for support of their aged relatives (thus instituting an informal system of social security). The courts proclaimed, too, that the head of a family was legally accountable for the actions of any of its members. Only after divorces had been considered by a full family council would the courts take action. Each person had to register himself as a member of his family and the village of his origin, and legally he remained a part of these groups forever.[19] In its educational program, too, the government ensured that the cultivation of modern aptitudes would not disrupt the traditional order, by ordering all schools in 1872 to inculcate reverence for family and emperor as the prime goals of education.

For those who entered the new factories, the government strove to create a social framework which would disturb traditional life in the least possible way. Workers usually remained in the same productive group permanently and were originally recruited on the basis of their previous status in the traditional order. Various social criteria determined the worker's rewards and his position in a complicated hierarchy. As a whole, the factory system exhibited a pronounced paternalistic spirit; employers regarded workers as parts of a large family.[20]

These various efforts to ensure the stability of traditional life, as well as the government's emphasis on light, decentralized industry, allowed Japan to avoid the social disorganization which industrialism occasioned in the West. Urbanism proceeded at a relatively slow pace, and the number of people engaged in agriculture remained steady; the sum of those living off the land declined by only 12 per cent between 1868 and 1940. Rates of crime, alcoholism, and other symptoms of social disorder did not skyrocket as they had in nineteenth-century Europe. Observers remarked on the "discipline" of urban laborers and their acceptance of the rigors of factory life. Militant trade unions did not emerge until the 1920's, and the entrepreneurs created by "guided capitalism" did not, as in the West, demand new political rights and power. In its early stages, industrialization for Japan became little more than the frosting on a cake of custom and tradition.

In Japan, therefore, we observe the remarkable case of a nation which truly lifted itself by its bootstraps and did so, even more surprisingly, without the wholesale destruction of tradition which economic growth normally entails. Unblessed with the resources or land or capital of Europe and Russia, Japan underwent a transformation which approached the miraculous. Certainly, the samurai relied on advantages which leaders of contemporary nations can seldom claim: they had a food surplus, export markets in Asia (provided when the Western nations had to withdraw from competition during World War I), and, eventually, colonies. The Meiji could also count on the allegiance of a peasant population long accustomed to national unity and discipline, and undisturbed by the longings for equality and affluence which have appeared in the new nations. Recognition of these differences should not, however, obscure the fact that Japan offers an exciting example of how a determined national elite once reconciled growth with the preservation of traditional society.

History's Relevance

> It is no great wonder, if in long process of time, while fortune takes her course hither and thither, numerous coincidences should spontaneously occur.
>
> GEORGE CURTIS

While the experience of Europe, Russia, and Japan cannot be translated unchanged into the middle of the twentieth century, still we can see that these nations achieved economic growth by overcoming five common obstacles. First, each society underwent commercialization. The accidents of history and the decisions of statesmen conspired to replace barter systems with the market, serfs with mobile labor, feudal lords with innovators. Secondly, men escaped from starvation, that state of recurrent famine which is always man's destiny in stagnant societies. The beetroot in France, irrigation canals in Japan, new plows in Russia: these apparently minor changes promoted agricultural revolutions which provided the indispensable granary for industrialization. Without it, the masses needed to fill modern forms of work could not have been released from subsistence toil.

Thirdly, the entrepreneurs, whether Japanese nobles or French Huguenots, secured and invested capital. In England industrialists extracted productive wealth from a new class of urban laborers and from the spoils of colonialization. In Russia the party squashed consumption in the service of heavy industry. In Japan the peasants bore the burden of capital accumulation. Although the elites accomplished it in various ways (and often with a severity which would not be tolerated in a democratic polity), they managed to amass a potentially productive surplus which, with proper cultivation, multiplied itself. Fourthly, new "human resources," from clerks to scientists, railroad workers to accountants, appeared in each society. These midwives of economic advance evolved more or less spontaneously in Europe but were deliberately and rapidly trained in Russia and Japan. Lastly, of course, each society applied its new resources to industrialization, a process in which machinery came to the aid of human productivity on a scale never before attempted.*

To call the roll of these common tasks implies that the newer nations aspiring to economic growth must resolve similar issues. And, in truth, I see no reason to hold out hope that these burdens can be avoided. But the historical record also shows that men have approached their common economic problems in a variety of ways. This very diversity is encouraging, for it suggests that the underdeveloped nations need not conform to a single mold of development.

Development has proceeded even in nations which lacked the supposed prerequisites for economic growth, such as "essential" natural resources. The Netherlands led the pace in Europe, although she possessed few mineral deposits. Denmark became a great agricultural exporter, even though her land was markedly less fecund than that of other nations. Missing coal, iron, and oil, Japan still achieved a fast rate of growth. Malta provides a classic example. Although virtually an "inhabited quarry" in the nineteenth century, the island developed advanced agriculture. Its peasants ground heavy rocks into pebbles, collected bits of soil from crevices, and mixed the two into a productive topsoil. Ingenuity and enterprise have often substituted for natural abundance.

Further, history does not lend strong support to those who insist that development occurs only when certain social preconditions for growth

---

* I use the term "industrialization" to mean simply the replacement of human energy with other sources of energy. Thus, in contemporary America, human muscles contribute only one per cent of the energy used in production, while in largely nonindustrialized nations such as India, human energy accounts for 60 per cent of production.

are provided. One group of experts, for example, led by Max Millikan and Donald Blackmer, has argued that two of the essential requirements for growth include "the expansion of the society's human resources; . . . (and) the laying down of basic transport, communication, irrigation, and power facilities." [21] Japan's experience (and, to a lesser degree, Russia's) confirms this generalization, for there the governments invested heavily in education and "social overhead capital" at the beginning of industrialization. In Europe, in contrast, industrialization preceded the building of railroads and dams, technical schools and scientific institutes. Economic development made possible these advances and, in some measure, initiated them. We should remain cautious, therefore, of those theories which arbitrarily allocate the highest priority to, say, education or to other enterprises which are not in themselves directly productive. On a simple economic level, as Albert Hirschman has ably demonstrated, the rewards of investment in a school rather than a factory must be carefully weighed in terms of a country's particular situation.[22]

We cannot find backing, either, for those such as Robert Heilbroner who believe that "an amalgamation of small farming units into large ones, and a displacement of a considerable portion of the peasantry from the land, is a necessity for almost every developing country, no matter how painful the procedure." [23] Certainly, this process of consolidation and eventual mechanization of agriculture did take place in Europe. And in Russia the Bolsheviks also attempted to communize the land, with disastrous results. Japanese farmers, on the other hand, produced a significant agricultural surplus without introducing mechanized techniques and without altering the structure of their "postage stamp" plots of land. Thus, the consolidation of land (and the consequent push of people into the cities) may under some circumstances aid food production. But the Japanese record offers convincing evidence that the traditional patterns of production and land tenure, so prevalent in the developing societies, can also be highly productive.

Two other important aspects of the Japanese advance must be underlined. Economic modernization in Japan did not entail the destruction of traditional society. Japan drastically altered her economy but managed to reinforce the structure of village life and of the extended family system. For those in the developing nations, caught up in the glamour of modern life but still retaining an admiration for traditional virtues, the Meiji policies offer a significant example of how some of the "social costs" of modernization may be avoided.

In addition, Japan aptly demonstrates that economic advance should not be identified solely with steel factories, steamships, and textile mills. Small-scale industries, calling upon the latent resources of the village, were the foundation of the new Japanese economy. As much as, perhaps more than machine tools, hand-looms gave impetus to Japan's advance. Again, for nations which sadly lack capital equipment, Japan's history gives reason for believing that economic growth may still proceed.

We should view with some skepticism, therefore, the long lists of prerequisites for economic growth which proliferate today. In some fashion, of course, developing nations must secure capital, increase food production, and apply new, productive techniques to their economic problems. The record indicates, however, that nations have advanced even while lacking resources or engineers, railroads or mechanized farms, fertile land or universal education. They have moved forward, most significantly, without the wrenching dislocations which authoritarians (as well as many scholars) regard as the inevitable price of economic growth.

In achieving an economic take-off in drastically different environments, men have attacked the problem with a variety of tools. We can take heart in this diversity, for it suggests that man's economic ingenuity has few limitations. In considering the essential topic which concerns us, the political framework of growth, the past presents an equally varied vista. Both liberals and authoritarians can call upon history to provide justifications for contemporary policy.

In defending their belief that only a centralized government wielding dictatorial powers can provide the base for economic growth, authoritarians (and intellectuals who reluctantly believe in the inevitability of dictatorship) can discover certain elements in economic history which sustain their position.

First of all, in most cases of economic change, centralized national governments played an important role. Economic growth has usually begun only in nations with long histories of political unity. Economic development in its earliest stages, Kenneth Galbraith has observed, "undoubtedly involves the building of organs of public administration and the provision of an educated minority, a nucleus of people who can build the system of public administration and, for that matter, everything else." [24] In the nations which we have surveyed, a sound public administration existed, and the state did a great deal to induce economic growth. Sometimes, as in Europe, this aid took the form of railroad building, protectionist policies, and colonial aggrandizement. At other times, in Japan and Russia, the government directly accumulated capital and undertook entrepreneurial risks. Unfortunately, in many of the currently developing nations, the state does not exhibit the same unity, capacity, or even probity as, say, the nineteenth-century English government.

Further, we should clearly understand that history issues no assurance that economic development will bring democracy in its wake. Germany achieved major industrial eminence long before military defeat forced democratic forms upon her. And the Japanese, who could brilliantly adopt Western technology, failed to emulate Western political forms. Even if the new nations can succeed in stimulating economic growth, the past offers little reason to believe that liberal democracy will be guaranteed.

We should also admit that economic development has usually, although not always, occurred under an authoritarian government, a regime which did not allow those people most affected by the burdens of industrialization any major role in deciding their fate. Whether ultimate power rested in the hands of a revolutionary elite, a noble class, or a small group of property owners, dictatorship and industrialization have often been tied in a marriage of convenience.

As Eugene Staley has cogently argued, a distinction should be drawn between the "early-comers" to industrialization (England and Holland) and the "late-comers" (Germany, Japan, and Russia). The early-comers had relatively more political freedom during their transition, since "it took a considerable degree of individual and intellectual freedom to make possible the invention and initial growth of the modern industrial system. . . . But once industrialism has been invented and demonstrated, it can be *taken over* and deliberately installed in unfree environments which could not have created it in the first place. . . . Nowadays we are dealing in the underdeveloped countries with a quite different kind of economic development which, in its first phase, is a development by borrowing ideas from abroad. The political atmosphere in which this process takes place can be either authoritarian or democratic." [25]

The utility of authoritarianism has not come from its greater economic efficiency or from an ability to avoid waste. Rather, its usefulness stemmed from the fact that authoritarian rule often facilitated capital accumulation, the transfer of an economic surplus from consumers to an elite (whether English industrialists or Japanese samurai) who invested it in productive activities. By excluding the lower classes from political participation, the controlling powers could suppress the discontent which this process entailed. It seems unlikely, for example, that the Japanese peasants would have welcomed the critically important land tax if they had the vote or that English yeomen would have willingly sacrificed their lands simply to expand textile production. And, certainly, history gives us little reason to believe that the Russian people would have given up their bread and homes in the service of industrialization, if they had really determined their destiny. It is this feature of authoritarianism—its ability, by choking off dissent, to quicken and direct capital accumulation—which lends it an economic appeal.

If that were all that history had to tell us, then contemporary authoritarians might have good cause for their opinions. We must closely scrutinize their claims, however, for history will not support the weight of many arguments which the authoritarians propose. Most importantly, the evidence does not confirm the belief held by Marxists that the rigors of economic development have *necessitated* a dictatorial government in one form or another. Political freedom and economic development have, in several instances, been successfully reconciled. One can point, for example, to Switzerland and Denmark as encouraging illustrations of liberal democracy's economic competence. In Denmark, a number of factors—the flexibility of the upper class, the existence of a free peasantry, the beneficent influence of the folk school movement —combined to create a stable liberal democracy which preceded the coming of large-scale industrialization. Democracy not only accommodated economic development in Denmark, but through various governmental actions—subsidies to capitalists, an early recognition of trade unions, the provision of technical education—actively stimulated economic growth. Similarly, in Switzerland, economic development went ahead within a democratic environment, even though the nation was racked not only by class conflicts but also by linguistic, religious, and ethnic battles. One of the more significant aspects of Swiss and Danish development was that both nations followed a path which resembled Japan's. Small-scale, artisan industries scattered through the countries established the base for economic advance, and both nations gave special attention to the development of progressive agriculture. While economic change was profound, it spread over these nations in a gradual fashion, affecting various segments of the population relatively equally. Capital did not need to be drained from the country to serve the city, for rural sectors advanced with equal rapidity. This decentralization of economic growth may provide one of the keys to understanding how political freedom can survive in an era of change.

Not only has growth begun despite political freedom, but there is evidence to suggest that authoritarian rule may, under some circumstances, have decisively retarded economic advance. In Russia, for example, greater freedom would in all probability have avoided the sad effects on agriculture of Stalin's attempt to force higher production. Similarly in Russia, more flexibility would have forestalled the immensely wasteful impact of trying to centralize all economic decisions and controls. One might wonder, too, about the possible effects of greater political freedom in Europe's development. If the Chartist demands had been fully granted, the workers would have gained greater dignity and initiative which might well have been reflected in productivity. If Owen's program had replaced the nineteenth-century sweatshop, perhaps the whole factory system would have enjoyed the flourishing prosperity of Lanark. If the French monarchs had not insisted upon the persecution of Protestant merchants, maybe France would not have lagged so far behind other European nations.

On close examination, many of the generalizations which contemporary authoritarians use to buttress their position fail to survive review. There is no reason, most importantly, to believe that the crushing of dissent must necessarily accompany economic advance or that centralized government control over the economy always results in a more efficient use of a nation's resources.

History can dispel some of the authoritarians' misapprehensions but it cannot guarantee the "inevitability" of either a liberal or an authoritarian regime in the developing nations. From such ambiguity, the liberal democrat can derive some satisfaction, for it suggests that he can, if he has the will, paint the familiar portrait of economic development anew with colors other than the black or red of dictatorship. As Hans Kohn has put it, historical perspective helps us in rejecting both "the utopias of enthusiasm and the utopias of despair." It is in that indefinite middle range between certainties that the liberal finds his proper domain in responding to the economic challenge.

IV

FINDING THE MONEY

Whosoever tries for great objects must suffer something.

PLUTARCH

Too often, in these days of uncertain progress, intellectuals abandon hope that any measures can alleviate misery in developing nations. Misinterpreting history as well as the passing scene of events, they fall into the despairing belief that ". . . for the majority of nations now attempting the long climb the outcome in our time will be defeat." [1] Immediate trends in the 1960's seem to confirm this opinion. At best, the "Alliance for Progress" founders in inertia. India's struggles have succeeded after fifteen years in augmenting per capita income by only one dollar per year. And during the last decade, some nations have not only failed to progress but have actually been sucked further into the mire of economic stagnation. Indonesian industry and plantations produce much less than they did under Dutch rule. After a promising start during World War II, Chile now has less real income per capita than before. In Peru, economic growth has fallen drastically behind the birth rate.

In foreign trade, too, the new nations function in a peculiarly unfavorable environment. Their few industrial products face the extraordinarily stiff competition of Detroit, Manchester, and Moscow; not surprisingly, the Volkswagen can easily defeat India's Ambassador car in a free market arena. The frequent total dependence of the under-developed nations on a single export product—cocoa, bananas, copper, coffee—subjects them to the vagaries of the world market. A collapse in prices for a particular commodity can destroy an entire economy, as the demise of tin's value shook Bolivia and the fall in coffee's price sent Colombia into chaos. Just the existence of highly industrialized nations (and of an intricately interlocked world economy) creates certain obstacles unknown in earlier periods.

Further, the already advanced nations did not suffer from some of the political and social hindrances to economic growth which handicap aspiring areas in the modern era. Entrenched military elites in South America, divisive tribalism in Africa, quietistic religions in Asia impose barriers which—while their equivalents were not unknown in Europe, Japan, and Russia—had been generally removed by the time economic progress began.

Above all, the populations of the "old" nations had not yet been infected with various doctrines, now widely propagated throughout the world. These new ideas sometimes operate more effectively than the usual economic factors to block action. In Africa, nationalism inhibits the creation of large, economically viable units, and racism, caught from Western colonialism, sometimes prohibits the use of foreign "white" experts who could provide crucially necessary advice and skills. In India, equalitarian dogmas force the government to adopt welfare and labor legislation which, while humanitarian in purpose, could hardly be adequately financed even in Scandinavia. In Indonesia, social-ism has driven out almost all foreign capital. Rubber plantations and factories (formerly flourishing under private management) languish from the neglect of economically untrained army officers and bureau-crats. Equalitarianism, nationalism, socialism, racism—these originally Western ideas—can sometimes be regarded as among the most impor-tant hindrances to economic progress in the new nations.

If one focuses on the massed obstacles to economic growth, it would appear that the new nations suffer from enormous disadvantages. Only those untutored in the economics of development could hope that these hobbled nations can really repeat the spectacular successes of an England, a Denmark, or a Russia. But these developing nations also have certain distinct advantages, some of which are unduplicated in economic history.

Like other countries before their jump into abundance, the under-developed economies have an unrealized potential. Some of these coun-tries possess capital reserves which, at the moment, the upper classes expend on flashy cars, Dior dresses, and American stocks. If these luxury expenditures could be converted into useful projects—technical schools, let us say, for Carolina de Jesus' children—we could anticipate tangible progress. Other nations have untapped mineral resources, uncultivated land, underpopulated virgin areas which could be put to use.

Most importantly, people go to waste. Villagers and, even more, city dwellers have to remain idle, although many crave work and the small rewards which employment could bring. And, in some nations, a mass of intellectuals fail to find useful employment, partially because their education has fitted them only for elegant exercises in the classics. As in the past, sensible economic policies, or brutal ones, could release these latent springs of progress.

Beyond these beneficial factors (which almost every country has at the commencement of its economic advance), contemporary underdeveloped regions have certain other, almost unique, advantages. To a limited but still critically important degree, they can call upon foreign aid from both the Western and Soviet blocs. While sometimes hedged with high interest rates or other restrictions, these grants compose about 30 per cent of all capital investment. Some countries also retain substantial benefits from their colonial heritage. However evil in other ways, colonialism in many cases did lay the base for a trained elite and civil service. It built much of the so-called "infra-structure" of railroads, dams, schools and highways which Europe and Japan lacked at the beginning of their development. And colonialism left enclaves of modern industry, mining, and advanced agriculture which, again, eighteenth-century nations did not possess in such abundance or technical perfection. The progress of science and technology can also be counted on the positive side of the ledger, for now developing countries can draw upon a fund of freely dispersed knowledge which did not exist previously. And, too, they can observe the models which history has provided of the relative efficacy of different political regimes in stimulating economic growth.

Objectively, the prospects are not as dismal as some prophets of gloom say. In theory, at least, the limited, specific aspirations of "transitional men" can be fulfilled. Whether the underdeveloped peoples can, in fact, capitalize on their potentialities and their unique advantages constitutes the fundamental issue: will their leaders have sufficient determination, knowledge, and humaneness to mobilize these positive elements in a sustained drive for economic progress?

Our review of history offers some hope in this matter, since it indicates that there are as many routes to economic welfare as roads to

Paris from the provinces. Whatever the method, certain critical tasks must be faced today, as they have been in the past by every advancing nation. These challenges—or better yet, one should label them dilemmas, for there are no simple solutions—can be reduced to four interrelated problems:

First, the developing nation must somehow accumulate capital, saved from the rigors of a subsistence economy; a surplus which can be invested in productive activities.

Secondly, the developing nation must revolutionize its agriculture, for without a vigorous rural sector a country cannot produce either the capital or the men for industrial undertakings.

Thirdly, a developing nation must encourage (or, at the minimum, tolerate) alterations in men and institutions.

Fourthly, all of these changes have to be channeled into the process of industrialization, where machines add their strength to the productivity of human or animal energy.

I do not mean to imply that the solution to these four tasks must proceed through preordained stages of growth. The breakthrough can come at any point or, most usually, through simultaneous advance along all fronts. If any element takes precedence over others, it would appear historically that an agricultural revolution has often been the main trigger of progress. But, in turn, agricultural advance has depended upon the investment of capital. The seventeenth-century English lord who improved his estates' productivity had to secure from some source the cash (or the labor) to finance alterations on his land.

Let us first face this *dilemma of capital,** the perplexing issue of how abysmally poor nations can find the money to initiate development. One fact about capital accumulation is that the rich get richer. There is no more valid precept in any economic textbook, for whether one considers individuals or nations, wealth begets wealth. A starving peasant, consuming what little he produces, cannot conceive of the possibilities for productive investment open to a Rockefeller or a Rothschild. And so it is with entire economies: before a nation can create the prerequisites of modernity, it must somehow scrape together a fund of capital.

* By capital, I mean "produced wealth, used productively." [2] This definition excludes land and other resources not produced by man, as well as consumer goods which are not used to further increase a nation's wealth. Under this rubric, I would include any investment which increased the productivity of land, resources, machines, or (through education) the productivity of man himself. Obviously, too, we cannot equate simple saving with capital formation since the hoarding of riches, as occurred in certain periods in France and other nations, can decisively retard economic growth.

With a fair degree of exactitude, economic theory has succeeded in estimating the relation between capital and economic progress. Economist Colin Clark has been able to reduce this complex relationship to a simple but workable rule of thumb: "It is only in so far as the rate of investment exceeds the rate of population increase multiplied by four that anything will be left for industrialization or for raising standards of real income." [3] Stating it differently, most economists believe that economic progress requires that about four dollars be invested to secure one dollar's worth of improvement in per capita income. This dry formula hardly reveals the extent of the staggering burden which capital accumulation imposes upon an underdeveloped nation. Harrison Brown has shown that an expenditure of $500 billion in developing regions would be necessary to accomplish the modest goal of shifting just one-fourth of the laboring force from rural into industrial work. For such nations to attain the current level of American riches would demand investment of the impossible sum of $3600 billion in capital.[4]

We have seen how some nations in the past have managed to save a surplus for investment. London workers, colonial peons, Russian kulaks, and Japanese peasants paid the price with their suffering. While an investing elite grew richer, the masses either restricted or reduced their consumption. Although Marx hardly intended the statement in the full meaning which we might give it, his observation concerning the genesis of capital still rings true: "If money . . . comes into the world with a congenital blood-stain on one cheek, capital comes dripping from head to foot, from every pore, with blood and dirt." [5]

Again, sacrifices will have to be made, for, in the great enterprise of economic growth, they cannot be avoided. But today, if reason prevails, the effort must be undertaken by all classes, particularly by those who have traditionally monopolized wealth in underdeveloped nations.

In developing countries it is true that the upper classes (not least, politicians) drain away potentially productive capital in luxuries and frivolities. I have visited homes in India, Indonesia, and Africa whose opulence might cause envy in a Texas millionaire. To take a single blatant example, six of the oil-producing countries of the Middle East received some three billion dollars in payments between 1945 and 1954. The greater part of this windfall went into the purses of fabulously rich sheiks, while their subjects continued to subsist on an annual income of about fifty dollars a year. If this same amount of money had been put into productive enterprises, the current income of these impoverished people would have increased by 50 per cent.[6] Instead, these nations have stagnated while the rulers enjoyed air-conditioned Cadillacs and voluptuously endowed harems. While not as extreme, a similar situation exists in other regions. In Puerto Rico, 10 per cent of the population receive 40 per cent of all income, and only a small proportion of this sum is reinvested. Even in India, not more than 50 per cent of business profits (and perhaps as little as 25 per cent) is plowed back into productive enterprises.[7]

The fault does not lie entirely with the "exploiting classes," as the Marxists would have us believe. Even the poorest transitional men in these societies, if they have any money at all, often expend it on items of questionable economic worth. The sales of beer, magic amulets, or "High-life" records sometimes exceed the money spent on plows, seeds, or medicine. Only a Dracula-like economic planner would wish to deny people the passing relief which a glass of arak or a religious icon brings a man. Nevertheless, if the choice is between spending money on a shot of whiskey or buying the quinine which could save a child from malaria, the nonessential pleasures have to be sacrificed.

How can it be done? Leaders of developing nations and social scientists have proposed three basic approaches: total confiscation of all potential capital by the government; a laissez-faire approach which would leave the responsibility to private sources; and a middle-of-the-road, pluralistic solution which would aim at collaboration between the state and private groups. Since, at base, most of the grand economic issues of the moment center on these politically volatile alternatives, we must examine the possibilities with care.*

Defenders of the view that the state should confiscate all "surplus" capital point to the glaring inequalities which obviously characterize developing nations. With ample reason, they contend that the cash now spent for haciendas and trips to the Riviera should be put into schools, factories, dams, and farms. As the mechanism for transforming this wealth into useful projects, those of the socialist persuasion argue for socialization of capital. Confiscation of all major sources of capital would, they assume, allow an "objectively rational" planning authority

---

* A fourth way of raising capital has been followed, sometimes unconsciously, by many nations, particularly in Latin America. This is the simple, but often catastrophic alternative of inflation. Such a policy can be disastrous not only in destroying the financial integrity of the country, but also in that the burden of inflation falls primarily upon the lower classes—those least able to bear it.

On the other hand, as Robert Alexander has shown, a policy of *controlled* inflation, combined with investment in productive activities can significantly aid in capital formation. As we have already noted, all countries during their period of initial growth underwent an inflation of some 8 to 10 per cent a year. *If* a government can truly moderate the inflation, there seems little reason to condemn deficit financing as one path to capital accumulation.[8]

to inject money into new, worthwhile enterprises. In fact, M. Bronfenbrenner (by no means an ideological advocate of confiscation) has demonstrated theoretically that expropriation of capital could significantly augment economic growth in developing nations. In one of the most important, if controversial, articles on economic progress, Bronfenbrenner has shown that a "Russian-style" confiscation of capital would increase development investment by some five times.[9] Under ideal circumstances, a policy of capital confiscation could dramatically expand the capacity of a developing nation.

Although the complex reality of underdeveloped economies often confounds the oversimplified doctrine of capital expropriation, the confiscators' gospel has won many adherents. At the opposite pole stands a minority group which totally opposes accumulation of capital in government hands. These believers in laissez-faire capitalism count in their ranks economists such as Milton Friedman and organized political units like India's Swatantra party. The London School of Economics (ironically, after its socialist history) represents one of the strongest fortresses of this position. Two of its leaders, Basil Yamey and Peter Bauer, have presented the "capitalist" argument with particular force and style.[10]

They reject, first of all, the socialist criteria of growth as simply an increase in per capita national product. Measured by this standard, they grant, capital expropriation might well stimulate a lagging economy. Rather, the "capitalists" contend that one should judge economic development by the degree to which it "widens the range of alternatives open to people as consumers and as producers."[11] They seek to decentralize economic decision-making and to diffuse incentives as broadly as possible. For Bauer and Yamey, the Soviet model is absolutely irrelevant, since forced capital accumulation (and the consequently high rate of growth in national income) did not bring with it an expansion in the choices open to individuals.

While I fully agree with Bauer and Yamey that economic growth should not be totally gauged by some sterile, often deceptive statistic of per capita income, I find a certain ambiguity in the standard they propose. How does one determine whether the expansion in Russia's economy will ultimately fail to "widen individual choice"? Temporarily, at least, the post-Stalinist period seems to have opened further the economic, cultural, and even political choices available to individuals. It may even be argued, as I will later contend, that industrialization exerts a powerful pressure toward such greater political freedom.

The goal is to expand the individual's freedom. In this basic intention, I side with Bauer and Yamey. Yet, we must at least entertain the distasteful vision that the end justifies the means and that dictatorship now (including the forced accumulation of capital) may bring freedom in some distant future.

As the capitalists portray the process of economic growth, it "usually requires a large number of small changes, each taking advantage of local opportunities and availability of resources and each in turn making further growth possible." [12] Consequently, they deplore any government monopoly over capital which would destroy the possibility for such local decisions.

They cogently argue that a centralized planning authority, particularly in a new nation, does not have enough information to make all the important decisions concerning the disposition of capital. Local people may know their own conditions, resources, and markets better than planners in some distant city. Thus, followers of the laissez-faire school wish to co-ordinate the knowledge available to the aggregate of all individuals through the normal mechanism of letting them compete naturally in the open market. In the end, so the argument runs, capital will flow to those entrepreneurs who are most capable and to those enterprises which reap the greatest profit; the benefits will come not just to individuals but to the entire society.

Further, capitalist theorists point out that no innate, self-correcting mechanism moderates the government's expenditure of capital. States, as well as individuals, can make foolish, self-interested investments. Ghana wastes millions on lush monuments; Egypt squanders money building rockets; Indonesia tosses its capital down the drain in an apparent unending search for national glory. A free market system, in contrast, provides a widely dispersed set of incentives and controls which can contribute to the efficient use and growth of resources. Automatically, the competitive market punishes the wastrel through his loss of profit and, eventually, in the evaporation of his capital. Who can so control the state, particularly if it is a dictatorship?

In consequence, devotees of laissez-faire theory insist that any means which divert large amounts of capital to the government act only to narrow competition and waste resources. They envision an economy where each investor makes his own wise decisions. Bauer and Yamey allow the state some role in capital accumulation and expenditure. Particularly, they favor government investment in those projects (such as malaria control) from which no individual could derive a financial profit, but which could add to the economic capacity of *all* individuals within the society. Further, they view the government as playing a useful role in providing the individual producer with sufficient information (say, on new forms of more productive seeds) so that he can truly make the wisest decision in his particular situation.

Each of the sides in this significant controversy between the "confiscators" and the "capitalists" has some obvious merit. Laissez-faire theorists can legitimately contend that dispersion of capital (and, therefore, of incentives) can make an economy healthily flexible. Certainly, too, they are right in asserting that the lack of self-correcting instruments to control government expenditure of capital has inherent dangers.

One has only to review the history of Indonesia in the 1950's to understand the distressing chaos which government expropriation of capital can cause. Inspired by nationalism rather than economic reason, the Indonesian government took over all Dutch-owned enterprises. Motivated by racial prejudice, they also harassed a Chinese minority, the traditional merchants, transporters, and middlemen of the economy. As a result, rubber plantations fell infertile, transportation collapsed, industries produced at only half their potential, and the nation's foreign exchange reserves disappeared. Sukarno poured capital (including some Russian and American foreign aid) into magnificent stadiums, tennis courts which could hold 10,000 spectators, Mercedes cars for bureaucrats, and various military toys for his army's adventures. When I visited Djakarta in 1962, a luxurious hotel (built with Japanese reparations) offered imported chocolate and soap to its guests, because the native economy, rich in material for such products, could no longer produce them. By the early 1960's, this potentially abundant economy tottered toward collapse. While Sukarno flew around the world in his jet airplane, peasants starved on the outer islands, simply for lack of ships to import Java's surplus rice. In the real world of underdeveloped nations, the ideally propitious circumstance assumed by the "confiscators" seldom obtain.

Governmental corruption, inefficiency, and greed can devastate capital resources when a nation is left ungoverned by either a self-correcting market mechanism or by the watchdog institutions of liberal democracy.

With justice, the "confiscators" can respond that not every developing nation suffers from the same governmental ineptitude as Indonesia. They can point to China, whose government, despite its brutality, cannot be accused of corruption, gross lack of economic ability, or flagrant misuse of capital. An efficient, dedicated elite can expend capital, the confiscators say, in a productive fashion unmatched by private economies. Yet, the argument contains a premise that we cannot grant: that a benevolent, intelligent Marcus Aurelius who rules today will not be replaced tomorrow by a Nero. Without solid institutional restraints, there can be no guarantee that the whims of a dictator will destroy an economy.

While hedging acceptance of the confiscators' arguments with these important qualifications, one must still admit that a government can at times act as a most efficient banker of capital. The state possesses immense powers of coercion, and if, as the authoritarians would do, its rulers used this power with unhesitating brutality and impeccable efficiency, consumption could be drastically reduced and, therefore, capital accumulated. Further, as in China or Russia, the authoritarian state can forcefully mobilize unemployed labor as a source of substitute capital. If an economy lacks tractors to build a dam, coolies can take their place. As the Russian experience has demonstrated, a government's galvanization of capital can achieve economic wonders. Thus, if the only issue at hand were the problems of capital accumulation, most social scientists—including those deeply committed to the cause of individual freedom—would have to grant the theoretical superiority of the confiscators' solution. Even the distinguished American conservative Henry Wallich has admitted that the forced extortion of savings has a powerful appeal:

The wartime experience of the United States is a case in point. We are ourselves on record, as regards the effectiveness of a dictatorial system, with actions that speak louder than many words—the nation's actions in two world wars. When the pressure was on, there never existed any doubt what had to be done; the United States shifted from a free system to controls. Patriotism made Americans willing to tolerate the severe repression of consumption that went with the system. There was no opportunity to discover what would have happened if the wartime system had been perpetuated, fortunately. But while it lasted, it delivered the goods.[13]

In terms of capital accumulation (and tested by a standard which estimates economic growth *only* in terms of whether it "delivers the goods"), the majority of economists subscribe to Wallich's reluctant conclusion: "A centralized system that is undemocratic, dictatorial and relies on force against its own people has two great advantages: It can extort more savings, and it need not worry about how to arrive at and execute a general plan that is acceptable to a majority." [14]

For those dedicated to political and cultural freedom, however, the expropriators' policy raises distressing specters of despotism. If indeed, a central government—even one which initially functioned as a liberal democracy—begins to dominate all capital funds, the danger of political tyranny increases. The defense of political freedom requires money. Capital is needed to finance the independent newspapers, the critical books, the opposition's political campaigns, the untrammeled scholars and their students, the unions and other autonomous organizations. If the government eliminates private sources of capital, unpopular opinions could not find means for their effective expression, short of revolution. Even in democratic India during the 1960's, intellectuals encounter difficulty in securing funds to underwrite research which criticizes or contradicts government policy. Very few equivalents of the Ford Foundation exist. If the Indian state, in a paroxysm of capital expropriation, took over all private capital (let us say, the funds of the Tata enterprises which do so much to support social investigations in India), the independent scholar would be financially forced to conform to the decisions of a single arbiter: the government itself.

To the degree that one wishes both bread and freedom, therefore, a program of capital expropriation must be viewed with dubiety. But the laissez-faire policies offer no greater hope for salvation to developing nations. It is all very well to glorify the free market, particularly as it operates in industrially advanced countries. In the newer nations, however, the profit motive does not, by any means, always work to increase the society's welfare. With rational self-interest, the rich in Latin America (and other areas) prefer to place their capital in the bourgeois security of Swiss banks rather than in risky domestic enterprises. If they do invest their savings at home, they quite naturally prefer dog-racing tracks, luxury apartment houses, or night clubs to more productive projects. After all, a person can turn a quicker profit by running a gambling casino than by constructing a steel plant, and his assets can be liquidated much more speedily. In developing nations, the free market mechanism does, of course, lead to high profits. In fact, the general rate of profit in developing economies usually surpasses the level in advanced regions. Yet, the free market too frequently fails to encourage substantial contributions to the most basic economic needs of an emerging society.

Even with the best of will, individual firms in the newer nations find that certain projects simply exceed their capacity for capital investment.[15] Steel plants, electric utilities, rubber-processing factories require amounts of capital far beyond the sums available to most domestic entrepreneurs. Such large-scale activities have to be undertaken either under the aegis of a foreign company, backed with Croesus-like capital, or by the government itself from its sources of revenue. In many situations, especially in those economies which are at the very beginning of their "take-off," the government must play the role which the Meiji state did in nineteenth-century Japan. It can serve as the primer of productive enterprises which ideally might then revert to private groups.

The state must assume importance, too, in the creation of "social overhead capital" or, to use Bauer and Yamey's useful term, in the provision of "indiscriminate benefits." Certain types of capital investments —irrigation canals, schools, hospitals, roads, dams, even railroads—may never return a profit to particular private investors. Yet, they confer benefits upon a wide range of people, vastly widening possibilities for economic progress. The building of a primitive road opens new sources of commerce between previously isolated towns. Aside from dispelling human suffering, programs of nutritional instruction diminish the diseases which so debilitate the economic capacity of transitional men. A simple campaign (such as that undertaken in Africa to eliminate the tsetse fly) frees land, which previously lay fallow, for cattle production. The provision of these services should not conjure up visions of authoritarian socialism, for such investments can be undertaken with equal facility by a politically free or by a tyrannical government.[16]

In a democratically developing country, the state has four important responsibilities: (1) it should avoid the lures of total capital expropriation, for this policy undermines the economic pluralism necessary for political freedom; (2) it must, as have all nations in their period of growth, restrict nonessential consumption, particularly that of the wealthier classes; (3) it must use capital for investment in productive activities (such as factories) which private interests cannot afford to undertake; and (4) it must invest capital in certain carefully chosen "social overhead" projects which, in themselves, would be unattractive to private entrepreneurs.

It is easy to list these prescriptions for the development and use of capital, but, as any harried finance minister can testify, it is far more difficult to put them into practice. The diverse experiences of the last decades have, however, demonstrated the effectiveness of certain measures for capital accumulation.

Almost every underdeveloped society needs to stiffen its taxation policies. Ironically, the governments of rich nations draw far more income from taxation than do poor countries. While America channels some 20 per cent of its national income into governmental sources, most Asian and African states contribute only 10 to 12 per cent in taxes, some governments impose even lower levies, and a few in Latin America have no income taxes at all. As Arthur Lewis has shown, this notorious discrepancy cannot be accounted for by the relative poverty of the new countries.[17] If the will existed, the tax revenues would be forthcoming. From whatever source (direct income taxes, indirect taxes on luxury goods, turnover taxes), the revenue must be increased to approximate the level (20 per cent of national income) which many economists regard as essential if progress is to be made.[18]

Capital investment can be facilitated in many other ways. Wise policies, as in India, can encourage private investment in productive enterprises by offering tax rebates, the construction of rent-free factory facilities, or even the temporary subsidization of new enterprises. Such measures can markedly increase the proclivity of private capital to seek productive outlets. Strict import restrictions on luxury consumption are also a necessity. Taxes on uncultivated land (such as the United Fruit Company controls in Central America) may also stimulate investment in progressive agriculture. And, as experience has demonstrated in such nations as India, Mexico, and Ghana, voluntary donations of labor by peasants can offer a most useful form of substitute capital. If a peasantry can be convinced that a particular project, such as a road, can make a direct contribution to their immediate, local welfare, they will eagerly give their free labor.

In other words, a variety of specific measures exists which can be employed by a government faced with the necessity of accumulating capital. The technical nature of these weapons of speeding up capital accumulation need hardly be detailed here, for they have been developed with great sophistication by such experts as Ragnar Nurkse, Benjamin Higgins, and Arthur Lewis.[19]

The tools for capital accumulation exist; the job can be done. But any conscientious commentator on the underdeveloped world would feel compelled to add two important qualifications to this optimistic conclusion.

First, as we have already mentioned, one of the more discouraging aspects of the problem is that newer nations today are simply much poorer than the rich countries at the start of their progress. In the most precise calculation possible in this field of vague, unreliable statistics, Simon Kuznets has shown that per capita incomes of most underdeveloped nations are only about 16 to 33 per cent of the comparable incomes of European nations a century ago.

While there are some important exceptions to this generalization (and Kuznets repeatedly warns of the difficulty of establishing comparable phases of development and of income), his judgment seems as close to the truth as we can get. Further, as Kuznets remarks, by ". . . the mid or late eighteenth century, many of the developed nations of today were already advanced economically—by contemporary standards; they had already experienced fairly sustained growth over the earlier centuries, and enjoyed political independence in doing so. . . ." [20]

Undoubtedly, in the developing nations, belt-tightening by restricting consumption will squeeze out useful capital. Nevertheless, we must recognize that even the strictest domestic austerities cannot possibly produce the enormous sums of capital once available to European countries and to Russia. Foreign aid and foreign private capital must fill the breach.

Secondly, the issue of capital accumulation—supposedly, a strictly economic concern—is, at base, a social and political problem. To paraphrase Plutarch, capital formation ". . . in things inanimate is but money-making, when exercised over men, becomes policy." Holding down consumption, the essence of capital formation, demands that a people wishes to save for its society's future. To convince an Indian peasant to relinquish his pitifully small "luxuries," to inveigle a traditional Brazilian landowner to buy tractors instead of a new villa, to request that Nigerian members of parliament voluntarily reduce their salaries (which, incidentally, exceed those of English M.P.'s)—these changes in a man's life style involve an altruistic dedication which taxes mortal capacity.

Yet, in the face of death and disaster, human ability has been able to surpass selfishness. In this prosaic matter of capital accumulation—which is, in fact, a battle of life and death—we must hope that transitional men and their companions in advanced nations will once again demonstrate that potential for sacrifice and wisdom which the achievement of all great objects imposes on man.

V

TRANSFORMING THE VILLAGE AND ITS LAND

> The future of the developing continents is . . . to be decided in
> the remote muddy villages where nearly 80 per cent of the people
> live, precisely as the course and character of American democracy
> was decided in our own rural areas.
>
> CHESTER BOWLES

When Mr. Tom Hughes-Rice first arrived in Machakos, Kenya, in
1951, he reputedly announced that all he could do "was to sit on top
of a hill and weep." [1] The government had charged him with the task
of revitalizing this rural area and restoring life to its dying land. Many
had tried before. All had failed.

Ravaged by erosion and mismanagement, the Machakos soil had
been stripped nude of vegetation. Bony cattle scrubbed in the bush
for what little fodder they could discover. Each year at harvest time,
the central government had to send out 200,000 bags of corn to keep
villagers from starving. In 1946, Mr. Creech Jones, the Colonial Secretary, reported that he had driven "mile after mile through hillsides
and plains swept bare in many places to the solid rock, through acres
where there was not a vestige of grass, through acre after acre of dead
and wilted maize. . . ." [2] Throughout the 1940's district officers had
attempted to terrace the eroded hillsides with caterpillar tractors, to
remove excess cattle, and to resettle 50,000 people in new areas—but
all of these well-intentioned schemes met with frustration. Who would
not weep when faced with the gigantic problem of transforming this
region, "a classic example of all the worst agrarian evils of modern
Africa," [3] into a productive, self-sufficient economy?

85

Indeed, the challenge of invigorating the village, whether in Africa, Asia, or Latin America, has seemed so frightening that many have given up all hope. Some politicians in the underdeveloped nations simply ignore the problem, presumably hoping that it will somehow evaporate. Even eminent economists and social scientists soberly advocate concentrating most resources, if not all, upon industrialization. They argue that once a modern sector develops, rural stagnation will cease; people will migrate to the cities, find jobs in factories, and gradually agriculture, too, will mechanize. In fact, with some prominent exceptions, this has been the historical pattern of economic development.

Yet, compelling reasons prevent us from trying to dismiss village problems with such dispatch. One could, of course, argue the issue just on grounds of humaneness. The great majority of transitional men live in miserable villages: something has to be done, and done now, to alleviate their suffering.

To put it simply, in today's world 85 per cent of people are hungry. In China, the traditional greeting upon meeting a friend has always been, "Have you eaten?" In Latin America, as Josué de Castro has demonstrated, pervasive malnutrition has spread apathy and disease.[4] Hunger causes rickets in many children: deformation of their legs, enlargement of their skulls and chronic fatigue. It also produces endemic goiter, which in certain sections of South America affects over half the school children. Such children need good food, and only the villages can provide it.

There are quite sound economic and social arguments why development requires rural transformation. On the economic level, one should recognize four basic reasons why a newly developing nation ought to concentrate a very high proportion of its energy upon a rural revolution:

(1) Investment in rural improvement conserves capital. This in itself assumes great importance, for the need for capital plagues all underdeveloped countries. Startling increases in rural productivity can be achieved with minimal capital outlay. Arthur Lewis has demonstrated that an expenditure of one per cent of national income can vastly increase agricultural produce, paying off much greater initial profits than a similar amount invested in industry.[5]

More specifically, Woddis has shown that the creation of a rural plantation in Nigeria involves about £500 of capital for each man put to work, while £2000 would be necessary to place the same man in a modern factory.[6] In Italy, one agricultural extension worker, sheerly by persuasion and education, raised the annual income of a village by 192 million lire, at a total cost for outside assistance of only 25 million lire.[7] Everywhere in the underdeveloped world, abundant evidence suggests that investment in the village pays off more, dollar for dollar, than any other type of capital outlay. In turn, since the rural sector forms the base for capital accumulation, an improvement in village prosperity—and a diversion of some of its new profits to productive investment—can go far in solving the problem of capital formation.

(2) Village development balances an economy in several important ways. An increase in rural productivity provides the necessary food and raw materials to maintain a growing industrial-urban section of a nation. Further, if the countryside stagnates, new industries will fail to find consumers for their products. Without vigorous villages as their underpinning, the most ambitious plans of industrialization cannot work successfully. In India, for example, precious foreign currency which could have been used for other investments has been expended on importing food, since the farms could not produce enough to support a growing population. Industry advanced, but people still starved.

(3) A transformation of agriculture can sometimes help to diversify an economy by introducing new products for export. Thus, in a drive to lessen its dependence upon cocoa exports as a source of foreign exchange, Ghana managed in ten years to double its export of kola nuts and to increase the export of coconuts by 500 per cent. Banana exports grew from virtually nothing in 1950 to 28,000 cwt's in 1958, and coffee production showed an equal rise. Such agricultural exports can help ease the cost of importing expensive capital equipment from abroad and consequently contribute indirectly to the growth of domestic industry.

(4) Most importantly, village improvement can go far in absorbing the excess population which so often cripples economic growth. At the moment, some 15 to 30 per cent of rural populations produce absolutely nothing. These hands must be put to work. As Guy Hunter has aptly observed concerning Africa, "it is only in the rural economy that the problem of employment can be solved." [8] Obviously, as population grows, so too must food production. In order to feed adequately the existing population in the underdeveloped world, the amount of food should immediately be doubled. If one assumes, rather conservatively, that population will increase at the rate of 2 per cent annually, food production must be doubled once again within only 35 years.[9] Almost everywhere such an increase can be achieved, if only full employment prevails and the right methods are used. Economist Colin Clark has calculated that good farming (following a Dutch or Danish model) could support 12 billion people, as opposed to the 3 billion the

globe maintains now. Further, this modernized agriculture could not only feed more people, but it could feed them at the opulent level now reached by the Dutch and the Danish.[10]

On the social and political level, there are equally compelling reasons for pursuing an energetic plan of rural development. Only a marked improvement in village life can stop the migrations to already overcrowded, festering cities. Only a village transformation can satisfy the limited, immediate aspirations which make up the "revolution of expectations" experienced by transitional men. They demand relatively little, but these demands have to be met on their own level—in the villages where the overwhelming majority exists. And only rural advance can moderate the politics of unreasoning passion which characterize transitional cities, for, as Chester Bowles has remarked, ". . . an unbalanced emphasis on rapid industrial growth is likely to *increase* rather than decrease political unrest in the cities and rural areas as well." [11]

But why then have most new nations chosen instead to invest more in factories (or even worse, in useless monuments) than in farms? Reasonable arguments have been advanced for this preference. Some geographic determinists argue that various elements—quality of soil, amount of rainfall, lack of nutritious minerals—drastically curtail the agricultural potential of many areas.[12] Neo-Malthusians believe that starving peasants will consume any extra food they produce and, consequently, by increasing their fertility, exacerbate the population explosion. Some social scientists hold the opinion that only an urban environment provides the right climate for innovation and the use of entrepreneurial talents.[13] One distinguished economist, Harvey Leibenstein, has concluded: "In sum, the growth agents [of economic development] are more likely to be stimulated in an urban, industrial setting rather than in an agricultural environment." [14] Leibenstein's position would seem both theoretically and historically accurate, if one granted an initial premise: that cities in underdeveloped nations could offer jobs and other opportunities to rural migrants. Unfortunately, at this point in history, this assumption has not been confirmed by reality.

With reason, some social scientists have emphasized the tremendous institutional obstacles to village development. The social barriers to progress may be even greater than the tangible obstacles of soil and climate. As John Galbraith has said, after his experience as American Ambassador to India:

Even the most eloquent agricultural extension expert cannot explain the advantage of growing two grains of wheat where but one flourished before if the peasant knows full well that both will go inevitably to his landlord. The best-considered forms of agricultural investment or the most sophisticated techniques of agricultural extension are worthless if the cultivator knows out of the experience of the ages that none of the gains will accrue to him.[15]

And even a cursory reading of Kussum Nair's *Blossoms in the Dust* reveals other social hurdles which must be cleared in order to change the village. As just one example, she records:

In the village of Budelpali the local agricultural extension officer had to go on hunger strike—he lay down in the village temple and refused to take any food—before he could persuade the peasantry to sow for a second irrigated winter crop of paddy. He had already brought 250 maunds of seed and distributed it to them. The peasants, however, had put forward excuses that: 'Paddy cannot grow a second time on the same soil; our Kharif production will fall; the water is without its electricity; where will our cattle graze?' But they would not readily agree even to try an experiment which promised straightaway to double their income." [16]

While we must respect these more or less reasonable objections to agricultural advance, they should not blind us to several salient facts: New nations do not possess the capital to promote *rapid* heavy industrialization; urban centers cannot economically tolerate an even greater influx of ex-peasants; and the farmer does not wish to leave his village, but feels forced to by the misery of its poverty.

Another, totally irrational—and perhaps most influential factor—has inhibited most developing nations from providing sufficient capital to stimulate agriculture. Arthur Lewis has called it "intellectual myopia" on the part of governing elites:

Failure to solve the problem of stagnant peasant agriculture is due principally to failure of government to take the responsibility for providing large sums of money for this purpose. . . . The most obvious feature of the past century and a half of development in the West has been urbanization with industrialization. It took some time to realize that this was made possible only by an equally profound revolution in agriculture, which increased the average farm family's output from enough food to feed one and a half families to enough food to feed ten families.[17]

And Marxists in many nations unfortunately believe that arguments for village transformation are simply a way of keeping the peasant "down on the farm." Basically, the communists argue that capitalists wish to keep underdeveloped countries in exactly their present position, as producers of rural commodities for consumption by luxurious Americans and Europeans. Tragically, one may grant some truth to this argument: Belgian behavior in the Congo serves as a relevant example. Yet, even the Chinese communists appear to be learning the lesson that the village cannot be ignored. In an underdeveloped country, food must come first, even if the communists or Americans, with their mania for spaceships, believe that high-quality steel is the most significant symbol of advancement.

Experience in many of the newer nations does not justify the theoretical (or the myopic) objections to rural advancement. Often, to our good fortune, average human ingenuity has surpassed the most elegant theories of social science as well as the most ill-informed policies of politicians. Three examples, taken from extremely diverse regions of the world—Egypt, India, and tropical Africa—illustrate the creative possibilities of man's mind when confronted with the challenge of village improvement.

Egypt offers an impressive illustration of what can be accomplished. Here, some 28 million people attempt to scratch their living from an area the size of Maryland. Until recently, only 3 per cent of Egypt's land could be cultivated, primarily the lush delta region where the Nile flows. Outside of this green belt stretches one of the most naked, rock-dry deserts in the world. When floods or drought ruined the delta, all but the rich starved. One of the few accomplishments of venal King Farouk was the completion of a series of dams which finally, after years of struggle, tamed the Nile's will.

When Egypt's army officers took power a decade ago, they dedicated themselves to the task of village renovation. Luckily for the peasants, many of the officers themselves came from a rural background. They had a sympathetic, intuitive knowledge of the farmers' plight.* The Egyptians faced a set of problems whose magnitude dwarfs that of

* Some writers (such as Eugene Staley, Donald Blackmer, and Max Millikan) have suggested that army officers in developing nations can act as *the* prime agents of modernization, following the model of Ataturk in Turkey. The validity of this belief depends critically upon the social background of the officer corps. If, as in Egypt, they do not come originally from the ranks of the traditional ruling class, they can serve a useful role. Unfortunately, in most nations, officers are drawn from the land-owning upper class, precisely the group most opposed to change.[18]

many African or Latin American countries. Nasser and his colleagues first had to increase production in order to feed the 800,000 people born in Egypt each year; large estates had to be broken up to give land to the landless without decreasing productivity; and they had to improve the lot of the peasant, not only by raising his income but also by introducing techniques which would better his health and education.

The success of their endeavors can be measured on a microscopic level by El Westiani, a village in the southern delta region. El Westiani typifies Egypt in that it is neither a model village (such as those on the Anchass plot, one of Farouk's former estates) nor is it one of the towns still untouched by the land reform agency. Until 1952 in El Westiani a single landlord owned 3,000 acres, and 10,000 people labored for him. Not only did they pay him 75 per cent of their produce in return for tenancy, but they had to take loans from him at 50 per cent interest during periodic famines. He used his power truly without restraint. Sometimes, he chose to exercise his *droit de seigneur* over young brides. One old peasant told me that, when the landlord drove through the fields, he carried bodyguards on the running-boards of his car. Anyone who got in his way was shot. "Nothing could be done," the peasant recalled, "since the police were in his pay. His word was law."

In 1952, the revolutionary Cairo government limited land ownership to 200 acres (in 1961, reduced to 100), and the peasants joyfully distributed the pasha's land. The landlord received government bonds in partial compensation and tactfully retired to a city villa. For the first time the farmers began to cultivate their own land. Production soared. Perhaps most importantly, El Westiani witnessed the birth of a sense of individual importance.

As one farmer—although unlettered and ill with both bilharziasis and trachoma—put it to me: "We gained dignity and independence for the first time. I now own ten acres. I am my own boss and doing well. I will even send my boys to secondary school and maybe they will want to come back and help me." Like other villagers, this man had to repay the government for the land in gradual installments, but the debt does not enslave him, as had the landlord's rule.

While land reform has not been as universally successful throughout Egypt as in El Westiani—the 1961 reforms touched only one million acres, enough to fulfill the needs of 300,000 families—it has paved the way for a remarkable improvement in agricultural efficiency. The government coupled land reform with "its own mixture of bribes and threats to deal with the dangers of fragmentation."[19] The land reform agency gives the newly freed peasant seeds, stock, credit, and expert advice, but in return the farmer must accept government marketing of his crops and a controlled system of crop rotation. Each co-operative governs the allocation of crops, but a government official supervises, and sometimes vetoes, its decisions.

The co-operative, as it functions in El Westiani, shows what can be done in rural extension. For five years, a government center has introduced villagers to modern, diversified agriculture. An experimental farm has taught bee culture, the raising of rabbits and chickens, the Japanese method of cultivation, and the use of chemical fertilizers. A prize Dutch bull (which was exhibited to me with enormous pride) serves the scrawny village cows, and new batches of calves are fattened in a co-operative barn. In an area previously dependent on cotton—and, therefore, at the mercy of plagues, weather, and world prices—this initiation into new practices has revolutionized production. Today, even the poorest peasant in El Westiani grows at least three crops on his land, owns several kinds of livestock, and enjoys an income which has increased by one-half since 1957.

The government has also made solid achievements in the battle against ignorance and disease. In El Westiani the villagers have a modern school building, even equipped with television to relay educational broadcasts. All children receive a primary education, albeit one heavily larded with ideology. Formerly in El Westiani (and all of Egypt) 65 per cent of farmers were ill with bilharziasis, a disease which contributed to the nation's cancer rate, one of the highest in the world. Eighty-seven per cent had trachoma, an illness which often resulted in blindness. During the last decade, however, the government has established small hospitals for each region of 10,000 people. In El Westiani and elsewhere, these little clinics give vaccinations, offer childbirth care, distribute American medicines, and handle minor operations. In return for free education, doctors now devote two years of their lives to service in the villages. Although one can hope for further advances—mothers recuperating from childbirth in El Westiani's four-bed ward were covered with flies—one must still cheer the progress. Trachoma now infects only one-fifth of the population, and bilharziasis has dropped to a rate of only 3 per cent.

Even in villages which have not benefited as fully from government attentions as has El Westiani, the most squalid regions have felt the changes. Barbara Castle, the British M.P., visited a village which had yet to undergo land reform. When she pressed a tenant farmer who had not been allocated land about what difference there was in his life now, he fingered his robe and replied: "Before I could only afford to wear one garment; now I wear three. And I buy three pounds of meat a week for my family." [20]

Much remains to be done. More money should be poured into the villages, rather than into factories and rocket missiles. The western desert needs to be opened. Even in 1962, engineers attempted to tap a huge underground water reservoir in the "New Valley." Conceivably, another 200,000 acres of previously raw desert may be opened for cultivation by these sources of irrigation. Completion of the Aswan Dam will also provide water for new land, but perhaps just enough to keep pace with the current population expansion.

Yet, already, an objective observer of the Egyptian scene can report tangible progress. It may seem insignificant to Westerners, but the Egyptian villager knows that a turn for the better has occurred. True, the Egyptian revolution has been guided by an autocratic hand, but the leaders evince a desire to create a base of self-government in the villages. Nasser has publicly exploded when he purportedly commented that he "looked over his shoulder" and found that the general population was not following the lead of Egypt's army, the core of its innovators. The 1962 Charter seeks to establish a mass movement behind the army and, within limits, lay a democratic foundation in rural areas.

The new regime will be led by a national union, an elite of "revolutionaries." While there seems little chance in the immediate future that the government will ease restrictions on civil liberties or its control over the press, the program does contain provisions for competitive election to the national chamber and, most importantly, for local government units. For the first time in their lives, the peasants in 1962 chose between alternative candidates for a variety of local offices. In one sense, the government had "fixed" these elections, since all candidates had official approval: indeed, in one village which I visited, the police had actually ordered a candidate to run. The new local governments nevertheless do have real power over such matters as road building, irrigation, and the resolution of local disputes. And these councils offer a channel through which village grievances can reach higher powers. So far, this allowance for criticism remains largely formal. At the 1962 national meeting for confirming the Charter, however, Nasser showed open, deep anger at the obsequiousness of the delegates. And, at the village level, I witnessed direct criticism of the government's handling of certain affairs and particularly of members of the local bureaucracy, some of whom dated from Farouk's time.

In one decade, therefore, the Egyptian government has made decisive inroads on such problems as land reform, improvement in rural production, and reduction of the toll of ignorance and disease. Institutional reforms, while carried out largely from above, have also made a halting start toward democratizing village life.

India has faced equally complex problems. Indian leaders have also desired to introduce basic land reforms, increase production, and ameliorate the peasants' suffering. In some ways, the challenge to India has been even more severe: the Indian government has had to deal with an infinitely more divided population of 330 million peasants; its reforms had to be worked out within a liberal-democratic policy, rather than within the tighter framework of a military autocracy; and India's overworked land has been notorious for its lack of fertility (its general yield per acre is about 25 per cent less than Indonesia's or Burma's). Further, Hinduism imposes tragic obstacles to those who fight for progress. Islam, dominant in Egypt, has not been noted in recent centuries for its innovative drive, but Hinduism, with its reverence for caste, its concept of reincarnation, and its aura of extreme fatalism makes the average peasant even less receptive to changing his "preordained" station in the world.

Despite these obstacles, India, too, has achieved miracles, even though they may appear minor when measured against either the hopes of its leaders or the unrealistic aspirations of Westerners. An ambitious village development program, begun on Gandhi's birthday on October 2, 1952, has affected 400,000 of India's 558,000 villages. Eighty thousand extension workers, similar to American county agents, have reached 300 million Indian farmers, spreading new ideas about crops, planting, and plowing. Village block programs, sustained by a principle of self-help, have encouraged road building campaigns, the erection of small dams, and the reclamation of virgin or waste lands.

In education, by 1955, 14,000 adult education centers had helped bring literacy to villagers (chiefly by the famed Laubach "each one teach one" method). Millions of children now attend schools which did not exist fifteen years ago, and, in principle, all children are entitled to a primary education.

Some of the greatest successes have been registered in reducing disease. Until 1951, one million people died annually from malaria. This energy-sapping disease afflicted over 100 million Indians. By 1955, the average number of cases had been reduced to 25 million. In 1962, largely because of a massive DDT campaign, the illness had almost been eradicated.

Major highly controversial efforts have been directed toward land reform. For centuries, India's peasants have been dominated by *zamindari* landlordism, in which the farmer financially enslaved himself to his local ruler. The yoke of subservience fell most heavily upon India's 48 million landless laborers, drawn largely from the ranks of untouchables. These unfortunate human beings could not even fall back upon the pitiful security which a small plot of land afforded to other farmers.

Two approaches have been followed in tackling this problem of providing the peasant with some property. Adhering to the Gandhian tradition, Vinoba Bhave has persuaded many landlords to surrender voluntarily over five million acres of land, particularly to untouchables. Bhave's movement began in 1951 when a group of landless peasants in one village begged him for eighty acres to plow as their own property. He called a meeting of peasants and landlords, pleading, "Brothers, are there any among you who will give land to your brothers so that they may not die of starvation? They need only eighty acres."

One man spoke up, "I will give one hundred acres." Thus commenced the *bhoodan* movement.[21] It has not been an unmitigated success. Only a small portion of land has actually been redistributed, much of it infertile; landlords have a heart, but not when it really involves their wallet. However admirable Bhave's movement may be, the issue of massive land reform has demanded government action.

Government efforts have taken the form of outlawing, in theory, the very large *zamindars* and replacing them with peasant proprietors. The state compensated former landlords for their property losses. Officials also tried to eliminate middle men and to establish a limit (25 per cent of produce) upon the rate of rent which could be collected by landlords. While millions of peasants have benefited from these legislative actions, land reform remains a central problem. Some provinces in India, still basically ruled by the landholding class, have hesitated in enforcing the law. In some areas, old vested interests turned new co-operative societies into instruments whereby they could, as before, control the market on tools, fertilizers, and seeds. Until now, the government has been unable to set up sufficient credit facilities for the newly freed peasant, thus throwing him back into the arms of the money-lenders. Tragically, Russia under its tsars (and America during its post-Civil War era) made exactly the same mistake; the technically "freed" slaves had to return to their original lords for financial support. Economic freedom did not accompany formal, legal freedom.

The hotly debated Nagpur Resolution, passed by the Congress party, aims at correcting some of these deficiencies. The new program seeks to set an absolute limit on landholdings, to introduce state trading in crops, and to establish more service co-operatives which, eventually, will become large farming co-operatives. Such a plan has much to recommend it, but, as Frank Moraes, the brilliant editor of *The Times of India*, points out, it also contains possible dangers. The proposed ceiling would limit farm families to an income of $720 a year: thus, in some of the more forward-looking sections of the country, it would discourage the farmer from producing more food. And what will the government do if the peasant refuses voluntarily to pool his land with others? Compulsion would seem the only alternative and, as Moraes contends, "The failure of [forced] collective farming in Soviet Russia and its revision in Poland and Yugoslavia carry a lesson for India. But the Congress Bourbons are evidently determined to learn nothing. . . ." [22]

Despite all of the difficulties, Indian food production has risen about 50 per cent from 1949 to 1964. Even this increase has barely kept pace with population expansion. India must still count on imports of America's abundant food surplus, if its people are to survive.

The triumphs and defeats of the last fifteen years of independence are illustrated in one more or less typical village, Alipur, which I had the opportunity of investigating fairly closely. (Of course no *really* typical village exists in India. The diversity in religion, language, ethnic group, and climate creates startling differences. Nevertheless, Alipur can be used as one illustration of what community development has accomplished in *most* of India.) Alipur, a village of about 1000 people, lies in the great plain which surrounds Delhi. The government (helped, at times, by the Ford Foundation) has supplied new types of seed and fertilizer, and the villagers have both diversified and intensified their farming. United in a loose co-operative, they till some of the land jointly and market their goods in common. On their own initiative, they have built a small school, a bare room roofed with straw, furnished with washable boards on which children inscribe their letters. Parents pay around 20 per cent of their income (a meager wage below the subsistence level requested by the UN) in school fees and make the further sacrifice, little appreciated by a Westerner, of doing the labor traditionally handled by children. One father who sent all of his four boys to school said with glowing pride: "It means I do all of their work in the fields, but it is worth it! *They will be educated men*." The children respond with joy to the school. The teacher had never encountered absenteeism or tardiness. In effect, illiteracy will all but disappear in the next generation. The village has also responded well to government programs for improved health. Malaria, yellow fever, and cholera, formerly endemic, have almost been eliminated.

One other aspect of Alipur's revolution deserves attention: the ambitious plan for democratizing local government. Prior to the development programs, as I have previously noted, a fundamentally authoritarian system governed social relationships in Alipur as in other Indian villages. The Panchayat Raj plan tries to decentralize political power in such a manner that every villager will have the right to choose not only his distant representative in parliament but also all the other officials who govern his life, from the provincial center down to the village of Alipur. So far, the people have tended to continue in their traditional pattern. The Brahmins are usually elected to reign over the village council. Increasingly, however, lower castes assert their numerical power, as they realize how this new instrument can be used for influence. By chance, I sat in on one judicial council in Alipur where an untouchable, elected as a judge, considered the case of a Brahmin who had embezzled $100 from the co-operative's funds. The untouchable ably led a discussion before a packed assemblage of village men. Two pictures, one of Gandhi and the other of Nehru, hung on the mud walls as we listened to the case. With the apparent approval of everyone, the untouchable sentenced the Brahmin to a fine, backed by a possible jail sentence.

All is not sweetness and light, to say the least, in Alipur. Annual family income has gone up substantially, but so have prices. Landless laborers still exist. In times of drought, the villagers put themselves heavily into debt. Infant mortality remains high, even though a nurse visits the village each month to give information and aid. Some of the farmers refuse to do their share of co-operative work, and 15 per cent of men are still idle for much of the year. The Panchayat Raj program has not, as yet, totally reversed the traditional pattern of authoritarianism; when a Brahmin, for example, first showed me around the village, he stalked into any hut he wished without requesting permission. When I questioned a villager if he minded the uninvited intrusion, he bowed and replied, "Whatever my master, the Brahmin, demands, I grant."

If India is truly to transform its villages, it must still grapple successfully with major problems. The land reform issue has to be resolved, hopefully, without resort to compulsion. Institutional reforms are required, particularly the provision of more credit to independent farmers. Somehow, population growth has to be held down; under the first five-year plan, the government built only 126 family-planning clinics. Fortunately, the third plan envisions the construction of 8200 clinics.

Perhaps the first requirement for a village revolution is that Indian leaders make up their mind about whether they really wish to transform the village. Allocations for village development have fluctuated wildly under the three five-year plans. These gyrations have occurred without economic justification. The planners, like stockholders in a panic, have increased their investments in years when harvests have been bad and dropped them when a chance change in rainfall has resulted in more food. The changes occurred because of the government's failure to develop a comprehensive long-range plan of rural development. The third five-year plan puts agriculture and village development very high on its list of priorities; one can only hope that the proposed allocations will materialize.[23]

Not all Indian leaders have committed themselves to the Panchayat Raj program, although publicly everyone endorses village self-government. Actually, allowing lower castes who formerly were helpless to have a political voice frightens some Indian politicians and intellectuals who believe that the conservatism and passivity of the villages has provided the surest base for the nation's stability. Such men genuinely wish for a true democracy, but they worry that a dictatorship may ensue. With the advent of a supposedly premature democracy in the villages, they fear that long-suppressed desires will have a potent outlet and that the scramble to satisfy a variety of local needs will overwhelm the central government. The 1961 election did, in fact, reveal a pronounced tendency for almost all parties to pitch their appeals to regional, caste, linguistic, or tribal interests. Instead of arguing for the development of India as a nation, many politicians promised to push purely parochial interests, such as making a minor dialect an official language. While it contains obvious dangers, I believe that this articulation of local concerns forms an essential characteristic of a liberal polity. India will certainly have to pay some economic price for the trend to local autonomy, but it appears to be the only way in which democracy can be solidly anchored in Indian society. The development should be welcomed, not privately bemoaned, by liberal and social democrats.

Tropical Africa's problems differ in nature somewhat from those of India, although the magnitude of the task is equally large. In general,

Africa has the good fortune of being relatively underpopulated. Large tracts of potentially cultivatable land rest untilled. In many sections, land-tenure patterns are traditionally communal; consequently, co-operative ventures in agriculture come more naturally to many Africans than to people raised in a rural economy based on individually owned, fragmented pieces of land. (The communal tenure pattern, of course, has its drawbacks, for no single individual may feel personally responsible for improving or even maintaining the land.)

African villages nevertheless have their share of serious problems too. Climatic conditions have ruined the soil in many regions. An unceasing battle must be waged in the rain forests against the encroachment of weeds and roots. Methods of agriculture remain highly primitive, although often fairly well adapted to the peculiar conditions of soil and rainfall.[24] Efforts to improve techniques of rural production often encounter tough resistance from social custom. An attempt to destock cattle from overgrazed land, for example, may well be blocked by a culture which views cows as wealth, particularly for buying brides.

Further, almost every African village has been drawn into a cash, market-oriented economy; the villagers have begun to desire products which cannot be produced by their subsistence agriculture. One African character in a novel remarked that Europeans suffer from a terrible disease, "The Wants." "It seems certain," Guy Hunter has observed, "that within the next ten or even five years, the remaining and dwindling proportion of 'African man' not yet infected will have caught 'The Wants,' and not from Europeans directly but from fellow Africans."[25] African agriculture, in its present form, cannot cure the disease. In consequence, as the desire for new, predominantly "Western-type" goods grows, African nations have increasingly imported food to meet the demand.[26] Ghana, in 1959, had to expend dear foreign currency to import 18,000 tons of fish, 45,000 tons of sugar, and 58,000 tons of flour—even though these items could, theoretically, have been produced more cheaply by Ghanaians.

As everywhere, change must come, and yet, so typically in these days of gloom, some Africanists have thrown up their hands in disgust at the purported stubbornness and laziness of the villager—his unwillingness to work hard for financial rewards. One expert, by no means a racial bigot, has concluded: "Certainly experience has demonstrated that all too frequently tropical man is unwilling to exert extra energies solely for financial reward, once his simple needs have been met. Agricultural officers recount . . . attempts made to increase productivity by the introduction of demonstrably better methods, only to find that output remained the same while land use or labour input declined." [27]

That the pessimism of this general judgment is unwarranted has been proved again and again. Let me cite just two of many illustrations: Awgu, Nigeria, and Machakos, Kenya.

Awgu, an area in eastern Nigeria populated by 150,000 people, depends on yams, cassavas, and various palm products for both food and cash. Like much of Africa, it suffered from the conservatism of elders; a general distrust of central government efforts to initiate change; a reluctance to "tamper" with land, since religious tradition sanctified it as belonging to tribal ancestors; and constant bickering about boundaries between the various villages.

I. C. Jackson, former principal of the Awgu Training Centre, and young village leaders overcame many, but not all, of these obstacles to community development. During the 1940's, village elders prohibited change and held down the younger men (many of whom had returned from army service) who wished to promote innovation. By 1952, however, a slate of younger men had won a majority of seats in the village councils. Aided by brief training courses in community development, this group inspired hope and vigor in their constituencies. Between 1950 and the end of 1953, 41 new village wells and five maternity homes had been constructed by villagers. Helped by a rather meager government subsidy, the people erected a modern hospital worth £36,000. The men of one-quarter of Awgu villages worked on the hospital for more than half the working days of 1953—and, simultaneously, carried on their farming. Donating their labor, they also built sixty miles of good highways and bridges. In agriculture, rice planting spread quickly and soon became a common (and highly lucrative) crop. A new rice mill transformed the product into a marketable commodity. Education in the use of artificial fertilizers helped increase the output of traditional forms of agriculture. In sandy upland areas, the villagers planted cashew trees in soil which had previously been considered totally infertile.

Of equal importance, community development radically changed certain social customs. I. C. Jackson recorded:

The greatest value from community development lies in the new social attitudes that it engenders. Leprosy is a case in point. In 1948 the only leprosy segregation village in the division was deliberately burnt down, and the people of the surrounding villages refused to help their sick kin in rebuilding their devastated homes. Yet four years later five segre-

*gation villages had been built, and the one which had been burned
down was reconstructed and was the best in the whole division.
. . . Leprosy was increasingly viewed as a dreadful but curable disease,
instead of as the awful and immutable punishment of God. . . . In-
fectious lepers who were concealing the disease grew more willing to
come forward for treatment. . . .*[28]

Jackson concluded from his work that community development can
achieve spectacular successes in welfare services (such as building a
hospital); smaller, but still substantial, gains in strictly economic development; and, in Jackson's words, it can ". . . clear the path for the
dynamic individual." [29]

The raped, eroded Machakos land—which caused the Kenyan development officer to cry at the prospect of his job—presented even more
formidable obstacles in 1951. Nevertheless, by 1955, "the nut on
which so many teeth had been broken had been cracked." [30] New forests had been planted (Christmas trees, incidentally), lush grass grew
in formerly barren areas, new hospitals and community centers had
gone up. As Elspeth Huxley observed the transformation: "Hillsides
were turning green again, raw red sores were healed, the walking hat-
racks had diminished in numbers and turned back into cattle, streams
were flowing in valleys where they had not flowed for twenty years, the
people were alert, co-operative and reasonably contented—about as
much as human beings ever are." [31]

Many elements combined to produce the Machakos miracle. For
the first time, the government provided massive funds for development.
New, more progressive chiefs came into power. Teams of experts in
agriculture, forestry, and veterinary medicine poured into the district
and, also for the first time, actually lived in the villages with the
farmers.

Well-trained, dedicated men, such as Assistant District Officer John
Malinda, worked with their own people, tactfully but persistently per-
suading them of the rewards for progress. They formed *mywethya*
groups on a clan basis and guided them in terracing the land, planting
grass, and enclosing the fields to prevent overgrazing by cattle. Each
clan competed with another and was called to its work with a traditional warrior's horn. As they labored, they often sang with rollicking
abandon to the beat of a drum.

> *The Askaris used to be strong and bold as lions.*
> *They went to fight and they were fierce as lions.*
> *But now it is we who are strong and bold as lions.*

Now we are strong as the Askaris.
Now we are stronger than the Askaris, stronger than lions.
Yeh! Yeh! Yeh! Stronger than Askaris or lions.[32]

All did not go smoothly. Land reform, for example, involved convincing people that they should *reduce* the size of their holdings, exactly the opposite of India's or Egypt's problem. Eventually, cattle which had foraged on thirty sparsely covered acres were confined to an average of one acre of verdant grass. Families which had tried without avail to handle seventy-acre plots were convinced that intensive cultivation of twenty or even ten acres would be more profitable for them. By 1955, poultry and new crops appeared—even popcorn to be sold in Nairobi movie theaters. All of this was accomplished by persuasion, not compulsion.

As for the future, it lies in the hands of the people. "Our great hope. . . ," John Malinda remarked, "is that they've seen with their own eyes that their country *will* recover, if they give it half a chance. They know now it's something *they* can do, not just some order from the Government." [33]

What lessons can be drawn from Machakos or Alipur or El Westiani? While the specific obstacles and approaches differed, their experience has several general implications which seem to have relevance for almost every underdeveloped country:

(1) Contrary to the pessimists, determined action *can* transform the village. Intensive, modern cultivation of the land dramatically increases its yield. (In Egypt, rural productivity has doubled in just ten years.) Crops can be diversified, new techniques introduced, old customs changed. Community development, including the voluntary labor of peasants, can create hospitals, schools, roads—and all this with relatively little capital investment. It is not easy but it *is* possible.

American experience in the Tennessee Valley can, in some ways, be considered a model for rural advance. Poverty, malaria, floods, and hopelessness had stricken the valley when Congress created the TVA in 1933. The new federal agency constructed a series of dams to control water-flow and it also offered leadership, technical assistance, and basic tools to the farmers. Today, floods have been conquered, malaria eliminated, and the average income of farmers has jumped by about 400 per cent. Barges now chug down the rivers carrying 12 million tons of produce, where, in 1933, only one million tons of commerce had moved. New sources of electricity have gone into action, while the cost of electricity has steadily decreased from 5.7 cents per kwh in 1933 to less than one cent in 1963. Even in the depths of its depression, of course, America had monstrous sums of capital available for TVA investment which most developing nations do not now possess. Nevertheless, TVA illustrates what can be done in a rural area if a nation decides to infuse it with money and wisdom.[34]

(2) The transformation must occur *voluntarily* and—if one wishes to use the corrupted word—it must take place democratically. By this, I mean that a large majority of the villagers affected must desire change and participate in it with enthusiasm. Such a generalization is not based on a simple sentimental attachment to democracy. Rather, experience has clearly demonstrated that peasants everywhere resist any attempt at forced change with supreme stubbornness.

To take Africa as one example, Guy Hunter has commented on Kenya that "the agricultural staff became convinced that compulsion was useless, and their greatest success has been through gaining voluntary co-operation in the use of new methods and in land consolidation."[35] In my own experience, I found that the most important advances in Nigeria took place either in newly founded religious communities (led by charismatic "prophets") or in traditional villages where local leaders took the initiative. In Eastern Nigeria, Ben Nzeribe, a selfless man with a Ph.D. in agricultural economics from Cornell, returned to his own village instead of taking the route of many intellectuals and turning his degree into hard cash. In just three years, he led his people in the construction of a hospital, schools, a farming cooperative, and in the opening of new farms for landless peasants. His people elected him to Parliament but he still spends most of his time in the village. One can only hope that his example will be followed by educated men throughout the developing nations.

Where compulsion has been used, food production drops; and this the currently developing countries, unlike Soviet Russia, can hardly afford. Poland learned its lesson well. Prior to the October Revolution, Stalinists tried forced consolidation of land, only to find that Warsaw's larders became increasingly empty. Agriculture all but collapsed. Gomulka wisely reversed this policy, offered the peasantry individual incentives, and (perhaps, only temporarily) restored personal ownership of land. As a result, food production has greatly increased. Hopefully, all nations will realize the futility of compulsion as an instrument for rural change.

(3) Paradoxically, the transformation must also often be initiated, and always sustained, from *above* the village itself. But mark it, this

does not mean political dictatorship or violent compulsion. In most cases of agricultural improvement, the agents of progress have come originally from outside the village. The central government, a private foundation, or sometimes an individual like Vinoba Bhave have spurred advance by stirring the village from its traditional fatalism. Usually, too, success requires that the government (or some other group) must buttress the village with direct subsidies, expert advice, marketing outlets, sources of credit, improved seeds, tools, fertilizers and insecticides. Beyond this, the government must often construct facilities which indirectly but vitally influence the rate of growth: dams and irrigation canals have to be built, erosion-control systems introduced, and, where possible, virgin land opened for those who wish to migrate. I shall long remember one Indian peasant, dedicated to improving his village, crying over the government's inability to provide sufficient credit to buy new seeds and its inadequacy in controlling floods which originated hundreds of miles from his village. "If only we had the money," he said, "what miracles could be done!" If improvement is to become self-sustaining, the desire must come from the villagers' hearts, but, of equal importance, governments in most underdeveloped regions must offer the original impetus *and* a lasting framework as the foundation for rural advance.*

(4) Land reform, in one shape or another, is an inevitable requirement for progress. Peasants who do not own their land must be provided with farms. Without the incentive of personal ownership, the enthusiasm and hard work necessary to expand production can seldom be generated. In some areas, such as tropical Africa, extensive landholdings should be reduced in size; in other regions, such as Indonesia, the job is to open the vast stretches of unworked land in Sumatra, Borneo, and the Celebes; and most difficult of all, the great feudal estates of Latin America must be transferred to individual peasant ownership.[36] Indiscriminate land reform can critically injure a rural economy. In the throes of its revolution, Bolivia chopped up the *latifundia* (huge farms owned by a small ruling class) and distributed them to the peasantry. While the government had good intentions and the farmers loved to own their own plots, production dropped, since the

---

* In most of the new nations, at this stage of their evolution, the introduction of mechanized agriculture would be undesirable. Tractors and combines can, under some conditions, improve output per acre, but their primary utility lies in reducing the cost of labor. In nations such as India and Egypt, which suffer from a surplus of unemployed men, one central objective is to provide work, not to increase idleness by replacing a man with a machine.

land had been overly fragmented. Contrary to the Stalinist view, no single panacea for land reform exists; sometimes consolidation of land-holdings in large co-operatives would be desirable; at other times it would be ruinous.

Voluntary co-operation by farmers, sustained help from outside the village, careful planning, and wise land reform make up the essential ingredients for village transformation. Such a transformation can and must take place, if the new nations truly wish to modernize their economies. Gandhi was both morally and economically right when he told an audience of notables at Benares College in 1916: "Our salvation can come only through the farmer. Neither the lawyers, nor the doctors, nor the rich landlords are going to secure it." [37]

VI

INDUSTRIALIZATION

> The workers in the mills of Bombay have become slaves. . . . If the machinery craze grows in our country it will become an unhappy land. It may be considered a heresy, but I am bound to say that it were better for us to send money to Manchester . . . , than to multiply mills in India. By using Manchester cloth, we would only waste our money, but by reproducing Manchester in India, we shall keep our money at the price of our blood, and I call in support of my statement the very mill hands as witnesses.
> MAHATMA GANDHI, in 1909

Gandhi detested industrialism. He felt revolted by the submergence of handicraft artisans, the exploitation of men by their managers, the wretchedness of the workers' lives. Yet Gandhi did not reject machinery in and of itself. "What I object to," he once remarked, "is the craze for machinery, not machinery as such. . . . If we would have electricity in every village home, I should not mind villages plying their implements and tools with electricity." [1] He sought, above all, to keep industrialization within the bounds of humaneness. He desired that industry should be dispersed throughout the country, based on village craftsmen, and aimed at satisfying people's immediate needs. In the current jargon, he wanted decentralized cottage or light industry rather than heavy industry.*

On this issue, Nehru had to part company with Gandhi. Nehru believed that only the most highly perfected, advanced heavy industry could offer eventual abundance to a developing nation: "The economy based on the latest technical achievements of the day must necessarily

---

* In this chapter, I shall follow Eugene Staley in defining "light" or "small-scale" industry as a firm which employs no more than 100 workers and utilizes inexpensive but modern technology.[2]

be the dominating one." [3] In 1946, he appeared convinced that the dispute had been settled:

Any argument as to the relative merits of small scale vs. large scale industry seems strangely irrelevant today, when the world and the dominating facts of the situation that confront it have decided in favor of the latter. Even in India, that decision has been made by these facts themselves, and no one doubts that India will be rapidly industrialized in the near future.[4]

Nonetheless, the issue has still to be settled in India. Among his other great burdens, Nehru has had to preside over India's Planning Commission. As we have seen, over the years of independence the various plans have fluctuated in their allocations for agriculture. Equally, the plans have varied—without any obviously apparent economic justification—in their expenditures for heavy versus light industries, though the latter have been, in general, notably supported in India. It would seem that the Planning Commission has not, as yet, fully committed itself to either Gandhi's 1909 opinions or Nehru's 1946 views. India as a nation has not made a collective decision.

In one fundamental sense, Nehru in 1946 did have reason on his side. Obviously, if machines can do a job, why should man? No one, except for a blind romantic or a dreamer, can argue that the process of industrialization should be stopped. Even if one wished to stop it, the gears of industry have been set in motion everywhere in the underdeveloped lands. Not even as persuasive a prophet as Gandhi could reverse the trend.

Clearly, we must all recognize that improvements in agriculture *alone* cannot bring about the radical economic advance so ardently desired in the new nations. While I have stressed the need for agricultural change, as well as improvements in village health and education, these efforts cannot initiate the "take-off." Industrialization, in some form, must accompany an agricultural revolution. This point has been ably demonstrated in Scarlett Epstein's studies of two Indian villages.[5]

These Mysore villages, Wangala and Dalena, closely resembled each other. Both lay near an industrializing city, depended on subsistence agriculture, and had the same political, social, and caste systems. In 1939, however, Wangala received the benefits of a new irrigation canal and quickly shifted to the production of more profitable "wet" crops (such as sugar cane). Its income went up, but the economic pursuits of the town, as well as its political and social fabric, remained essentially traditional.

Dalena, the "dry" village, did not directly reap benefits from the new irrigation canal, since the water did not reach its fields. Instead, some men went to work in a small factory constructed to fabricate the sugar cane produced by Wangala farmers. Others became contractors to build bridges and roads servicing the canal. One man constructed a sugar-cane crusher, another built a flour mill, and some bought carts to carry sugar cane to the new factory. By chance, Dalena entered more fully than Wangala into a modern cash economy.

The economic difference between the two villages had wide ramifications. In Wangala those powers which had run the village continued to dominate it. The people of Dalena, in contrast, "competed and co-operated with new sets of people, entered into new master-servant relationships; they encountered new authority, had new experiences." [6]

Consequently, in Dalena the old master-servant relationship disappeared, since the servants found independent wage labor. The village *panchayat*, while still functioning ineffectively, became a truly elected, competitive body rather than one based on hereditary transmission of authority. While both towns became more prosperous, a higher proportion of Dalena's people invested money in improving their houses and their village; they had learned that such investments eventually pay off. Wangala's peasants spent their higher income paying for more elaborate festivals—a rather significant fact when one considers the national requirements for productive capital accumulation.

From the experience of Dalena and Wangala, Wilfred Malenbaum, an expert on the Indian economy, has concluded: ". . . If efforts for change focus on agricultural improvement alone, there is less prospect for benefiting from the forces for change in political and social fields as well as in economic habits and institutions, and there is less prospect for actually achieving the important political and social changes themselves." [7]

The implications are apparent: a nation can achieve real advances only if agricultural change and industrialization complement each other.* The only significant issue which statesmen must now decide is what *type* of industrialization they desire for their nation.

---

* Such a statement gets one entangled in the continuing battle which rages amongst economists concerning the so-called "balanced growth" doctrine. On the one side stand economists such as Ragnar Nurkse who, putting it very generally, argues that economies must develop along many fronts—agriculture, heavy and light industry—in as simultaneous a fashion as possible. In opposition, economists like Albert Hirschman believe that balanced growth is impossible and, further, that it is not a realistic view of how growth actually pro-

Some men have already decided. For many scholars (and all Stalinists) the advancement of heavy industry looks like the primrose path of economic development. Adherents of heavy industrialization can muster powerful arguments for their position; the reasons for their preference fall into two classes: strictly economic arguments and sociopolitical contentions.

On the economic level, they present five generalizations in defence of heavy industry. First, to state the obvious, heavy, highly advanced industry can usually produce more goods more efficiently than any other form of economic activity. A large-scale textile factory can put out at least fifteen times more cloth than can a small-scale, handloom factory. The Ford Motor Company today can turn out millions of more cars in its mechanized, mass production plants than could Henry Ford and his few mechanics in their early garages. The same situation applies in an underdeveloped nation, some theorists say. In consequence, one finds fully automatic refineries in Bombay, a highly advanced water filtration plant in Djakarta, and an automated beer factory in Lagos.

Second, some economists maintain that a concentration on heavy industry will accelerate capital accumulation. The argument runs that an emphasis on dispersed, small-scale production will lead only to an increased demand for consumer items (shirts, shoes, food) and will hinder the process of capital formation. A village-based economy, such as that envisioned by Gandhi, would lead peasants to eat more of their produce and would tempt workers to demand more consumer goods; in the end, inflation would result, since these desires could not be satisfied. In contrast, defenders of this view believe, the big businessman (in a private economy) has already satisfied his needs and, therefore, would be willing to invest his profits from heavy industry in other productive enterprises. (This position is based on the assumption that the tendency to save, and reinvest, is greater at higher levels of income than at lower levels—a generalization which is far from proved.) Similarly, in a socialist society, the government could more easily control profits from heavy industry and could, therefore, quicken the pace of capital investment.

Third, advocates of heavy industry point out that agriculture or small-scale industry has fewer "linkage" effects than does heavy industry. By this they mean that a steel plant widely stimulates economic growth, since it must purchase its raw materials from other sectors of

ceeds. They generally argue for the creation of heavy industry, even if it is out of balance with the rest of the economy, on the basis that industry will spontaneously induce further development.[8]

the economy, while simultaneously, it processes the steel which eventually will be used in other industries. Since a small-scale enterprise can often be more self-sufficient, it has fewer "links" with the rest of the economy. H. B. Chenery (Assistant Director of American AID) and T. Watanabe have compared the degree of interdependence of various industries in Italy, Japan, and the United States. Their results suggest that heavy industry does, in fact, have greater "linkage" with the other parts of an economy:[9]

AVERAGE DEGREE OF INTERDEPENDENCE OF ECONOMIC SECTORS
IN ITALY, JAPAN, AND THE UNITED STATES

	Purchases from Other Sectors	Sales to Other Sectors
Iron and steel	66	78
Processed foods	61	15
Agriculture and forestry	31	72
Fishing	24	36
Trade	16	17

From such evidence, economist Albert Hirschman drew the conclusion: ". . . The industry with the highest combined linkage score is iron and steel. Perhaps the underdeveloped countries are not so foolish and so exclusively prestige-motivated in attributing prime importance to this industry!" [10] *

Fourth, those enthralled with heavy industry believe that no efficient technology exists which would fulfill the Gandhian dream of village craftsmanship. Thus, economist Benjamin Higgins (by no means an unreasoning advocate of heavy industrialization) has been led to the opinion that, for the most part, "There *is* no technology which can be applied to a wide range of productive activities," one which would make small-scale industrial programs reasonable investments.[11]

Fifth, many believe that heavy industry, once established, will *inevitably* drive small concerns out of business. Certainly, history justifies this belief, although it may not justify its moral and political implications. It seems certain that efficient mass production can destroy artisans. This conviction pushed Nehru to inquire in 1946:

---

* Of course, one must make the original assumption that there are pre-existing industries and markets with which to link the steel factory. The assumption may be valid for nations such as India or Brazil, but hardly for the majority of developing areas.

Is it possible to have two entirely different kinds of economy in a country—one based on the big machine and industrialization, and the other mainly on cottage industries? This is hardly conceivable, for one must overcome the other, and there can be little doubt that the big machine will triumph unless it is forcibly prevented from doing so.[12]

Those who favor steel factories do not rest their case solely on economic grounds. They also turn to sociological and political arguments against Gandhians. At bottom they believe that only industrialization, following a Western or Soviet model, can create the men and institutions necessary for a modern society.

On a socio-political level, people of this opinion contend that a government can co-ordinate and plan an economy based on heavy industry with greater efficiency than one scattered in many small units and farms. To the degree that centralized planning organs are considered desirable, one must grant that it is easier to control a heavily industrialized society than a peasant society.

Some social scientists further argue that underdeveloped nations critically lack skilled workmen, engineers, and managers. A highly automated plan conserves these vital human resources, since relatively few workers are required to run advanced machinery. In this same vein of argument, Albert Hirschman has maintained that the installation of a highly complex hydroelectric plan, for example, *forces* a government to operate and maintain it with great care. The sheer expense involved in such showpieces "places [a government] under a far stronger compulsion to 'deliver' than if it were to spend the same funds on a large number of small projects." [13] Hirschman argues that laborers in such a hydroelectric plan perform better than in craft industries, since machines pace the operation and workers' mistakes are so costly. Workers *have* to learn the necessary skills, if they wish to retain their positions.

David McClelland, although personally not in favor of the ideology of heavy industrialization, has developed another sociological argument in support of this position. McClelland's studies indicate that any policy which entirely focuses on rural development will only reinforce traditionalist attitudes and fail to produce the entrepreneurs necessary for an "achieving society." [14] He criticizes those who hope for a continuance of village life, on the grounds that they ignore the revolution of expectations. In McClelland's opinion, the developing peoples will not be satisfied until the full material benefits of industrialization come to them. Thus, he views with some skepticism the advice which Stuart

Chase offered to the villagers of Tepoztlan, Mexico, in 1931. Chase hoped that the peasants would retain the charm and virtues of their old culture; he suggested, ". . . If I were you, when and if the new highway comes looping over the mountains into your village street, I would buy all the boxes of extra-sized carpet tacks I can afford." [15] McClelland responded:

The advice, though well-intentioned, was obviously unrealistic in almost every particular. . . . The discussion is romantic, not of course in terms of ultimate values, for who is to say that a simple peasant community achieves less in human happiness than rich industrialized city life? It is romantic in the sense that it believes that peoples will be satisfied with simplicity or backwardness, once they have had contact with advanced material culture.[16]

Proponents of heavy industrialization put forward a final argument, composed more of fervent nationalism than economic sense. Many leaders in developing lands wish their economies to become totally self-sufficient. They want to divorce themselves from the current world market. The development of domestic heavy industry would seem to many of them the only way of assuring such economic independence. When Chou En-lai spoke at the Bandung Conference in 1955, he expressed not only his own aspirations, but those of many genuine liberals and social democrats: "The majority of our Asian and African countries, including China, are still very backward economically, owing to the long period of colonial domination. That is why we demand not only political independence but economic independence as well." [17]

The technical aspects of this position have been elaborated by Raoul Prebisch, an eminent economist. For Latin America, Prebisch contends, the international division of labor has worked to the detriment of the continent. He maintains that Latin America has been forced into being an exporter of primary products (such as bananas and coffee) and an importer of manufactured goods from North America. Meanwhile, he contends, world prices for commodities have declined, while the demand for industrial goods has increased, thus placing South America in a most disadvantaged position. (Whether, in fact, there has been a downward secular trend for raw commodities remains an issue of considerable debate in economics.) "There is no other way of correcting the effects of this disparity," Prebisch has concluded, "than the promotion of industrial production in underdeveloped countries." [18]

Few would question the need for developing nations to avoid dependence on a single export product. Yet, the fact remains that every new nation, including China, must import capital equipment in the foreseeable future. These nations must—in one way or another—pay for the imports. Total self-sufficiency may be attained by a primitive village, but not by an entire state bent on modernization.

A country's attempt to count itself out of the world market can have disastrous results, as Argentina's recent history sadly demonstrates. When Perón took power, Argentina had the highest literacy rate in Latin America, the second-highest per capita income, an extensive railway system, and a sound industrial base. But Perón dreamed of converting Argentina into a totally industrialized economy. Utilizing a surplus derived from beef exports (temporarily, world demand for meat had been very high), Perón bought out foreign interests at a cost of $400 million. He then set his hand to a program of rapid, heavy industrialization. Inevitably, food production fell, exports dwindled, and peasants sought work in the cities, lured by wages artificially pegged at a high level. Imports rose, and the economy went into an inflationary spiral. Between 1948 and 1955, the gross national product fell by 7 per cent. Why did Argentina regress? As one Latin American expert explained it: "Argentina's troubles spring from Perón's clumsy but well-meaning attempts to make it economically and industrially independent." [19] In today's world, unfortunately, attempts at complete economic independence are doomed to failure.

Nevertheless, when one passes in review all of the arguments for heavy industrialization, they present a rather handsome front. Indeed, for a handful of developing nations—perhaps Mexico, Brazil, Uruguay, Argentina, and India—an ultimate goal of heavy industrialization *may* be economically sound (although the social and political repercussions should be carefully weighed). These economies could roughly be classified as "semi-modern." They have already achieved a relatively high degree of industrialization and urbanization. Some have a fairly respectable rate of literacy, a pool of skilled labor, a well-trained elite, and a competent civil service. They also possess most of the "infrastructure" of railroads, highways, dams, and electric power. In contrast, the rest of the underdeveloped world might be called "semi-traditional." Nations such as Pakistan, Nigeria, and Indonesia still lack a large industrial base, an extensive infra-structure, widespread literacy, or sufficient manpower to run a complex of heavy industries. The semi-traditional areas face economic challenges quite different from, let us say, Uruguay's.

For the majority of developing regions, particularly of the semi-traditional variety, I am convinced that the program originally conceived by Gandhi offers more hope than that enforced by Stalin. The reasons for preferring light, decentralized industries seem clear, almost self-evident.

First, we will touch only lightly upon the costly errors made by governments hypnotized by heavy industry. In Eastern Europe, ill-conceived planning forced the cancellation of half-finished steel plants and, in East Germany, the elimination of an entire aircraft industry. Egypt manufactures a Ramses car and jet planes, when foreign imports would be much cheaper. Venezuela's Jíminez spent some £1000 million, derived from oil exports, in building a vast hydroelectric station when there was no demand for electricity; and he purchased a steel works, without any coke ovens or coke supply. Indonesia imported an entire French water plant simply because of its shiny modern look, and Sukarno wanted to replace the little Opelettes with new buses, even though the small trucks provided better, less expensive transportation. These errors testify to the follies committed in the name of industrialization and modernity. They are human mistakes which any government might make, but the more you invest in heavy industry, the more you lose if the gamble fails. As Barbara Ward (Lady Jackson), the distinguished British economist, has observed:

It is said of Mayor LaGuardia that he once said: "I make very few mistakes, but when I do make a mistake, it's a beaut." I think you can say the same is true of governments. They do not necessarily make mistakes in the development of heavy industry. But if they do make a mistake, it tends to be a very large one—in short, a "beaut." [20]

Even if one assumed that a government had infinite wisdom, there are many other reasons for giving preference to light, small-scale industries. On economic grounds, to reiterate the obvious, two problems plague most underdeveloped nations: scarcity of capital and constant underemployment. The creation of heavy industry does little to allay these burdens, but a program of small-scale industry could.

Light industries have the pre-eminent virtues of both conserving capital and putting idle men to work—thus, striking at the core of a developing country's immediate economic problems. Such enterprises are "labor intensive"; that is, for the same investment of capital, more workers can find employment than if the money were put into heavy, "capital intensive" factories. This point has been well illustrated by P. S. Lokanathan in his investigations of the Indian textile industry, one of the most important sectors of the Indian economy. His results can be seen in the following table: [21]

CAPITAL AND LABOR INTENSITY AND PRODUCTIVITY
IN THE INDIAN TEXTILE INDUSTRY

Mode of Production	Capital Investment per Worker (Rupees)	Production per Worker (Rupees)	Ratio of Capital to Production	Amount of Labor Employed per Unit of Capital
Large-scale industry (modern)	1,200	650	1.9	1
Small industry (power loom)	300	200	1.5	4
Cottage industry (automatic loom)	90	80	1.1	13
Cottage industry (hand loom)	35	45	0.8	34

Several conclusions may be drawn from Lokanathan's study. Clearly, large-scale industry produces more, *but* small industry puts four times as many people to work (for each unit of capital invested) as does heavy industry. Further, small industry produces 23 per cent more textiles, *per unit of capital*, than does heavy industry. In other words—at least for Indian textiles—small industry saves scarce capital and also provides a higher rate of employment. While this generalization does not hold true for all types of manufacturing in all nations, it is more or less valid for many other branches of industry, particularly the production of consumer goods.[22]

When speaking before Indian scholars and students, John Galbraith made this point succinctly: ". . . It is a mark of wise development planning to copy from the countries in the more advanced stages. And it is also a mark of wise planning not to do so. . . . Not long ago, in a neighboring Asian country where there is much unemployment and where wages are low, I saw expensive automatic gates imported from abroad being installed at the railroad crossing. These are a necessary development in those countries where no one is any longer available for the reflective life of the railway gateman. But not here. Had the distinction I am making been more clearly in mind considerable money would have been saved and the gatemen would have remained gratefully at their posts." [23]

The small-scale, decentralized approach can lay claim to other important economic virtues. Such a program does not necessarily require an advanced transportation system, highly skilled labor, or sophisticated managers. Under proper circumstances, it can use nearby raw materials, locally produced implements, and seasonal labor. And, in some areas, light industry may actually be more efficient than heavy industry. Eugene Staley has demonstrated that small concerns can often out-compete large industries in the manufacture of certain kinds of products: bricks, clothes, backed goods, precision instruments, and several varieties of specialized machinery.[24]

A further important point, too often overlooked by statesmen bent on heavy industrialization, has been well clarified by Arthur Lewis. A scheme of development which concentrates on heavy industry entails what Lewis has called "hidden overhead costs." To run a large industry, someone must provide an extensive transportation system, sources of power, electricity grids, specialized buildings, technical schools, as well as housing and many other services for factory workers. As Lewis has pointed out:

Workers are often attracted away from areas which may already have schools, hospitals, and other facilities, into [new urban centers] where the full range of public facilities now has to be provided. And the cost of this falls not on the new industries which cause it, but on the government, and through the government on industry as a whole, wherever it may be located.[25]

Unfortunately, many governments fail to compute these hidden costs or to realize that decentralized, small industries would avoid much of this toll.

Small enterprises may also better fulfill the nationalist goal of economic self-sufficiency, sought by so many politicians in developing regions. The little industries are best adapted to production of consumer items. Like the advancement of agriculture, the development of small-scale, consumer-oriented industries could significantly aid in resolving the recurrent balance-of-payments problem, since it would reduce imports. Indonesia, to cite one illustration, would no longer have to expend its capital on the importation of Lux soap and Hershey chocolate bars, if it created—as it easily could—village shops to produce soap and candy.

Thus, on the level of economics, a concerted drive to establish light industries offers several benefits to most developing countries: expensive mistakes could be averted, scarce capital conserved, unemployed labor utilized, hidden overhead costs avoided, and imports of consumer products reduced. Perhaps even more basic arguments for light industrialization come from the social and political realm:

First, decentralized, small-scale production can give immediate satisfaction to the pressing needs felt by the peasantry. Not only would
more peasants find work but they could produce by themselves many
of the industrial products which they desire. A genuine self-sufficiency
could be created in the village and with it, possibly, a newly regained
sense of dignity.

Second, decentralized growth—following the path first blazed by
Japan—avoids urbanization and the suffering which, as we noted, characterizes transitional cities. If left unchecked, heavy industry gravitates
toward urban areas. Heavy industries (which are not geographically
tied to a particular raw material) tend naturally to concentrate in
cities, since an urban environment normally offers a large market, the
best transport, superior banking facilities, and various other economic
advantages. A policy of decentralized, light industry, on the other hand,
would help to stop the migration to cities. It would bring industry to
the peasants, not peasants to the city. Paul Johnson's comments concerning Latin American cities apply with equal force throughout the
developing regions:

*They have all expanded far beyond their economic limits and now im-
pose a crushing, ravenous burden on the rural areas. A third of Argentina lives in Buenos Aires, a quarter of Chile in Santiago; Mexico City
with 4.5 million, Caracas with 1.5 million, Lima and Bogota with a
million each—all are far too big for the depleted productive workers
who must feed them.*[26]

Third, development of light industries would help to avoid the
seething political discontent which arises where there exist enclaves of
heavy industry surrounded by a stagnant village society. Arthur Lewis's
studies have shown that mass political unrest and the dangers of anarchic mob rule reach their peak in those nations where pockets of heavy
industry appear without a balanced development of village economies.
To quote Lewis once again:

*The high incomes earned in the more productive industries . . .
create tensions in other industries. Civil servants, bus conductors, plantation workers, farmers . . . keep trying to catch up, through trade
unions, farmers associations, or other political activity.* **The more rapidly heavy industries develop, the greater the industrial and political
unrest in other industries.**[27]

For a multitude of reasons, then, it is critically important for a newly
developing nation to place very high priority upon building a small-

scale, village-based, decentralized economy. But can it be done? This seems the most basic question posed by opponents of such a program. Typical of the pessimists, Robert Heilbroner has argued:

> . . . *One could imagine the growth of a modern, highly productive "cottage industry," capable of supplying many consumer items and even some industrial equipment. . . . As yet, however, such a technology does not exist. . . . Nor does small-scale industry seem capable of providing a substitute for the vast capital agglomerations of heavy industry, as evidenced by the very disappointing results of the Chinese "back-yard" steel furnaces.*[28]

While I agree with Heilbroner that the task would hardly be simple— *no* approach is easy in the struggle for economic development—I fear that he, along with many other Western social scientists, underrates the potential creativity of transitional man. The development of small industry will require careful planning, training programs, the provision of outside aid of many types and, in *some* cases, the invention of a new technology. Yet, we know that the job can be done, for, here and there, it has *already* been done.[29]

I will choose only a few examples (from many) to illustrate the village's capacity for light industrialization. To refer again to some towns which we have previously examined, one could call as evidence the experience of El Westiani, Egypt. El Westiani's agricultural progress has been closely coupled with industrialization. In the last five years, a small brick-making plant has been established which now furnishes all of El Westiani's building needs. A hand-craft furniture shop, staffed by five men, makes chairs and tables. A cotton-fabricating plant, employing some 100 people, processes El Westiani's crop. These industrial advances have been partially subsidized by the government but are now self-supporting. Wisely, the Egyptian government has tried to decentralize its industries—thus, instead of building the cotton-processing plant in Cairo, they placed it ten miles from El Westiani. Men can work in the factory without deserting their original homes.[30]

Even the gigantic textile mills which eventually turn El Westiani's cotton into cloth have been located near villages, so that workers will not have to sever their ties from their home environment. For its large industries, Egypt has provided excellent training programs for the new workers. In one textile plant which I visited, employment of workers had increased from 500 to 10,000 men within the last decade. At first, inevitably, the new workers made many mistakes. "They were not used to industrial discipline," the plant's director, a former brigadier told me, "they didn't even realize that one cannot simply leave a machine running in order to take the time to go to the bathroom." Eventually, for good or ill, the workers learned to accustom themselves to factory life. Now, the plant produces cloth which approaches Germany's in quality. With further improvements in the workers' skills, they hope to surpass Germany within a few years. One other aspect of Egypt's industrialization deserves mention: Workers' representatives sit on the management board. This is a start toward industrial democracy, although, in fact, the managers (mostly ex-army officers) still make most of the basic decisions. Also, workers, by law, receive 25 per cent of the profits of their plant, a device which goes far in increasing incentive.

In Alipur, India, a little furniture factory, brick kilns, weaving looms, and a small soap-producing shop have been introduced. The government provided the money for the initial implements and established a training center to offer brief courses in the necessary skills.

In Kenya, an entirely indigenous industry grew up under the stimulus of a single chief. In a region where wood-carving had not been a traditional craft, this *Askari* taught young men of his clan how to carve small statues from wood. Eventually, he established a compound of buildings where today many carvers, mostly adolescents, whittle away making statues. Elspeth Huxley observed:

It is mass-production without machinery. Perhaps a carving expert could detect subtle differences between one elephant and another, between the innumerable antelope lying with their fawns at foot, between the various rhinos and tortoises and giraffe-headed salad-spoons, but to the ordinary eye they appear identical. Yet there does not seem to be any pattern laid down, still less a master-carver in charge of it all. Marketing is organized by one or two traders. . . .[31]

In 1961, exports of these carvings brought some £150,000 into the village, significantly, from an industry started without any outside stimulus or help whatsoever.

Such examples could be infinitely multiplied. Ghana has built numerous small-scale canning factories, processing plants, and small roofing mills near existing villages. In Vicos, Peru, Cornell anthropologists have initiated a process of rural and industrial development which has been so successful that the Indians have become moneylenders to less fortunate villages. In Punjab, India, Peace Corpsmen found that American AID had sent an electric wheat-grinding machine which did not work because its plug could not fit Indian circuits. By simply installing a round-pronged plug, a new industry commenced. The lesson is apparent: Sufficient human inventiveness can create thriving small industries anywhere in the world.

For the next decades, decentralized, balanced, small-scale industry offers *most* developing nations (at this stage of their evolution) important economic, social, and political benefits.* Too often, planners have ignored these advantages in their bedazzlement with heavy industry. For a few semi-modern economies, the pursuit of heavy industrialization may be a valuable endeavor. Yet, even in these societies, the development of village industry can be neglected only at great peril. Mexico, for example, stands very high on any list of industrialized nations. During the last decade, its advancement of heavy industry has been most impressive. But, as Karl Meyer, an editor of the *Washington Post* has observed:

> *The visible truth is that progress has been centered in the cities, and the peasant has been the symbol but not the beneficiary of a revolution consecrated to his plight. . . . What you miss is any driving sense of urgency about transforming a countryside where life can be nasty, brutish, and short.*[33]

Again, as in the case of agricultural change, the development of small-scale industries requires careful planning, an infra-structure (of dams, electric power, implements, and the like), and, usually, governmental guidance. A successful program normally demands that the government or some other institution initiates change. It must also make provisions for credit and marketing facilities. One promising approach, used in India, has been the establishment of widely dispersed "industrial estates," or communities where the government builds common workshops and provides power, advisory services, and even housing. Here, the fledgling entrepreneur rents the necessary equipment. If his enterprise fails, he does not lose as much as if he had invested all

---

* Of course, qualifications must be added. Clearly, small-scale industries depend, to some degree, upon heavy industries. It is hardly advisable to build power looms for village use, by hand. Eventually, small-scale and heavy industries should be complementary. Basically, I would subscribe to Willem Brand's view: "The future course would seem to be: (1) to modernize cottage industries or small-scale industry in general in order to raise their productivity and minimize the cost of keeping uneconomical, but socially advantageous, forms of production alive; (2) to expand more productive industrial and other activities outside the primary sphere in order to open up additional employment opportunities." [32]

of his own savings. By reducing the risk, such a method can encourage industrial innovation.[34]

In many instances, some agency must undertake to provide the people to staff new industries. I mean this not only in the trite sense that men have to be trained to use new tools, but also that the program must have at its disposal a corps of well-qualified managers. As Barbara Ward has said:

The desirability of widespread and diversified enterprise does not . . . answer the question whether there are enough entrepreneurs to undertake the expansion. And where they are lacking, as in large parts of Africa, government must inescapably play a part in helping an entrepreneur to begin.[35]

A wise government, such as the Meiji regime, must consciously plan to produce an elite to run its new industries. Indeed, one may legitimately say that all of the dilemmas of development which we have discussed—the problems of capital accumulation, agricultural improvement, and industrialization—can be resolved only if another tough problem can be overcome: that of transforming men.

VII

TRANSFORMING MEN

> Growth cannot be measured only by indexes of industrial produc-
> tion. . . . What is fundamental is the man behind the machine.
> G. L. MEHTA

In 1928, a British team investigating the Anchau area of northern
Nigeria discovered that sleeping sickness had reached epidemic proportions. Forty per cent of the 50,000 people who lived near streams
suffered from the disease. The solution seemed simple. Tsetse flies
which carry the germ can live only in a relatively cool environment.
If the government could persuade Hausa farmers to chop down brush
surrounding the river banks, the flies would disappear. British officers,
ruling "indirectly" through local emirs, ordered that the job be undertaken. In turn, the emirs issued commands to their subordinates. And
then the trouble began.

The British overlooked several salient aspects of Hausa culture: The
peasants believed that sacred spirits inhabited certain clumps of bush.
They did not share with the British the same definition of sleeping
sickness; they identified the illness solely with its most severe form,
total somnolence, rather than with its more common symptoms of
constant fever, headache, and chronic weakness. The peasants believed
that evil spirits caused the disorder and that it was highly contagious.
Further, they condemned the man who came down with the disease
as an outcast and, consequently, the victim felt loath to admit its
presence.

Because they did not take these beliefs into account, the British attempts to educate the peasantry failed. Farmers refused to cut down the flies' shelter along the river. Village headmen quit in protest against the orders. Even the chief emir began to feel his power had been shaken, and it appeared for a time that the whole political structure of the region might collapse in chaos. Non-Hausa peoples imported from the French Sudan had to cut down some of the more sacred patches of brush. The British resorted to fines for Hausa peasants who did not co-operate. After years of struggle, the British won, and sleeping sickness disappeared from Anchau.

Yet, even in 1960, when sociologist Horace Miner returned to the region and questioned villagers, he found basic attitudes unchanged. The Hausa continued to cut down the flies' cover, but only under orders from the emirs, now freed of English rule. One-quarter of village headmen had no idea whatsoever why the emirs wanted them to do the work. "The interviews produced that rarity in social science data, unanimous concurrence. When asked if they would continue to clear the streams if they were not forced to do so, every headman replied, 'No.'" [1] Both the British and Nigerian elites had failed effectively to integrate the new program of stream clearance with the local problems and beliefs of Hausa peasants.

Again and again, those concerned with development encounter replicas of the Hausa problem, not just in the field of health, but also in agricultural change, industrialization, the initiation of new fiscal policies—in virtually every aspect of a developing nation's life. We have finally come to a groping realization that transitional men's habits, institutions, customs, and beliefs must undergo certain changes, if their new aspirations are to be fulfilled. Galbraith has well phrased the challenge:

> . . . In many countries any serious look at the larger system must soon come to focus on the shortcomings of the social order. . . . On even the most preliminary view of the problem, effective government, education, and social justice emerge as critically important . . . in diagnosing the barriers to advance, it is lack of these that is of critical importance.[2]

We have already mentioned several of the social and cultural issues with which modernizers must struggle. No one can conceive of economic development in Latin America without considering the role of the Church, the traditionalist ethic adhered to by feudal barons, and the social function of the military as a governing class. In Africa, no one can sensibly examine the prospects for growth without paying close attention to the impact of tribalism, the economic effects of an extended kinship system, and the prejudices against such "aliens" as Indians, Syrians, or Lebanese. Nor can one analyze Asia without a concern for the economic relevance of quietistic religions, of governmental corruption, of religious, racial, and linguistic divisions. The list of social problems seems virtually endless.

The specific social obstacles to growth differ radically for each country; in fact, *within* each country. Though all these social evils cannot be discussed individually here, there are three issues concerning the transformation of man which most developing nations face in common:

How to control the population explosion?

How to educate men?

How to produce creative innovators?

We will examine each of these questions, for almost every developing nation must deal with them—consciously or unconsciously, wisely or irrationally.

The Population Explosion

> Every time your pulse throbs, the population of the world will have grown by more than one human being . . . almost 100 more a minute . . . 6000 an hour . . . 140,000 a day.
>
> WILLIAM VOGT

The facts are simple, even though many leaders in underdeveloped nations choose to ignore them: At the current rate of population increase, Mexico will double its people in less than 24 years. Indonesia has already doubled its population in less than 27 years. India's population expands each year by about as many human beings as live in New York City, despite the fact that India's rate of fertility is less than that of the United States.

By the year 2000, 663 million people will live in Africa, 651 million in Latin America, and over four billion in Asia. And these United Nations estimates made in the 1950's do not take into account new evidence, such as China's recent census which revealed a much larger population than anticipated.

If the prevailing rate of growth has not been reversed, five and one-half billion people will try to live in the underdeveloped areas by the end of the century. In contrast, the economically developed regions

(North America, Europe, Russia, Australia, and Japan) will have to support only one and one-half billion people.[3]

The significance of these facts has not yet been fully comprehended. Unless a miracle occurs—and even the briefest examination of agricultural problems suggests it won't—the globe simply will not have enough food to feed these new people. While food production in the developing countries has increased during the last decade, the per capita amount of food in 1961-62 was slightly *lower* than in prewar years.[4] The breeding of babies has outpaced food production. Even if America distributed all her abundant food surplus to the existing billions of hungry people, it would only suffice to give each person two extra cupfuls of rice every nineteen days.[5] And experts know that it normally takes two acres of land to feed a person on a minimally adequate diet. Fifty-five million people are born every year. How could farmland possibly expand at an equal rate? Unless a change in birth patterns occurs, mankind would, in effect, condemn these new children to death, in the classical Malthusian way.

Aside from the problem of food, the population surge has other important consequences for economic development. Ansley Coale has demonstrated that effective birth control would aid in providing productive employment for men by achieving a faster rate of growth in capital per worker.[6] In India, for example, the current incidence of birth will probably add an additional 150 million people in 25 years. If India's industries supported these human beings, fifteen million new jobs would have to be created. This requires about $50 billion in capital. To meet the total needs of a growing population, India would need $100 billion in additional capital within 25 years. The provision of such sums is utterly impossible.[7]

As Paul Hoffman has said, "Many countries are having to run hard just to stand still." [8] In Egypt, the completion of the Aswan Dam and connecting irrigation canals will open two million acres for cultivation. Food production should increase by 45 per cent as a result. But, with its current birth rate of 2.5 per cent, Egypt will not have added to the total amount of food available. Ten years of labor on the dam will not put more meat or milk in children's stomachs.

One would think that these facts speak for themselves: man has managed to reduce death rates in the developing nations but has failed to decrease birth rates. Clearly, our duty is to introduce birth control, if transitional men are to have any chance of fulfilling their hopes. Nevertheless, three powerful groups—the communists, the Roman Catholic Church, and some optimistic social scientists—have formed a strange alliance in opposing an effective attack upon the problem. Their arguments deserve attention, for they influence millions of people.

The communists, with varying consistency, have opposed birth-control programs on theoretical grounds. Orthodox Marxists have traditionally believed that overpopulation is a mere "relative surplus" of labor. When the millennium of a socialist society comes, all will be employed and the population issue will disappear. A typical spokesman for this position, T. V. Ryabushkin, has told a United Nations conference:

> *Every social system has its own concrete laws of population. . . . In conditions of capitalistic mode of production a certain part of the population systematically becomes relatively superfluous. . . . In socialist society . . . the problem of excessive population no longer arises.*[9]

After inquiring whether birth control would aid a people's well-being and whether Malthusian theory may still obtain in developing areas, Ryabushkin concluded, "To these questions we . . . give a sharp negative answer." [10]

Because of their misconceptions, most communist nations have helped to block United Nations action on birth control. In 1962, a resolution authorizing the United Nations to give technical assistance to countries requesting birth control aid failed to pass the General Assembly. Its defeat took place for two reasons: a massive vote of rejection from Catholic nations and an extraordinary number of abstentions. The Soviet bloc (and the United States) abstained. Brave Yugoslavia voted for the resolution.

Even China, however, now seems to recognize in practice the folly of Marxist doctrine. China has reversed its policy on birth control several times since 1949. At first, the regime encouraged contraception; then, in 1958, Mao demanded *more* babies, and the program of contraceptive instruction abruptly halted. By 1962, the failure of the "Great Leap" became apparent. Critical food shortages began, because the rulers had neglected to advance farming. Mao commanded another change in policy. In 1963, a huge propaganda campaign called for contraception, sterilization, postponement of marriage, and abortion. Posters told young people that they must not fall in love, because it was unpatriotic. China had to change its policy, for the population now exceeds 700 million and grows annually by more than 2 per cent. Food output dropped by 10 per cent between 1958 and 1963; but in 1963, the government had to feed 50 million more Chinese. The elite attempts to reconcile its actions with Marxist dogma by concentrating publicity on health and welfare, never mentioning the population problem itself. Outsiders cannot estimate the success of the newest approach, but some observers in 1963 reported few signs of change in the countryside where 85 per cent of Chinese live.[11]

The Roman Catholic doctrine of birth control approaches orthodox Marxism in its blindness to the facts of life—and death—in developing nations. The Church makes its case on a moral basis: the "rhythm method," periodic continence, seems to the theologians more "natural" than other ways of controlling fertility. If man used "artificial" techniques, this would violate God's will. The opinion can be traced originally to Saint Paul, who believed that the only reason for sexual intercourse was procreation and, possibly, the relief of lust—"It is better to marry than to burn." A definitive pronouncement by the Church during the twentieth century allowed the rhythm method. Actually, one may regard even this as an advance in the Church's theology, since previously any attempt to regulate births systematically had been condemned.

Today, along with their moral doctrine, various Catholic theologians put forward social and psychological arguments for their opinion. Some contend that periodic continence has good physical effects, helps cement family ties, aids self-discipline, and brings man closer to God. Regardless of the validity of these hypotheses, one fact has been relatively well established. Exclusive reliance on the rhythm method leads to "accidents," unwanted children, among 30 per cent of couples who practice it.[12]

One other fact has to be kept in mind. In spite of Church edicts, many Catholic couples *in economically advanced nations* practice "artificial" birth control. One major study in the United States indicated that the great majority of Catholic couples married ten years or more tried to regulate births, and of these, only 44 per cent relied totally upon the rhythm method.[13]

Particularly in South America, the Church's concept (in addition to many other factors) has had a disastrous impact upon the fertility of an illiterate population. In tropical Latin America, population grows each year by 3 per cent; in Venezuela, by 4 per cent.[14] At this speed, tropical Latin America will have doubled its population in 23 years; Venezuela, in less than eighteen years. Their battered economies could not tolerate the strain.

Will the Church change its position and give Catholic areas some chance for survival? One can only hope for such a reversal, but on this issue the matter seems literally in the hands of God. The Church has changed its mind on various other matters, such as usury. Whether it will again change would seem to hinge partially upon the development of technology. Perhaps scientists can work out methods which the Church will consider "natural." Even now the most eminent Catholic gynecologist, Dr. John Rock, has tried hard to convince the Vatican that new oral contraceptives which control the menstrual cycle are as natural as the rhythm method. In any case, we must unfortunately anticipate that Rome will probably continue its opposition to effective birth control.

Although the Church has immense political influence, it cannot completely dominate all Catholic countries. Against opposition from the priestly hierarchy, Puerto Rico has introduced a widespread birth control program. And, in the debate over United Nations technical assistance in this field, two Catholic countries (Chile and Costa Rica) voted *for* the resolution. Haiti, Mexico, Nicaragua, Panama, and the Philippines abstained, rather than joining with other Catholic delegations in sinking the proposal. Perhaps the governments of other Catholic nations will have the same vision in the future.

A motley assortment of scientists whom I would label as the "optimists" joins with the Church and orthodox communists in fighting birth control. Some people hope for the harvesting of seaweed, the manufacture of edible algae, the opening up of deserts, and even exporting men to the moon or distant planets. They believe that advances in technology or a gigantic application of existing knowledge could solve the population problem, without resort to birth control programs.

Some of the optimists point out that since 1800, the globe's population has trebled, and so far, technology has managed to keep up with the boom. Why, they ask, can't science do the same job for the future? Such an argument overlooks a few facts. In 1800, vast stretches of land in Europe, America, and elsewhere could easily be cultivated. This is no longer true. In addition, the trebling of population has *not* left mankind in a bettered position. There is good reason to believe that many Indians, Chinese, and Latin Americans have less to eat now than they did in 1800.

A reasonably moderate advocate of the optimistic view, economist Colin Clark, has argued that population increases should not really be considered a significant problem. He points out that Denmark and the Netherlands manage to feed 200 people per square kilometer of cultivatable land. If Danish methods of agriculture were used in all nations, he rightly says, they could support four times the earth's present population. He maintains that "nothing could be more futile—apart from the morality of it—than to attempt to distribute contraceptives among people who do not wish to use them." [15]

Yet, there are a few problems which these scientists neglect to mention in their glowing portrayals of the future. Theoretically, we might be able to feed properly all the current population of the globe. To do this, however, would mean irrigating the Sahara, opening Australia for migration, reforming land-tenure patterns in South America, chopping down Africa's rain forests, re-educating billions of peasants—in short, heroic efforts that would involve social, technical, and political changes which not even the most Micawberish social scientist can sensibly envision. Even if man could somehow double food production in the next forty years, he would only keep step with projected population growth. The majority of mankind would still starve. As for packing people off to the moon—assuming they wanted to go—this alternative at best could be used on a mass scale only ten or twenty years from now. By then, without birth control, economies such as Venezuela's may already have fallen apart.

There can be only one solution: programs of birth control, coupled with other measures of economic advance, must be actively promoted in almost every developing nation. But this conclusion raises the really critical questions: Do cheap, effective contraceptives exist? Can transitional men be convinced of the necessity for birth control?

For many peasants, having a large family has traditionally been a source of pride. And, in the bleak world of the peasant, one of the few pleasures left in this life is sexual intercourse. Naturally, he is reluctant to relinquish it. Some of the peasants with whom I have talked also believe, with some rationality, that children are an economic boon, since they can work in the fields. Even in those regions where religion has not sanctified large families, the task of changing these attitudes is of enormous magnitude.

Simple ignorance constitutes another barrier. In India, discouraging experiments included one in which government clinics passed out strings of beads to women for use as an aid in the rhythm method. The success of the experiment depended upon the women's carefully using the beads to count the days of their menstrual cycle. They liked the beads so much that they began to exchange them as currency in the village. Needless to say, the experiment failed.

Nevertheless, the picture is not as desolate as it might appear. Reports increasingly show that even the most illiterate, traditionalist peasant can alter his attitudes toward procreation. In 1956, Puerto Rico initiated a project of distributing oral contraceptives to women. Among those who followed the schedule (most did), none had pregnancies. In Japan, Dr. Y. Koya, director of the National Institute of Public Health, conducted a simple educational program in three rural villages. Between 1948 and 1954, the birth rate of these Japanese peasants dropped by 66 per cent. In Singur, a peasant area outside of Calcutta, relatively untrained personnel taught villagers the use of inexpensive means of birth control. Within four years, the birth rate in villages which received the education had gone down 15 per cent, while in adjoining "control" villages the birth rate remained stable. In Ceylon, a Swedish group—working intensively with a somewhat more literate peasantry—reduced fertility by about one-third.[16]

As usual, one problem is money. Most developing countries do not have the capital or the personnel to conduct extensive birth-control campaigns. Outside aid must back up the program. If peasants could be educated in the use of contraceptives, there would still be the problem whether they could afford to buy the necessary equipment. The oral contraceptives used in some experiments cost approximately six dollars a month, an impossible price for a peasant woman to pay. Science affords some hope on this front, too, since a really inexpensive oral contraceptive will probably soon be developed.

Intra-uterine contraception may have even greater promise. Gräfenberg, a German gynecologist, invented this technique during the 1920's. Essentially, it involved the insertion of a small silver ring in a woman's uterus. It could be removed when the woman desired children. In 1959, reports from Japan recorded that 19,000 women who had had ring insertions over a twenty-year period experienced great contraceptive success with this approach.[17] It may prove technically feasible to manufacture rings from rubber at a price of about three cents. Even the poorest woman could afford the cost of this permanent contraceptive.

If its plans mature, Egypt will have mounted the most effective birth control program in the developing world. Nasser, like Mao, has changed his mind radically about birth control. At first, he wanted the population to expand, presumably adding greater glory and power to the United Arab Republic. Gradually, the responsibilities of power added a more sober note to Nasser's policies. He authorized medical clinics to provide contraceptive information to women who had borne more than five children. Later, he told the clinics to pass out instructions to all women. By 1962, as a potential food crisis loomed, plans evolved to establish birth-control clinics throughout Egypt. Most importantly, the plan called for the importation of a German factory to manufacture oral contraceptives. The government would distribute these free to any woman who wished them. If Egypt can, in fact, achieve its goals, it should have controlled its population explosion within a decade. One can hope that other developing countries, assisted by the economically advanced regions, will follow Egypt's lead and initiate similar crash programs. As Karl Sax has outlined the stark alternatives:

> *We have the knowledge and the potential resources to provide a good life for all of the world's people if population growth can be controlled. . . . Modern man can choose either a future based on ignorance and superstition, or a future based on science and rational thought. In the future, as in the past, population growth will be controlled by war, famine, and disease—unless birth rates in all parts of the world are soon reduced to moderate levels.*[18]

Educating Men

> A dollar or a rupee invested in the intellectual improvement of human beings will often bring a greater increase in national income than a dollar or a rupee devoted to railways, dams, machine tools, or other tangible capital goods.
> JOHN KENNETH GALBRAITH

In nearly every emerging nation, the people demand education for themselves and, particularly, for their children. Most often, they conceive of education solely in "materialistic" terms. For adults, literacy may provide them with ways of winning a factory job or some other solid reward. For their children, the adults view education, especially on the university level, as an entree to coveted positions in the civil service or business. Some, too, crave education simply for enlightenment and the enrichment of their lives.

Whether dictator or democrat, no politician in the developing world can long ignore the people's will on this matter. If he is to retain power, the politician must at least make gestures toward providing educational facilities.

Even if one tried to dismiss political realities—and attempted to forget the benefits which education can confer upon an intellectually benighted people—there are cold-blooded economic reasons why a developing nation must invest in education. We have touched on some of these: the success of birth control, peaceful taxation reforms, agricultural improvement, and industrialization depend critically upon education.

On a theoretical level, William J. Platt of the Stanford Research Institute has shown that investment in education plays a highly significant role in all aspects of economic growth. "Education is both investment and consumption," he has commented, ". . . one of those delightful economic commodities in which we can be investing while we consume." [19] While well-recognized by Adam Smith, this fact has too often been underrated by contemporary social scientists, who have tended to treat education as simply another consumer item like candy and Cadillacs. Theodore Schultz, in a 1961 presidential address to the American Economic Association, chided his colleagues for disregarding investment in "human capital." Surveying the growth of the American economy, Schultz maintained that capital outlays for education were actually *more* productive than investments in such hard goods as factories or railroads.[20] And Galbraith has contended that even the most esoteric types of education may pay off for an emergent economy:

> *Not even the artist, as an object of investment, may be ignored. One of the most successful industries of modern India is motion picture production. This industry flourishes only in the presence of a secure artistic tradition in the theater, music, ballet, and the visual arts. . . . No one ever invested in an artist with a view toward helping the balance of payments. Yet India's artistic tradition is serving admirably to earn foreign exchange.*[21]

Every developing nation needs more education, but the restatement of such a truism does little to reveal the problem's scope. Experience in the last decades has uncovered numerous pitfalls to progress in education. The cost is fabulous. Arthur Lewis has calculated that universal primary education in Nigeria would eat up 4 per cent of the gross national product, while in the United States only one per cent is required.[22] Many reasons account for this discrepancy, including the relatively higher pay of Nigerian teachers. A conference of African countries in 1961 found that the fulfillment of modest educational goals by 1980 (postulating a moderate rate of economic growth) would demand one billion dollars more annually than they could possibly afford.[23]

Social and political obstacles have also hindered the advance of education. In some nations, universities have copied uncritically from the West; for instance, they have taught classical French literature or traditional economics to students who later face tasks which have little to do with Montaigne or Keynes. Quite often, too, university education has inculcated an "elitist" posture among students which inhibits them from dealing with the real problems of their countries. Many do not want to soil their hands with the dirty work of economic development. In consequence, some 20 per cent of university-educated Indians are technically "unemployed." And in Nigeria, many university graduates report that they are unemployed, even though they may be doing very useful work as teachers in secondary schools. These nations need all their intellectuals—as teachers, let us say, or community-development officers. But for a man trained in the law, such work seems below his dignity. In some regions, only a civil-service post appears appropriate to the status of a college-educated man; thus, in certain nations of French-speaking Africa, 60 per cent of the national budget goes to support an artificially enlarged bureaucracy.[24] For such men, a *secondment* to Paris is ultimate paradise.

Another difficulty has been the need felt by leaders in many new nations to "equalize" education. In India, so as to establish equality of opportunity, quotas for different castes have been set in various universities and even in apprenticeship trades. While admirable in its goals, such a policy can often mean that a medical school denies admission to a well-trained Brahmin to make room for a relatively unqualified lower-caste student. The search for equality of opportunity may lead to a downward, rather than an upward, leveling. Equalization of educational opportunities has regional ramifications, too. Each subsection of a new nation may demand exactly the same educational facilities. In Nigeria, for example, an expensive university has been built in the eastern region because of political pressures, although an expert commission of educational planners did not recommend the additional expenditure.

Each developing nation, then, needs more education, but statesmen must grapple with the intricately involved issue of assigning priorities to the types of education best suited to their country. It would be delightful if—as in California, where I am now writing—*every* child could be guaranteed a free education through two years of college. Yet, developing economies cannot afford the capital to train teachers, build schoolrooms, and provide all the other educational amenities. And it would seem out of the realm of political possibilities for economically advanced regions to supply all the additional money and men which would be necessary.

Therefore, in working out a strategy of education, statesmen in emerging nations must make two basic decisions: How much of the economy's resources should go into education, as opposed to other productive enterprises? How should a government distribute the available resources among different types and levels of education?

Unfortunately, no one can furnish a single comprehensive answer to the question of how great a priority should be given to education. No IBM machine can yet produce a model which will show definitely that a school will eventually help an economy more than a textile factory. Some economists lean to the view that education should assume top priority; others tend to the opinion that too much money has already gone into education, particularly primary schools.[25] The problem has to be resolved flexibly, pragmatically, and in terms of the specific goals of each region. Economists like Frederick Harbison and educators such as Paul Hanna have set to work on this task in areas as diverse as East Africa and the Philippines.[26]

One point, however, is abundantly clear. Governments must closely co-ordinate educational planning with economic planning. In some African territories, an overemphasis on primary education has created a group of déclassé young men who can read and write but find no jobs. In contrast, one African nation constructed a complete sewing-machine factory, but the government could not locate workers with the proper technical capacities to man it.

If and when a country can decide how much to expend on education, a second issue of allocation remains. How much of the money should be put into primary, secondary, university, technical, or adult education? William Platt has stated the possible alternatives:

Newly developing nations cannot yet afford universal education. . . . They can decide to spend their education budgets according to a variety of strategies. The ranges of strategy can be visualized as manpower pyramids. . . . A given budget can be spent in either a broad, stubby pyramid or a narrow, tall one. The broad one, or the equalitarian one, might include universal primary education. . . . The same total funds might be spent for more selective training of an elite, with only literacy training being universal and large funds available for secondary and higher education.[27]

Platt does not commit himself, except to suggest that "these are worthy areas of inquiry." [28] It seems to me, one may make an abstract decision between the alternatives rather easily. Solely in terms of stimulating economic development, the most profitable course lies in training an elite, not only of managers and civil servants but also of secondary personnel such as technicians, mechanics, accountants, and typists. Economist P. N. Rosenstein-Rodan has gone so far as to argue that "the *first* task of industrialization is to provide for the training and skilling of labour." [29] In other words, as in Meiji Japan and Soviet Russia, technical and high-level education should take precedence over broad primary education. Governments should pour money into selective secondary schools, technical institutes, and universities, rather than dispersing it throughout many primary schools.

The political dangers in this policy are, unfortunately, obvious. Without a broadly educated majority, how can viable democracies survive in the newer nations? And, as Paul Hoffman has said, ". . . No popularly elected political leader of the underdeveloped world would be likely to stay in office for long if he so much as wondered aloud whether expenditures for primary education might better be diverted to selective secondary schooling." [30]

It would take bravery of the highest order for a democratic statesman to tell his people the *real* alternatives involved. Yet, without such courage, the chances of rapid economic development seem dim indeed. What we need in educational policy, then, is imagination of the best quality. Underdeveloped economies require technicians and a well-educated elite for economic progress, but the people's demands for a minimum level of education must somehow also be met. Fortunately, one can detect many signs that imaginative, unconventional ways of mass education are being developed in the newer nations, just as Denmark once evolved its unique folk-school system to enlighten its nineteenth-century peasantry.

Ghana, Cuba, and Guinea have attempted massive, rapid campaigns to spread literacy, often by a "one man teach one other" method. As yet, observers have difficulty in evaluating the success of these efforts. Some have advanced claims that such an approach can eliminate illiteracy in one quick sweep. My own limited experience in Ghana indicated that the campaign had significantly helped many people, but that in some cases the effects were short-lived. The people forgot the alphabet which they had temporarily memorized. After a burst of initial enthusiasm, these campaigns may burn out, leaving the majority of the population still unlettered.

One group in Ghana has experimented with "programed," machine-operated teaching of basic mathematical concepts.* One advantage of

---

* In passing, we might note that an educational team in Ghana (led by Professor Patrick Suppes of Stanford University) had laid to rest a myth fostered by colonialists. Ghanaian and British businessmen have often complained that

this approach lies in its conservation of scarce teachers' time. UNESCO plans projects on a much larger scale which would involve the use of teaching machines for instruction in many subjects on all levels of education. In parts of Africa, UNESCO has also tried radio as an educational device. Powered by solar cells and costing only one or two dollars, small radios can transmit educational broadcasts on a mass basis.

On a somewhat different front, a few nations have called upon unconventional human agents of education, other than formally trained teachers. In Pakistan, the Sudan, and Egypt, army men have taken a major part in all forms of education. In some countries, plans have been developed to use journeymen with no prior experience as instructors to train artisans in new attitudes and skills. Actually, experiments hint that journeymen who have been on the job a long time train apprentices *more* effectively than do regular teachers.[32] In Ecuador, the National Planning Board is contemplating the use of such techniques in an effort which would affect 225,000 persons now engaged primarily in handicraft activities.

Private foreign industries can also be useful, that is, if they are not prohibited from operating by an unreasoning nationalism. Aluminium of India, a company owned primarily in Canada, has perhaps the most comprehensive program of education furnished by any firm. The training covers all areas of the enterprise, from the original education of unskilled workers, through a technical training institute, up to a management educational program at the University of Geneva, Switzerland. In a few short years, the productivity of Indian workers in this plant has approached that of Canadians, a rather remarkable feat when one considers the difficulty of transforming a peasant into a skilled industrial worker. Olivetti of Italy, led by humane, enlightened managers, has accomplished similar successes throughout the world. Aramco, an oil company operating in Saudi Arabia, has followed a conscious policy of subcontracting to Arabians and training them for their jobs. As a result, many new indigenous industries have mushroomed. Owned by Arabians, these small companies produce concrete, electrical materials, plumbing, and ice.[33]

To be sure, the provision of this education has its cost in the profits eventually removed from the country by foreign companies, but train-

---

West Africans lack mathematical ability. The Suppes group administered a relatively culture-free test of fundamental mathematical concepts to both Ghanaian children and American children at the *start* of their education. The results showed no significant general differences between the children. Their findings underline once again that brains, if not money, are equally distributed throughout the world.[31]

ing of any sort has a price-tag. The foreign companies can supply a pool of trained personnel and experience which most countries, particularly a primitive one such as Saudi Arabia, would take years to develop.

Technical assistance from economically advanced regions and the United Nations can, of course, aid in promoting education. Indonesia has benefited from the Ford Foundation's exchange of American economists to serve on university faculties. In Liberia, professors from San Francisco State College are engaged in building an entire public-school system for Monrovia. They will assist in all phases of the process, from consultation on school building to the training of Liberian teachers, and the actual administration of the system for a period of three years. Russian engineers who aid in constructing the Aswan Dam will leave behind them not only a pile of concrete but a pool of skilled Egyptian labor. Helped by Harvard University, Nigeria has a new, "comprehensive" high school, combining vocational and academic instruction. On Formosa, the Stanford Research Institute is facilitating the third four-year plan by assisting the various ministries concerned through economic and educational planning.[34]

Potential resources exist to conquer ignorance, but it will take courage, imagination, and technical ingenuity to mobilize them. These forces must be brought together, however, for investments in transforming men may well be the most important gamble that any nation makes. Theodore Schultz's comments on the growth of the United States economy have equal relevance to other developing areas:

Truly, the most distinctive feature of our economic system is the growth in human capital. Without it there would be only hard manual work and poverty except for those who have income from property. There is an early morning scene in Faulkner's Intruder in the Dust, *of a poor, solitary cultivator at work in a field. Let me paraphrase that line, "The man without skills and knowledge leaning terrifically against nothing."* [35]

The Need for Creative Innovators

> Where are those who will come to serve the masses—not to utilize them for their own ambitions?
>
> PETER KROPOTKIN

Whether they serve in governments or factories, hospitals or universities, villages or business offices, creative leaders are sorely needed by every society. Particularly in a developing country, the economic innovator—a man willing to introduce new techniques, bear the risks of failure, and assume responsibility for change—must take the lead. Clearly, creative men are urgently needed on every strata of society, from the prime minister down to a "Mr. Khrishna," leading his village co-operative.

If one considers solely the demand for talented industrial managers, he immediately perceives the indispensability of innovators. In 1947, to pick an illustration, Dr. Joseph Stepanek went to Asia where he helped in building modern small factories in several areas. He soon found that the enterprises' success depended not only on capital, planning, and expert advice, but most importantly upon "individuals eager and able to seize the opportunity to develop." [36]

Stepanek argued that no emerging economy suffered from an oversupply of managerial innovators. He noted that even Hong Kong, overrun in 1949 by an immigration of penniless "entrepreneurs" and former managers from mainland China, soon absorbed them into an already burdened economy. Stepanek's experience has been repeated throughout the world: stagnant economies can always use innovators to lead them into an economic "take-off."

Few would disagree with this statement, but several social scientists have gone a step further. They have argued that the innovator is the crucial element in economic growth and that only a unique social and psychological climate can produce or tolerate him. Such a view, if true, would have great significance, for by implication it condemns many contemporary economies to the prospect of perpetual inertia. In recent years, the position has been advocated most prominently by Joseph Schumpeter, J. H. Boeke, David McClelland, and Everett Hagan.

Joseph Schumpeter, in his review of the history of economic development, presented a classic defense of entrepreneurial talent as the key factor in economic growth.[37] At least in the evolution of capitalism, Schumpeter believed that the introduction of innovations (changes in methods of production or supply) contributed the essential ingredient in stimulating an economy. The entrepreneur, willing to utilize new techniques, stood at the center of the process. Schumpeter held a dim view of capitalism's future, although personally he favored it as an economic system. He thought that a variety of trends—the introduction of organization "teams," changes in the Western intellectual and political climate, governmental interference with business—would eventually eliminate the entrepreneur. Without entrepreneurs, an economy reposes in a state of equilibrium. Although he did not deal specifically with contemporary underdeveloped regions, Schumpeter's general ideas would lead naturally to the view that "antientrepreneurial" policies—high taxation, labor legislation, any measure which would decrease private accumulation of capital—slow down economic growth in an emerging country.

Dutch economist J. H. Boeke had direct experience in underdeveloped areas, which led him also to place special stress upon entrepreneurial drive. Boeke believed that sociological factors prohibited major economic advances in South and Southeast Asia. In contrast to Western societies, he contended, in Eastern economies, people had limited needs and would not work hard to better their position. He believed, too, that men in places such as Indonesia valued commodities for their social value, rather than their economic importance—a cow had significance as a symbol, not as meat, butter, or milk. Further, he supposed that Oriental peoples would not accumulate capital and that they had an aversion to taking risks. All this forced him, with great reluctance, to conclude that significant innovations would not take place spontaneously in Eastern economies.[38]

More recently, psychologist David McClelland has constructed a social and psychological theory of economic growth which bears some resemblance to that of Boeke and Schumpeter. In *The Achieving Society*, McClelland proffers a fund of evidence to indicate that a strong, deeply rooted need for achievement motivates entrepreneurial men.[39] This drive (empirically measured in a number of ingenious ways) seems less prevalent among men in underdeveloped countries, who appear to be motivated more by desires for affiliation or power. Since the need for achievement is created early in life by parents who stress mastery and self-reliance, McClelland thinks that social and economic plans should be directed to creating (or conserving) achievement motivation. He agrees with Schumpeter that economic development requires numerous, vigorous entrepreneurs, but he believes that they are motivated by much more profound drives than a simple desire for profit. McClelland hopes that emerging societies may be able to create men with a built-in drive for achievement; he does not share Boeke's pessimism.

Everett Hagan, an economist by training, has arrived at a theory which also heavily emphasizes social and psychological elements—indeed, to the point of excluding all the traditional economic elements normally considered by economists. Hagan served for two discouraging years as economic adviser to the Union of Burma. Burma's officials avowed a desire for economic development but failed to use the resources available to them in an effective manner. After his return to the United States in 1953, Hagan began to re-evaluate his Burmese experience. He asked:

Why have the people of some societies entered upon technological progress sooner or more effectively than others? Since it seemed clear to me that the differences were due only in very minor degree to economic obstacles, lack of information, or lack of training, I turned my attention to other possible causes of differences in human behavior— to differences in personality, and hence personality formation and the social conditions affecting it.[40]

His investigations eventuated in a general theory of economic and social change. Calling upon psychological evidence, as well as the histories of England, Japan, Colombia, and Indonesia, Hagan concluded that the transition from a stagnant to a dynamic economy occurs in four stages: In the beginning, a static elite oriented to traditional values rules a complacent peasantry; for some reason (perhaps, a colonial intrusion), people in the society undergo a "withdrawal of status"; a period of "retreatism" ensues for several generations while men search for a new set of values; eventually, a class of innovators appears that feels alienated from the old order and strives to establish a new economic system.

For Hagan, the questions of economic growth can be reduced to a conflict between two personality types: the "authoritarian," prevalent in peasant societies, and the creative reformer, found in economically progressive economies. Change originates in the outsider, the person who does not believe in the transitional order or who cannot achieve status by following the usual paths to power. Hagan's work has two undeniable virtues. He shows that men alienated from the old society (*Antiqueños* in Colombia, Quakers in England, certain clans in Tokugawa Japan) have had important roles as innovators. He also demonstrates that economic progress can occur in the absence of supposed material prerequisites (such as minerals and capital), *if* these dissenters wish to turn their energies to economic activity.

The attitude of Hagan, as well as of the other social scientists who adhere to what might roughly be called the entrepreneurial school, leads to certain implications as to policy. It could produce deep pessimism, for scholars of this persuasion seldom demonstrate exactly *how* the motivations of man can be changed. By stressing the individual character of the entrepreneur, they implicitly announce that changes in the broad socio-economic system have to await alterations in man's deepest motives. Indeed, Boeke gave up all hope for striking economic advance in Eastern states, and Hagan believes that at least several generations will be required in most former colonial areas before innovators emerge. If individual motivation were the crux of development—and if it were further true that early family experiences determined the level of achievement drive—this would be sad news. It means that somehow governments have to manipulate radically the family structure, child-rearing practices, and kinship customs of their entire nation —a task which even a regiment of psychiatrists would hesitate to undertake.

Hagan and McClelland do make cautious, specific recommendations about policies that might accelerate economic growth. Hagan believes that an increasing understanding of technology, or tensions among an existing elite, or the intrusion of outside forces which change existing social relationships *might* start a chain reaction in peasant societies. Nevertheless, he holds out very little hope that these forces would really alter the basic values and motivations of peasant society.

McClelland appears more optimistic concerning the possibility that some agency could alter fundamental motives. He thinks that ideological campaigns or religious movements may induce the necessary fervor for achievement. In addition, he advocates the spread of education and the emancipation of women. And he argues for the introduction of heavy machinery and training programs by foreign industries as ways to promote modern, entrepreneurial attitudes.

Are these propositions adequate, comprehensive descriptions of economic advance? In reviewing the economic history of Europe, for example, we must admit that, by and large, those states which did make the greatest progress were dominated by the innovative, entrepreneurial spirit of early Protestantism. Yet we should also recognize that some of the most Protestant areas of Europe were economic backwaters, while some of the Catholic sections (the Catholic part of the Netherlands, northern Italy, and the Rhineland) made impressive progress. It would appear, therefore, that to the degree a nation had entered the market system, a new kind of "commercial ethic," stressing individual responsibility, appeared. These commercial values were highly compatible with Protestantism but did not, apparently, require a specific religious framework for their emergence. Further, it would appear that the innovative potential, so long assumed to be a part of the Protestant ethic, failed—in the advance of a market system—to stimulate economic growth.

It remains unclear whether economic growth in itself may *call forth* latent entrepreneurial qualities from the population. One finds great difficulty, for example, in explaining the differential growth of northern and southern France or northern and southern Italy on the basis that more entrepreneurs originally resided in the northern sections. Availability of transportation, markets, capital, and natural resources seem to have assumed greater importance than the number of entrepreneurs in each area. While it may seem a curious stance for a sociologist, I must defend the place of traditional economic factors as necessary ingredients in any theory of economic growth.

Even Everett Hagan's own figures concerning the role of English dissenters in the evolution of British industry give rise to some doubts about his thesis. In one calculation, he shows that more English businessmen came from the ranks of religious nonconformists than one would expect, given their proportion in the eighteenth-century English population. But one should equally emphasize that the *majority* of entrepreneurs emerged from the traditional elite of Anglicans. His tables also show that the innovators were most often raised in families of high or moderate income, only a handful coming from poor families. In absolute numbers, therefore, the old ruling class led the "outsiders" in promoting industrialization.

On the contemporary scene, Arthur Lewis has commented:

Certainly the underdeveloped countries have no shortage of the commercial instincts (despite all that we hear about religious and cultural barriers to economic growth), and their peoples demonstrate as great a fondness for trading and for taking risks as one can find anywhere. There is a marked surge of entrepreneurship in road transport, in entertainment, and in building. Why then is there a shortage of entrepreneurship in manufacturing industry? [41]

He proposes several answers: Potential entrepreneurs lack markets for manufactured goods because of agricultural stagnation; peasants do not have money to buy the goods. Also, entrepreneurs do not have skilled technical manpower to aid them; many have not administered large-scale organizations; and they lack capital for financing big industries. They suffer, too, from various restrictive practices and prejudices handed down from colonial times: "All former British territories have inherited the social prejudices of Queen Victoria . . . social snobbery towards fortunes made in trade . . . serves to discourage entrepreneurial activity and to persuade the bright young man to devote his energies to other fields." [42]

Lewis is convinced that a great pool of entrepreneurs exists but that primarily *economic* rather than social and psychological factors prevent them from utilizing their talents in industrial activity. My own experience, particularly in Africa and Indonesia, confirms Lewis's observations. Small traders, independent little businessmen, market women, abound in minor commercial transactions. The bustling open markets in Djakarta, Delhi, or Accra overflow with potential entrepreneurs who are as shrewd and calculating as America's legendary "robber barons." But they must confine themselves to selling imported pots and pans rather than manufacturing them because of their nations' economic structures.

Consequently, in weighing theories of economic growth, we must inquire whether many transitional men may have already undergone the psychological changes which the entrepreneurial school regards as essential. Commenting upon McClelland's thesis, economist Benjamin Higgins noted that the proposed policy recommendations would take generations to implement. He inquired:

> *Will underdeveloped countries wait that long? And is not the very fact that many of them will not wait that long sufficient evidence that the change in motivation has already taken place, at least among the elites? Could we not conclude from Hagan's theory that any country which has gone far enough to produce an economic development plan that has become a matter of public discussion has already met the psycho-sociological prerequisites of growth?* [43]

In my judgment, the weight of evidence lies on the side of Higgins and Lewis. Latent entrepreneurial talent exists in almost every region; proper economic planning can bring it into action.

The moral as well as the economic consequences of the policies embraced by some who follow the entrepreneurial school must be carefully appraised. McClelland's evidence, as an illustration, suggests that boys raised away from their fathers have a greater need for achievement than boys reared with a father present at home. McClelland does not say that underdeveloped nations should try to remove fathers from their sons and, in fact, he comments: "The men would have to undertake to become less authoritarian (or be forced into it by feminism), or else start a few wars or promote the merchant marine. Unfortunately, none of these alternatives seems very practicable." [44]

And yet, if one takes McClelland's general view really seriously, practical policies *do* exist whereby fathers could be absented from their homes. In Africa today, thousands of men leave their families for prolonged periods to work in cities or in mines. If it so wished, a government might dispense its resources in such a fashion that men would be economically forced to leave their homes. But should a government pursue such a policy? Aside from ethical considerations, there would seem to be strong economic reasons why most planners avoid an economic program now actually followed in South Africa and Angola. Drawing men from their villages into copper mines not only destroys families, but it increases the burdens of urbanization and decreases the chances of rural development.

I would argue that the social and psychological evidence—although often empirically sophisticated and elegant—does not as yet justify planned efforts to alter complete social structures and cultures. Knowing so little of the interaction between motivation and economic growth, governments should be highly cautious of setting out deliberately to erode an entire tradition. Whatever social measures are undertaken should be limited to specific areas (such as education in birth control or malaria eradication) where the relevance to economic advance has been solidly demonstrated. Every nation needs entrepreneurs, and these innovators undoubtedly need help in the form of training and capital and implements. Yet this does not imply as Hagan and McClelland seem to suggest and Robert Heilbroner directly says, that the old culture must be forcibly wrenched from its moorings.

Implications

> Our . . . Negritude is humanistic . . . it welcomes the complementary values of Europe and the white man, and indeed, of all other races and continents. But it welcomes them in order to fertilize and reinvigorate its own values, which it then offers for the construction of a civilization which shall embrace all mankind.
> LÉOPOLD SENGHOR, commenting on the concept of the "African Personality"

The thesis can be stated succinctly: men and institutions in developing nations must change, but in the process of transforming man, no government has a duty to dismember an entire tradition. If an economy is to blossom, some agency (usually the government) has to initiate changes in transitional man's customs and attitudes. Sometimes, this may mean creating new institutions, such as farming co-operatives; at other times, it may involve undermining the influence of groups which oppose economic progress, as Nkrumah took away the power—although not the symbols—of Ashanti chiefs. Almost universally in the emerging world, three specific obligations have to be met by those who desire economic advance:

(1) Mass birth-control programs should be undertaken. Experiments indicate not only that technologists can invent very inexpensive contraceptives but that most of mankind, if given a chance, wants to prevent the birth of children whose only prospect is an early death.

(2) Developing regions must concentrate a good proportion of their resources upon education. Ideally, educational strategy should focus upon structuring an elite and a secondary corps technically equipped to fight their country's economic battles. Simultaneously, educators have to call upon imaginative, unconventional ways for furnishing literacy and enlightment to all, since no emerging country can yet afford universal formal education. Governments have to co-ordinate closely their educational tactics with general economic planning, if a society's balanced progress is to be achieved.

(3) Transitional societies must seek out, train, and tangibly aid their potential innovators. Creative entrepreneurs proliferate, but their energies need diversion into more economically productive activities.

Contemporary sociologists will not greet these propositions with wild enthusiasm, for many "functionalists" believe that *any* change in a social order necessarily entails other alterations in a country's social and economic fabric. They picture society as an intricate interweaving of many elements; if change takes place in one sector (say, the economic), it inevitably leads to shifts in values, family organization, and social status. Sociologist Wilbert Moore, for example, has maintained that economic development demands changes in concepts of property, the break-up of an extended family tradition, the growth of a "rationalized" bureaucracy, and an over-all increase in social mobility.[45] Many social scientists regard the piecemeal reforms which I have advocated as both insufficient and impossible to implement without much more fundamental social changes.

In one respect, these sociologists are right. Obviously, economic development does give birth to social changes. Innumerable studies have demonstrated this fact.[46] Taking only two illustrations out of many, one can cite Oscar Lewis's investigations of Mexico and Alex Inkeles's analysis of Russians.

Lewis revisited the village of Tepoztlán, Mexico, in 1943, some seventeen years after another anthropologist, Robert Redfield, had originally studied it. Lewis returned again in 1956 to see what changes Mexico's economic progress had brought to the village. Although much remained the same, Lewis did find distinctive alterations in the people's style of life. He noticed a greater willingness to use modern medicine, more readiness to sell land, greater interest in education, and more travel to the city. Child rearing had moved in the direction of greater permissiveness, and arranged marriages had disappeared. The young people were more restless and had more ambition, not only for material success but also for education. Many factors—the entrance of a doctor, teachers, radio, the *bracero* immigration to the United States—had injected new elements into Tepoztlán culture, particularly an increase in individualism.[47]

In an entirely different area, sociologist Alex Inkeles has interviewed Russian emigrés concerning what effect the Soviet Revolution had on their attitudes. He compared two groups, one raised during the Tsarist period, and another which had experienced the Revolution, with all its economic and political impact. Specifically, he examined the people's attitudes about child-rearing and their occupational goals. Inkeles concluded that the postrevolutionary sample showed greatly decreased concern about inculcating traditional values in their children and increased emphasis upon secular norms. His findings led him to the opinion that:

> . . . *the middle generation, responding to its experience . . . under the Soviet regime . . . turned away from the pattern of child rearing under which it had been raised earlier and in its approach to the new Soviet generation stressed goals and values of a different sort. It appears, furthermore, that this training of the youth in new value orientations was relatively successful.*[48]

Undeniably, economic alterations change values, habits, and customs. Yet the obverse does not necessarily hold true. Social and cultural factors may or may not affect an economy adversely. Bert F. Hoselitz has usefully clarified this question by drawing a distinction between a social "tradition" and a "traditionalistic" ideology. Hoselitz points out that a traditionalistic ideology, whose adherents dream of maintaining forever an unchanged culture, can have catastrophic effects upon economic growth. He notes Greece's military adventures in the 1860's, the 1880's, the 1890's, the 1910's, and the 1920's as a case in point. In a futile scramble to restore the Byzantine Empire, Greece poured all of its energy and money into useless wars. Because of an ideology which extolled Greece's past greatness, the country lost its opportunity to make any economic progress.

Yet, Hoselitz effectively demolishes the view that whoever seeks economic development must necessarily get rid of tradition. We have already noted that Meiji Japan moved forward vigorously while *reinforcing* some of its traditional culture. In contemporary terms, Hoselitz presents many instances where preservation of an original culture may actually *promote* economic growth. In India, for example, the presence of an extended kinship system allows an ambitious artisan to borrow from his family in a situation where no other funds are available.[49]

With careful planning, therefore, it seems that underdeveloped regions can achieve economic growth without uprooting their whole tradition; a melding of the new and the old can take place. But, clearly, economic plans have to be based upon intensive social research into the specific culture of particular areas. Without knowledge of a region's tradition, the best-intentioned schemes will run into trouble—as the British attempts to eliminate sleeping sickness in Anchau demonstrate.

In the transformation of men, the alternative which should be followed is what Max Millikan and Donald Blackmer have called "the third choice." They have noted that in most developing societies the battle lines are drawn between "traditionalists" who desire to preserve the old culture at any cost and the "modernizers" who seek ". . . the radical destruction by extremist measures . . . of the whole political, social, and economic fabric of traditional society." [50] Millikan and Blackmer go on to say:

> But these two choices, fortunately, are not the only ones men perceive. There are almost always some traditionalists and some modernizers who, with varying degrees of clarity and hope, perceive a third choice—the gradual modification of the institutions, practices, and structure of the traditional society in the direction of modernization while retaining some of its traditional cohesive features.[51]

If wisdom prevails, the leaders of emerging societies will choose this third path, one fraught with difficulties but the only one which offers any promise of peaceful, voluntary evolution.

VIII

THE ROLE OF ADVANCED REGIONS

> Immediate reality [for the Westerner] is the new car, the new 'telly,' the cosy suburban house. How can one look through the picture window with vision enough to see the starving men, bundled in rags, lying on Calcutta's pavements? Just so did the nobles of France ignore the peasants starving at their castle gates.
>
> BARBARA WARD

We have sketched an anatomy of possible economic development, with muscles of decentralized, light industries; vigorous, productive villages; and an educated citizenry. But again and again, it has been necessary to say that the blood stream of development is money.

If it lacks capital, no economy can grow. And without doubt, most contemporary nations do not possess the domestic sources of revenue to finance extensive development. They most certainly do not have the money to advance simultaneously along all fronts—invigorating agriculture *and* building new industries, creating dams *and* schools, launching birth-control programs *and* extending transportation. Yet, it must be clear by now that only by such complementary, balanced efforts can underdeveloped nations lift themselves from the economic quagmire.

Admittedly, greater austerity in some emerging countries will help. In Peru, to take just one glaring example, 100 families own 90 per cent of the wealth, $1,334,000,000. Thirty families control 80 per cent of this sum. The rest of the population subsists, barely, either by farming or other work which brings in an average of $53 a year.[1] If some of the money of these 100 oligarchs could be siphoned into productive activities, an inroad could be made into Peru's problems—perhaps its illiteracy rate of 65 per cent could be reduced, and maybe that half of the population which has never seen a doctor might receive some medical care.

Nevertheless, even the severest domestic program will not always extract the necessary funds. In most developing areas, particularly India, the magnitude of the task exceeds the economy's capacity. Only external aid from those nations which have already crossed the border between murderous destitution and economic affluence will sufficiently quicken the pace of capital accumulation. Advanced regions—the West, the Soviet Union, and Japan—must come to the financial rescue of developing countries. They not only have a moral duty to help, but, in an age of a "great equalizer," the Bomb, simple self-interest commands that they must.

The need for external aid may appear awesome when stated in round figures—and indeed it is, for underdeveloped areas—yet it constitutes merely a tiny portion of the incomes of advanced countries. Naturally, one encounters difficulty in arriving at exact estimates of the amount of foreign assistance required. The fact that definitions of "aid" fluctuate compounds the difficulty. Currently, the United States counts as part of her assistance program such items as 8 per cent commercial loans and the massive sums devoted to supporting the military. As we shall see, this "aid" hardly constitutes tangible help to an underdeveloped nation and can often be considered a burden.[2]

Experts have managed to arrive at some rough figures which reveal the urgency of the need for external assistance. India by itself will have to receive an extra $7.5 billion from abroad in order to fulfill the objectives of its third five-year plan.[3] And the plan is by no means immodestly conceived—by 1966, for example, India hopes to furnish electricity for all towns containing more than 5,000 people, *but* this will cover only 29,458 of India's half-million villages.[4]

If one considers the plight of just a few more nations, the sum grossly expands. Paul Hoffman has estimated that additional capital of $3 billion *each year* will be necessary to achieve the United Nations' goal of doubling per capita income in a handful of emerging countries during this decade.[5] Using the same base, Andrew Shonfield, economic editor of *The Observer*, has said that this would be inadequate and that some $4 billion annually has to be forthcoming.[6] It must be remembered that these figures apply to only ten or fifteen countries which seem lurching on the brink of economic progress.

If a truly global program of economic aid were to be achieved, at least $15.5 billion more would have to be spent between 1961 and

1976. In a very conservative approximation—one which *excludes* from the computation all expenditures for food imports, health, education, armies, and social development—Professor P. N. Rosenstein-Rodan has made the following judgment concerning the required inflow of "hard" foreign capital between 1961 and 1976:[7]

PROJECTED NEED FOR INTERNATIONAL AID TO UNDERDEVELOPED
COUNTRIES, 1961-1976
(*in millions of dollars*)

	1961-66	1966-71	1971-76
Africa	430	605	740
Latin America	1,550	1,495	1,010
Asia	2,520	2,910	2,270
Middle East	640	750	400
Totals:	5,140	5,760	4,420

During the last decades, the advanced regions have fallen far short of providing even these minimum amounts of foreign aid. The United States, the largest single donor country, has expended about $22 billion in assisting developing countries between 1945 and 1960.[8] This might appear an impressive total, but it hides certain distressing features of America's aid program. Thirty-four per cent went to subsidize armies whose function has too often been the staging of coups d'etat. Another 10 per cent went for "defense support." Of the remainder, a substantial proportion has to be repaid with interest by underdeveloped nations. And one should remember that during this same period, America spent $500 billion on defense and amassed $5,653 billion in its national product.[9] Russia's record has been even less glowing. Not only has she given a great deal less, but much of Russia's aid has come in the form of loans at very high interest rates.

Adding together all sources of aid from rich nations to poor nations, one finds that foreign capital entered underdeveloped regions at a rate of $3.25 billion annually in 1950-55, $6.8 billion between 1956 and 1959, and a high of $8 billion in 1960.[10] The increasing pace of investment should be welcomed, yet it still does not supply the *extra* three or four billion dollars each year which these economies need.

Further, the inflow of capital has run in a remarkably uneven stream. In 1958, South Korea, South Indo-China, and Formosa received $700 million in American assistance. This represented about one-third of all American foreign aid, even though these countries had only 50 million

people.[11] Similarly, American private capital has been drawn dispropor-
tionately to the oil of Venezuela, Arabia, Iraq, and Iran, while British
capital went in huge lumps to Kuwait and Rhodesia because of their
oil and copper. The combined population of these nations amounts to
40 million people. Clearly, political considerations and a desire for
quick profits have often taken precedence over the general welfare of
all developing peoples in governing American and British policy.

If only they had the vision, the rich could do far more to initiate
economic growth. The total capital donations of the affluent countries
add up to only 0.4 per cent of their combined national incomes, and
much of this pittance returns to industrialized areas in the form of
profits and purchases.[12] Humane, enlightened governments in advanced countries could easily triple their aid without the slightest suffering to their own peoples.[13] In fact, contrary to America's self-con-
gratulating stereotype of itself as the most generous people on earth,
France already devotes more than one per cent of its national income
to underdeveloped nations. (Between 1905 and 1913, England exported capital to the tune of 7 per cent annually.)

And, as Gunnar Myrdal has ably explained, the gap between rich and
poor continues to widen rather than narrow. In the 1950's, America,
West Europe, Japan, and Russia savored increasing prosperity. In the
underdeveloped nations during the same decade, each individual received a raise of approximately one dollar a year—not exactly a record of
progress. Advanced countries must assume much of the blame, for
they had the capacity to triple or quadruple this snail's pace.

What can the rich nations do to meet their obligations more effectively? Three complementary ways exist: Industrialized countries
can step up the pace of private foreign investment. The rich regions
can help the poor by stabilizing world trade, and reducing the dependence of emerging areas upon a single export product. Most importantly, they can increase the amount of direct foreign aid.

The Role of Foreign Enterprise

> What results from an expert mission is usually a report. When
> private enterprise operates, the oil flows out of the pipeline.
> J. B. CONDLIFFE

Although vituperously condemned by some politicians in the new
countries, private foreign investment can buttress an economy's de-

velopment. It has been a misfortune that cannonades against foreign companies have been fired indiscriminately by both the left and the right in underdeveloped lands.

Leftist opposition to foreign firms has drawn heavily upon Lenin's theory of colonialism. Radical nationalists have indicted foreign capitalism as just another tool by which "imperialist" states maintain their economic domination over former colonial areas. In this view, the sole function of nonnational companies has been to plunder minerals and other resources from underdeveloped countries, replacing political with economic slavery. The position has been enunciated in typical fashion by U Nu, former Premier of Burma:

The capitalists . . . want profits. . . . Because of this profit motive, there is exploitation. . . . Human greed led the capitalists, who were making profits, to want to make ever larger and better profits. This, in turn, stimulated a search for territories from which raw materials could be obtained cheaply and plentifully. . . . This search for territories, for raw materials and controlled markets, led to imperialistic expansion, and to wars between imperialist powers.[14]

History offers substantial support to such a portrayal of foreign capitalism. Many Western companies have, in fact, merely exploited underdeveloped economies without contributing in the slightest to the peoples' welfare. Oil profits from the Middle East have gone into the bulging coffers of Western companies and Arab princes, seldom trickling down to the masses. In typical mining industries throughout the developing world, less than a third of income returns to domestic workers as wages. Venezuela's oil could bring its six million people some $4 billion of income; actually, they receive only one-fourth of this.[15] The lion's share goes to foreign interests. U.S. Steel in Venezuela pays only one *bolivar* per ton, although iron ore sells for about $7 at embarkation.[16] In Central America, if domestic agencies owned banana production, six countries would receive $708 million annually in profits. Instead, they get around $192 million yearly. Much of the rest stays in the hands of the United Fruit Company, a North American corporation.[17] Whatever his political persuasion, no one in the developing nations can say that foreign capitalists' hands are lily-white.

Right-wing nationalists often join with socialists in their bitterness over foreign enterprise, but not on quite the same grounds. Rightist military men, for example, resent the political power exercised by such octopus corporations as Shell, United Fruit, or Unilever. The mere size of these giants dwarfs the prestige and power of nationalist leaders. In consequence, orators call for expropriation of foreign capital—and with some reason, too, for there can be little doubt that international companies own certain nations lock, stock, and barrel. United Fruit's political influence in Central America and the actions of the Union Minière du Haut-Katanga in the Congo testify to this fact, as did Cuba's history before Castro's revolution. In Cuba, absentee owners controlled sugar production, 90 per cent of telephone and electric services, and 50 per cent of public railways.[18] Naturally, Cubans disliked their treatment as little vassals of a North American colossus, regardless of their personal attitudes toward capitalism itself.

While nationalist opposition to foreign capital has much to vindicate it, passion sometimes stifles reason. As many leaders from Nasser to Nkrumah have gradually come to recognize, the proper kind of foreign private investment can energize a lagging economy. An infusion of foreign enterprise into an underdeveloped region has many advantages. Most obviously, it can relieve the inevitable burden of capital accumulation which in past history has fallen brutally upon the poor. As economist Robert Alexander has commented:

In effect, when the citizens of a highly industrialized country establish a factory . . . in an underdeveloped nation, the unindustrialized country is receiving a "loan" of that factory. It does not have to put aside immediately sufficient income to pay for it. It receives it without any reduction of current expenditure, and pays back the cost of the equipment out of future income.[19]

Further, foreign companies automatically furnish a cadre of entrepreneurs, skilled managers, engineers, and technicians which a developing economy badly needs. Through educational programs and imitation, modern attitudes and techniques can be transferred to domestic workers and managers. Establishment of a foreign company normally brings with it the most advanced techniques and machinery available on the world market. Thus, developing nations can avail themselves of patents and innovations which otherwise would be closed to them. And the very fact that a self-correcting profit motive determines a foreign firm's operations may well work to the advantage of an emerging nation. Private capital (foreign or domestic) *has* to pay off. The same compulsion does not inhibit public enterprises. Rightly directed, private capital can move into the most productive channels, while public expenditures may be wasted in scattered, "pork-barrel" projects.

The potential utility of foreign capital can be seen in the current operations of the United Africa Company. This firm has long functioned in Africa on a very big scale. Largely due to a rather unpleasant past record, it has often been indicted by nationalists. Yet the company has actually played a most beneficent role in recent years. Since 1929, it has reinvested in Africa $180.6 million of its profits. The company has also furnished supplies, advice, and financial support to thousands of African entrepreneurs. In West Africa alone, each year it lends $5.6 million to over 6,000 Africans, who, in turn, sell about $70 million worth of goods. Africans handle most of the firm's trade in cocoa, palm oil, peanuts, and rubber. United Africa has stimulated home industries by giving both capital and managerial advice. In Nigeria, as an illustration, United Africa has built a singlet factory which Nigerians own and manage. The plant uses fabric supplied by its foster company and has a guaranteed market in United Africa's merchandising outlets.[20] It should be recorded in passing that, contrary to the usual belief, "metropolitan" nations have invested much more money in Africa than they have taken out.[21]

Responsible statesmen should welcome rather than condemn the assistance of companies like United Africa. Such enterprises can furnish capital and skills unavailable from other sources. Unhappily, many nationalists have allowed ideology to blind them to these economic facts. "The difficulty with the nationalist ideology," political scientist Paul Sigmund has correctly said, "is that it does not distinguish between the new-style, economically productive business innovators and the old-style, non-productive absentee landlords and moneylenders. There is still a lingering suspicion of the businessman's role as essentially exploitative. . . ."[22]

Slowly, reality seems to be dissipating this suspicion, as well as its counterpart of distrust in the minds of Western businessmen. In recent years, T.W.A. has helped Ethiopia to build a fine airline; Kaiser Aluminum has been assisting Ghana in constructing the Volta Dam; Armco Steel has launched factories in India; Abbott Laboratories has built plants in Pakistan, as has Singer Sewing Machines in Indonesia. Manufacturing investment has crept up in the last five years, and sales by American-built factories producing in underdeveloped lands have increased from $4.1 billion in 1957 to an estimated $6.3 billion in 1962.[23]

There is no sound reason for totally prohibiting these foreign factories from competing peacefully with nationally owned industries, public or private. In India at the moment such competition already exists in steel production. (Up to this point the "native capitalist," Tata Industries, appears to be beating its opponents.) Public, private, and foreign enterprises often complement and stimulate each other.

The erection of a foreign plant, for instance, can have manifold effects in emboldening, instructing, and materially aiding local groups. And, of course, the opposite holds true, as Andrew Shonfield has observed concerning the relation of public and private sectors of India's economy:

> *For all the grumbling among Indian businessmen that the public authorities are trying to capture too large a slice of an exceptionally rich cake, the fact is—and some of them even realize it—that the cake would not be nearly so rich without the contribution of public enterprise towards the making of it. It is after all a commonplace of experience in the developed countries that when a state corporation commits itself to a long-term programme of expansion, e.g. on the railways or on electric power, this has a revolutionary effect on the profit expectations and the investment of capital in the privately owned concerns supplying the state industries. And that in turn helps to stimulate more private investment elsewhere. A clear and generous policy towards the underdeveloped world . . . would itself reduce the demands that have to be made on the public purse for carrying it out.*[24]

All the indications suggest, therefore, that emerging nations should seek out private foreign capital and that wise businessmen in advanced countries ought to welcome the opportunity of new markets, resources, and challenges. But two qualifications have to be appended to this position.

First, developing countries must not tolerate the exploitation which has scarred the past—and which the corrupt venality of certain states helped to make possible. Responsible governments have a right to expect that foreign companies will adhere to the law, stop meddling in local politics, use domestic resources, and add to, rather than subtract from, the economy's strength. Governments also have a clear duty to demand that a substantial portion of the profits should be reinvested in the developing economy and that local personnel should join the firm, either as owners, managers, or workers.

Mexico, Brazil, Ghana, and Nigeria appear to be working out sensible policies along these lines. For example, Brazil's request that a foreign automobile industry must, within a reasonably specified period of time, create all its own supplying industries could act as a model for using foreign capital to induce further growth. Similary, a recent agreement reached between an Italian oil company and some Middle Eastern countries (whereby they retain 75 per cent of oil profits) serves as a good illustration of the ways that countries can control the supposed influence of "monopoly capitalism."

Foreign investors, in turn, must have the assurance that their efforts will not be in vain. Reasonably, they should be able to expect that reimbursement would follow any policy of nationalization. Without such a guarantee, only a fool would put his money into new enterprises in a developing economy. A very useful, although perhaps politically unfeasible, device would be the establishment of banking institutions (either through the United Nations or on a national level by each industrialized nation) which would guarantee investors a return of their capital in the event of an unexpected nationalization.

Also, most economists predict that no *great* upsurge in foreign investment will take place in the near future.[25] Among many other reasons, they point to the relative attractiveness of investment opportunities "at home" as opposed to the riskiness of ventures in emerging nations. Although this opinion may prove overly pessimistic, we must anticipate that foreign capital will not play the same role which it traditionally has (as, for example, British capital did in stimulating American and Argentinian growth).

Additional avenues of external assistance need to be explored.

Balancing World Trade

> Sooner or later we will have to comprehend the fact that trade *is* aid, and that every limitation on the ability of the underdeveloped world to sell its products to the industrialized nations ultimately retards by just so much their eventual well-being.
>
> ROBERT HEILBRONER

The advanced nations can also help by taking effective measures to protect the marketing of exports from developing countries.

Too often, the public fails to realize the great significance of world trade to a growing economy. Whether they like it or not, the world market has locked advanced and underdeveloped economies in an embrace which cannot be severed. "No nation or area," one economist has candidly said, "is or can be self-sufficient, and least of all the developing nations." [26] At the moment, the principal flow of trade allows advanced regions to sell capital equipment and consumer goods to developing regions. In exchange, they export raw commodities—minerals, food, and oil—to industrialized countries. This pattern gives the underdeveloped lands some of the equipment which they desire—electricity generators, locomotives, machine pumps—and it gives advanced regions basic commodities without which they might not survive.[27]

Of all forms of aid, profits from exports have assumed greatest importance in developing nations. As Peter Kenon has shown, most poor countries underwrite their imports for development from their export incomes. In India during 1957, just $13 out of every $100 which India spent on development came from grants or loans from foreign nations. About $70 derived from Indian exports, and the remainder was drawn from accumulated reserves.[28] This interweaving of industrial and nonindustrial economies grows tighter as the years pass. Between 1953 and 1960, trade between the rich and poor nations went up 24 per cent (and trade among underdeveloped countries increased 20 per cent.) [29] Unfortunately, the world market has not always worked to the benefit of emerging economies.

Part of the problem stems from World War I, which markedly changed the pattern of trade. Until 1914, Great Britain, at that time the greatest lender nation, invested heavily in regions then developing. But in World War I and even more in World War II, Europe partially fought its battles by liquidating investments abroad, stopping the outflow of gold, and borrowing from its colonies. Ironically, ". . . the poor countries helped to finance the conflicts of the rich among themselves. . . ." [30]

The resulting complex of trade has often had a bad impact upon emerging countries. One difficulty has been that the demand for primary commodities has fallen slightly, while the developing regions' need for industrial goods has remained steady or has increased. Thus, in Latin America between 1955 and 1961, the price index of imports did not change, but the profits from exports fell 16 per cent.[31] The market's operation has forced many developing regions to buy dearly but sell cheaply. Indeed, Mario Rossi has estimated that throughout the underdeveloped world, the last decade has placed emerging nations in a position where the same amount of their exports buys one-fourth less industrial goods.[32]

Another related problem has been the fantastic movements in prices for raw commodities. The price of copper shot up 42 per cent in 1955, then fell 34 per cent in 1957 and another 34 per cent in 1958—sending Chile into chaos. Wool prices collapsed by 50 per cent between 1952 and 1958, and cocoa fell by the same amount in just one year, 1956. In 1957, because of a recession in the United States, commodity imports dropped disastrously. "The result," Robert Heilbroner has noted, "was that the poorer nations received some two billion dollars less in actual purchasing power, *which was more than all the 'aid' they received that year."* [33]

If advanced regions seriously care about the destiny of underdeveloped lands, they obviously must co-operate with them in balancing the teeter-totter of world trade. Some modest instruments already operate to stabilize commerce. The International Monetary Fund lends money to developing nations which find themselves in a temporary squeeze for foreign exchange. The "Aid India Club" (made up of some industrialized countries) has furnished funds to stabilize India's exports. International bargains between the West and developing countries have helped to steady the price of such commodities as cocoa, tin, and rubber. While useful, these first tentative efforts have not yet conquered the problem. Brazil's economic fate, for instance, still hangs precariously on whether coffee prices go up or down by a penny in the New York Commodity Exchange.

Bolder, more co-ordinated endeavors—involving the Soviet Union and Japan, as well as the West—are needed. Imaginative but realistic proposals abound, if the advanced regions only have the will to implement them.

Stockpiles of commodities could be put under the control of an international agency. When prices fall, the authority could purchase commodities as a buffer; when prices rise above a prescribed level, the agency could sell its stocks on the open market. A similar idea has been put forward by Yale economist Henry Wallich. He suggests that rich nations ought to make direct loans to poor nations at times of declining commodity prices. The raw materials themselves would secure the loans and would be withdrawn from the market during a crisis, thus strengthening the price level.[34]

The funds available to the IMF should be greatly increased, so that underdeveloped nations could handle the inevitable, continuing gold shortage which they face while going through the initial stages of economic progress. And the long-debated UN dream that militarized powers gradually reduce their armaments and devote the subsequently freed money for economic development may eventually be realized. Part of these funds could be set aside to establish a "buffer-stock" agency or to aid the IMF.

Developing nations can initiate some effective measures by themselves. Perhaps the three most important steps which they could take unilaterally would be to diversify exports, to replace consumer imports with domestically produced goods, and to increase trade among themselves through economic federations.

Diversification of exports can reduce a developing economy's reliance on the world market's vagaries. If new forms of exports could be created, Ghana would not be ripped apart by a fall in cocoa prices, and countries such as Chile or Bolivia could survive a declining market for copper and tin. The possibilities for diversification are not very strong. It would be unrealistic, for instance, to assume that emerging nations can successfully compete on the world market with developed regions in the manufacturing sector. Nevertheless, room for maneuver does exist in the diversification of certain commodities. Theodore Schultz has shown that, for the next two decades, the demand for forest products in the United States may move up 20 per cent, the need for farm products should increase 40 per cent, and the requirements for minerals and fuel will go up some 80 per cent. With its own resources, the United States will not be able to meet the demand.[35] A developing nation, like Nigeria, could jump to take advantage of this trend by stepping up its production of oil, lumber, tin, and aluminum, thereby relieving its economy from dependence on palm products and cocoa.

Replacement of consumer imports also deserves serious attention. Clearly, developing nations will continue to depend upon imports of highly perfected industrial goods—not only because this represents the cheapest path to industrialization but because advanced regions will refuse to buy commodities unless they receive a *quid pro quo*. But developing nations could safely reduce their importation of consumer goods and, consequently, ease the balance of payments burden.

For example, in Agra, India (home of the Taj Mahal), 40,000 handicraft workers produce shoes. These shoes not only circulate in the home market, replacing imports, but India trades them to the Soviet bloc in return for heavy industry. Since Russia has a surplus of heavy industry and a lack of shoes, India makes an ideal trading partner. "The great advantage of the Agra method," Andrew Shonfield has remarked, "is that it produces foreign exchange with the minimum amount of equipment—no more than a wooden last and a hammer. Cheap and abundant labour is the complete substitute for capital." [36]

Such a policy implies an international division of labor which, in the end, would produce more wealth for everyone.* The world already has

* This statement involves one in the very complicated issue of tariff protection for new industries in emerging countries. Some economists argue that absolutely free trade will ultimately produce the best results. Certainly, this argument has some merit. India now produces very expensive automobiles and all but prohibits the importation of foreign cars by exacting a high customs duty. The Renault Company applied for a license to build a plant in India, but the government refused, on grounds that the Renault competition would

an excess of heavy industry, as economist Rosenstein-Rodan has demonstrated.[38] For developing nations to add further heavy industry would not only constitute a tremendous sacrifice on their part but also a simple waste of the earth's resources. A concentration on consumer industries and commodity production would nicely complement the needs of developing *and* developed areas. This program, of course, postulates that emerging nations would stress the building of light, "labor-intensive" industries. The nature of the world market adds one more reason to those arguments advocated in Chapter 7 for preferring light to heavy industrialization, since light industry is best adapted to the processing of most raw commodities into products for domestic use.

A third approach, increasing commerce within developing regions, also holds out promise. Faltering steps have been made in this direction. As illustrations, India now barters some of its textiles for Burma's surplus rice. In consequence, both countries avoid a drain on their precious foreign currency. In another area, the establishment of the Latin American Free Trade Association of nine nations has led to some reductions in the tariff barriers which they had previously imposed on one another. Brazil's Cia. Vale do Rio Doce now furnishes Argentina with 150,000 to 300,000 tons of iron ore, exempt from duties. Chile imports cotton from her neighbor rather than from the United States and has built a paper plant to triple its exports to LAFTA countries. Remington-Rand brings in typewriters from Brazil to Chile, other items from its Argentine factories into Brazil. Central America, too, seems groping toward an economic federation, as are Malaysia, and some French-speaking sections of Africa. The creation of an African Development Bank, composed of 32 countries, is another step in the right direction.

---

crush India's infant car industry. Renault could produce a cheaper, better car. Free traders contend that competition between, say, Renault and India's Ambassador cars would force down the price and improve the quality of India's automobiles.

Yet, without going into detail, it would seem that the protection of certain industries—particularly consumer industries—is essential in most new nations. In general, I agree with Robert Alexander, who has said, "An underdeveloped nation is justified . . . in extending protection to industries that will provide as many as possible of the basic goods the consumers of the nation are going to need regardless of whether there is a war in Europe, a depression in the United States, or whether the prices of the country's exports are good or bad." [37] This means that governments ought to protect industries that produce textiles, shoes, processed food, canned goods, flour, building materials, and other essential goods. It does not mean that India should protect its car-making industry simply in a futile effort to become totally self-sufficient.

Without such co-operation among themselves, only a handful of very large nations—maybe India, Nigeria, Brazil—could even hope to survive. Yet, to everyone's detriment, nationalist rivalries may prevent economic federations. Sad experiences in the Congo, India, the U.A.R., and Nigeria demonstrate the economic havoc which can be wrought by ideological, tribal, linguistic, or racial divisions. Whether the new nations can overcome parochialism for the sake of economic advance remains to be seen.

Economic co-operation between developed nations and developing ones, as well as co-operation within underdeveloped regions—these measures are the only possible ways to stabilize world trade. But the harsh realities of the Cold War, of tariff barriers, of divisive nationalism may well defeat the most rational of policies. Since other measures may fail, we must examine the potential of a last, critically important source of external assistance.

Foreign Aid

> It has never been clearer in human history that all men are brothers; the economic facts of today's world point unfailingly at total interdependence.
>
> PAUL HOFFMAN

To all—except those blinded by nationalism or isolationism—it should be evident that only direct aid from advanced regions will suffice to quicken the rhythm of growth in developing lands. Stabilizing world trade and increasing private foreign investment are very important stop-gap measures. But only foreign aid (in some mixture of technical advice, "soft" low-interest loans, and direct capital grants) can permit emerging nations to break through the barriers to sustained economic progress. India alone requires billions in foreign capital, and not even the rosiest optimist would suggest at this point in history that these sums can be gained domestically or through increased exports or through more private foreign investment.

Nevertheless, in Accra and Washington, Bonn and even New Delhi, influential leaders have voiced their dissatisfaction with foreign aid, and the rumbles may be increasing.

Critics in underdeveloped nations have feared that foreign aid may be a concealed weapon in the Cold War, a device to draw unaligned countries into the camp of one antagonist or another. Too frequently, this view has been correct. American "aid" to Guatemala, South Vietnam, Korea, Formosa, and other countries has hardly been motivated by humanitarian concerns. And equally, Soviet and Chinese "aid" to Cuba, North Vietnam, and Africa has had plainly political and military goals. Nevertheless, in countries such as India, states as diverse as Russia and America, Austria and Japan have co-operated in substantially assisting economic growth, without damage to India's political autonomy.

In advanced regions, responsible critics have also aired grievances about foreign aid. The "Clay Report," prepared by a presidential panel of American experts, has lashed the United States program as wasteful and as a drain on America's gold stock. (Actually, 90 per cent of America's foreign economic assistance takes the form of food, goods, or services—not dollars. A cut in America's foreign assistance program would adversely affect her exports, rather than cutting down the balance-of-payments deficit.) [39] The panel argued against the use of American money to establish public industries which compete against private firms, and it demanded that aid should go primarily to "border areas," whose military and economic strength directly contributed to American power. The supposedly realistic group concluded, ". . . We are convinced that reductions are in order in present military and economic assistance programs . . . the committee recommends [that] deductions be phased over the next three years." [40]

The arguments which underpin the Clay Report are based on baleful predictions about the future of underdeveloped economies. In its rational form, the position has been most directly stated by Eric Sevareid, liberal American commentator:

We are all obliged, it seems to me, to take an unblinking look at the estimate . . . that if the backward countries got all the aid they could absorb, used it well, and if the populations increase by one-fourth in the next 15 years, the average personal income in those countries would be increased by no more than $50 a year.

We have to ask ourselves why we assume that intervention by foreigners in totally alien cultures can produce economic levels, political institutions and social mores in 10 or 20 years of the kind produced in Western societies only after many generations.

We have to ask ourselves why we think we can produce even a respectable fraction of such results in lands where we have no enforcement powers, when we cannot elevate life in the West Virginia mining areas or get on top of the problems of poverty, illiteracy, crime, and crowding that are swamping welfare planners in our own urban sprawls.[41]

No foreign-aid official would dispute Sevareid's contention that overseas assistance confronts numerous obstacles. Military aid, in particular, has been an almost total waste. "Sending guns to Latin America is shocking, a disgrace, and a waste of funds," Alaska's Senator Ernest Gruening has said. "It ruins the efforts of people who want to do the decent thing and get the South American economy off the ground." [42] And until now, the Alliance for Progress has done very little to prime the South American economy. Much of the blame has to be assumed by the recipient countries themselves: only three countries (Colombia, Bolivia, and Chile) had submitted development plans by 1962; Paraguay and Guatemala had no income taxes; Argentina and most other countries refused to initiate required land reforms. And some South American bureaucrats had no conception at all of the Alliance's goals. In El Salvador, one government leader announced to United States Ambassador Murat Williams, "We'll need $80 million."

"Fine," said Williams. "Submit your plans and I'll see what I can do for you."

"Plans?" the Salvadorean repeated.

"Why, certainly. We're not just ladling out money. We're giving it for specific purposes. Submit your plans. We'll examine them. And if they look good, you'll get the money."

The Salvadorean thought for awhile. Finally, he said, "Mr. Ambassador, how do I go about drawing up plans?" [43]

The situation in other areas has seemed equally depressing. Millions of francs and dollars have disappeared in Vietnam with no tangible progress in the people's welfare, and Indonesia presents a classical picture of disillusion. Western nations have donated $1.5 billion to Indonesia between 1949 and 1962, while the Communist bloc contributed $563 million. As the people starved, Sukarno used much of this money to crush rebellions and invade West Irian. Japanese reparations went to building an $11 million hotel, surrounded by hovels. Russia constructed an Asian Games complex, including a beautifully useless stadium seating 100,000 persons. And America built a four-lane, neon-lighted highway, whose sole function was to connect the hotel with the Games site. By 1963, misjudgment and mismanagement had led Indonesia to the edge of economic disintegration.

All this is grist for the mills of those who wish to ax foreign aid.

Yet, the bleak picture has another side, too often ignored by both scholars and the public.[44] On the brighter side one should record some of the happenings in Libya and parts of Latin America, even in Indonesia and Formosa.

Libya, once the poorest nation in the world, has had the good fortune of striking oil, and the government has wisely set aside 70 per cent of its revenue for development. United Nations commissions and Western aid have helped the new state in a variety of meaningful ways. In one year, 1960, the United Nations persuaded farmers to plant 600,000 new fruit trees in formerly barren desert. The United Nations and the West have supplied civil servants to staff government ministries, operated training institutes, built a system of communications, surveyed the economy's resources (making possible some oil discoveries), and furnished expert help in agriculture and the development of small industries. In another decade, Libya may well have a self-sustaining economy.

While progress has been slow, small enclaves of enlightment and progress have appeared in Latin America. Alliance funds had built 360 new hospitals, 15,000 miles of roads, and 17,000 new school rooms by 1962. In Peru, workmen had begun building water and sewage systems, and in Venezuela American tractors had harrowed new land. Both adults and children had begun to receive the blessings of literacy, if not yet economic liberty. Undeniably, these advances are pitifully inadequate, but they do represent a solid beginning.

Although the government has wasted much of its resources, the people of Indonesia can still claim some lasting benefits from foreign aid. American assistance has provided many training schools, at all levels of education. The Colombo Plan nations have sent grants of machinery, serum, books, hospital equipment, and a cement plant. The United Nations has lent experts specialized in agriculture, education, and health. Some Japanese reparations have gone for ships, fertilizer, railroad equipment, and irrigation—rather than for luxury hotels. The Soviet countries have built roads, phosphate plants, a hospital, and twelve chemical factories.

Even America's military outpost of Formosa has made considerable economic progress through foreign assistance. Huge sums of United States money and technical assistance have achieved beneficial results. Between 1952 and 1958, agricultural production increased by 41.6 per cent, putting Formosa in the front ranks as a producer (per hectare) of rice and as a rice exporter. Industrial production rose 85.6 per cent. Although population also went up phenomenally (3.3 per cent a year), real income for each individual was augmented by 24.4 per cent.[45] If

America had channeled proportionally equivalent sums of aid throughout the developing nations, what real advances might have been achieved!

Patchy though it is, the record of foreign aid deserves commendadation, not recrimination. To be effective, foreign assistance requires the sincere co-operation of statesmen in developing countries. No amount of money sent into a country like Paraguay, ruled by its oligarchs and military, can dramatically improve the people's welfare. And foreign aid must be well planned and well timed, for there exist certain critical junctures where each developing nation needs *different* types of help. For post-traditional economies, including most of those in Africa, foreign aid must concentrate on education, transportation, agriculture, the building of an infra-structure, and surveys of potential resources. In semi-modern societies, such as those of India and Mexico, attention might best be given to heavy investments in industrial establishments, for here much of the foundations for rapid growth have already been laid.

If advanced regions and the developing areas assumed their moral responsibilities—if, most importantly, affluent countries stepped up their aid appropriations by some $3 billion a year—there seems little reason to doubt that our times can justify the title suggested by the United Nations, "The Decade of Development."

The Future's Promise

The stakes are high and still mounting. They include even more than the destiny of faceless billions of people, at the economic mercy of the earth's advanced regions. They also number the fate of the dieting minority that lives off the fat of the globe. In a contracting world where China will possess an H-bomb before 1970 and even Indonesia imports nuclear equipment, the rich can no longer afford the luxury of ignoring "barbarian" hordes at their door. To avoid an atomic Armageddon, the West must utilize all of its wisdom, good will, and abundance in aiding underdeveloped lands. If the advanced nations retreat from their obligations, it will be the greatest, and maybe the last, moral abdication in history. Surely, we can have the vision to recognize the debt which rich nations owe to the poor.

For centuries, Europe bled its colonies of resources and capital, in financing its own development. For centuries, the United States has pirated prizes from Latin America. Some American companies have taken 500 per cent profits annually, leaving in their wake ruined land which once fed people adequately. And the ironic fact that under-developed countries subsidized Europe, Russia, and America in World War II should give rise to feelings of atonement even among hardened isolationists.

The most elementary concept of justice dictates that the rich should pay back in some meager measure the gold they extracted from the poor, and, what is ironic, this could be done without any suffering at all. Atomic reality and simple ethics require that advanced areas must become their "brother's keeper." Paradoxically, if the rich nations accepted their responsibilities, the resulting increase in world prosperity would redound to their own economic self-interest. An increase of one per cent of per capita income in developing countries during the next decade would mean that exports from industrial regions would climb by some $320 billion.

The means are ready at hand. Sufficient determination on the part of both industrialized and nonindustrialized nations could greatly ex-pand the flow of capital into underdeveloped regions. But, clearly, any major effort requires close co-operation among all countries. In the Cold War epoch, man may not have the courage (or the time) to change and advance. During the last decades, the West, Russia, China, and the unaligned states have at times acted sordidly. While "Death and Eternity sat glaring," mankind has concerned itself with petty rivalries, which often have ruined the best-laid plans for external assistance and economic development.

China's invasion of India, for example, may well cripple the chance for Indian growth. Because of a combat over barren rocks, India in 1963 had to increase its defense expenditure from a projected $790 million to an actual $1 billion.[46] In 1964, Indians have had to spend $1.8 billion—while starving men die on Calcutta's sidewalks. On a more microscopic, but still lethally important, level, China has done what it could to disrupt Western foreign aid throughout all of Southeast Asia. As a single instance, one might recall the "Tilapia Fish Story." [47]

In South Indochina, American aid brought in nutritious, rapidly breeding tilapia fish to stock lakes. A new industry sprang up (at a cost of only $20,000), and the Vietnamese took to this "miracle" fish with such gusto that, in 1952, airplanes had to fly in new stocks of eggs. But then the communist radio and Chinese cadres stepped in with propa-ganda. With enormous success, they discredited the tilapia. They man-aged to get lepers to eat tilapia and then travel from village to village demonstrating that the fish "caused" leprosy. Inevitably, the industry collapsed, and the people lost their new source of food.

America has more than its full measure of guilt, too. We have isolated and attacked Cuba. We have kept oligarchs on their shaky thrones in the Middle East. We have overthrown an elected government in Guatemala and drained millions of aid to our puppet dictatorship, all in the name of Dulles's "realism." We have spent one million dollars a day for ten years in Southeast Asia to "defend freedom"—with such notable results that, in 1963, Vietnamese peasants had been herded into concentration camps, Buddhist priests burnt themselves to death because of religious persecution, and the greatest Vietnamese writer of this century killed himself in protest against Ngo Dinh Diem's dictatorship.

In Latin America, the United States has ladled out money and medals with the greatest of largess to military men. The sole impact has been to reinforce a rule of blood, as historian Edwin Lieuwen found after studying our "assistance":

Recent events in Colombia, Argentina, Venezuela, and Cuba seem to show . . . that the movements which have unseated dictatorial regimes in those countries represent a widespread popular striving toward the ideal of stable, democratic government. And the fact is that the fallen dictators were all military men.

These events have shown also that, insofar as the [U.S.] military aid programs have increased the political influence of the armed forces, the prospects for democracy have suffered. For the military, far more often than not, resort to nondemocratic procedures to achieve the internal order and stability which both they and the United States, for quite different reasons, so ardently desire.[48]

To make real progress anywhere in the world, America—and Russia, as well—must look beyond the Cold War's horizon. And underdeveloped countries must stifle the bickerings among themselves. It would indeed be a tragedy if India and China, or northern and southern Nigeria had learned nothing from Europe's centuries of nationalistic self-destruction.

Co-operation *is* possible. Southeast Asian territories have submerged their quarrels (such as who owns which sacred temple), and together they are developing the Makong Delta. Perhaps Indonesia, Malaysia, and the Philippines will join in an economic federation, forgetting the age-old dispute as to who has a "right" to North Borneo. Arab co-operation seems to grow, and even in Africa, economic forces may forge a unity which colonialism, tribalism, and nationalism have so far prevented.

Of even greater importance, many indications suggest that the Soviet Union and the West may reach an uneasy détente. In Ghana, Poles and Englishmen, Germans and Russians, Americans and Israelis work side by side with Ghanaians in attacking the problems of development. In India and Egypt, co-ordination between Russia and the West mounts, almost proportionately to China's military aggressiveness. In Poland, America contributes hospitals and food, while Russia (after Stalin) aids in industrial development. In Afghanistan, Russians have built an airport, Americans staff it, and a Swede manages it.

With growing maturity, the Soviet Union appears to comprehend that its national interest does not lie in fomenting "world revolution" in underdeveloped areas. Rather than attempting to frustrate all of the noncommunist efforts to achieve economic growth, Russia may increasingly co-operate with the West *and* with developing countries in building a peaceful, prosperous globe. A specter of an atomically armed China stalks Russia as well as the West today. Regardless of what surface changes occur in the Soviet "party line," mere words cannot eradicate the dangers inherent in new nations' toying with nuclear weapons, intoxicated with visions that they could escape destruction.

The Soviet Union and the West must join hands in aiding emerging countries, just as they have managed to co-operate in such less significant endeavors as exploring Antarctica's ice and, tentatively, in thrusting science into outer space. If these faltering steps toward world co-operation were reversed, *all* of our societies could meet *and deserve* the fate which has destroyed other civilizations. With her usual eloquence, Barbara Ward has described the choice:

Our wealth and comfort hold us back. We find it easier—as do the wastrels of any age—to "sit down to eat and rise up to play" . . . Marie Antoinette playing shepherdess at Trianon when the peasants, not the sheep of France, were eating grass, Rome bemused with bread and circuses while the barbarians gathered at the gate, the Cretan Kings drinking deep behind the walls of Knossos with Mycean fleets waiting to take the city in the night—all these are symbols of the fate that awaits the complacent and the comfortable when they let their good fortune stifle their good will.[49]

It may be that the gods will scatter us in atomic dust, if the advanced nations are not willing to enroll everyone into the family of mankind—a starving Indian, a leperous Congolese, a blind Egyptian,—as well as a Swedish businessman stuffed on *smorgasbord*. Is this too much to request of the fat and comfortable nations? Let us hope not.

PART THREE

The Search for Freedom

IX

THE BATTLEFRONTS OF FREEDOM

> If a friend of mine were suffering from an incurable disease, I
> would not be inclined to give him a vivid description of the na-
> ture of his disease. . . . On the other hand if I believed my
> friend's disease curable, and if an understanding of his difficulties
> were a prerequisite for the cure, I would be inclined to describe
> his disease to him and to project its course into the future as best
> I could.
>
> HARRISON BROWN

In 1961, I discussed the prospects for Nigerian democracy with leaders
of the nation's "Action Group." At Lagos, the federal capital, this
party served as a vigilant opposition, championing political liberty and a
form of democratic socialism. At Ibadan, the Action Group held power
as the ruling party of the Western Region—perhaps the most economically advanced, progressive section of the country.

To a man, these statesmen voiced their disgust with the one-party
systems on the ascent throughout the rest of Africa. They had a cautious optimism that Nigeria's federal union could survive the vicissitudes of nation-building. "The very fact of our peoples' diversity forces
compromise and imposes a system of checks and balances," Chief A.
Rosiji, a member of parliament, told me. "The interdependence of
each region upon the others means that no single group can achieve
the ascendancy necessary for autocracy."

Obafemi Awolowo, head of the Action Group, talked in a similar
vein. Affectionately known as "Awo" by his constituents, he had been
born in a small village, worked his way through school, and eventually
earned degrees in commerce and law at the University of London. Awo
fervently believed that Nigeria's traditions of free speech, village assem-

blies, and elected rulers provided impregnable safeguards for political freedom. Indeed, he thought that human nature itself offered the best defense against dictatorship. In his autobiography, Awo wrote:

> Government by dictatorship is maintainable only by the use of force and by various acts of repression and oppression against those who disagree with or are critical of the dictator. One of the lessons which history has repeatedly taught, however, is that, however repressed it may be, mankind cannot permanently attune itself to the base and inhuman conditions of a dictatorship. Sooner or later (and in these modern times it is now sooner than later), those who have been repressed make an adamant and irrepressible bid for their liberation.[1]

He felt repulsed by African leaders (and their Western apologists) who talked of "new forms" of democracy and the inapplicability of Western institutions to the African environment:

> . . . There is a newfangled theory now being propounded with erudition and gusto in the countries of the so-called Western democracies. The proponents of this theory hold the view that it is inappropriate and hardly fair to expect a newly emergent African nation to practice democracy as it is known and practiced in the countries of Western Europe and the United States. Every mortal blow that is struck by an independent African nation at the vitals of democracy is rationalized by these theorists as the African's peculiar method of adapting democratic usages to his barbaric and primitive environment. The denial of fundamental human rights, the destruction of the rule of law, and the suppression of opposition have been brilliantly and felicitously rationalized. The outrageous declaration by an African leader that a one-party system is in accord with the democratic way of life has been ably defended by these spokesmen. . . .[2]

For Awo, the *basic* defenses of freedom—a rule of law, an institutionalized opposition, jealously guarded rights of criticism, privacy, and assembly—did not magically change their nature simply because of geographical area. He believed that in Nigeria as well as along the North Atlantic seaboard, freedom could flourish with equal vitality.

Yet, by 1963, the voices of Awo and Rosiji had been silenced.

In 1962, financial scandals and a split within the Action Group caused the downfall of the Western Region parliament. The federal government brought Action Group leaders to trial on charges that they had run guns in from Ghana. Ruled by ethnic groups opposed to the West's Yoruba, the government refused Awo's plea to be defended by English lawyers (who held legitimate credentials before the Nigerian bar). Even an American lawyer who had no connection with the case was precipitously ejected from Lagos airport when custom guards discovered his profession—presumably on suspicion that he might give Awo a proper defense. The government, of course, secured the convictions it desired and promulgated broad laws giving it the power to suppress criticism. In 1963, Awo began to serve a prison sentence, and it appeared that Nigeria was sliding into a swamp of dictatorship.

The experience of these Nigerian leaders is hardly unique, for the momentum of history seems to pull all developing nations in an authoritarian direction. Even in India—an outwardly solid bastion of liberal democracy—events in the 1960's may push the nation toward either a totalitarian solution of her problems or utter disintegration.

In 1962, for example, I sat in on meetings of India's Praja Socialist party as its members performed a post-mortem on the last election. The party had gone to the people carrying a banner of national unity, political freedom, and limited socialism. Its leaders—men like Asoka Mehta, R. Dave, and Nath Pai—looked weary and discouraged, for the party had suffered disastrous reverses at the polls. Of the Indian parties, only the Socialists had more or less consistently made their appeals on an "all-India" basis: pleading for national economic development, preservation of the Indian Union, and elimination of regional hatreds. Other political units cast their slogans on a much lower, but more popular, level of sophistication. The Jan Singh promised to make Hindi a compulsory language. The Communists artfully set one caste against another in their search for votes. Despite Nehru, the Congress party based its local platforms on various conflicting pledges to specific linguistic, tribal, and caste groups.

The Congress and the Communists came out on top as the dominant parties, although neither could command an absolute majority. In consequence of their devotion to ideals of national unity, the Socialists dwindled from the major opposition party to a powerless minority. Heads of the party ruefully concluded that only a reversal in their basic policies could have saved them in the election. Privately, some admitted that the next party manifestoes would have to drop the emphasis on Indian unity and the over-all development of the country. Many of the most thoughtful statesmen in the group foresaw only two, equally baleful, alternatives for the future—a forced centralization of power in New Delhi, or a Balkanization of the nation into caste, linguistic, and regional divisions.

The scene of events in the mid-1960's only too easily promotes discouragement in champions of liberty such as Nehru and Mehta in India, Rosiji and Awolowo in Nigeria, Busia of Ghana, or Hatta of Indonesia. Their weariness is compounded because such men realize all too well the interrelation between the polity and the economy. They wish to preserve an open, politically liberal society and, simultaneously, give more bread, clothing, and shelter to their people. But, all too bitterly, they are well acquainted with the political and economic obstacles to the achievement of this aim.

They know, for example, that an economic price sometimes has to be levied for preserving political liberty. India's experience since independence gives many illustrations of the fashion in which the compromises inherent in a democratic system can at times shackle economic growth:

In 1957, to take one instance, Assam (one of the least developed of Indian regions) benefited from the discovery of oil reserves. The central government faced the decision whether to build a refinery in Assam or in another area. On rational economic grounds, they chose a region where trained workers, power, and transportation were readily available. Assamese politicians let out a wail of affronted "nationalism." "Every drop of oil in Assam is as sacred as a drop of blood of every Assamese," one member of Parliament proclaimed. "We cannot allow it to be sucked by others." [3] Because of political pressures, the government eventually made the economic sacrifice of establishing an expensive refinery in Assam.

As another example, two other areas—Andhra and Mysore—have long wrangled over the division of irrigation water coming from the Tungabhadra Project. Mysore felt that its water had been "stolen," since 55 per cent of its irrigation flow and 80 per cent of its produced electricity went to neighboring Andhra. To appease the discontent, the government placed half of the headworks in Mysore, at excessive expense. But this in turn lighted another political battle, since Andhra farmers felt overly dependent on another province—a political entity which they considered alien and hostile.[4] The internal nationalistic sentiments *within* India boil over into combats that are sadly reminiscent of European history.

Enmeshed in democracy's pushes, pulls, and conflicts, Indian planners must steer a treacherous course—one which will assure economic growth and also satisfy the conflicting political demands of different regions. As Maurice Zinkin has shown, political considerations inevitably color economic decisions.[5] The Indian planner cannot establish new railroad connections, factories, or dams simply on the basis of economic calculations, since this could mean that underdeveloped regions such as Assam would receive no new enterprises at all. He has to appease the political demands of each region, even though this may entail less rapid economic advance for the country as a whole. And it seems most likely that political claims for pieces of the economic pie will increase exactly in step with socioeconomic progress. As Selig Harrison has perceptively commented about India's "most dangerous decades":

> In the decades between glimpse and fulfillment "development" releases a new social awareness that soon becomes, in the uniquely compartmentalized Indian social setting, a militant group awareness. The promise of progress is the signal for a political and economic competition that intensifies as new claims to equality arise and as population growth presses the claimants into closer and closer quarters.[6]

The pressures for freedom—social, economic, and political—are mounting steadily throughout the developing world. The desire for liberty cannot be equated with a simple need for bread, although this demand in itself has vital, perhaps paramount, importance. Beyond the quest for bread lies another basic goal: a search for freedom in many of its varied garbs. The Tamil wants protection of his native culture against the usurpation of Hindi. The Egyptian peasant welcomes his release from a landlord's arbitrary political rule with as much enthusiasm as he does the increased food produced by his own lands. The Yoruba in Nigeria looks with suspicion upon the political inroads of northern, feudal Hausa, ill-acquainted with Yoruban traditions of self-government. Against this traditionalist backdrop, concepts of individual progress, equality, and social justice, originally Western, infiltrate ever deeper into the minds of emerging peoples.

Thus, the liberal or social democrat in emerging nations finds himself fighting battles on two intimately related fronts. A Nehru or a Busia, a Betancourt or a Mehta tries to build an open society with some elbowroom for dissent and individualism. But he must also fight to advance the pitiful economic condition of his people. This twin quest for bread and liberty proceeds without a battle plan, for history provides only a grand strategy, not specific tactics for winning on both fronts.

In this chapter, I intend to portray (in the blackest of colors) the political difficulties which confront statesmen persuaded that neither liberty nor bread should be exclusively pursued. These are the men who believe that even a Rolls Royce in every garage could not make up for the indignity of servitude, the degradation of being an untouchable, or the stifling of creative individualism. They look toward a new society like America—without its McCarthys; Russia—without its Stalins; or France—without its Robespierres.

In bringing this dream down to reality, such democrats face frightening obstacles. The nature of their political problems can be seen anywhere in the developing world. I shall choose just two quite diverse regions, India and Bolivia, as illustrations of the difficulties which hamper those who fight on the battlegrounds of freedom. And I shall draw the worst possible case against my own beliefs, for only by understanding the grounds for pessimism are we in a position to overcome it.

India

> The future is in the hands of the gods but as far as I can judge, the centrifugal forces will prevail, and . . . the nation may be compelled to go through a period of political anarchy, and face the risk of fascism, which is Nature's way out of disorder and misrule.
>
> C. R. RAJAGOPALACHARI, first Indian
> Governor-General

In 1952, Patti Sriramulu, an ascetic believer in linguistic autonomy, conducted a fast, aimed at encouraging the establishment of a separate Andhra state within India. Until then, a Telugu-speaking minority had sat alongside various other linguistic groups in a unified Madras Assembly. Sriramulu and his fanatic followers viewed this cultural diversity as intolerable and demanded autonomy for the Telugu.

Sriramulu fasted unto death in December of 1952.

His mortal gesture ignited violence throughout the region. Communist-led hysterical mobs massed in the streets. Unable to control waves of destructive vandalism, Nehru reluctantly granted the independence of an Andhra state. By so doing, he opened a Pandora's box, as other regions began more vociferously to claim their own independence from the center.

The Andhra incident illustrates the intensity of the many centrifugal forces which threaten to tear the Indian Union into shreds. Those who wish to preserve India's unity and her democratic institutions face the task of moderating these divisive forces whose virulence seems to grow as economic progress proceeds. The cracks in India's polity run along three separate, although not unrelated, seams: linguistic divisions, caste hatreds, and economic rivalries.

Linguistic problems constitute one critical threat to India's survival. India is a conglomeration of language regions, miraculously patched together by British rule and the charismatic influence of Gandhi and Nehru. Officially, Hindi serves as the national language, but actually only 37 per cent of the population (at the most generous estimate) can understand the language. The remainder of the people speak one of the nation's nine other major languages: 10 per cent communicate in Telugu, for example; 8 per cent in Marathi, 8 per cent in Tamil, and 7 per cent in Bengali. As a result, India faces a political problem which surpasses in magnitude the obstacles that confronted Switzerland, or the Austro-Hungarian Empire before World War I. A Ganges hinterland has tried to impose its language (Hindi) upon restive minorities who wish to preserve the integrity of their own cultural traditions. The disintegrative potential inherent in India's multilingualism has led one leader to warn: "India stands the risk of being split up into a number of totalitarian small nationalities." [7]

That this prediction has much to sustain it can be seen in many sectors of Indian life. On the political level, English currently serves as the medium of communication in the national Parliament, since not all M.P.'s can understand Hindi. In most regional assemblies, delegates talk in the particular region's dominant language, often to the consternation of minority members who cannot understand Hindi or Bengali or Telugu. Moreover, command of English—always limited to a tiny minority—is declining precipitously as the decades move on. Regional languages, in contrast, assume more and more importance, while Hindi remains confined to those who speak it from birth.

One essential political danger, therefore, is that regional elites will gain increasing power and will have no way of communicating with one another. Even today, some regional politicians must take translators with them when visiting New Delhi. This inability to comprehend another person's language and culture could easily lead to a bifurcation of Indian states, each battling the other "foreign nations."

The disintegrative impact of language can perhaps best be portrayed in India's educational system, whose basic unity (established by Macauley's recommendations in the nineteenth century) could crumble into antagonistic linguistic units. At every strata of education, English and Hindi appear to lose ground to the native languages of each region. The economic and political effects of this disunity are many. In universities accustomed to teaching in English, the change to a regional language could be disastrous, for an entire new staff might need to be hired. The Vice-Chancellor of the University of Madras pointed out this difficulty when politicians argued that Tamil should become the official language of instruction at his university:

I tried to look into the figures of the people who would be in a position to teach through that particular language and I found to my surprise that practically all colleges would have to reshuffle their teaching staff. For very important subjects, where recruitment of the teaching staff is not on a provincial basis but on an all-India basis, it will mean that there will be an absolute halt to the progress of higher education.[8]

As another instance, Gujarat University found that it would cost nearly one million dollars to translate essential textbooks into Gujarati —if regional politicians required the dominance of their own language. Fortunately, up to 1964, most universities had preserved English as a common means of communication.

The national civil service, long a model of rectitude and dedication, has not escaped these linguistic battles either. Now, the government phrases examinations for the civil service or the army in English, the real *lingua franca* of India's elite. If regional languages conquer, each province would have its own mode of communication and, consequently, its own methods of selecting an elite corps. No longer could the civil service act as a cosmopolitan group serving the entire nation's interest, standing above the immediate stresses of regional politics.

Most objective commentators contend that the rise of regional elites, each speaking its own language and attached to a parochial culture, would severely damage still other aspects of Indian society. In all probability, if the movement gained in force, courts would conduct legal affairs in a language which cannot be comprehended by courts of higher appeal or of other districts. (Even now, reports and legal decisions written in a regional language molder in New Delhi files, unread by national leaders.) India's intellectual milieu would suffer, too, since the spread of linguistic divisions might well encourage an already booming tabloid press, one which catered to the interests of the local group in power. The total impact of India's linguistic revolution has been well summarized by Selig Harrison:

In each region writers and intellectuals will be caught in an atmosphere of political ferment that will, in most instances, emphasize and honor parochial rather than universal values. The decline of English has already led to a sharp decline in educational standards. . . . Intellectual activity in each region will to a considerable extent be a pulp culture of popular writers who will address themselves to the swelling millions of new literates in the regional languages. This pulp culture will, by its very nature, be predominantly parochial in its horizons. Men of stature in the new generation of Indian leadership will attain their full height in spite of, but only in spite of, this intellectual climate.[9]

The political future in India, then, may bode ill for those who seek national unity. New regional parties, a new breed of civil servants, a pulp press, and a degraded educational system could dominate the Indian scene, if the movement toward cultural disunity intensifies.

Often intermixed with linguistic issues, caste divisions complicate the difficulties created by language. Ironically, as economic development goes forward in India, the vehemence of traditional caste hatreds mounts. The ideal of *individual* equality of opportunity becomes debased into concepts which stress the wishes of one caste *group* versus the others. Political scientist Myron Weiner has rightly commented about the fashionable prediction that economic progress will melt traditional differences:

On the contrary, as economic growth has occurred in India and political awareness has increased, the number of community associations has grown. Before 1947 the most prominent division in Indian life was between Hindu and Muslim groups; and after 1947 among the most prominent groups were those that emerged from linguistic-regional sentiments. Tribal and scheduled-caste bodies are now multiplying; and within political parties ascriptive identifications are playing a more prominent role.[10]

Organized groups, some ready to use violence, have come forward to press the claims of each caste "community." On a nonviolent level, they demand, among other things, that industries, universities, and the civil service set aside particular quotas for each caste—regardless of the individual merits of aspirants to the positions. To an increasing degree, Indian leaders have given in to these pressures.

At times, caste organizations have resorted to open violence. In 1959, Madras festered with severe riots produced by conflicts between Maravar and untouchable sections of the population. In contrast to the past, when caste battles could be limited to particular villages or local areas, this combat engulfed an entire province.

In India's four southern states, political parties based exclusively on
caste (and linguistic) antagonisms have sprung up. The DK and the
DMK parties represent the interests of Dravidian castes against the
supposed tyranny of "Aryan" Brahmins. The parties have fought the
use of Hindi as a national language, violently demonstrated against
Brahmin merchants, destroyed Hindi religious idols, and contended
that the various five-year plans have favored the north (and thus, the
"Aryan" Brahmins) to the detriment of southern groups. The DK and
DMK can play on several different but interrelated themes: regional
jealousies, linguistic differences, and caste oppositions. In consequence,
their political power has grown astonishingly. In 1957, DMK candidates ran for office for the first time and won fifteen seats in the Madras assembly. By 1962 they had gained fifty constituencies. As their
popular vote doubled between 1957 and 1959, they secured control of
the Madras Corporation, upsetting the Congress party by a substantial
margin.

The rise of an organized competitive caste system is a new phenomenon in Indian history. Previously, as Charles Drekmeier has brilliantly
shown, the caste system served an integrative function and often acted
to reduce conflict.[11] Today, in contrast, caste differences intensify linguistic, economic, and political conflict. Selig Harrison has well described the place of castes in India's hectic new environment:

*To enshrine equality is in effect to tell all castes that it is every man—
which is to say every group—for himself. Caught in a never-never world
of frustration, somewhere between newly aroused desires for equality
and the scant spoils of progress that are actually available, it is inevitable for a man to turn to a loyalty he knows and understands to fortify
his quest for equality with those above him and to assure that he is
"more equal" than those below.*[12]

Inevitably, caste and linguistic differences have become enmeshed
in the crosscurrents of India's economic problems. The close connection between these various elements can perhaps best be illustrated in
the pervasive Indian suspicion of Marwari economic power.

The Marwari merchant castes of Rajasthan have traditionally been
the moneylenders and entrepreneurs of India. Used loosely, the term
Marwari applies to over four million people who speak the language.
In the Indian political context, most groups direct their hostility specifically to the Vaisya castes in the Marwar area of northern India (particularly the Oswal, Agarwal, and Maheshwar castes).

Since the early nineteenth century, these communities have served as middlemen in the Indian economy. Perhaps driven by a "chosen people" complex based on a myth of their descent from Rajput kings, the Marwari have exhibited exceptional business acumen and energy. Their economic power as landholders, bankers, traders, and industrialists spreads over all of India. They include in their ranks such notable industrialists as G. D. Mirla, as well as numerous village merchants and bankers. At the highest sectors of the Indian economy, Marwaris in 1947 owned 16 jute mills, 54 cotton mills, 35 rice mills, 24 oil refineries, 15 sugar factories, and 11 *dal* mills. By 1960, eight Marwari families held seats on the board of directors of 565 banking and industrial firms.[13] Moreover, the Marwari exhibit a remarkably tight familial and caste solidarity. Wherever a Marwari may live in India, he feels that he is a member of his clan and is treated as such. Their unity and success has created widespread hatred of Marwaris by the less enterprising Indian communities, a kind of parallel to the West's tragic history of anti-Semitism.

Politicians have depicted the Marwaris as the archvillains behind every Indian problem. Because they defend Hindi as a national language, Marwaris have been blamed for imposing this alien tongue on Telugu- or Tamil-speaking regions. Their economic affluence has been lashed by socialist orators such as Congress leader N. V. Gadgil, who charged in 1952 that Marwari "capitalist insects" and "parasitic elements" had stolen the economy of Maharashtra and Bengal.[14] In charges ranging from crushing the peasant to promoting disunity, the Marwaris have been the whipping boys.

When demands for an independent Vidarbha state became rampant, newspapers charged that the movement could be traced to Marwari interests. Actually, most Marwari leaders favored a united Maharashtra province (including Vidarbha) for the obvious reason that the influence of their own population was greater in that unified state. In the south, much of the money behind nationalist "independence" movements (including the Communists) comes from the coffers of non-Marwari landholders and merchants. Originating from high castes themselves, these capitalists quite rightly believe that they would prosper if "northern" Marwari influences simply evaporated. In the classic manner of vested interests, the Tamil entrepreneurs use elevated, nationalistic slogans to defend their economic flanks against the Marwari.

The conflict of the Marwari against other groups is only one illustration of the political consequences of mixing linguistic, caste, and economic rivalries. Caste differences also debilitate the trade-union movement. Rather than acting as a unified force, trade unions are divided along strict linguistic and caste lines. As a result, responsible leaders often find it impossible either to guide a united group of workers in pressing legitimate demands or—when the workers succumb to messianic visions—to moderate exorbitant claims. In consequence, an undisciplined, disunited trade-union movement plagues the Indian economy.[15]

As the vision of economic progress seeps deeper into Indian minds, economic conflicts mix with other sources of political instability. While there has indeed been some economic progress, the hopes of increasing numbers of people vastly exceed reality. Organized or spontaneous violence has been the result, not only among the labor movement but in other strata of the population. Student dissatisfaction, for instance, has often erupted into mass disorder. Riots forced the closing of Lucknow University in 1953 and Benares University in 1958. An increase in bus fares led to student riots at Patna. Police had to fire at Patna students, as well as Gwalior students in 1950 and Indore students in 1954. Today, some professors even feel compelled to carry pistols in the classroom.[16]

Numerous incidents in Calcutta indicate the magnitude of economic unrest:[17]

In 1953, a tram company attempted to raise its fares by approximately one-quarter of a cent. In response to this announcement, mobs poured into the street, closed down shops, factories, and colleges, and demanded a boycott of trams. Mobs pulled people off the trams. Students joined in, barricading themselves in university buildings and stoning the police. During riots in the city square, police had to fire on the people. On July 18, the West Bengal government called for troops, since rioters had taken total control of the southern section of the city. Finally, the government restored order, and a commission arbitrated the fare-increase issue.

Again, in 1954, Calcutta teachers struck for higher wages. Among other instruments of protest, they (abetted by professional hooligans) burned cars and buses, smashed traffic signals, and looted stores. In a wave of destruction, four persons were killed and 65 seriously injured.

In April, 1958, the Calcutta fire department announced the opening of 100 new posts (at a salary of $11 a month). More than 10,000 men appeared the next day to apply. The authorities could not cope with the crowd and decided to suspend interviews for the day. Profoundly angered, the applicants smashed houses and furniture; police had to stop them with a *lathi* charge. During the same year, refugee elements broke loose, protesting a government decision to resettle Bengali refugees outside the region. Rioters stopped traffic and daily engaged in battle against the police.

Such examples could be multiplied, but the lesson seems obvious: the convulsions of economic development have produced mobs whose anarchic violence has too often paralyzed India's economy and its government.

Many thoughtful men cannot foresee a clearly illuminated path out of India's political difficulties. Language differences may render the Indian Union into a multitude of antagonistic cultures. Traditional caste divisions, now organized into violent pressure groups, enfeeble the ideal of individual opportunity. Economic conflicts mix with the other issues, endangering not only India's pluralistic federation but also its opportunities for economic progress. As villagers disengage themselves from traditional society, a new uprooted generation has entered Indian politics.

The combined impact of these centrifugal forces has not been witnessed on such a scale in previous history, except perhaps in eastern Europe. As Hans Kohn has shown, the rise of regional divisions within the Austro-Hungarian Empire led to the emergence of nationalistic leaders, proclaiming the "self-hood" of each province and promising a chauvinistic, utopian future to those who followed them.[18] This similarity of the past to contemporary Indian events has led Arnold Toynbee to the question: "Will India succeed in carrying out [its] experiment, without bringing on herself eastern Europe's tragic fate?"[19]

Three groups have proposed an answer to Toynbee's question: authoritarians wish to centralize all power in a totalitarian state; regionalists would like to Balkanize India; and a beleaguered, but wise group of leaders hopes to preserve India's balanced pluralism.

Authoritarians of the left and right consider that only a total consolidation of power in New Delhi will save India. From the right wing, the late Subhas Chandra Bose championed one form of totalitarianism. He set the basic policy for the R.S.S., a group dedicated to a Nazi-like "rejuvenation" of the country. Bose flatly declared that India "must have a political system—a State—of an authoritarian character . . . a government by a strong party bound together by military discipline."[20] He believed that the trend of world history would lead to "a synthesis between Communism and Fascism, and will it be a surprise if that synthesis is produced in India?"[21]

The Communists have come forward with equivalent pleas for an enforced Indian solidarity. In theory, of course, they look to a dictatorship of the proletariat, one which presumably would override all linguistic, caste, and regional divisions within India. In actuality, the Communist party has come close to power only when it used these traditionalist divisions for its own political advantage. In Andhra and Kerala, Communist parties could not mobilize support behind the usual socialist slogans. Instead, they turned with great success to caste hatreds as the basis for their electoral appeal. A legislative Communist victory in Kerala can be traced almost completely to the party's sole emphasis upon the interests of numerous Ezhavas to the exclusion of other groups. And in Andhra, contrary to doctrine, the Communists have chosen to side with the Kammas, a rich proprietor class. Thus, the party has fattened its purse with financial support from the Kammas, at the expense of less fortunate castes. With pragmatic acuteness, India's Communist party has discarded Marxist doctrine in the tug of war for political power. Perhaps this development was inevitable since, as an editorialist in the Lucknow *National Herald* rightly observed:

Probably Marx, even Lenin or Mao would have wilted in the Indian climate. The inchoateness of the class situation, the indeterminate, undefined, intermediate forces which are largely British-made, the peculiarly hard social structure defy analysis.[22]

Neither the Communists nor right-wing "communalists" have offered workable solutions to India's problems, for the exotic nature of the Indian social structure does defy the usual doctrinaire nostrums. Even the national meetings of the Communist party have broken up into caste, linguistic, and regional strife. If the party cannot unite its own dedicated members, how could it patch together all of India? Perhaps backed by a massive show of military force, the Communists, the R.S.S., or some other authoritarian group might conquer regionalism. Yet the odds seem overwhelming against any national party attaining such support. An authoritarian solution to India's dilemmas hardly seems a practical alternative.

A second possibility, the complete disintegration of India into separate nations, is more likely. With seeming inevitability, the Congress party is losing its grip as a molder of national unity. As one instance of its failure, the party has yet to resolve conflicts between Bengal and Bihar. In comic-opera fashion, these states—*both* dominated by the Congress party—have bitterly disputed their borderlines. Each government has argued, in effect, for the destruction of the other, although leaders in both provinces supposedly adhere to a mutual party platform.

In 1954, disputes between Bengal and Bihar reached the point where Nehru had to plead with them "to stop behaving like two independent countries on the brink of war." [23]

The trend toward provincialism may even be built into India's constitutional system. Indian law has specifically given to each state the right to collect taxes from agricultural production, the greatest source of revenue in the nation. Thus, the federal government has partially lost one of the most important instruments through which national unity can be preserved: the power to exercise financial control over its various units. Since landowning castes tend to dominate regional governments, the central government has been unable to reap substantial tax income from the rural sector. At most, one per cent of the value of gross agricultural output returns to the government in taxes. China in contrast levies 25 per cent.[24] The Chinese government has, of course, the advantage of ruling a relatively homogeneous population, long accustomed to unity and discipline.

From their vantage points, some pessimistic experts see India's disintegration into financially, culturally, and politically independent units as almost preordained. The dynamic forces which rip India apart lead a number of observers to conclude that a realistic view of the future "must rest on a clear recognition that the odds are almost wholly against the survival of freedom . . . the issue is, in fact, whether any Indian state can survive at all." [25]

India's Balkanization would entail a tragedy of Homeric scope. Minorities in each new state would have to be ejected or eradicated by dominant majorities. Caste against class, language against religion, village against city—these battles, with all of their subtle intermixtures—would inevitably result in a bloodbath. India's quest for freedom and bread would culminate in disaster.

A handful of leaders—Nehru, Jayaprakesh Narayan, Vinobha Bhave, Asoka Mehta, Frank Moraes—saw beyond the immediate horizon. In differing ways, they offered an intermediate, pluralistic solution to India's apparent alternatives of bloody centralization or an equally murderous Balkanization. We shall have occasion to examine their proposals for India in a later chapter. But for the moment, let us briefly review the obstacles which confront another, apparently quite diverse state: Bolivia. Although strikingly different in past history, geography and culture, Bolivia faces equally pressing problems in her quest for freedom. While India's future will probably decide the fate of Asia, the success or failure of Bolivia's revolution could have as profound an importance for the destiny of Latin America.

Bolivia

> The United States has given me just enough rope to hang myself.
>
> HERNÁN SILES, ex-President of Bolivia

In the summer of 1963, Bolivian tin miners sat behind machine guns guarding the single railroad running into Catavi-Siglo Veinte. They had gone on strike because the mining company wished to dismiss 1,000 workers in an effort to "rationalize" operations. Ironically, the miners aimed their machine guns at a peasant militia, not at "exploiting Capitalists." A decade before, the workers and peasants had been comrades in a common battle against feudalism. Their revolution triumphed in 1952. As one result, Bolivian leaders nationalized the tin mines, hoping to use the profits for the entire nation's welfare. Yet, a decade later, the revolutionary leaders found themselves enmeshed in an explosive conflict with their former supporters.

Bolivia is one of the very few Latin American nations which has undergone a genuine social revolution. The MNR, the revolutionary party, has distributed land and guns to the peasants, broken the power of Bolivia's tin barons and landholding class, and has striven to ameliorate the lot of Bolivia's destitute Indians. Moreover, the government carried out all the reforms within a democratic framework—a free press has functioned vigorously, free speech and elections have remained inviolate, autonomous organizations such as the tin union have flourished outside governmental dictation, and huge portions of the population, formerly voteless, have entered politics.

One would think, then, that Bolivia could serve as a brilliant example for the rest of Latin America. The peasants have not been casually forgotten (as in Mexico after her revolution), nor has individual liberty been destroyed (as in Cuba). Nevertheless, few progressives in Latin America look to contemporary Bolivia for inspiration. John Gerassi has curtly summarized the current state of affairs: "The MNR has ruled ten solid years; the social revolution has been carried out—democratically and with all possible vigor—and Bolivia is in a mess." [26]

Before these words see print, army officers, a fascist party, or left-extremist groups may well have toppled the MNR from power. The reasons for Bolivia's serious political difficulties must be traced to her past history and to her present socioeconomic structure. Without understanding these elements, it is impossible to comprehend how such a well-intentioned government could be so endangered.

Prior to 1952, a small elite had run Bolivia as a feudal domain. Four per cent of the population owned 70 per cent of the land. Tin constituted Bolivia's major export, and this lucrative industry was tightly controlled by three families. They ran the mines with a brutality that might have revolted even a seventeenth-century capitalist. Owners punished union organizers by murder. A handful of families owned gigantic latifundia and ran them with unmasked contempt for their Indian serfs. By law, the landowners bound the peasants to their estates. Among other legally imposed duties, the serfs had to contribute their labor freely as domestic servants for certain parts of each year. For their work on the land, the serfs did not receive wages and had to exist within the confines of a barter economy.

Landlocked and mountainous, Bolivia seemed eternally isolated from modern life. Although the size of Spain and France combined, Bolivia's 3,500,000 people occupied just one-tenth of this area, subsisting in barren, treeless hamlets 10,000 feet above sea level. The majority of people spoke only Aymara and Quechua, even after centuries of Spanish influence. During the brief periods when Bolivia functioned on paper as a democracy, the elite still retained power by the simple expedient of restricting the franchise to literates. Since the governments expended almost no funds on schooling, this technique effectively cut off the great majority of the nation from political participation.

Perhaps this system could have been maintained in a state of stagnation for centuries more. The elite, however, made one disastrous mistake: embarking on the ill-starred Chaco War with Paraguay between 1932 and 1935. Desiring to win back the prestige lost to Chile and Brazil in previous combats, the elite launched a border battle which was doomed from the start. Paraguay's army had good leadership, intimate familiarity with the Chaco terrain, and short supply lines. The Chaco adventure decimated both nations. Paraguay lost 40,000 men and Bolivia 60,000.

The Chaco defeat had profound, unexpected repercussions on Bolivia's political structure. Since the country desperately needed all of her manpower, the government conscripted peasant masses. For the first time since the Spanish invasion, the Indians were exposed to an unfamiliar outer world greatly different from their traditional servitude. They experienced a new sense of nationality and became intensely aware of their degraded position within Bolivia. Bolivian expert Richard Patch has well described the psychological impact of the war:

> For many of the Bolivians who called themselves "whites" or gente decente, it was an unparalleled experience to serve in an army with "Indians." The white and mestizo officers suddenly found themselves

dependent upon the infantry of the once despised indios. *For the Indians it was an equally strange experience to conceive of Bolivia as a nation, and to become the object of propaganda designed to persuade them that they were citizens of a single nation, no longer Indians, a people apart, but* gente, *or "persons," in the same sense as the "whites."* [27]

Awakened from the anesthetic of traditional servitude, the Bolivian masses began to flex their muscles. Indian uprisings sputtered episodically throughout the country. At the risk of death, tin miners began to organize trade unions. And student groups inspired by liberalism or socialism lent their support and leadership to liberation movements. The political pendulum swung directionless between outright military dictatorship, the usual traditionalist governments, and shortlived liberal governments. When unshakily in power, the liberals attempted to pass peasant reforms. Each minor advance, even if later reversed by succeeding dictatorships, made the serf more poignantly aware of his humiliation and more eager to change his lot in life.

The rumblings of discontent reached a crescendo in 1952 when miners, peasants, disaffected army officers, and intellectuals joined in overthrowing military rule.[28] The change came abruptly and relatively easily; even the police themselves passed out guns to the revolutionaries. Hernán Siles, Juan Lechín, and Victor Paz stood at the head of the revolution. Siles and Lechín personally led the attack of peasants (sometimes armed only with spears) against a German-trained army, fighting with tanks and modern artillery.

The revolution handed power to the MNR (Movimiento Nacionalista Revolucionaria), a curious, uneasy alliance of many social groups. Founded in 1940 by Victor Paz, a former professor of economics, the MNR brought together a coalition of young army men, liberal intellectuals, and, eventually, union workers, peasants, white-collar workers, and splinter Marxist groups. The party gained increasingly popular support and was even allowed to contribute cabinet members to the temporary government of Major Gualberto Villarroel, head of a secret army cabal which took over the government in the 1940's. Villarroel eventually dropped MNR members from his government and, in 1946, was hung from a lamppost by an angry mob. A succession of military and unstable civil governments followed, until President Urriolagotia announced free elections for May of 1951.

The government—that is to say, the feudal and military rulers—mistakenly believed that they could retain their influence without rigging the elections. The Bolivian constitution specified that a president could win only if elected by an absolute majority or, failing that, by a vote of parliament. Since many candidates took to the field (and peasants could not vote), the government thought that a split vote would require its puppet congress to choose a "proper" candidate for the presidency. Although the MNR's greatest influence lay with the non-voting peasantry, Victor Paz received 45 per cent of the highly restricted number of votes which were actually cast. The MNR garnered six out of nine senatorial seats. Discomfited by electoral reverses in supposedly safe districts, a military junta seized control—thereby inciting a mass MNR revolt in 1952. Significantly, even a member of the junta itself, General Seleme, joined forces with the MNR. After 3,000 deaths, the MNR triumphed and called Victor Paz back from exile to assume the presidency.

Led by Paz and Siles, the MNR precipitated fundamental reforms. The government nationalized tin mines, some other metals industries, and certain oil wells—with recompense to their former owners. Guarantees for freedom of the press and speech were firmly established, and unions gained the ability to organize freely. All men, literate or not, received the right to vote. Most importantly, in 1953 the government broke up the huge landed estates and distributed plots to formerly landless serfs.

At first, the MNR had vacillated about the type of rural change to undertake. Many of its city-dwelling leaders feared the breakup of large, market-oriented plantations into small subsistence plots. Another branch of the MNR knew more intimately of the peasants' deep longing for land of their own. The *campesinos* themselves resolved the theoretical debate when they began forcefully to confiscate the estates. With some reluctance—since they realized the possible effect on Bolivia's rural productivity—the MNR leaders promulgated a basic reform in 1953, liquidating the latifundia. The peasants joyfully took over the land. Unfortunately, the new smaller pieces of land could not be farmed as efficiently as the old feudal domains, and the government failed to provide sources of credit, supplies, or advice to the peasants. While the peasants gained a sense of dignity and independence, the nation's food supply began a decline which has yet to cease. Here, then, is still another case where an essentially political decision damaged an economy. The peasants had asserted their will so strongly that no national government, particularly one dedicated to the peasants' welfare, could defy it. Yet the economic effects were disastrous: Bolivia has had to import increasing amounts of foodstuffs and, by 1962, was expending $90 million of hard-earned foreign currency simply to keep its people from starving. Some of the MNR's most basic political difficulties stem from its inability to reconcile economic reality with the yearnings of peasants for privately owned land. The rural sector can no longer sustain Bolivia's cities. And peasants, spurred by new aspirations, have flooded urban areas seeking nonexistent jobs. Disillusioned with their independence, the Indian urbanites are malleable clay for demagogues' oratory.

Other tough obstacles have hindered the revolution's advance. The world situation itself, outside the control of MNR's leaders, has created some of the worst problems. Bolivia desperately needs a port, for example, to export its products. But Chile has yet to grant Bolivia's request to return part of a coastline ceded to Chile after an early war.

Even more serious are the difficulties presented by the world tin market. Bolivia has traditionally depended upon tin as her greatest source of external revenue. The Korean War temporarily created a great demand for tin, but at its end the United States canceled tin contracts with Bolivia. The price for tin plummeted. It dipped even further when Russia entered the world market and sold tin which undercut Bolivia's price. Because of these conditions (as well as the depletion of Bolivia's highest-grade ore), the nation discovered that the price of production exceeded the revenue received on the world market. In 1956, President Paz announced that the cost of tin production averaged $1.25 a ton, while by 1959 the world price hovered around $.90 a ton.

This gap forced Paz and Siles to try to reduce tin workers' wages, artificially enlarged during the Korean War, and to end "featherbedding" practices introduced by the unions. Paz has further tried to resettle 10,000 tin workers in a new sugar industry and has promised them $700 each as recompense. The MNR has no alternative but to make the tin industry more economical, for without its revenue Bolivia's economy has no chance of progress. Any reasonable government would have to undertake similar measures. Nevertheless, some politicians have taken advantage of the tin crisis in their search for personal power. Most prominently, Juan Lechín, a former leader of the revolution—an "organizer who calls himself a miner but whose main physical effort in life has been to play soccer" [29]—has incited some Trotskyite unions to revolt. It is these who have implanted machine-gun nests in the mountains. The majority of union members and peasants still adhere to the MNR, but in 1964 no one could foretell whether the government would survive the newest armed revolt.[30]

Plagued by an agricultural decline, miners' revolts, and inflation—since 1956, housing prices alone have risen 2,452 per cent—the MNR flounders in confusion and frustration. Possible resources abound in the potential development of other minerals for export, relocation of peasants on new land, the establishment of rural co-operatives, and the erection of consumer industries. Yet, the open anger of miners, the smoldering resentment of city immigrants, and the actions of irresponsible orators may blow up Bolivia before substantial progress can be made.

A massive infusion of foreign capital would save Bolivia. Indeed, the United States has given more aid per capita to Bolivia than to any other Latin American nation. Nevertheless, much of this money has had to be devoted to currency stabilization, a useful but hardly sufficient instrument for economic advance. Again and again, during his term as president, Siles tried to hold down inflation by a combination of domestic restrictions and stop-gap American funds. Siles attempted to keep prices and wages locked at an austerity level. Eight times he threatened to resign as president when various groups attacked his anti-inflationary programs. But, fortunately, Congress supported him each time until his 1960 resignation, a retirement enforced by Bolivia law.

While Siles and Paz have received support from a majority of the people, dissident elements have continued to agitate. During Siles's regime, Lechín prompted strike after strike. At one point, he closed down the railroads for several weeks. The right-wing fascists felt equally incensed by the moderates' policies and abortively tried an armed coup d'état against Siles. Precariously, the middle sections of the MNR have held on to power, but the United States has furnished them with just enough "rope to hang themselves"—not enough assistance to galvanize Bolivia's near-bankrupt economy.

The United States aid program has been admirable in intent and, until now, has succeeded in its basic goal: sustaining leaders who rejected authoritarianism either in its feudal or its modern forms. Nevertheless, the program has suffered from grave deficiencies. The customary mixture of loans, direct monetary grants, and donations of foodstuffs has not met the demands of a peasantry aflame with revolutionary passion. Most U.S. projects have been limited to urban, Spanish-speaking areas. They have often been conceived as long-term programs, taking years to mature. Transportation systems, the development of small industry, and the opening of virgin land have all been neglected. Inevitably, untrained American officials have been guilty of waste and inefficiency.[31] Above all, the United States has sought Bolivia's economic "stability" as a basic goal—an unrealizable aim in a nation caught up in waves of revolutionary sentiment.

The situation today does not seem hopeless, only unpromising. The government has distributed some three million hectares of land—but not established community co-operatives to increase production. The oil and tungsten industries have expanded—but the country's total production index has gone down. American aid has built some new roads and clinics—but an unthinking hatred of America by fascists, communists, and Castroites also seems to increase. Political freedom remains intact—but politicians use their liberty to whip the people into a frenzied madness which no government could cure.

"The crux of the matter," Richard Patch has noted, "is that Bolivia's political and economic difficulties have been intensified, not reduced by the basic social changes of 1952." [32] Most significantly, both Bolivian and American statesmen have failed to gauge accurately either the needs or the power of newly freed serfs: "They have underestimated the profound nature of the social changes that follow the emergence of the *campesinos* from their previous status as serfs, changes that will make social and economic institutions unstable for a long time." [33] In Patch's assessment of U.S. assistance, he concluded that the basic difficulty has been American inability to fit its programs to the real needs of the peasantry:

*Long-range development programs have too often been stressed, rather than smaller-scale, short-term schemes which would raise living standards for the majority of underprivileged peasants. . . . To the campesinos' desire for seed, land and water, the agricultural service has too often responded by offering insecticides, sprayers, fertilizers, and a school for training tractor mechanics. These innovations, while potentially valuable, are not adapted to the level of agricultural techniques practiced in most of Bolivia.[34] ***

All is not lost. Bolivia today has sound, progressive leadership and a potentially strong economy. But the survival of the Bolivian revolution, the only truly democratic one in Latin America today, will require a profound reorientation of both MNR and American policies. For its part, the MNR must pay much closer attention to satisfying the immediate desires of the peasantry. And America must commit herself to a much more massive aid program. As one expert concluded in 1962:

* As one instance of this shortsightedness, the United States established a training station at La Tamborada, complete with prize bulls designed for breeding. The starving peasants slaughtered and ate the bulls.

If the Alliance for Progress really wants to help push reforms, it should back the MNR still more. With $1 billion limited to roads, electricity, and farm machinery, Bolivia could be totally self-sustaining in two years—even without a port. Whole fertile regions could be opened to life and industry.[35]

Let us hope that historians will some day record that the United States had the vision to back up its slogans with action.

The Dilemmas of Nation-Building

> Venezuela, . . . and all the other countries of Latin America, is perfectly capable of organizing itself in an economic, political, and social order. We are a people who can be governed democratically and legally. We are resolved to follow our own course, to make our own history. . . . We are a people who are accomplishing something that will be the pride of the new America.
>
> ROMULO BETANCOURT, President of Venezuela

All progressive men desire that Betancourt's description of his nation's destiny will prove to be more than a passing illusion. Yet, in 1964 Venezuela's reformist government seemed in grave danger of collapse. Terrorists set off bombs in the capital, the army talked of a possible rightist revolution, and the United States government leaked news that marines might be landed. As Juan Bosch fled the Dominican Republic, army officers grabbed power in Africa, and Algeria's Ben Bella proclaimed a one-party state—few observers of the developing nations believed that these regions could be "governed democratically and legally."

Whether in Venezuela or Nigeria, India or Bolivia, the storm signals indicated to pessimists that the cause of freedom would be engulfed. It hardly requires emphasizing that responsible leaders of the new states —men who desire to release their people from both political *and* economic servitude—confront unprecedented obstacles imposed upon them by the vagaries of history. In attempting to build politically open societies, they must grapple with certain universal dilemmas:

They must muzzle the centrifugal forces of tribalism, regionalism, and parochialism which threaten to destroy their politics. Particularly in former colonial areas, nationalism served as a rallying cry to unite diverse groups. Now that independence has been achieved, the old slogans have a hollow ring. Other interests—class, caste, linguistic, ethnic, religious—take precedence over national welfare. As Mario Rossi has rightly observed, "In the Third World, independence preceded viability, so that in a sense the traditional pattern of evolution to nationhood was reversed." [36] For liberal and social democrats, the necessity of maintaining a stable, effective government at the center—while not breaking down a system of checks and balances—poses a delicate problem. At a conference on the ancient island of Rhodes in 1959, democrats from Western nations and emerging states debated whether political democracy could take root in countries which had not passed through the long evolution of Europe and America. Edward Shils, the distinguished American sociologist, summed up the uneasy spirit of the conference: "This was the passionately felt urgency: some enhancement of the social unity of the new states. Yet, at every turn, there was an equal awareness of the need and rightfulness of diversity." [37] In one fashion or another, progressive leaders must harness the forces of *internal* nationalism—they must, in Bertrand de Jouvenal's apt phrase, invest their new states with "majesty"—without eroding the fundamental bases of individual liberty.

Then, in many nations such as India, some of the less happy political legacies of colonialism must be eradicated. These inheritances from the past take many forms. One is a sense of racial inferiority, a sentiment well expressed by General Carlos Romulo of the Philippines: "We have known, and some of us still know, the searing experience of being demeaned in our own lands, of being systematically relegated to subject status not only politically and economically and militarily—but racially as well." [38]

He warned his colleagues not to fall into a chauvinistic counter-racism, as China has: "There is no more dangerous or immoral or absurd idea than the idea of any kind of policy or grouping based on color or race as such. This would, in the deepest sense, mean giving up all hope of human freedom in our time." [39]

A side-effect of the degrading colonial experience, political scientist Lucian Pye has cogently argued, has been to destroy the basic sense of identity of many national leaders.[40] Today's elite has been subject to the intrusion of an alien, dynamic, modern culture often in direct conflict with ancient traditions. Pye contends that leaders caught in this flux suffer from deep feelings of insecurity and distrust:

> In such a psychological and political climate trust disappears, intrigues flourish, and personal dangers multiply further still. Failing trust and predictability, it is impossible to build the "adaptive and purposeful" organizations on which the modern nation-state must rest. . . .

Disappointment, bitterness, confusion, and passivity add their burden as the leader descends the long spiral to the point where he can no longer make a real contribution to the nation-building task. His identity and function lost, the society about him grows confused about its competence and its image as well.[41]

Another political impact of colonialism, all too apparent in India, has been to create a posture of oppositionalism, regardless of the issues at hand. Dissatisfaction with the government in power, whatever it may do, becomes a habitual attitude. Without homogeneity of values, constructive agreement becomes difficult to reach. With a touch of bitterness, socialist leader Asoka Mehta has described this attitude in emerging countries:

The apochryphal story of the Irishman, ship-wrecked on an island, asking: "what is the government here?" and without waiting for enlightenment, asserting, "I am against it," has an element of truth in it. Whether the Irish are like that today I do not know, but prolonged foreign rule fosters such an attitude among subject peoples.[42]

Further, as a result of these forces, progressive leaders have to create institutions and symbols which promote modern democracy but also meld with traditional social forms. Raghavan Iyer of Oxford has nicely summarized this challenge: "How to establish and operate new democratic institutions and forms while also preserving the best elements in national traditions and indigenous ideas?"[43] Men such as Gandhi and Nehru have managed to bridge this gap and maintain the stability of a democratic regime. It is problematic whether leaders of sufficient stature will emerge in the future to fulfill similar roles. The new class of intellectuals and politicians appearing in Asia, as one illustration, seems to many commentators to lack the unity and dedication of the old generation of leaders. Asia expert Michael Edwardes has noted:

Without any background of agitation, or any simple and overriding ambition to throw out the foreigners, the younger generation is prone to disillusion—for the scene is now one of extreme complexity, in which issues are no longer clear-cut or emotionally inspiring . . . the feeling of being a lost generation is very strong amongst students and young intellectuals, who still to a large extent look for employment in government and politics as a right they have gained through their education. . . . A sense of scepticism is strongest among those who cannot be absorbed into the system, and who feel that their education entitles them to preferment in the halls of government.[44]

Finally, statesmen in all areas must face the dilemma of reconciling economic progress with the preservation of political liberty. In India or Bolivia, perhaps the greatest challenge is to develop a political leadership which can forge links with the village level—an elite flexible enough to comprehend and meet the immediate aspirations of the peasantry. To some degree, Nehru had managed to accomplish this goal, and certainly he clearly recognized it as the crucial problem of our time: ". . . How to combine democracy with socialism, how to maintain individual freedom and initiative and yet have centralized social control and planning of the economic life of the people. . . ?"[45]

The complexities involved in Nehru's question have led many scholars to despair. Social scientists such as Herbert Spiro, Immanuel Wallerstein, and Robert Heilbroner seem to perceive no political future for developing nations except for one-party, plebiscitarian states. Both scholars and politicians contend that emerging nations lack the historical background for democracy, that economic progress can proceed only by crushing dissent, and that the disparate fragments which make up developing nation-states have to be coerced into unity.

Such pessimists—and I have been playing their role to the hilt in this chapter—see only the problems and not the accomplishments of societies trying to develop in a democratic fashion. I have detailed the frustrations and complexities which face liberal leaders in countries such as India and Bolivia. To keep the record in balanced perspective, one should note the favorable trends which characterize these nations. India, for example, in the face of all her political problems, has maintained her plural system and managed a steady rate of economic growth. Despite various economic mistakes, India has registered important gains: national income has gone up by 40 per cent since 1953, the rate of investment has doubled, food production increased by 50 per cent, steel output has tripled, electric power has quadrupled, life expectancy has climbed from about 27 years to over 40, and 70 per cent of Indian children under twelve now attend school. Admittedly, India's squalor is still appalling, but its record of achievement over the last decade offers hope that democratic means can handle the problems of emerging countries. And, of course, all India's economic advances were accomplished in a political climate of stormy dimensions.

Nonetheless, from all parts of the "Third World," the need for an authoritarian system is still trumpeted. "The whole nation from the

President downwards must form one regiment of disciplined citizens," Nkrumah of Ghana has declared.[46] * Until executed by Baghdad mobs, dictator Karim Kassem of Iraq echoed Nkrumah's opinion that institutionalized dissent was merely "mischief-making": "The parochial groupings and party affiliations at this time are of no benefit to the country . . . my party is the entire people, and I belong to the party of the people." [47] And Sukarno of Indonesia, in defending the introduction of his so-called "guided democracy," lectured Indonesian students:

I have said over and over again, our political atmosphere is an unhealthy one, a liberal political atmosphere, an atmosphere of "freefight liberalism." . . . It is a situation where there is no order and no unity, no one yielding to the other. . . . We must abandon this freefight liberalism completely, if we want to develop and build up in the right way.[48]

All these pronouncements boil down to a premise enunciated by Robert Heilbroner: "Mild men will not ride the tigers of development. Neither will mild political or economic systems contain or impel it." [49] The validity of this assumption can be gauged in two ways: by the yardstick of contemporary experience and by the measure of history. In the next chapter, we will be concerned with whether current authoritarian systems live up to their well-advertised claims of superiority.

* This opinion was passionately shared by former Information Minister Adamafio of Ghana—at least until he, too, found himself behind bars.

X

THE AUTHORITARIAN SOLUTION

> Dictators ride to and fro upon tigers which they dare not dismount.
>
> WINSTON CHURCHILL

Leaders who mount the tiger of dictatorship seldom do so irrationally. Nkrumah, Castro, Ho Chi-minh, Mao Tse-tung, and others like them began their political lives longing for the freedoms provided by a liberal polity. Even after they gained power over their nations, politicians such as Nkrumah and Sukarno had an apparently sincere conviction that liberal democracy would work. Michael Edwardes's views about the contemporary Asian ruling classes apply with more or less generality to other parts of the world:

> *From books by Western political philosophers and politicians [the nationalist] acquired the shibboleths of democracy, those high-faluting and intoxicating phrases which again and again have driven men to the barricades to fight against tyranny. He read, too, of the right of rebellion, and that the history of democracy seemed to be a record of positive action against political evil. . . . The colonial nationalist who now rules in Asia . . . has not altogether lost his faith in the essential rightness of the democratic idea. The use of democratic phrases . . . is not entirely an exercise in propaganda.*[1]

Raised as many of them were on Western concepts of liberty, why, then, have so many leaders discarded democracy's institutions and used only its "high-faluting phrases"? Essentially, it is because they have become converted to a new ideology which, under one label or another, pervades the newer nations. "What you think, you become," Gandhi once commented, and his aphorism describes all too cogently the transformation of men such as Nkrumah. This new ideology of authoritarianism, which has invaded and too often conquered the intellectual atmosphere of emerging countries, derives its appeal from three basic generalizations.

The first argument rests on the conviction that economic development has supreme importance in advancing the welfare of emerging peoples. The authoritarians assume that in a nation's urgent scramble to survive and grow, political liberties are a luxury which cannot be afforded. Therefore, they say, an all-powerful state has to crush dissenting opinion, mobilize resources, and centralize all important economic decisions. Without such a big push, the chances for economic progress will supposedly evaporate.

The argument runs that a liberal political system has inherent faults which impede economic growth: such governments cannot make full use of their natural resources, utilize technological innovations to the utmost, draw without restraint upon unused labor, or co-ordinate the planning of different economic sectors. The "frills" of democracy have to be sacrificed in the more fundamental quest for bread. Richard Hughes, an English journalist who observed the Chinese revolution, has convincingly stated this aspect of the authoritarian position:

I knew Shanghai when it was the gayest city in the Far East—gay, that is, if you were a foreigner or a Chinese millionaire. But there were corpses in the street every night, 20,000 died a year from hunger, cold and exposure. And there were swarms of beggars. And the childish streetwalkers, and the sweating rickshaw coolies, with a professional life expectancy of eight years if they didn't smoke too much opium.

Now no one goes hungry in Shanghai.

Who can strike the balance between freedom from starvation for the majority against freedom of thought for the minority? The comparison, one must keep repeating, is not the China of today with the Western world of today, but the China of today with the China of yesterday.[2]

For those who choose "freedom from starvation for the majority," it often seems that parliamentary democracy has in practice proven a major block to economic improvement. As one Egyptian general put it to me, while justifying the abolition of opposition parties: "All that parliamentary forms did in Egypt was to give free reign to corrupt, selfish interests—to those wealthy ones who could buy votes or newspapers. Why give these unprogressive forces a political voice? Western countries do not allow ordinary criminals to vote. Why should we allow people who are figuratively or literally equivalent to murderers *any* civil rights?"

A second argument is that emerging countries lack the historical experience and proper social structure to produce anything remotely like Western liberal democracy. Those who profess an authoritarian creed seldom express this view publicly, although it often plays a very important private part in their decisions. A. J. Balfour, British Conservative leader, openly stated this opinion while defending imperialism before the House of Commons in 1910. Countering criticism of British rule in Egypt, he argued:

You cannot treat the problems with which we have to deal in Egypt and elsewhere as if they were the problems affecting the Isle of Wight or the West Riding of Yorkshire. They belong to a wholly different character. . . .

Let us look at the facts of the case. . . . You may look through the whole history of the Orientals in what is called, broadly speaking, the East and you never find traces of self-government. All their great centuries—and they have been great—have been passed under despotisms. . . . Conquerer has succeeded conquerer; one domination has followed another; but never in all the revolutions of fate and fortune have you seen one of these nations, of its own notion, establish what we, from a Western point of view, call self-government.[3]

Because he had to protect Britain's colonial policy, Balfour conveniently overlooked the grassroots, village kind of democracy which existed in many parts of the Empire. Despite its somewhat tarnished heritage, Balfour's assumption has been expropriated by the new nationalist leaders and by their abettors in the West. Current apologists for authoritarian governments assert, "Because the underdeveloped countries . . . consist of disparate fragments without a coherent political history, they must be coerced into 'nationhood' for their own good."[4] Certainly, the internal disputes which ravage India or Bolivia lend credence to the assertion that nationhood does not come into being without pain and ferment. During the critical stages, the authoritarians say, dissent and disunity cannot be allowed. Only after a coherent political unit has taken form can internal dissension be countenanced.

A third argument is based on the belief that a "new" form of democracy will emerge from the decades of turmoil. Often quite sincerely, the authoritarian hopes that he can evolve a novel system of democratic participation, a form of government which can give real power to the people. An independent judiciary, conflicting groups grappling for power, competing parties, constitutional guarantees of personal liberty —all of these are mere conventions in the authoritarian's eyes. In the Rousseauistic, populist tradition, the authoritarian hopes to create utterly new institutions which will give man a voice in deciding his destiny. Usually, these new forms of democracy are conceived of in "communal" terms, as expressing the general will of the people; they are premised on the assumption that people in developing lands do not portray themselves as individuals with separate rights, as do Westerners. In his enthusiastic account of the new China, Felix Greene recounts again and again the way in which the people collectively support the regime. He has speculated:

Is the structure of the unconscious itself different? After all, the Chinese developed their society for four thousand years uninfluenced by Western concepts and behavior patterns. Is it possible that the highly separate, individuated consciousness which some of our psychological historians believe developed in Western man only at the time of the Renaissance, has never had to evolve here? In other words, that the consciousness of I being separate from you is not so sharp here as it is with us? Me and not-me tend to merge in the collective we? [5]

Thus, authoritarian leaders generally subscribe to three beliefs: a radical cultural relativism which pictures each society as developing its own unique type of democracy; a scorn for Western political institutions as inappropriate to the exigencies of nation-building; and a conviction that, in any case, economic progress must come first. Except for a few instances of megalomania, leaders in developing nations have not rejected free institutions out of a simple thirst for power. Most authoritarians genuinely hope that a new form of liberty will emerge, *after* the crises of development end. Until that point, they subscribe to Lenin's dictum: "Liberty is precious—so precious that it must be rationed."

The claims of authoritarians cannot be dismissed lightly. They have to be measured against the realities of development, as it occurs today and as it has taken place in the past. Three nations—China, Ghana, and Indonesia—provide salient examples of how authoritarian systems actually function in emerging countries. Today each of these nations presents a model of what sociologist Edward Shils has correctly described as the most likely alternatives to democracy in the new states: "totalitarian," "modernizing," or "military" oligarchies.[6] China is undoubtedly the most important example of a totalitarian oligarchy, a regime which unrelentingly suppresses dissent in its search for modernity. The government imposes its will with whatever brutality the situation demands. Simultaneously, the elite flaunts a doctrine adorned with democratic airs. Ghana has been described as a modernizing oligarchy, one which suppresses civil liberties but maintains at least the outer forms of parliamentary life. (Some might prefer to describe Ghana as a monarchy, since ultimate power seems to rest with one man, not a group.) An elite rules with highly concentrated authority, but whether for reasons of expediency or compassion, the government refrains from the more brutal practices of totalitarianism (such as mass execution). Indonesia, like most Moslem countries, is essentially a military oligarchy. Although nominally led by a civilian, the nation's government rests primarily in the army's hands. As a supposedly uncorrupt, united group, the army charges itself with seeking the country's development.

All of these types of authoritarian regimes are bent on modernization. All claim to build new, "progressive" societies. How well have they succeeded?

China: The Asian Colossus

> We are told: "You are setting up a dictatorship!" Yes, my friend, you are right. . . . We are told: "You are not benevolent!" Exactly. . . . To hostile classes the state apparatus is an instrument of oppression, of coercion and not "good will."
>
>   MAO TSE-TUNG

One-quarter of mankind now subsists in the "empire of the blue ants" where perhaps the most significant experiment of our age is being ruthlessly, pragmatically, and efficiently conducted. By any estimation, China represents the pre-eminent example of a totalitarian approach to the problems of development. Despite the ostrich-like American posture, we must pay the closest heed to this experiment, for its success or failure will affect the ultimate destiny of all men.

The great endeavor began in the 1920's, when a dedicated and brave group of revolutionaries first plotted to overthrow Chiang Kai-shek's autocracy. At its inception, the Communist movement seemed to have almost no chance of gaining power. Riddled with dissension, bereft of mass support, lacking weapons, held in contempt by Stalin—and at times actively hindered by him—the party undertook the seemingly impossible task of toppling a well-armed dictatorship. Contrary to Marxist doctrine and to Stalin's explicit orders, Mao and some of his followers made the wise decision of turning to the peasantry as the foundation for their movement.[7] In the battle against Chiang, the Communists consistently and effectively appealed to the peasants, by living with the people, redistributing land in "liberated" areas, and espousing the farmers' interests against those of landlords. By the 1930's, the small elite of intellectuals who began the movement had forged the formidable Red Army out of the hordes of peasants who swarmed to their flag.

For decades, this army fought with the greatest valor against the better-equipped Japanese and Kuomintang troops. Inspired by a vision of the future, Mao's guerrillas overcame what seemed to be insurmountable odds. Perhaps their most heroic and historically important feat was the famed "Long March."

Due to military errors and the technical superiority of Chiang's forces, the Red Army in 1934 found itself encircled in Soviet Kiangsi, a small area where the Communists had temporarily established their power. The leadership made the bold decision to move the entire "Soviet Republic" deep into China's interior, where it would prove more difficult for Chiang's troops to infiltrate. For one year, Mao and his army—some without shoes, all dressed in light cotton tunics—marched 6,000 miles on foot. They fought more than 200 battles. They crossed deserts as well as the 15,000-foot Great Snowy Mountain. They passed through eleven provinces. They suffered continuous bombing and machine-gunning from the air. When the column finally came to a rest in northern Shensi, only 20,000 people out of the 100,000 men, women, and children who had begun the march remained alive.

Despite the decimation, Mao managed to establish a base of operations from which Chiang never dislodged him. The Long March was not only a brilliant military accomplishment, a testament to what human beings can endure, it was—in Mao's words of the time—"A manifesto, an agitation corps and a seeding machine. It declares to the . . . two hundred million people of eleven provinces that only the road of the Red Army leads to their liberation." [8]

History vindicated Mao's judgment. Everywhere his army went, it won lasting support from the peasants. The army freed the peasant, if only temporarily, from the terror of Chiang's "blue-shirt" secret police and of the local warlords. The army distributed land and paid for its supplies, rather than looting the countryside as Kuomintang soldiers did. The leaders offered a model of honesty and austerity which contrasted sharply with the opulent style of Chiang's officers. The Long March and the spirit of dedication which it engendered allowed Mao to establish his new "republic" in Yenan, to repulse Japanese and Kuomintang attacks, and eventually, in 1949, to sweep Chiang Kai-shek into the sea.

As Americans too easily forget, the demise of Chiang's dictatorship was well deserved. Venal, corrupt, and incredibly cruel (Chiang's minions had a taste for burying their opponents alive), the tyranny collapsed of its own weight. The Kuomintang made fantastically stupid mistakes which eroded the support Chiang could once have legitimately claimed. When he retook the Communist enclaves of south China, for example, Chiang undid the Communist land reforms and returned all land to the landlords. Despite enormous American *and Russian* aid, the despotism lost its "mandate from heaven" through a total inability to understand or reach the peasant masses.

Since 1949, Mao has constructed a powerful, relatively prosperous state out of the debris of civil war. Today, outside observers radically disagree in their evaluation of this new Chinese polity, but few dispute its basic political characteristics:

(1) Indubitably, China is totalitarian. As even the nation's former minister of communications has declared, "China is composed of five hundred million peasant slaves ruled by a single god and nine million puritans." [9] In principle, the person owes everything to the state and cannot expect any aspect of his private life to be left inviolate. Even the ancient customs of filial piety have been scrapped. In a manner reminiscent of Nazi Germany, the *Current Affairs Handbook* of 1952 instructed women to inform on their relatives:

Sisters, if your own father, brother, husband or child has committed any of the above-mentioned crimes, you must rid yourselves of any scruples and courageously prevail on them to confess or you must report them. . . . Everybody must understand that it is a glorious thing to induce your own relatives to confess or to report your own relations. . . . [10]

The regime has never felt any inhibition about using terror to achieve its goals. Between 1949 and 1950, an official announcement proudly reported that 1,176,000 "counterrevolutionaries" had been executed.[11] By 1952, some fourteen million people had been liquidated.[12]

(2) Mass persuasion has been effectively combined with terror. Hundreds of thousands of Communist cadres have poured into the countryside exhorting the people to greater effort and instructing them in the current dogma. Successive educational campaigns have been waged against religion, laziness, "warm-feelingism," waste, inefficiency, and individualism. Indeed, as one observer has said, the indoctrination has been directed "against private aspirations, private ties, private life and all—aimed at destroying all public and private bases of resistance to the relentless production drive. People had to be remoulded into completely conditioned human machines, as similar as possible to such biologically conditioned insects as the ants or the bees." [13]

The radio in particular has been used extensively as a means of telling the people their duties. One Indian visitor to China, after noting "the dull uniformity" of the country, reported:

> . . . no one can escape . . . the ubiquitous loudspeaker. I first heard it at the frontier station of Shum Chun when I boarded the train which was to take me to Canton. The radio haunted all my waking and many of my sleeping hours till I left the same frontier station. . . . The voice blares away at one in the bus, in the train, in the tram, in Pullman sleepers and dining cars, on street corners, in villages, towns, and cities—just about everywhere. . . . And what does the radio pour out day and night? The answer: everything that the government approves and wants to convey to the citizen.[14]

(3) Except for the exceptional interlude of "The Hundred Flowers," the state has smashed dissent and criticism. Only one prophet, Mao, sees the truth. The official line has been clearly expressed by the *Peking People's Daily*:

> Today in the era of Mao Tse-tung, heaven is here on earth. Once the Party calls, tens of millions of the masses jump into action. Through scientific Marxism-Leninism he can see the future. Each prophecy of Chairman Mao has become reality. It was so in the past; so it is today.[15]

Despite its confidence in Mao, the party in 1957 briefly allowed direct criticism of national policy. For reasons as yet unknown—perhaps because of fear that the Hungarian uprising might be repeated in China, perhaps to uncover "subversives"—the state allowed dissent to sweep over the country between May and June of 1957. For a short six weeks, the cauldron of discontent boiled over.

The universities not unnaturally emerged as the first source of dissent. Professor Ko P'ei-ch'i of Peking University said:

During the campaign for the suppression of counter-revolutionaries in 1955, an untold number of citizens throughout the country were detained by the units where they were working (this did not happen to myself). A great many of them died because they could not endure the struggle. No matter how strong the "reasons" were for detaining the citizens, . . . this was, after all, a serious violation of human rights.
This is tyranny! This is wickedness! [16]

Other universities followed the example of Peking, and by June of 1957, students and faculty had rioted in Tientsin, Shanghai, Nanchang, Wuchang, Hanyang, Futan, and Canton. "Democratic Walls" appeared everywhere in the universities as students affixed posters advocating a "garden of democracy," free debate, and a China where discussion would be as unfettered as in Hyde Park.

Once unleashed, the spirit of criticism engulfed the country. By July of 1957, armed revolts had taken place among workers and peasants in Honan, Kwangsi, and Manchuria.

Of the utmost importance, members of the inner elite of the party began to voice their dissatisfaction. Lo Lung-chi, a cabinet minister and member of the party's ruling committee said to a public meeting, "Chairman Mao is a very shrewd and crafty man, much more ruthless than any other ruler in our history." [17] Ke Yang, editor of the *New Observer*, told Peking students: "In the past, to be a Party member one had to regard oneself as either a lunatic or a corpse. One could speak one's own mind only in the privacy of one's own bedroom." [18] Hu Feng, once officially hailed as China's greatest poet because of an ode to Mao, wrote about this work: ". . . Before I started, I felt disgust. . . . After I had set to work, I could not help crying. How came there to be such an imbecile, such a rotten beast?" [19] About a speech he had once written for Mao, Hu Feng commented, "Mao's address is essentially not realism. . . . Under present circumstances, it is liable to kill people." [20]

The brief interregnum of open discussion ended abruptly when the party leadership comprehended the extent of popular disagreement with its policies. Confessions from generals to students flooded the newspapers. Members of the elite, as well as common people, suffered: high officers of the "Central Headquarters of Mid-China Generals" disappeared, while middle-school boys in Hanyang were publicly executed. In published estimates, the government revealed that 1,300,000 "counterrevolutionaries" and 250,000 additional "rightists" *within* the party were uncovered, and a further 810,000 party members demoted. Various cabinet ministers, generals, provincial governors, vice-governors, and other leading Communists lost their jobs or their lives.

Since 1957, the security police has been most careful in preventing the blooming of another hundred flowers. Because of the terror—and because half the present Chinese population has been weaned on propaganda—one may doubt if such criticism will appear publicly again.

(4) Like Meiji Japan, the government has consciously set out to integrate its policies with certain traditional aspects of Chinese culture. In restructuring family relations, for instance, the party has apparently achieved great success.[21] Most importantly, the party has taken China's native traditions of authoritarianism and poured them into a modernized mold. To good psychological effect, Mao has increasingly been depicted as the great God-Emperor. School children memorize songs such as:

> *Mao Tse-tung is like the sun:*
> *He is brighter than the sun.*
> *Little brother, little sister,*
> *Everyone clap hands, come and sing.*[22]

With symbolic reference to the past, Mao has given up his peasant habits and now occupies the Imperial Palace of the Forbidden City. In some peasant homes, his picture has replaced that of the kitchen god, and people are taught to say this grace before eating: "Thanks to Chairman Mao for our good food." Mass bowing before Mao's picture often commences public meetings.

The extent to which Mao has become a god is illustrated in two not uncommon quotations from party sources. In 1950, the Peking Municipal People's Soviet suggested:

> *Formerly we worshipped Kuan King who was said to be omnipotent. Where is his omnipotence? Whom shall we worship? To my mind, we should worship Chairman Mao.*[23]

And in 1955, the Governor of the Yi national minority declared:

> *The sun shines only in the day, the moon shines only at night. Only Chairman Mao is the sun that never sets.*[24]

What has happened, then, is that the party has manipulated China's native authoritarian attitudes to its own purposes. It is of the greatest significance to realize that China, unlike such countries as Ghana and Indonesia, *never* possessed a heritage of individual freedom or of limited self-government.* Indeed, the Chinese language in 1900 did not even have a word to express the concept of "liberty." When Western ideas began to infiltrate the Chinese elite, it tried to find some parallel concept for liberty, but most usually translated the idea into the Chinese equivalent of "unrestricted license."

China's history has been one sorry parade of dictatorship after dictatorship. Some have effectively united the nation for a time; others, like Chiang's, failed to achieve total control over this gigantic area. In any case, we should clearly understand that Communist rule has not broken with China's most ancient political traditions. It is not an alien intrusion, but rather a continuation of the past, a solidification of warlord dictatorships into a single monolith. The Communists can and do point with pride to their ancestors in China's past. As early as 9 A.D., Emperor Wang Mang anticipated the current scene of events when he established state ownership of natural resources, declared strict price and wage controls, and killed those landlords who refused to participate in his policies. (Wang Mang's regime collapsed because the peasants eventually became infuriated at his officials' corruption—a warning from history that the present government would be wise to heed.) A thousand years later, Chancellor Wang An-shih built a state which closely resembled modern China. He nationalized all industries, established semi-communes, had history books rewritten, used education for political indoctrination and executed critics with abandon. Defenders of the present state place Wang Mang and Wang An-shih in the pantheon of lesser gods who preceded Mao. Because the most recent dictatorship has so pragmatically combined the new and the old, one historian, Amaury de Riencourt, has been led to observe, "Red China is a more up-to-date, more ruthless, more efficient version of what the Celestial Empire had been for thousands of years." [25]

This new "Celestial Empire" has combined several policies with astute practicality. The uninhibited use of terror, unceasing indoctrination of the peasantry, the smashing of intellectual dissent, and the integration of an initially authoritarian culture with a modern type of totalitarianism has eventuated in a state which may well become the most powerful on earth. Few question the political stability of the

* In recent times, China has had political movements which have understood and sought to build liberal institutions. In 1947, for example, the Democratic League argued for the establishment of a Western-style parliamentary system. The League had many adherents and stood as a third force between Chiang and the Communists. The League's popularity prompted Chiang to persecute it out of existence. General Marshall and other experts believed that the League would have gained millions of votes in a free election.

present government. It has successfully crushed internal revolts, expanded its territories, and reduced domestic critics to silence.

While admittedly stable, is the government popular with the people?* Only history can pass the final verdict on this issue. Contemporary observers differ drastically in their opinions. Many diplomats and other visitors believe that the government enjoys the overwhelming adulation of the people. After interviewing foreign diplomats in Peking, for example, British journalist Felix Greene concluded that from 80 to 90 per cent of the people would vote for the present government in a free election.[26] In contrast, other equally unbiased writers believe that support for the regime has been generated more by fear than by genuine enthusiasm. Generalizing from the Hundred Flowers period, another observer of China concluded:

> *Students all over the country were in a violent mood. They hoped to stage a "second Hungary." For Mao, the students—the products of his own regime—were the greatest shock. . . .*
> *For a brief six weeks, the truth came out. The people judged. The Chinese Communist press produced massive documentation of the fact that Mao Tse-tung was the most hated man in the country, and that his Party was detested by the people.[27]*

Sripati Chandra-Sekhar, director of the Indian Institute for Population Studies and an invited guest of China, found that the Chinese seemed to hide their real feelings behind a mask of uniform discipline. "In China," he commented, "I did not find a single person who talked freely to me as man to man, and all the courtesies that were extended to me resulted from the directives of the people in power." [28] In many visits to communes, Chandra-Sekhar noted:

> *Even the most casual observer could not have helped seeing that the average adult looked sullen and unhappy. He followed official directions and did his duty, but dejection and misery are impossible to conceal. We have incredible poverty in some of India's villages, but such poverty has never been a barrier to banter and humor, and even, oddly enough, gaiety. This I completely missed in the communes and the countryside of China.[29]*

---

* This issue concerns me only as it affects the permanency of the regime. I most emphatically do not regard popularity as equivalent to good government. The most vicious crimes against humanity have been committed by popular rulers such as Hitler.

Who can really say, at this juncture of history, whether seven hundred million Chinese revere or hate the regime? The very fact of the government's survival suggests, however, that the government has forged some kind of consensus behind its program. The final trial of the government's stability will depend on its capacity to cure the curses of famine, disease, and hopelessness which have plagued the Chinese peasantry. On this essentially economic issue, we can—at least tentatively—draw a balance sheet.

Has the revolution materially benefited the average Chinese? Any summary of China's economic situation has to be divided into two fairly distinct stages: the period of consolidation and splendid advance between 1949 and approximately 1960, and a time of retrenchment or even retreat from 1960 to 1964.

Up until 1960 (some would date the transition in 1958 or 1959), China seemed to have wrought economic miracles. Her economy had not only recovered from the war's devastation but had moved forward at an astounding pace. Electricity and coal production, the bases of industrial energy, increased at the astronomical rate of 25 per cent annually. Steel production went up at an almost equivalent pace.[30] Overall industrial production leaped ahead at a rate of 15.7 per cent each year.[31]

Agriculture did not lag far behind. Between 1950 and 1957, agricultural production rose by about 33 per cent, grain production by perhaps as much as 92 per cent.[32] In the best microscopic study available, anthropologist W. R. Geddes closely examined Kaihsienkung, a village on the Yangtze plain. His 1956 study is unique in that conditions in the same village had earlier been researched by another anthropologist, Fei Hsiao-tung, in 1936.* Thus, Geddes could estimate in detail the changes which had occurred over a twenty-year period. Geddes found many alterations in the village, but, most importantly, he concluded that the state of near-starvation which had characterized the peasants in 1936 had ended. Rice production had increased since 1936 by 120 per cent, and average household income has risen by not less than 60 per cent.[33]

The Communists not only put more food on peasant tables, they also mobilized human talent in a fashion unknown in old China. By 1959, the average peasant worked 300 days a year, on one project or another,

---

* Fei also revisited the village in 1957. He published his findings, some of them critical, in the *People's Daily*. Later he was forced to recant and undergo corrective labor. Since 1958, nothing has been heard about this greatest of Chinese anthropologists.

where in 1949 he could find employment only 130 days a year. In formal education, the government registered similar gains. Illiteracy declined from 80 per cent of the populace in 1948 to 30 per cent in 1960. Enrollment in universities jumped 636 per cent between 1948 and 1960.

These dry statistical records hardly suggest the tangible ways in which the fate of the average Chinese has improved. For the first time, the peasant could enjoy some minor "luxuries" which fate had previously denied him. One visitor to a Chinese commune in 1959 has recorded the basic pleasure which the peasants took from a simple meal:

> *It consisted of meat dumplings . . . which we dipped into a hot sauce, a sweet dish, and endless cups of hot tea. Everyone enjoyed the lunch and the Director, obviously satisfied and happy, recalled his days as a landless farmhand in this village before the Liberation.*
>
> *"These meat dumplings were a great luxury then, because we couldn't afford meat. We had this dish only once a year during a festive occasion. Now we can have this delicacy any time we want." And he served me a few more hot dumplings.*[34]

The scope of the Chinese triumph between 1949 and 1960 can best be seen by comparing her economic evolution to that of India. In 1950, China and India both had per capita incomes of around $50, and 80 per cent of their populations were engaged in agriculture.[35] Both initiated large-scale development schemes at the same time and from roughly similar economic bases. In the judgment of most experts, India had the economic advantage over China:

> *If anything, India gave promise of greater progress in view of its advantages in basic resources per man, in transport facilities and modern industry, and in training and leadership attributes. Thus, India apparently had greater scope for using its surface water potential and for exploiting the intensive margins of agricultural cultivation. With the same relative efforts, therefore, larger returns could be anticipated in India than in China.*[36]

In 1950, then, one would have thought that India would outstrip China in economic performance. Yet, by 1960, the obverse situation prevailed. Gross national product in India had increased by about 15 per cent, while China had approximately doubled her economic capacity. China's superiority appeared in every sector of the economy.

Chinese steel production, for example, increased at a pace seven times faster than India's, and the amount of grain grown in China was about double India's production. In some of the most decisive sectors of the economy—coal, cement, fertilizer, electricity—India began its development at the same level as China. By 1960, however, Chinese output in these areas exceeded India's by 200 to 700 per cent.[37] Felix Greene has summarized this contrast and its potential meaning for other underdeveloped areas:

> *I know the attitude in the West is that India is going slower because she is accomplishing her revolution through a politically democratic process, more gradually, more humanely. But when we move from political theory to the mathematics of human survival, we face the fact that a Chinese child today has better health, better food, better work-prospects, more education, and greater security than an Indian child. . . .*[38]

Many factors contributed to China's accomplishments during the 1950's. China invested much more capital in productive activities and apparently used it more efficiently. By 1959 (as opposed to 1950), the rate of investment in China had increased five times, while India's had doubled. China's greater regimentation allowed her to squeeze out larger sums of capital, particularly from the rural sector of the economy.

Perhaps half of China's advantage over India can be explained in terms of the accelerated pace of investment.[39] But other very important elements played a role in China's progress. China drew upon her human potential much more efficiently than did India. By investing relatively more money in agriculture and small industry, China's government provided productive outlets for her idle labor. The nation also spent very heavily on formal education. Some 12 per cent of national income went to schools, about twice the sum that the Chinese spent on their military establishment.

Because of its strait-jacket control and co-ordination of the economy, China was in a good position to limit the consumers' freedom of choice, impose rationing, and totally direct the flow of imports to productive enterprises. The government also exhibited exceptional flexibility in its economic planning. Reacting to dynamic conditions within the economy, the government pragmatically altered its plans; for example, it quickly moved away from an initial concentration on heavy industry.

In addition, the significance of the Russian contribution cannot be overemphasized. Not only did Russia send technicians and some $3 billion in capital to China,* but, most importantly, the two countries synchronized their economic planning. As one expert observed in 1960:

Every underdeveloped country is familiar with the difficulties repre-sented by the lack of stable markets for its limited range of exports. . . . The synchronization of Soviet and Chinese economic plans elim-inates such difficulties to an extent that is hardly possible between countries with liberal economies. In fact, instances are known when domestic output of certain commodities was reduced in the Soviet Union by 2 to 3 per cent, in order to facilitate the absorption of cor-responding Chinese exports. In reality, the existence of the Soviet bloc market . . . has enabled China to develop her exports with excep-tional rapidity. . . . Inversely, this same close collaboration enabled China to obtain all the essential machinery and other supplies in the required moment. . . .[40]

Up to 1960, the essential ingredients of the Chinese model of de-velopment included: co-ordinated planning both within China and in co-operation with an advanced industrial nation; a relative restriction of consumption (but not its diminution) and a consequently high rate of capital accumulation; the massive training and investment of idle labor as substitute capital; and a concentration upon agricultural de-velopment and rural, small-scale industries.

It should be underlined that almost exactly the same policies could be adopted by a politically free society as by a totalitarian one. A liberal polity would not allow the same degree of regimentation as did China. It is also true that a nation like India does not have China's mono-lithic, disciplined population. Because of these qualifications—some of which are historically determined and, thus, unchangeable within the near future—it is doubtful whether a liberal democracy could repeat China's economic advance between 1949 and 1960. Nevertheless, with some modifications, most of the Chinese program—denuded of its totalitarian aspects—could fit the economic requirements of many new nations. After their extensive comparison of Indian and Chinese per-formances, economists Wilfred Malenbaum and Wolfgang Stopler concluded that China's superiority could be traced to its pragmatic economic policies rather than to any specific element of its political system. They commented:

* A great deal of Russian aid had to be repaid with the usual commercial in-terest. Thus, China, like every other developing nation, had to create export in-dustries which would fit the needs of an advanced nation.

The advocates of neither democratic nor Communist methods can find in the experiences of India and China . . . evidence of a systematic relationship between ideology and the rate of economic progress. . . . Their relative success was due to the degree to which they geared their development programs to the existing structure of their economies. [In China] cold and objective appraisals were made of the stages necessary to achieve a state of continuing progress from inadequate starting points. Throughout, they demonstrated flexibility in selecting courses of action.[41]

Since 1958, the Communists have failed to show the same wisdom as they did in the preceding decade, and the nation's advantage over India has begun to fade. In their eagerness to achieve "The Great Leap Forward," the Chinese planners made a series of costly mistakes symbolized in the wasteful "backyard steel furnaces" experiment and the attempt to communalize the countryside. Most seriously, the planners cut back on their previously large investments in agriculture.

Simultaneously, of course, the feud with Russia flared, and co-operation with the Soviet bloc disappeared. Apparently, during the last few years, Russia has stopped all significant aid to China and has recalled Russian technical advisers—many of whom reputedly left with the blueprints of unfinished construction projects in their pockets.

The combined impact of these blows severely damaged China's economy. Food production has dropped since 1958, while the Chinese population has continued to grow. In consequence, the government has had to expend $782 million from its slender cash reserves to import food. By most estimates, industrial production has remained stable at the 1959 level. Education has been cut back: the government reduced the number of students 20 per cent in 1962 and another 20 per cent in 1963.

With characteristic flexibility, the party has responded to the crisis with a series of measures which may get the nation back on the road of economic growth. Millions of people have been sent back from the overcrowded cities to work on farms. Private farming enterprises were allowed to function again in 1961 and have produced well for the market. The commune system has been revamped, so that the typical farm unit now consists of 25 to 40 families who can exercise considerable autonomy over their agricultural policies.

While the crystal ball is cloudy, most observers agree that China will resolve her current problems and will, after some decades, emerge as a self-sustaining economy.[42] And, beyond doubt, in comparison to 1949,

China can lay claim to great economic advances which have substantially bettered the miserable condition of the masses. As such, China should still be regarded as the most successful economic experiment undertaken within an authoritarian framework. Probably the most balanced estimate of China's gains and losses during the Communist period has been drawn up by Tibor Mende, an objective reporter with no sympathy for totalitarian atrocities. After a recent extensive tour of China, he summed up the impressions of most visitors:

> Only too painfully visible in a number of Asian countries, I have seen in China no evidence of malnutrition. People as a whole, and children in particular, look healthy and vigorous. There is no unemployment and no one goes around in rags. . . . Peking has created a collective society which offers to countless millions security in a new and powerful China. . . . Those unable to fit into this new pattern are inevitably ruined. The small minority of intellectuals are probably unhappy in their strait-jacket. But the overwhelming majority, whose material conditions have probably never been better, may well consider acceptable things as they are.[43]

Due to many factors—its alliance with Russia, its cultural tradition, its pragmatic economic policies—the Communist state had by 1963 helped to lift its people from the dregs of poverty. Another authoritarian experiment, that of Ghana, conducted under quite different conditions, has had less happy results.

Ghana: The Price of Nkrumah

> If men would but heed . . . a sense of accountability could be awakened that could result in our world becoming a happier place to live in. The astronauts say that the view from the upper regions of space is indescribably beautiful; what we need is an aroused sense of accountability—to make this earth of ours describably fairer.
>
> K. A. Busia, former leader of the
> parliamentary opposition in Ghana

Flying from Nigeria in late 1961 on an errand of social research, I approached Accra with high expectations. The Preventive Detention Act had resulted in the imprisonment of some opposition members, but I felt reluctantly prepared to be persuaded that the "exigencies of the situation" required this repression. Nigerian intellectuals had frequently expressed profound admiration for the vigor of Ghana's regime and contrasted it to what they regarded as the bumbling, compromising ineffectiveness of Nigeria's democracy. And, quite frankly, my initial exposure to Accra's superhighways, to its new ten-story buildings, and to the thoughtful efficiency of the Information Ministry (whose director later faced execution) contrasted sharply with the unorganized bustle of Lagos and Ibadan.

As I heard the popular "high-life" bands singing "Ghana is free now," I felt inclined at first to agree with the opinions expressed by so many Western liberals and socialists, that Ghana's social revolution demanded and justified a high degree of unity, even of repression. Patrick O'Donovan's comment in *The New Republic* typifies this view:

> *In Ghana, President Kwame Nkrumah is trying to achieve a revolution in a non-revolutionary situation. . . . Opposition cannot really be tolerated. Only a united and disciplined effort will work the miracle.*[44]

I soon learned to question this opinion. The revolution has, indeed, triumphed in Ghana, but its fruit was the death of individual liberty and, at best, a rather uncertain improvement in the people's material welfare.

Today political power in Ghana centers solely in the supreme leader, Nkrumah. To replace the real popularity which he had once earned from his people, Nkrumah's minions have built up a cult of personality. In 1961, for example, Tawai Adamfio (a close colleague, later jailed) composed this eulogy:

> *What is going to happen in Africa? It is to one man that everyone looks for the answer: Kwame Nkrumah . . . his name is a breath of hope and means freedom, brotherhood and racial equality; to us, his people, Kwame Nkrumah is our father, teacher, our brother, our friend, indeed our very lives, for without him we would no doubt have existed, but we would not have lived; there would have been no hope of a cure for our sick souls, no taste of glorious victory after a life-time of suffering. What we owe him is greater than the air we breathe, for he has made us as surely as he made Ghana.*[45]

On September 7, 1962, the Ghanaian parliament offered to make Nkrumah president for life. Nkrumah graciously declined the honor but only on the implied condition that "The people shall vote—for Nkrumah." [46] When, as during the 1962 assassination attempts, Nkrumah's dominance seemed endangered, he struck back with terror. The simultaneous imprisonment of Foreign Minister Ako Adjei (formerly the most "right-wing" man in the cabinet) and of Information Minister Adamfio (the most leftist) suggested the undiscriminating nature of the dictatorship. All voluntary organizations, co-operatives, and unions had been digested as corporate units of the Convention People's Party. Except for bombs, the opposition had no instruments left to express its disagreement with the regime.

In his search for unanimity, Nkrumah had suppressed all public liberties. The newspapers carried no criticism of the *Osagyefo* (the redeemer); they performed such remarkable feats of nimbleness as praising Adamfio for exiling Anglican bishops who had criticized Nkrumah's youth corps and, three days later, demanding that the same minister should be hanged since he had lost the leader's approval. The formal opposition has been gobbled up by Ghana's prisons. Some 300 to 5,000 people languished in jails. In response to the courts' "quibbling" about the legality of the Preventive Detention Act, the government crushed an independent judiciary; all judges received personal appointments from the president while the chief justice trumpeted the need to revise the law to fit the people's will. (In 1963, Nkrumah dismissed the chief justice, for he had the temerity to declare the innocence of three of Nkrumah's political opponents.) The civil service, previously the best in Africa, well-trained in the apolitical British tradition had to publicly announce its adoration for the leader. Rather unsuccessfully, the government attempted to indoctrinate every sector of the society: one of the more tragic sights in Accra was watching phalanxes of "Young Pioneers," aged twelve, chanting their oath, "Nkrumah is always right! Nkrumah will never die!"

One incident symbolizes for me the pervasiveness of Nkrumah's attack on personal privacy. With a young professor at the University of Ghana, I had been discussing Nkrumah, the role of opposition, and particularly, the disintegration of the university itself. He described the waves of fear which swept the college of its European professors and had sent most of its best Ghanaians into exile or prison. Respected college administrators had been dismissed in favor of youthful stooges whose primary duty consisted in monitoring classes for any sign of "subversion." His words ended in a strangely abrupt manner, however, when we heard a knock at the door. As a repair man entered the room and began to dismantle the telephone, my friend collapsed into frightened silence. Later, as we strolled through the beautiful Legon campus, he most unnecessarily apologized for his timidity: "You just never know these days who is an informer. I dared not talk in front of that man; he might have been a spy and these chaps get a good price for each person they report."

In sum, on the political level, Ghana was a society of fear. So far, Nkrumah has refrained from executions. When the whim took him, he could still indulge in gestures of generosity, such as the release of 130 political prisoners in July 1962. Even this relaxation carried with it the proviso that the maximum term of political imprisonment would be raised from five to twenty-five years. Since a person could spend three years in prison for voicing any criticism of the president, no one with whom I talked—from cabinet ministers, who discussed their fears privately, to taxi drivers, who defiantly displayed pictures of the Queen rather than Nkrumah in their cabs—felt themselves exempt from the threat of repression. It should come as no surprise, therefore, that someone tried to assassinate Nkrumah on August 1 and on September 9, 1962, and again on January 2, 1964. In a society festering with fear of terror, counterterror comes all too naturally.

Was this tyranny unavoidable? Was it justified by Ghana's need to pull itself loose from a swamp of poverty, illness, and ignorance? Responsible answers to such questions will indicate Ghana's future, for these issues rest at the heart of the nation's problems. Those who would apologize for Nkrumah—and there were precious few of them left among the educated in Ghana itself—contended that Ghana's social structure could not tolerate the stresses of liberal democracy. This position, I am convinced, neither reflected Ghanaian realities nor contributed to creating a truly open society in Africa.

The belief that African nations must sacrifice democracy in order to sustain a social revolution has been defended by anthropologist Stanley Diamond, among many other Western intellectuals. Diamond has contended about Ghana that colonialism destroyed the original culture, thus leaving a political void, and that the opposition party was hopelessly parochial and reactionary. He concluded that "the revolution . . . can hardly tolerate an opposition." [47] As one of Ghana's economic planners put the same argument to me: "We require a strong army and decisive internal measures to prevent the total disintegration of the nation. The opposition resorted to violence; if we wanted to prevent anarchy, we had to reply with violence. The only way to cure tribalism, to provide a sense of nationhood, lies in forging a unanimous national front, gathered around the leader."

Such an argument radically oversimplified the West African situation. Admittedly, in Ghana, the opposition party did partially draw its backing from tribal groups opposed to change. At the same time, one can hardly have labeled a party led by such progressive men as Dr. J. B. Danquah, Professor K. A. Busia, and Joe Appiah as merely a reactionary clique. While perhaps lacking in political skill, they too sought economic advance, but within a framework of decentralized political power.

Further, apologetic arguments for Ghana cast a pall of inevitability over events which were well within the scope of human choice. In Ghana's last free election in 1959, Nkrumah received 97 per cent of the vote. Exactly what implacable forces *compelled* this still immensely popular figure to impose despotism? Surely, enriched by such mass support, he could have governed the nation without resort to coercion.

The reasoning behind Ghana's dictatorship did great harm to the cause of freedom and economic progress in Africa. First, as I hope to show, Ghana in the 1960's was no less prepared for democracy than Europe at the beginning of the nineteenth century. High per-capita income, a literate educated public, undivided loyalty to the nation-state, long practice in self-government—all these supposed prerequisites of liberal democracy—did not exist in Europe as it began its transition to democracy, nor did they in the new countries of West Africa. Secondly, by any standard, Ghana had greater luck than almost any other emerging nation: at liberation it boasted of an extraordinarily high average income ($169 yearly), the best educational system in tropical Africa, and a magnificent civil service. Although tribal antagonism hampered the creation of a viable state, Nkrumah had, to his credit, welded a basic consensus by 1959 without resort to violence. His integration of traditional symbols with modern democracy could have ensured Ghana's stable evolution.

Thirdly, despite CPP claims, Ghana never seriously suffered from subversion or threats of internal violence until Nkrumah himself opened the Pandora's box of political terror. Admittedly, both the CPP and the opposition called upon strong-arm men to break up opponents' meetings, but any blame for this storm-trooper atmosphere must be laid on the CPP, for its members first used this unloved instrument. Admittedly, an abortive, clumsy attempt to murder Nkrumah may have been planned in 1959, as two out of three members of a British investigating team reported. The courts, however, could have quashed this assumed coup with dispatch under existing criminal laws; instead, Nkrumah used the incident to suspend the rule of law, dismiss dissenting judges, enact the Preventive Detention Act, and initiate mass arrests. Admittedly, Ghana consisted of a diverse collection of primitive Moslem northerners, Ashanti peasants, and Westernized southerners—a disparate collection whose allegiance to the national state may have been ephemeral. Yet, surely, Ghana's diversity did not approach that of India or Nigeria, both of which managed to create a system of checks and balances. Nkrumah, in contrast, had stripped tribal chiefs of power (by incorporating their land as part of the Crown possessions) and, in 1960, destroyed the regional assemblies which were among the few genuine sprouts of local democracy in contemporary Ghana. Thus, the attempts at assassination did not reveal "inherent" tendencies to violence. As responses to the tyranny, they could have been the work of any one of several groups: intellectuals, cocoa farmers, or workers. Nkrumah's totalitarianism may not have justified attempts at tyrannicide, but it certainly explained them.

Why did Nkrumah feel compelled to resort increasingly to totalitarian methods? Until 1959, when the terror began, Nkrumah headed a party whose commanding majority had reduced the opposition to the role of ineffectual critic. The CPP's adroit combination of modern political techniques with a clever manipulation of traditional symbols —oaths to the party chief, incantations before meetings, sacrifices of animals before an election—had a unique emotional appeal for the masses. Despite this vast support, Nkrumah destroyed the institutions of liberal democracy, with mounting and eventually frenzied attacks.

Aside from his immense megalomania, the reason lay in Nkrumah's belief, shared by his Western apologists, that an authoritarian social revolution must take precedence over democratic institutions. As he commented back in 1958, "Even a system based on social justice and democratic constitution may need backing up during the period following independence by emergency measures of a totalitarian kind. Without discipline true freedom cannot survive." [48] To judge the validity of this view that modernization cannot proceed within democratic forms, one must assess most carefully the objective progress of Ghana's revolution. Even the severest critic has to admit that the nation made some significant advances in the last decade.

Nkrumah approached the three most crucial economic problems of emerging nations—agricultural reform, extension of education, and the creation of industries which draw heavily on labor—with intelligence and a flair for innovation. In agriculture, the government conquered the swollen-shoot disease which threatened Ghana's major export crop of cocoa; it mobilized the agricultural unemployed into "Workers' Brigades" (units, modeled on the CCC, engaged in building public works and co-operative farms); it initiated some diversification of farming, thus alleviating Ghana's dangerous dependence on fluctuations of the world price for cocoa. Between 1950 and 1960, exports of bananas rose from nineteen cwt to over 28,000 cwt, tobacco increased by 300 per cent, coconuts by 500 per cent, rubber by 250 per cent, and coffee by 300 per cent. In education, during the same period of time, the primary-school population more than doubled, secondary-school pupils increased in the same proportion, and adult illiteracy was cut in half. In industry, light manufacturing units—canning, cement, timber processing—sprung up, the gleaming new port of Tema (a city of 30,000 created from a village) commenced operation, and, of course, the great Volta project entered construction. Up until 1960, per-capita income had been augmented at a modest but steady rate of some five dollars a year.

Such progress should not be dismissed lightly. Even more significant for Western liberals is the recognition that authoritarian methods facilitated and, in some cases, made possible these achievements. When persuasion failed to convince cocoa farmers of the necessity for felling some diseased trees to protect others from the swollen-shoot blight, the government introduced punitive measures and saved the cocoa crop. When Ashanti leaders demanded a confederacy, with each region having the right to spend its own income, Nkrumah anticipated that this would mean a dearth of funds for national development. He acted by dismissing regional assemblies and gathering all power to the center. When farmers protested against the Marketing Board's arbitrary reduction in prices (a measure aimed at diverting the surplus from world prices into government hands), Nkrumah responded first by announcing, untruthfully, that the farmers had "voluntarily" accepted the cut; the farmers' co-operative of 14,000 members repudiated the claim, and the government reacted by destroying the association and absorbing its remnants into the CPP. When community development officers first entered the villages, the peasants voted democratically for the projects which they wished to undertake. Typically, they chose splashy but useless projects, such as post offices in areas where no one could read. The officers dropped the façade of democratic choice and ordered the villagers to engage in economically more significant endeavors.

Each of these government actions made good economic sense; without them, Ghana might not have achieved the material progress which it has. Yet, each action involved direct government suppression of democratic choice or dissent.

This contradiction between the economic demands of modernization and the rights of opposition entered a more intense stage in 1961. Faced by a financial crisis, the government promulgated an austerity budget; imports were severely curtailed, truck and gas taxes were raised, personal income tax drastically increased and, most importantly, workers faced with a wage "pause" and a compulsory savings scheme which automatically deducted 5 per cent of their salaries. Workers in Takoradi and other areas struck in opposition. The government responded by imprisoning leaders of the "old" opposition, respected intellectuals such as J. B. Danquah, Joe Appiah, and K. K. Butu. Yet, as Irving Markovitz pointed out, an even more significant repression took place: trade union leaders and workers who had previously stood resolutely behind Nkrumah found themselves in jail for subversion.[49] Even K. A. Gbedemah, the finance minister who had introduced the budget but had, in response to the strikes, advocated moderation, fled into exile.

Again, defenders of Nkrumah argue that the pressures of the economic situation forced these Spartan measures. Sidney Lens, for example, observed ". . . give the Ghana unions such full rein, permit them to win wages as high as uncontrolled power would permit, and the revolution would founder." [50] Truly, Ghana did need the revenue which supposedly will issue from the new measures. Its foreign exchange reserves have dwindled to a new critical low, and prices for its traditionally exported commodities continue to drop. Development will stop unless the government's coffers can be replenished.

It must be admitted, however, that the nation's crisis stems, in no small part, from exactly this authoritarianism. The death of political freedom brought some immediate gains, but it also penalized the economy in ways which are only now becoming apparent.

To understand fully the price of authoritarianism, one must keep in mind the rather different stages of Ghana's economic evolution. Between 1946 and 1951, the colonial government then in power launched the first development plan. It envisaged the expenditure of some £61 million over the next ten years, primarily to establish communications and transport systems. The government set up the Cocoa Marketing Board, whereby it could buy up the entire cocoa crop and dispose of it on the world market. This device served two purposes: it gave the government a source of potential profits for investment, and allowed it to maintain internal economic stability by adjusting Ghana's cocoa sales to world price fluctuations.

In 1951, Ghanaians themselves increasingly took over the reins of political power from the British. A new development plan was announced which involved the expenditure of £74 million in some six years. This ambitious program concentrated on building roads, railways, schools, and new industries in the Tema and Volta areas. Despite a drop in world cocoa prices, this infusion of capital into the economy resulted in a steady, high rate of growth.

Beginning in 1955-56, however, the fall in cocoa prices (and a high volume of imported consumer goods) resulted in an adverse trade balance. The government, too, began to run a substantial deficit, since it refused to reduce expenditures. Finance Minister Gbedemah urged import restrictions, taxes on luxury goods, and warned, "Government expenditures . . . have to be related to the total available resources. Stability will be preserved only if there is no overstraining of those resources." [51] The left wing of the CPP did not heed Gbedemah's warnings but instead wished to step up the rate of government expenditure. In May 1961, Nkrumah removed Gbedemah and announced that government spending would be increased to a total of £119 million annually. Since government revenue did not mount at the same pace, the nation ran a budgetary deficit of £36 million that year. Rather than set its goals more modestly, the government attempted to squeeze additional money out of the people by severe domestic measures—thereby igniting strikes and rioting. The result was economic stagnation. By 1961-62, the budgetary deficit had increased to £46.7 million and, most significantly, economic growth came to a halt. An objective report on Ghana's economic condition in the early 1960's indicated that "the real rate of growth was negligible if any at all." [52]

Thus, from one point of view, the austerity budget of 1961 was a rational measure which any government *at that point in time* would have been forced to promulgate. It must also be stressed, however, that authoritarian measures and economic miscalculations largely created the chaotic economic situation which necessitated this budget.*

The economic cost of authoritarianism in Ghana can be gauged in four areas. First, since the government did not tolerate criticism of its members or policies, corruption in high circles was rampant. The gold-

* While the drop in cocoa prices certainly played a major role, the government had the means at its disposal to soften the impact on the domestic economy. As Bruce Ferguson has rightly commented, "It should be noted that a downturn in world trade might have relatively little effect on the domestic income or standard of living in Ghana, as long as the Cocoa Marketing Board could keep up the fixed payments to cocoa farmers which were the backbone of the economy. A recession was possible only when the cocoa crop was small (total payments being related to volume, not to the world price) or when Government expenditure, the other main factor in the economy, was greatly reduced." [53] Between 1957 and 1959, the opposition parties urged that cocoa reserves should be run down and invested in productive activity; the government chose instead to manage the economy on a deficit basis.

plated bed of "Crowbar" Edusei's wife only epitomized the graft which enriched all government employees. The fact that officials could escape the threat of criticism, unless Nkrumah himself intervened, opened the gates to graft. It was not uncommon for officials to possess three houses, each worth $50,000, while supposedly existing on a $3000 salary. Part of this corruption derived from the West African tradition of "dash": the custom, wholly honorable in a tribal context, of paying for the chief's services with gifts. A more important stimulus, however, came from the temptation to gain something without risk.

A second consequence of the lack of responsible criticism was that spending for nationalistic prestige proceeded unbridled. Expenditures for economically useless baubles assumed breath-taking proportions. Nkhumah purchased a $600,000 yacht and remodeled Christianborg Palace, a former slave prison, at a cost of some $6 million. Massive buildings for party units, glittering squares (some blinking with neon signs spelling Nkrumah), and a fine superhighway—leading pointlessly from the airport to Accra—blossomed throughout the city. Prestige projects received priority over more mundane activities; instead of improving the inadequate domestic transportation, for example, Nkrumah purchased a fleet of Russian jets which traversed the continent, carrying an average of two persons a flight in grand isolation. Even the new port of Tema, an economically feasible endeavor, suffered from prestige spending; to impress workers, its docks sported immense German cranes, which stood idle, since the freighters used their own equipment. From his depleted treasury, Nkrumah lent $28 million to Guinea in an attempt to ensure that nation's allegiance.

A third consequence has been the alienation of urban masses who previously adored the regime. The strikes indicated this change in attitude, but the malaise ran deeper. Not a single urban worker or merchant with whom I talked in private expressed support for Nkrumah. One dock porter, for example, voiced common complaints about loss in wages, but he also despaired of some of the government's political measures. "Did you know," he said, "that Danquah and Appiah are in concentration camps? That's not right to lock up some of our best men. I don't like all those Russians coming in either. They will try to take us over." Such dissatisfaction with the regime probably did not percolate down to the peasants (although, of course, the cocoa farmers had their own specific grievance); but widespread discontent did characterize urban people, exactly those groups whose skills, initiative, and assumption of responsibility are indispensable for economic growth.

The erosion of Ghana's elite constituted a fourth and, perhaps, the most serious price of Nkrumah's policies. The intrusion of dogmatism and terror into universities, courts, and the civil service has decimated Ghana's elite. Aside from those in prison, thousands of Ghanaians—many of them intellectuals, professionals, or technicians—fled to Nigeria, Togo, or Europe. Nkrumah attempted to replace these losses with foreign imports, but each foreigner was approximately three times as costly to employ as a Ghanaian. In contrast to pronouncements about "African independence," more foreigners than ever administered Ghana. One section of the elite, the army, maintained an apolitical role in support of the regime. Bribed with the most modern equipment —another severe drain on foreign exchange reserves—the officers remained quiescent. Nevertheless, disillusionment had begun to affect even this most solid sector of support by 1961; Nkrumah felt compelled to appoint political commissioners in every army unit to "inform" the army about its proper role. (Apparently, high police officials were implicated in the January 1964 assassination attempt against Nkrumah.)

One finds enormous difficulties, therefore, in writing a balance sheet on Ghana's economic progress or in arguing, on the basis of expediency, that the "social revolution" justified political tyranny. The disappearance of an elite, conspicuous government consumption, graft, and alienation of the urban masses had all taken a massive toll. Yet, Ghana's economic advances under authoritarian rule still tended to exceed those of her most similar neighbor, relatively democratic Nigeria. In 1961, Ghana's rates of capital accumulation and over-all growth appeared to be about one-third ahead of Nigeria's in these first years after independence, which means that, in exchange for freedom, Ghana may have purchased a slight bit more productivity.

Some still believe that this authoritarian state will wither away, once economic abundance is achieved. Perhaps. For my part, Ghana's stuffed jails, the stifling of all voluntary organizations, the collapse of the rule of law, the pervasive use of irrational indoctrination suggest, as Lewis Coser has put it, ". . . that once a totalitarian regime is in power there will be a long night." [54]

The long night has descended on Ghana. It may end, as many Ghanaians predicted to me, in Nkrumah's assassination and the army's assumption of power. Or one may cling to the tattered hope that counsels of moderation will prevail—that the CPP will realize that terror can produce Christianborg Palace, a monument to past and present slavery, but that it has never yet created a free society.

While the Ghanaian form of authoritarianism has led to relative economic stagnation, the dictatorial measures chosen by a third country, Indonesia, have literally pauperized a potentially rich region.

Indonesia: Rebels in Paradise

It's time someone spoke out. We can't all remain silent. . . .
All that we moderates can hope to do is to try to stop the situation from getting any worse. . . . I still believe in miracles. I believe that out of this chaos a young nation will grow up under wise leaders, a nation which will be ready to work and accept responsibility in the world. It will come.

SHAFRUDDIN, Ex-Prime Minister of Indonesia,
ex-president of the National Bank,
ex-president of the rebel "Republic of Sumatra"

"This last try on Sukarno's life?" The young Indonesian journalist smiled at my inquiry about the motives behind an assassination attempted in 1962. "I think it was a complete fake, rigged by Sukarno himself," he responded, "just one more way of building up the President's prestige. No extreme Moslem—and they were blamed—would shoot a man at prayer. Even the Caliphs who died from assassination were always killed after their prayers." Someone, supposedly a member of a fanatic Moslem group, had shot at Sukarno while he took part in a public prayer. The bullet missed its mark, as have many others directed at Indonesia's leader. Whether the attempt on Sukarno's life was in fact a fake, no one outside the government can really say. But it did undoubtedly increase the aura of omnipotence which already surrounded the man in 1962. Peasants took his escape from death as one more quite literal sign from heaven that God was on Sukarno's side.

Much of Indonesia's political life in the 1950's and 1960's drew its sustenance from exactly such mummery. In every field, symbols had taken precedence over economic sense. In Djakarta, the beautiful Hotel Indonesia—replete with built-in radios, air-conditioning, French cuisine, a string orchestra, and a *maître d'hôtel* from San Francisco's Mark Hopkins—dominated a city in which three million people subsisted in shacks. Many Indonesians starved while military officers munched on filet mignon in the hotel's dining room. Overhead, Soviet MIG's cracked the sound barrier, sometimes shattering the thatched roofs below. They demonstrated Indonesia's power to seize West Irian, a wasteland which had cost the Dutch millions of guilders to support.

An elegant Ministry of Atomic Science occupied one spot on the main government square in a nation possessing, at most, two engineers remotely qualified even to discuss nuclear science. The Asian Game complex of stadiums sprawled over one section of Djakarta, an area in which malaria and rickets still afflicted a high proportion of the inhabitants. Such contrasts inevitably produced a degree of skepticism among the educated minority, whether about threats on Sukarno's life or his claims of the nation's greatness.

Since 1959, Sukarno has ruled Indonesia as a guided democracy, indoctrinated with "Manipol," his manifesto which instructs the people to adhere to the spirit of revolution, establish socialism, and defend the Indonesian identity. All the people, whatever their private beliefs, have to subscribe to Manipol. Today Indonesia functions as an authoritarian regime, although its harshness has been somewhat mellowed by the gentle Javanese character and by sheer mismanagement. Indonesia has not always been a dictatorship; like Ghana the nation has conducted a flirtation with democracy. For a period after independence, Indonesia was a remarkably free society. An acute observer of Indonesia, Guy Pauker, has recorded the burgeoning of freedom between 1949 and 1955:

Half-way through its first decade of independent existence Indonesia seemed to be headed for democracy. Political activities were unrestricted beyond the norms of more mature systems . . . the Press enjoyed a freedom which was used to the point of licence. The individual felt that he lived in a free society. The rural masses experienced governments less inclined to interfere in their lives than any that had preceded them for generations. Low pressure characterized all aspects of public life in Indonesia, thus giving meaning to the slogan merdeka *[Freedom] in the name of which the struggle for independence had been fought.*[55]

Yet, the situation has now been reversed. As in so many Asian nations, the leadership has turned away from the principles of liberal democracy to embrace authoritarian rule. The downfall of democracy in Indonesia came in a brief space of years. Its nemesis lay in the nation's colonial heritage, drastic internal disunity, a series of catastrophic economic decisions, and, eventually, open revolt.

Indonesian democracy had seemed to blossom under the provisional constitution of 1950, after the new nation had finally won its independence from the Netherlands. For centuries, the Dutch had ruled the islands until Japanese conquerors routed the Europeans during World

War II. At first the Indonesians welcomed the Japanese as liberators, but they soon found that Japanese tyranny could be just as harsh as the Dutch. Nevertheless, under the Japanese they learned the unforgettable lesson that Asians could defeat Dutch forces. Further, the Japanese trained Indonesian military units for potential use against European invaders.

By 1945, Japan had capitulated, and the Indonesians felt more than ready to guide their own fate. As the globe's sixth-largest country in population, rich in resources, and as big as the United States, Indonesia appeared ripe to become an independent power. A series of unfortunate nationalistic decisions temporarily frustrated Indonesia's hope of independence and peaceful evolution. Instead of accommodating themselves to the desire for independence, the Dutch made the incredibly short-sighted decision of ordering Japanese troops to "maintain control" until Allied forces landed. When British troops came on the scene, they imprisoned the Japanese and assumed power. Indonesia's leaders, however, refused to accept this new colonial intrusion and proclaimed a republic. Lashed by guerrilla fighting, the British rearmed Japanese soldiers to fight against the republicans. Dutch troops eventually moved in, despite a peace pact with Indonesia signed in 1946. They engaged in sporadic attacks on the new government and imposed a strict naval blockade.

To the discomfiture of the Dutch, the battle continued for years, as young Indonesians—sometimes armed only with bamboo spears and homemade Molotov cocktails—managed to contain Dutch soldiers in urban areas. Wearied by a fruitless war and by liberal criticism at home, the Netherlands government finally recognized Indonesia's independence in the Hague Agreement of 1949.

Rather than pouring oil on troubled waters, the treaty created rancor among Indonesians. Among other articles, it provided that Dutch property would remain inviolate, that fifteen puppet states (separate from the Republic of Indonesia) would be recognized as sovereign, and that Indonesia would assume the huge debts of the former Dutch East Indies. The treaty also required the maintenance of Dutch civil servants in power for at least another two years. Indonesians recognized that the civil service could be of great benefit to the new nation, but Dutch actions eroded the possible good will which might have existed between the civil service and the nation. Just before the Hague Treaty took effect, the Dutch government promoted the entire Indies civil service by many ranks, thus adding an enormous burden of expanded salaries and pensions to the fiscal problems of Indonesia.

A co-operative relation between Holland and Indonesia might well have evolved if the Dutch had not so stubbornly resisted a peaceful transfer of sovereignty. After all, the Indonesian elite had been immersed deeply in Dutch culture, the country needed the Dutch civil service, and the Indonesian economy had critically important links with Holland. Each nation depended on the other. Nevertheless, Dutch actions left behind only deep resentment and a nationalism as virulent as their own.

They left behind, too, a society which was hardly equipped to bear the economic and political problems accompanying independence. Unlike the British in India or the French in Africa, the Dutch had consciously followed a policy of totally indirect rule. They made little effort to train Indonesians beyond the level required to staff menial positions. They offered the people no introduction to the institutions of modern democracy but, instead, left traditional Moslem culture relatively intact. In terms of education, if an Indonesian wished to enter the elite, he had to meet the very strict standards of Dutch universities. As Lucian Pye has noted:

> . . . There was no room for the transitional man, the man who sought to become Westernized without necessarily losing all of his traditional values. . . . For the Dutch there was no place, no recognition, for the counterpart of those within the British territories who could identify themselves with some pride of "Oxon, B.A. (failed)!" [56]

Because of stringent restrictions, very few Indonesians had the chance to receive the privileges of education. In 1940, when the population stood at 70 million, only 240 students graduated from high school and a mere 630 attended Indonesian universities.[57]

Beyond the fact that the Dutch failed to create a modernized civil service or a middle class, such as those which evolved in India, the government did all it could to encourage divisive regionalism. Following a policy of "divide and conquer," the Dutch allowed Chinese immigrants to enter retail business, but they discouraged Indonesian entrepreneurs. The government rightly believed that a Chinese middle class dependent on Dutch protection could serve as an alien buffer group between the government and the Indonesian masses. On the political level, the Dutch established new native regents, each with his own court—and all ultimately directed by a Dutch governor. "Judged strictly by the standards of good administration, such a dual system might seem clumsy," James Mossman has written, "But judged politically the system can be seen as an astute means for a foreign power to maintain its grip on a vast and diverse colonial empire by committing large sections of the native ruling class to preserving . . . the foreign power's interests." [58]

As its heritage, Dutch colonialism left bitter feelings, a dualistic system of political authority, and a population almost devoid of trained men. Partially because it allowed him to juggle conflicting interests, Sukarno retained the dualistic mode of political administration. After independence, he made it even more complicated and cumbersome. In 1961, as an illustration, Bandung was the headquarters for the governor of West Java, the regent of Bandung regency, the mayor of Bandung, and the army commander of West Java. Each official acted independently; each had large separate staffs performing overlapping functions.

After the revolution, this inept bureaucracy (which had grown to over one million people in 1963) had to rebuild the transportation system, reconstruct economic facilities, and provide essential medicines and food for a war-weary people. It also had to contend with bands of guerrilla fighters drawn from the 100,000 men who had taken to the hills in revolt against the Dutch. Many of these turned into Communist revolutionaries or simple bandits, ravaging the countryside at will. Further, irresponsible nationalists demanded the total and immediate eradication of all Dutch influence in the Indies. To no avail, moderate Indonesian leaders pointed out the country's need for skilled personnel and foreign capital. In 1957, with disastrous economic effects, Indonesia nationalized all Dutch property and ordered 46,000 Hollanders to leave the country forthwith.

In such a chaotic situation, one could hardly expect liberal institutions to operate effectively. Yet, to their credit, some Indonesian leaders did try to establish a democratic regime. In 1955, the first (and last) free election took place. Five parties emerged on top: The Nationalists (PNI), led by Sukarno, sought to establish a moderate socialist state. The Masjumi party wanted to create an Islamic-oriented nation. The Moslem Scholars (NU) were a conglomeration of religious people which aimed at a total theocracy. The Communists (PKI) received support from Javanese peasants and urban workers. The Socialist Party, led by Sjahrir, sought to establish a decentralized, "communal" form of social democracy.

These diverse groups—some of which had no respect for parliamentary institutions—were charged with the task of drafting a permanent constitution. The provisional assembly spent more than three years in debate. At the end, they could agree only on a national flag, an anthem, and a national language—but no constitution. With ample reason, Sukarno dissolved the assembly. Instead of calling for new elections, however, he and the army imposed a ban on "destructive" political activities and appointed a puppet parliament. Launched on a path of "guided democracy," Sukarno hoped to restore order and unity to a divided nation. He soon found that the promulgation of supreme decrees could not suppress dissent.

Three separate, only vaguely united revolutions challenged the continued existence of guided democracy. The first, conducted most violently between 1957 and 1962, spread terror throughout Java. The Darul Islam movement claimed that it desired a purified Moslem state. Darul Islam was actually a mob of brigands who lacked any coherent ideology, except for a desire for loot. Bandit raiders descended on Javanese villages, robbing, burning, and raping as they went. Theii leader, Kartosuwirio, planned a systematic campaign of destruction. In those regions which he commanded (including much of rural Java), opponents had little chance of survival. Among other unpleasant habits, Kartosuwirio beheaded those victims who refused him plunder. He would then carve a crescent on the corpse's chest as a warning to others.

On the Celebes and Moluccas between 1957 to 1959, the Permesta movement followed an entirely different path of violent dissension. Led by disaffected army colonels, this group aimed at greater regional autonomy of the outer islands from Java's rule, and a more equitable share of the profits from produce shipped to Djakarta. The Permesta leaders rejected the greed, disorder, and dictatorship of "guided democracy" as well as what they considered Javanese imperialism. At first ardently supported by the people of their islands, the Permesta declared its independence from Djakarta.

In 1958, a third—and most significant—revolt emerged in Sumatra. Its leaders included Shafruddin, a liberal leader of the old republic; Oatsir, former head of the Masjumi party; members of the Socialist party; and various dissident army commanders such as Colonels Kawilarang, Simbolon, and Jambek. These men had all played heroic roles in the fight against Dutch rule; the traditionalists among them looked to the revolution as a means of restoring lost liberties. James Mossman, one of the few correspondents who covered the Sumatran revolt, has well summarized their basic attitude:

When the revolution swept the nobility away, many of the new leaders spoke of the rediscovery of an older, more truly Indonesian order; a golden age, when the peasants had stood firmly on the ground of their liberties and the economy had been varied and vital. . . . The democratic spirit [was] not new to Indonesia. Before the Dutch arrived, society in both Sumatra and Java was only mildly authoritarian. The peasants had powerful customary rights which the native aristocracy dared not challenge. . . . To restore these liberties, said the traditionalists, men who had never even experienced them had fought and died in the war against the Dutch. . . . We fought, they said, not simply to be free of the Dutch, but to restore the lost liberties to the regions and to all Indonesians as individuals. It seemed to them to be this aspect of the revolution that Sukarno had betrayed.[59]

Whether of a secularist or traditionalist orientation, the Sumatran rebel leaders united in their opposition to communism, in their desire for a federalist union based on village democracy, and in their disgust with Sukarno's increasing assumption of personal power and glory. The movement drew mass support from Sumatrans, who may have been only vaguely aware of the leaders' ideology, but who felt a deep distrust over Javanese dominance. They had sound economic reasons for their displeasure with Indonesia's central government, for Sumatra produced 71 per cent of the nation's foreign exchange but received only a pittance in return for development and welfare. Until 1961, the rebel movement held effective control of the gigantic island of Sumatra.

During the Sumatran revolt, the United States played an ambiguous, ineffectual role. According to rumor, the CIA dropped small-arms supplies to the rebel government. In a curiously bungling fashion, these supplies were sufficient to infuriate Sukarno, but too little to turn the tide of battle. The rebels pleaded for more help. Three jet fighter planes, they said, could have ensured the movement's success. America —so rumor has it—provided only five outmoded Mitchell Bombers through the good graces of Chiang Kai-shek but refused the jet fighters.

Debate about America's policy in 1958 and 1959 is pointless. Whatever the "might-have-beens" of history, the rebel government—the last powerful source of liberal democracy in Indonesia—collapsed in 1961. Central government troops routed the rebels and led Shafruddin, the rebel leader, to swear a humiliating oath to Sukarno as the "great leader of the revolution." All the most prominent rebels on Sumatra followed suit in this submission, except for a few army commanders who still held out in 1964, fighting a lost cause of guerrilla warfare.

Sukarno had also broken the back of the Permesta movement by late 1961. A tight blockade had enfeebled the economies of the Celebes and the Moluccas. Resultant austerity measures alienated the people from Permesta goals and sapped their will to fight against invasions by the central government's crack Suliwangi division. By 1964, a few scattered units still held their ground in the Celebes, but most Permesta leaders had submitted to Sukarno's will.

Sukarno, backed by his immensely able chief of staff, General Nasution, next turned his attention to the Darul Islam bandits. Fortunately for Indonesia, the government apparently destroyed these terrorists. Reports circulated in Djakarta in July of 1962 that Kartosuwirio, his "finance minister," and the band's major leaders had surrendered. The government's flair for exaggeration created some doubts about the story—I was repeatedly advised in 1962 not to travel at night over country roads for fear of Darul Islam—but at least the bandits no longer caused quite the terror they did in the past.

All who look to Indonesia's welfare welcomed the decline of Darul Islam. The defeat of the "Republic of Sumatra" and of "Permesta," however, served only to smother military rebellions, not to redress the economic and political grievances which prompted them. By geography and history, Indonesia is a highly decentralized area. Military force can impose an artificial unity, but it does not cure persistent longings for greater regional autonomy and individual liberty.

Any conscious policy aimed at some degree of regional autonomy— —so necessary in this ethnically and religiously divided archipelago— had been scrapped by 1964. The central government appointed regional governors who often came from the dominant group of their area, but who had (on paper) no independent power. Freedom of speech existed only to the degree that the state machinery, as it often did, failed to apply sanctions with efficiency. Many people languished in jail for political crimes. Estimates of the number of political prisoners ranged from 100 to over 5000. However small the actual number of political convicts, the threat of imprisonment sufficed to create an air of fearful caution. Troops thronged the streets, and thus spread an impression of force and arrogance which profoundly disturbed not only Indonesia's thin stratum of intellectuals but much of the peasantry, too.

Thus, Indonesia today has become an authoritarian regime, dominated—although hardly governed—by one man and the army. Despite his slogans, Sukarno has taken no action to build the institutional base of a liberal society. All decisions—and tragically few were made—percolated down to the local level from Sukarno's palace. And caught in

Indonesia's strange mixture of dictatorship and anarchy, the local war-lords can ignore or even countermand Djakarta's injunctions.

While Indonesia may be considered as an oligarchic regime headed by a charismatic figure and backed by military might, it has not become a truly totalitarian society. Many factors hindered the development of an untrammeled regime of terror. For one, the technical facilities available to the government did not permit total control. The barely developed mass media, the sheer lack of communications between hundreds of islands, and the uncertain loyalty of Indonesia's army prohibited totalitarianism. In addition, the Indonesian character —if one may be permitted to call upon an abused, but still useful, stereotype—emphasizes gentleness, humor, politeness, and dignity. These traits, when honored by a whole people, play havoc with the creation of a totalitarian regime. Also, during the 1960's the political balance of power trembled so delicately in the scale of history that, as one official told me, "We cannot apply thoroughgoing coercion, for the enemies of today may be our bosses tomorrow." Because no one in power could predict the future, the political prisons of eastern Java more closely resembled summer resorts than concentration camps. Most prisoners apparently lived under a tolerant, even indolent, "house arrest."

The balance of power today shifts uneasily between the Communists, the army, and Sukarno. The Communists largely control urban workers and a significant section of the peasantry on Java and in southern Sumatra. Undoubtedly, they could win free elections, if they are ever held. Communist "Houses of Solidarity" stand prominently in the center of almost every Javanese village. While prejudice against the Chinese continues and the abortive attempts of Communists to gain control in the 1940's has not been forgotten, the Communist party— inspired by Mao's dictums about the relation of the peasantry to revolution—has made decisive inroads into the rural population.

The army, on the other hand, wields more or less effective military control over all the islands. By defeating the various revolutions, the loyal section of the army has gained in prestige, morale, and of course, in experience. The army's leaders, such as General Nasution, speak in terms of national unity and use mildly pro-Western language. In all probability, the army's primary opposition to the growing Communist movement stems not so much from ideology as from a desire to retain its close control over the richer sections of the economy. After nationalization of the economy in 1957, army officers assumed direction of factories and plantations. Today, like story-book capitalists, they earnestly defend their prerogatives against the encroachment of other forces. As Guy Pauker observed the transformation of Indonesia's army in 1962:

> A self-denying group of young revolutionaries, modest and egalitarian in spirit, who took to arms and uniforms for the sake of a nationalist ideal are now turning into middle-aged militarists, enjoying the perquisites of office, symbols of status, and benefits of power . . . the officer corps of Indonesia is deeply divided, within the branches of the armed forces as well as among them, by personal jealousies, conflicting outlooks, and special interests.[60]

Ruling over the two factions of Communists and army officers, adroitly playing one against the other, Sukarno retains shaky control over Indonesia. At times, he throws the Communists a bone. During the period of nationalization, many Communists received ministerial portfolios, and the party had full freedom in the press—and in the streets. At other times, the army received his nod. In 1962, in a presumed bid for American support over the West Irian issue, Sukarno dismissed Communist cabinet members and replaced them with army men (loyal to Nasution) or nationalists (loyal to Sukarno himself).

It will always remain something of a mystery why Sukarno maintains his influence—as do the explanations of Napoleon's, Caesar's, or Hitler's hypnotism of their peoples. Perhaps Sukarno exercises his power because he has come to symbolize an ideal blend of the modern and the traditional. He paid homage to religion, he took several wives in the best sultanic way, he spoke with emotion of Indonesian culture —and simultaneously he talked of socialism, heavy industry, and modernization. "Bung" (Brother) Karno has become an almost unchallengeable folk-hero, whose surprisingly frequent escapes from assassination deified him in villagers' minds.

While proclaiming his desire for industrialization within a socialist framework, Sukarno apparently had no understanding of how such development could be accomplished. One of his colleagues told me, "Bung Karno hates Keynes, he loves big buildings—here his knowledge of economics ends."

This disdain for rational economic policies has brought Indonesia today to the brink of catastrophe. While the government refuses to release official statistics, unofficial estimates indicated that prices had risen one thousand per cent between 1960 and 1963, brutally striking at exactly those groups whose involvement in a market economy would normally qualify them as the elite of modernization. Foreign exchange reserves had fallen to only $10 million in 1962 and, while the government talked sternly about import restrictions, favored officals had little difficulty in buying luxury foreign cars. A dollar in Djakarta, officially pegged at 45 rupiahs, could easily fetch 1000 rupiahs in the black market.

Fiscal anarchy was accompanied by breakdown in transportation and distribution systems. Ten freighters sat in Djakarta harbor in 1962 waiting to transport troops to West Irian, while the economy of the outer islands ground to a halt for want of supplies. As a result, rubber plantations in the Celebes lacked shipments of ammonium necessary for their processes. And on Sumatra, workers went on permanent strike, since shipping had failed to bring the rice which was normally utilized as their wages. Famine struck certain islands, while on others food rotted on idle docks.

Hampered by a lack of supplies, by the inefficiency and corruption of its managers, Indonesia's few factories produced at 50 per cent of capacity. Export sectors of the economy were particularly hard-hit. In 1940, Indonesia had been the world's third-largest producer of sugar; by 1963, production had dropped 66 per cent, and the nation had to expend its meager foreign currency to import sugar. Almost all other aspects of Indonesia's economy suffered an equivalent decline. Since 1940, rubber production has dropped 25 per cent, coffee 50 per cent, tobacco 60 per cent, and copra 75 per cent. For Indonesia, guided democracy has meant a great leap backward.

This breakdown did not originate in any inherent economic weakness, for Indonesia has been richly endowed by nature. The demise of Indonesia's economy has to be traced to the nation's social structure, particularly its political situation. As in Ghana, the authoritarian system itself has to bear much of the blame:

(1) The internal revolts, largely ignited by Sukarno's desire to centralize power in his personage, ravaged the economy.

(2) Unchecked by institutionalized criticism, Sukarno followed a policy of conspicuous national spending on useless luxuries. He built the world's biggest mosque, purchased jet airliners, and bought a variety of other tinseled monuments. While the market economy collapsed, Sukarno frittered away capital on prestige symbols.

(3) Military adventures, encouraged by Sukarno, further depleted the economy. The battle over West Irian represented one such indulgence. Whatever the legal justifications, the squabble over a stone-age territory (which cost the Dutch more to support than it returned

to the Netherlands) represented a very costly exercise in national pride. And, in 1963, the Indonesian navy spent its energies blockading Singapore in a display of anger over the formation of Malaysia. While this use of force hurt Singapore's trade, it also deprived the Indonesian people of vitally needed imports, particularly medicines.

(4) Wastes of the nation's economy characterize every aspect of current Indonesian life. During the West Irian crisis, as just one example, the army commandeered the Bank of Indonesia's fleet of trucks to carry spectators to the flamboyant Asian games. As a result, bank employees could not come to work, and the national financial system stopped functioning. But the circuses went on.

(5) The dictatorship's ill-considered policy of socialism, mixed with anti-Chinese prejudice, further hindered Indonesian development. The 1957 nationalization of Dutch property may have been emotionally satisfying to Indonesia's elite, but it crippled the nation. As we have noted, the Dutch bore much of the guilt, since they had reserved all "managerial" posts (even that of mailmen!) for European immigrants. Nevertheless, the fact remained that Indonesia by itself could not provide the personnel to service an industrial economy. Army people took over the nationalized industries, but they could hardly create the clerks, let alone the managers, to run Indonesia's economy efficiently. Despite the realities of economic life, the government proceeded to chase out the Dutch.

On top of this badly advised policy of nationalization, Sukarno mounted a campaign against the Chinese middle class. Waving aloft banners of socialism and "Indonesia for the Indonesians," the government forced the Chinese to emigrate or to try to recoup their fortunes by entering fields other than trade. Both Communist and Nationalist China protested the prejudiced actions of the government, but their complaints had no effect. Temporarily at least, the government forced Chinese merchants to quit retail and distribution businesses. Since the Chinese, like many alien groups in today's emerging countries, represented an invaluable pool of talent, their decimation created more economic problems than it solved.

(6) Another element in the Indonesian crisis of the 1960's is governmental corruption. Since no court or legislature can effectively question the ruling group's actions, almost everyone in the elite takes his private slice of the public cake. A chauffeur driving one of Djakarta's new, government-owned Mercedes taxis, once asked me, "Why do you think the word 'taxi' is just painted on the back window?" When I admitted that I did not know, he smiled slyly and said, "As soon as the Asian

Games are over, the officers will take over these cars. They can erase the taxi sign easily and use the car as their own." In 1962, no one expected that the officers would pay for their Mercedes; it just "wasn't done."

Again and again, one ran into corruption. A merchant, flying with me on Garuda, the nationalized airline, explained the textile market's operation: "I buy cloth from government factories very cheaply, after paying the customary bribe. Since the government wants to encourage Indonesian business (rather than Chinese), I get it easily. Then, I hide it. When the next crisis comes and people want clothes, I sell it for eight times the cost." This man salted away his handsome profits in Hong Kong banks.

On one other instance, I talked with a French salesman who was attempting to sell some Caravelle jets to the Indonesian government, which already had lost a fortune on its American-built Electras. While he was an engineer whose job was simply to explain the technical superiority of the Caravelle, he had a special assistant whose sole occupation was to bribe the proper officials within the government. Probity was unknown, since no institution could enforce it.*

If a free press, a vigilant opposition, and an independent judiciary existed, much of the corruption, economic irresponsibility, and militarism of the regime might have been held in check.

Theoretical solutions to Indonesia's crises abound in the 1960's. With eminent rationality, Indonesia's eight-year plan places the resumption of export production and the achievement of self-sufficiency in food and clothing at the head of its priorities—yet no one in the chaos believes that the plan will be fulfilled. The government has announced its intention to "transmigrate" some of Java's 66 million people from this most crowded spot on earth to virgin areas—but the transport of each person to another island costs $250, a sum which the government cannot mobilize. In consequence, the birth rate on Java exceeds by ten times the number of émigrés to less populated areas. Sukarno has established a commission to serve as a watchdog over civil service corruption, but no one seriously believes that this group, bereft of real power, can end government and army graft. The National Planning Council has announced admirable goals to transform rural life. Each village by 1969 should have a library, clinic, school, mosque, and co-operative—but the ministry charged with this task was filled with

* Only the Communist party seemed above suspicion. As one person told me in 1962, "Just the Communist members of parliament give up the big cars, the Mercedes and Cadillacs. They drive through the streets on bicycles and motor scooters. The people see this. The Communists will win!"

young students who had no experience at all in community development.

Solutions exist, but their implementation would require a profound reorientation of the government. If Sukarno and his followers would take a few steps toward the realization of democracy, a healing air of opposition and criticism could prevent some of the more blatant mistakes of the regime. If the outer islands could achieve some relative autonomy, the resulting decentralization of power would promote greater realism in the formation of national policy and lessen the intense antagonism felt toward the Javanese. If, after the West Irian affair, the government would renounce similar adventures, Indonesia's resources could be devoted to the realization of the eight-year plan.

Today few observers of the Indonesian scene are willing to take odds that such a transformation will actually occur. Indonesia's few genuine democrats—who are most numerous among the younger intelligentsia—lack an organized social base or military support. The Communists have great popularity but no desire to end the chaos before the advent of their own utopia. And the army, while representing a potential source of modernizing talent, is riddled with corruption and exhibits little eagerness to relinquish its fat place in the *status quo.*

Indonesia, then, represents one of the world's most relevant examples of authoritarianism's failure: "guided democracy" has neither promoted economic growth nor has it evolved a new, higher form of democracy. An unpropitious combination of historical circumstances (as well as disastrous decisions by the Dutch and Indonesian leadership) has subverted Indonesia's democratic traditions and all but ruined a potentially affluent economy. In the short run, Sukarno's form of authoritarianism may prevail, but its continuing failure to mobilize a national consensus behind its goals eventually dooms it. As Guy Pauker has predicted:

> *Political oscillations of increasing amplitude have led to the establishment of a personal dictatorship backed by the military. This coalition of forces may seem to bring to a temporary halt the motions of the body politic, but far from solving basic problems, it is likely to make the underlying pressure more explosive and the formulation of solution of lasting value more difficult or even impossible.*[61]

In the foreseeable future, the army or the Communists might succeed for a time in imposing a stricter, more brutal regime. A truly totalitarian rule, á la China, could not be sustained in Indonesia, for it would prove extraordinarily difficult to reconcile the demands of dictatorship with Indonesia's ancient democratic traditions, its geographic diversity, its cultural pluralism, and the people's character. In the long run, only a polity which recognizes Indonesia's inherent pluralism, welcomes dissent, and allows a decentralization of power conforming to the islands' natural divisions can ensure the nation's stable evolution.

The Inadequacies of an Authoritarian Solution

> When societies first come to birth, it is the leaders who produce the institutions of the republic. Later, it is the institutions which produce the leaders.
>
> MONTESQUIEU

History has granted the new nations, particularly those which have most recently won independence, an almost unique opportunity. Their leaders may start a new body politic. They may create economic and political institutions which the world has never known. Like the Founding Fathers in America, Mao, Sukarno, Nehru, Nasser, and other new leaders have had enormous, although not unlimited, latitude to build societies which offer food, freedom, and hope to their people.

Unfortunately, many of these charismatic heroes have chosen to follow a path already well trodden in the past: by the Wang Mangs, Caesars, Bismarcks, Hitlers, and, indeed, the old colonialists. The ideologists of the most recent wave of authoritarians affix fancy labels to old techniques. Today, dictatorship hides under such appelations as a "people's," "guided," or "tutelary" democracy. Slogans, however, cannot conceal the facts. As they have for thousands of years, generals, redeemers, emperors, or "chairmen"—all-too-mortal in their decisions—enforce their will over the people with coercion and indoctrination. And as ever, the frustrations of human existence provide a sufficient number of true believers who think that *this* time the millennium has arrived and all will turn out for the best.

Current trends offer scant justification for such hopes. The recent histories of Indonesia, Ghana, and China can give little, if any, substantiation to the claims put forth by contemporary authoritarians in emerging nations or by their sympathizers in the West. After having reviewed three species of authoritarian rule as it operates in practice, we are in some position to measure authoritarian generalizations against reality:

First, is it true that the exigencies of economic development require the establishment of a central state armed with dictatorial powers? Does such an authoritarian regime give more hope than a liberal polity to those societies launched into the storms of development?

China's experience, at least until 1960, appeared on the surface to lend credence to authoritarian presumptions, for it seemed apparent that dictatorial rule had finally freed the Chinese from starvation. If Mao and his men do not repeat the mistakes of the "Great Leap Forward"—or worse, commit the majestic errors which Perón did in his attempt to industrialize Argentina forcefully—one can hope that the richly fertile economy of China will fulfill its promise. Nonetheless, to generalize from China to the majority of emerging nations, to argue that they should all adopt totalitarian methods, would be a superficial and dangerous assertion.

It must be remembered that the Chinese people, like those of Meiji Japan, had long submitted themselves to the discipline and terror of dictatorship. To their advantage, the Communist elite had at its disposal a society already cowed by centuries of despotism. Most emerging peoples, in contrast, have a proud tradition of liberty (partially derived from the Western Enlightenment, most of it inherited from prior centuries of self-government). Would an Ibo in Nigeria, lacking even a concept of chieftancy, accommodate himself to a "God-Emperor"? Would the village republics of India permanently surrender sovereignty to a single, overarching ruler? Would Bolivian tin miners let their union become simply one more organ of an all-powerful party? I doubt it, *if* they had any informed role in the decision. A political system has to adhere more or less closely to a nation's dominant culture, if it is to survive permanently. China and a few other countries have never tasted the sweetness of freedom, but for most of the world, indigenous political and social relationships do not conform to a totalitarian model.

We must raise a further question about China's economic advances: Did totalitarian methods, "the elimination of freedom of thought for the few," really play a significant role in China's material progress? Conventionally, most commentators assume that China's improvement could not have been accomplished without the extermination of millions of "counterrevolutionaries." Yet, as we have noted, most objective scholars attribute China's success to specific, flexibly applied *economic* policies—a high rate of investment, mobilization of rural masses as the spearhead of advance, an emphasis on small-scale industry, education, and agriculture—all measures which do not, in and of themselves, require totalitarianism. Indeed, China's strictly economic policies for attaining growth resemble those of nineteenth-century, democratic

Denmark as much as those of Stalin's Russia. The Chinese achieved a faster rate of growth (until 1960) than did the Danish, but after all, China had many economic advantages: more abundant resources, foreign aid, virgin land, larger markets, experience with industrialization, and close collaboration with another large nation. The question cannot be answered dogmatically, but there seems a real possibility that China's growth should be attributed to sensible economic policies which could be followed with almost equal ease by a free nation as by a terrorist regime.

Even in China's case, therefore, we must be highly cautious in assuming that any direct relationship exists between economic growth and the use of authoritarian methods.

When one examines authoritarian rule in Ghana and Indonesia, the scaffolding of those who desire dictatorship becomes even shakier. Ghana's despotism has helped some of the people economically but has now entered a stage of stagnation. In Indonesia, a personal, military tyranny has ravaged the economy, while similar regions like the Philippines and Malaysia have forged ahead, even though they have been handicapped by internal revolts and the supposed burden of democratic constitutions. A comparison of Indonesia and the Philippines redounds to the advantage of a democratic approach; the more popular pairing of India and China purports to show the superiority of an authoritarian solution.

Such comparisons suggest that *the success of a drive for economic growth depends not on the degree of political coercion involved but rather on the unique culture of the nation and on particular economic policies followed by the government in power*. An authoritarian regime, as in China, may possibly aid in stimulating economic advance; it may, as in Indonesia, cause a potentially irrevocable depression. A democratic polity may make economic mistakes, but they seldom have the permanent effect of errors committed by a dictatorship.

At the very minimum, an unbiased observer has to conclude that authoritarianism provides no panacea for poverty. Even if they ignore the human sacrifices involved, leaders in emerging nations should hesitate to adopt strong-arm methods. Certain potential economic dangers are an inherent part of any politically authoritarian system:

First, a government which controls all capital, all natural resources, and all labor can expend them in any fashion it wishes. Sometimes, such an authoritarian state makes wise decisions, as in China between 1949 and 1960. At other times, like Sukarno's, the regime can fritter away the "riches of the Indies." Inevitably, an unleashed authority will make some economically foolish decisions. What then will happen if all dissent, all counterbalancing institutions have been systematically eliminated? The significance of the problem has been well stated by African scholars Susan and Peter Ritner, who view the growth of one-party states with apprehension:

> Sooner or later the acting government, the Founder or Deliverer, the single party, the elite, the what-have-you—sooner or later he or they must stumble, lose their grip, and when their hour strikes the helm of affairs will need to be plucked from their hands. There exists no doctrine, no party, no charismatic hero, no scientific management, no all-knowing it or they which infallibly can plan economic, social, and political policy which is forever selfless, tireless, incorruptible.[62]

A second danger in the authoritarian approach—particularly in those societies unhabituated to the rigors of dictatorship—is that the more pressure a government applies, the less realistic its sources of information become. In the emerging countries, where some degree of economic planning has to be maintained, a lack of reliable intelligence on the state of the economy can have dire results in the formation of policy. In Indonesia, for example, rational planning cannot take place, since factory managers falsify their reports, merchants hide their profits, and the peasantry refuses to report the full extent of its produce. Distrust of the state machinery, bred by coercion, can lead to economic breakdown.

Third, in the disunited situation characteristic of most developing countries, authoritarian coercion can drain the people's initiative and lead to direct economic sabotage of the system. In Ghana and Indonesia, disaffected elements antagonized by state policies ignore or countermand the state's directives. Thus, a significant proportion of Indonesia's produce is smuggled to the Philippines and Singapore, rather than sent through the central government's export outlets. In Ghana, since strikes have been forbidden, workers' "slow-downs" hamper production, and cocoa farmers avoid government restrictions by smuggling their product to other countries.

A fourth, long-term danger—one which it is difficult to gauge without historical perspective—is that the perpetuation of an authoritarian system can stifle the spirit of inventiveness and innovation so necessary to economic growth. Already, Ghana has lost much of her entrepreneurial talent, and Indonesia has decimated her Chinese "middle sector." China has rid herself of many of her most creative intellectuals. No one can foretell the eventual effects of these repressive policies, but it seems reasonable to speculate that the loss of innovative leadership, exactly at the moment when it was most needed, will badly hurt these economies.

Solely in terms of economic performance, the record of authoritarianism does not lend itself easily to the contention that total political control over a society represents the soundest approach to economic development.

The second defense of authoritarian rule postulates that new nations are so chaotic and disunited that only a dictatorship can provide a solid barrier against anarchy. Certainly, even the briefest glance at India or Bolivia, Ghana or Indonesia indicates that these regions do suffer from intensely divisive forces. And in a few areas, such as the Congo, it is probable that only military rule suffices to maintain a minimum degree of order.

The Congo is not, however, a typical representative of new nations. As we have noted, in some countries the belief that a "state of emergency" justifies exceptional measures is specious. Despite overwhelming, freely given support from his people, Nkrumah chose to impose a dictatorial strait jacket on Ghana. History did not force his hand. In this case and many others, the leadership had won decisive approval from the great majority of their people. What national good was served by persecuting a minority opposition?

Further, in those states where a national consensus has not emerged, there seems little warrant for believing that suppression of dissent will do more than push it underground. Forbidding opposition does not extinguish it—at least, not until many years have passed. The opposition only modifies the form it takes, and, usually, this means a turn to violence, as in Ghana and Indonesia. As Edward Shils has commented, after reviewing the problem of consensus in new states:

> *Totalitarianism depends on organized force at the center and demands enthusiastic conformity in untraditional practices in a large part of the society. There is no reason to believe that a totalitarian oligarchy can create this social unity better than any other type of regime can. It can undoubtedly create the* appearance *of unity better than a more democratic regime can, but it cannot do any better in the creation of the reality.*[63]

As for the final argument—that somehow a "new" form of democracy will be spawned out of contemporary authoritarianism—one can hardly put a great deal of faith in this claim. Despite talk of the internal democracy of the single party, the fact remains that when real disagreement has been voiced, the authoritarian state quickly stifles it. When Ghanaian workers disagreed with government wage policies, or Chinese students requested an iota of free thought, or Indonesians demanded greater autonomy for the outer islands, the façade of democracy disappeared and the single party cracked its whip as effectively as possible. No "new" free constitutional forms have yet appeared in emerging countries, and it would be foolish to hope that a ruling elite will relinquish power, once having enjoyed its rewards.

Too many people in the emerging countries cling to the hope that the "invisible hand" of modernization will in its own right produce political freedom in some indefinite future. Some look to industrialization, others to education as the magical propellants of new constitutional forms. Such an argument conveniently overlooks the evolution of Germany and Japan, where industrialization certainly did not lead to democratic attitudes. As Henry Kissinger has aptly written:

> . . . industrialization, rather than producing democracy, may remove the economic incentive for it. When the government does not impede economic development but systematically encourages it, the more enterprising members of society, far from opposing the existing system, will identify themselves with it. . . . In both Germany and Japan industrialization was achieved by an alliance of industrialists and the landed aristocracy. In both countries the managerial group proved more interested in nationalism than in liberalization. The success of economic development enhanced the prestige of the form of government promoting it.[64]

Again, the spread of education cannot be counted on as a force promoting a spirit of free inquiry. Education can lead to independent political judgment, to skepticism, and to reflection about the nature of freedom and authority. But in a society where the government controls publications, hires only politically reliable teachers, and encourages strictly vocational training, education becomes just one more instrument for indoctrination.

All of this suggests that developing societies are not in some "transitional" political stage where dictatorship will just evaporate, once modernization has been achieved. On the basis of contemporary experience, we have no reason to believe any of the authoritarian claims:

(1) Centralized, repressive states have yet to demonstrate that their *political* approach—regardless of the culture or economy upon which it is imposed—will produce an affluent utopia.

(2) Authoritarian states, as a general rule, have not been any more

successful than liberal polities in resolving the internal disunities which characterize new nations. Suppression *may* produce surface unity but it can also lead to bombings, violent revolts, and economic sabotage.

(3) The "total state" exhibits little inclination to evolve into a new, higher form of democracy. As Montesquieu knew, institutions, once firmly anchored in the social body, do not easily lose their grip.

If the authoritarian approach does not offer a high road to bread and freedom, what path can be followed? No one has an infallible answer, but, if anywhere, solutions should be sought in historical data—particularly in the first springtime of freedom which the world experienced a century ago.

XI

THE FIRST SPRINGTIME OF FREEDOM: EUROPE

I should have loved freedom, I believe, at all times, but the time in which we live I am ready to worship it.
ALEXIS DE TOCQUEVILLE, 1857

"We may evolve a truly democratic society in Poland," a Communist leader, high in the power elite of the nation, told me in 1961. "But first, we must accomplish the social revolution. We must destroy the old forces and lay an economic base for a new society. As economic development occurs and stability increases, personal liberties will be protected. Only economic stability can create democracy."

We sat in his office at the top of the rococo Palace of Arts and Sciences, and mused over Poland's future as twilight encased Warsaw that October evening. As a member of the hundred-man Party Secretariat, he held direct responsibility for the country's economic development, after Poland's almost total destruction by Germany. And as a person nurtured on Western culture, he felt a deep commitment to the cause of individual liberty. "But," he commented, "we cannot repeat the nineteenth-century pattern of evolution by gradually developing the forms of parliamentary democracy. We must forge our own new path to the liberation of man."

Like his comrades, this director of Poland's fate privately admitted the failure of Marxism as a general theory of history. Nonetheless, he clung to certain elements in the Marxist-Leninist conception of social change. He believed, for example, that a beneficent elite would eventu-

247

ally relinquish power to the people, once the stage of "true" communism had been reached. And he portrayed liberal democracy as merely another weapon in the hands of the bourgeois class. For him, the unfolding of democracy in the eighteenth and nineteenth centuries served only as a negative model, one which contemporary Eastern Europe could not and should not emulate.

Two months later, I talked with the parliamentary leader of Ghana's Convention People's party in Accra's government compound. Although not a Communist, his words strangely echoed the Warsaw conversation. In justifying Ghana's political repression (much more severe than Poland's), he argued that certain conditions which he assumed characterized England in the nineteenth century could not be duplicated in Ghana. "Clearly, when Europe built her form of democracy, she had distinct advantages over us: a high level of industrialization, abundance, and literacy; a well-educated, sophisticated public imbued with a sense of national unity, practiced in the arts of deference as well as in self-government." He justified the Ghanaian dictatorship by the implicit theory that democracy resembles an orchid, which can grow only under rare conditions. He contended that Ghana's level of socioeconomic development did not have this very special kind of fertility.

In a not wholly articulate fashion, both the Ghanaian and the Pole operated on the basis of a theory—a view of the necessary conditions for establishing a liberal polity. On the foundation of certain historical generalizations, they have set their course. Their first job, they believe, consists in creating the proper base for democracy by the expedient instrument of dictatorship.

At all times, a nation's policy rests upon implicit or explicit sociological generalities of this type. In Ghana and Poland, a philosophy of social change—quite sincerely held, I believe—has condoned authoritarian rule as a temporary but necessary first stop en route to "real" democracy. How valid is the widely-held conviction that underdeveloped nations lack the social and economic prerequisites for a liberal political system? We can answer such a question, if at all, only by turning to history.

It is necessary to analyze carefully those conditions which in the past have preceded the building of stable liberal societies, for history serves as our only possible guide to the future. As Lord Acton wrote, "The recent Past contains the key to the present time. All forms of thought that influence it come before us in their turn, and we have to describe the ruling currents, to interpret the sovereign forces, that still govern and divide the world. . . ." [1]

The Social Origins of a Liberal Polity: The Case of Europe

> The events in Holland and Switzerland, in England and America
> are the most important events in modern history.
>
> IMMANUEL KANT

As Lord Acton recognized, the nineteenth century marked the first
time that "man consciously sought liberty," not only in the religious
realm but legally, politically, and socially. The events in the seventeenth, eighteenth, and nineteenth centuries were truly unique in world
history. Previously, dogmatism and despotism ruled the earth, stifling
diversity and criticism. The American and French revolutions symbolized the beginnings of an entirely different political order. "It was a
new and revolutionary civilization," Hans Kohn has remarked, "based
upon the belief in the equal rights of all, irrespective of religions, an-
cestry or class; upon the concern for the dignity and humanity of every
individual; and upon the right to intellectual and political opposition
and criticism." [2] No other society evolved such a panoply of rights and
privileges as did Western civilization during this era. No other civilization has yet equaled the Western achievement. Indeed, emerging nations today still live on the political ideas developed in this epoch. For
this reason, I propose to examine the European experience as the classic
historical instance of the transition from an authoritarian to a liberal
polity, as the first springtime of freedom.*

Rooted in earlier periods but sweeping to triumph in the nineteenth
century, the ideas of liberal democracy became the basis for a new political structure in a handful of European nations: England, the Scandinavian countries, Switzerland, the Lowlands, and, more shakily,
France. The advance toward a more open, liberal society moved

---

* Discussion of the paths followed by America, Canada, and Australia is generally irrelevant in this context, for their histories are so unique. Although
Seymour Lipset has drawn some interesting comparisons between these areas
and England, none of their patterns seems applicable to the challenges faced
by contemporary nations.[3] America during its colonial period cannot be treated
as a "new nation" in the same sense as contemporary Ghana, Indonesia, or
India. Blessed with unlimited frontiers, the absence of tradition, and the lack
of a feudal elite, America and Australia did not have to face traditionalist opposition. As historian Louis Hartz has ably demonstrated, these nations were in
a sense "born free." [4] In contrast, liberal forces in eighteenth- and nineteenth-
century Europe confronted challenges from the old aristocracies resembling
those faced by progressive movements in contemporary developing states.

roughly through three stages. First, the old elites granted legal democracy (equality for all under the rule of law, with protections for religious and other forms of dissent). Secondly, more and more people in northwestern Europe achieved the privileges of political democracy. Establishment of a competitive political system and extension of the franchise ultimately promoted a greater "circulation of elites." Thirdly, in the 1880's and 1890's, social democracy emerged, as the movement toward universal education, minimum social security, and the broadening of economic opportunity gained increasing impetus.

Yet, this evolution was confined to only parts of Europe. Other nations in the nineteenth century—Russia, Italy, Spain, Germany, the Austro-Hungarian Empire—failed to develop the full framework of a liberal polity or did so only briefly. What elements allowed some countries to make this leap into freedom while others could not?

Recent efforts to explain this difference—a contrast of tragic importance for the twentieth century—fall into four general theories: those which stress the role of economic affluence, those which emphasize ideology, those that look to strictly political differences, and those which assign pre-eminent importance to the growth of socioeconomic pluralism in the nineteenth century. The differences between each of these schools of thought is not absolute. Nevertheless, even the most minor variations in theoretical emphasis can have major importance for the setting of policy in today's new nations.

The doctrine which has gained the greatest popularity in underdeveloped countries regards a liberal polity as simply one among many results of economic abundance. In his brilliant *People of Plenty*, historian David Potter has stated the general position succinctly: ". . . to succeed as a democracy, a country must enjoy an economic surplus to begin with or must contrive to attain one."[5] Sociologist Seymour Lipset has carried the theory further by establishing correlations between the stability of democracy and such measures of affluence as per capita income, number of doctors, telephones, and newspapers which a country possesses.[6] Such analysts believe that economic abundance not only reduces the bitterness of class differences but also lays the base for other conditions which they regard as prerequisites for democracy: universal literacy and mass education, for example. Placing abundance first and democracy second (either implicitly or directly), this theory has earned respectful attention in underdeveloped countries. It appeals not only to authoritarian politicians who seek excuses for their actions, but to serious scholars of the problems of development as well. Kalman Silvert, one of the most distinguished observers of contemporary Latin America, has flatly concluded: "Economically retarded countries cannot, by definition, enjoy democratic politics." [7]

Such exclusive emphasis upon economic affluence does not do justice to the facts of the nineteenth century. The theory may possibly aid in explaining the long-range stability of a democratic system, but it falls short of elucidating the origins of a liberal polity in Europe.

The theory suffers from its exceptions. By any standard of abundance, Germany ranked high with other nineteenth-century states, yet democracy curdled in the Teutonic atmosphere. Scandinavian countries had a significantly lower level of national income, but there a liberal system planted firm roots. A theory which ignores such signal cases remains questionable.

The very concept of "abundance" also exudes ambiguity. Per-capita income in Europe during the first part of the nineteenth century averaged $175. This sum hardly constitutes affluence by contemporary standards, and, indeed, many developing countries today have already reached this level. Judged by modern standards, nineteenth-century Europe was poor, and yet it was there that the world witnessed the beginning of liberal societies.

Further, at the beginning of the nineteenth century, Europe had a literacy rate of approximately 30 per cent (not far from that of contemporary Egypt), and mass education did not commence until the 1880's, long after the franchise had been extended deep into the population. In northwestern Europe, universal literacy was a result, rather than a cause, of a liberal polity.

One finds it difficult, therefore, to view economic abundance and its concomitants as prerequisites for democracy. Indeed, the fact that the level of income in some contemporary emerging countries (Ghana, Egypt, Mexico) equals or exceeds that of Europe in 1800 offers a reason for political hope that these nations' leaders too readily ignore. The correlations reached by Lipset and others might just as easily, perhaps more reasonably, be read as indicating that a stable liberal democracy *creates* more doctors or telephones or literacy, rather than the reverse.

A second theory—one which stresses the primacy of ideology—stands at the opposite pole. Subscribers to this point of view believe that a liberal polity flourishes only when certain values have filtered down to the masses. Political scientist Massimo Salvadori has contended that the development of a unique set of ideas in the seventeenth and eighteenth centuries alone made possible the later blossoming of liberal democracy.[8] Salvadori has argued that the cumulative influence of Bacon and Newton, Descartes and Voltaire, Condorcet and Locke created a new framework of political discourse. The impact of the Protestant revolution, scientific discoveries, and of the Enlightenment; the emergence of men willing to attack tradition, laud individual reason, welcome dissent, and conceive of society's perfectability—these forces, he believes, provided the necessary foundation for European democracy. For Salvadori, factors other than ideas do not explain the emergence of democracy in one nation as opposed to another:

Neither race, geographical environment nor economic conditions explain why the ideas and institutions of modern liberal democracy were born in the countries bordering on the shores of the North Atlantic Ocean.

When a clear-cut differentiation began to appear between a liberal Western Europe and an authoritarian central Europe, the economies of Great Britain, France and the western section of the Germanies . . . were not basically different from those of the neighboring countries to the east (Italy, most of Germany, etc.) where liberal democracy had no spontaneous growth and appeared later as a foreign influence struggling against native authoritarianism.[9]

Salvadori's emphasis upon ideological commitment serves as a welcome antidote to those who view history as merely the wastebasket of implacable economic forces. But it smacks of Hegelianism to suggest that philosophies, abstractly floating above social reality, totally created a new society. Such a position does not really clarify the fact that the new set of ideas epitomized in the Enlightenment influenced some countries and not others. Like the economic approach, it does not explain the German failure. Surely, intellectual currents noted by Salvadori had a profound influence upon many Germans. Why, then, did this nation which had been the cradle of many Protestant and Enlightenment thinkers fail to evolve a stable democratic system? It would seem that the most seminal ideas can lie fallow in an infertile social environment. Conversely, as Lipset has shown, liberal democracies can function in environments with strikingly different value orientations—in America, say, with its lawless, equalitarian tradition, and in Great Britain, where the people still accept the dominance of an elite.[10]

A third school of thought cites strictly political factors as primary in accounting for the origin of liberal polities. Proponents of this opinion, including the leaders of many underdeveloped countries, argue that a stable democracy requires that people place their loyalty in the nation-state and accept the national rule of law as legitimate. Stated in this form, one cannot quarrel with the position, especially since nationalism accompanied the rise of liberal political systems in Europe. When extended, however, to the belief that cultural or national homogeneity *must* precede democracy, the argument becomes shaky. On the one hand, it should be remembered that Switzerland—although extremely divided ethnically, religiously, and linguistically—evolved perhaps the most stable of all liberal systems.[11] And it should also be kept in mind that a nationalistic search for unity and homogeneity can hasten the downfall of a liberal polity, as the events in Germany during 1848 testify.

Other scholars emphasize that self-government is a precondition for democracy. With its gradual evolution of restraints on the king, parliamentary institutions, and constitutional protections, Great Britain offers support to those who believe that only a solid "yeomanry," long accomplished in ruling themselves, can provide the human material for a liberal society. Yet, one cannot apply the same standards to Denmark or Switzerland. The Danish peasantry lacked almost all experience in self-government at the beginning of the nineteenth century, but it still became the bedrock of Danish democracy. Before the advent of democracy, Switzerland's cantons were ruled as often as not by tightly closed elites. Nevertheless, in both cases, power devolved upon the people, and they rose to the occasion by successfully adopting parliamentary institutions.

Clearly, national homogeneity, or the existence of an electoral system which compels compromise, or long practice in self-government may in certain instances aid the development of a fully liberal polity. Nonetheless, it should be underlined that nineteenth-century Europe abounded with examples of nations which lacked these advantages but still managed to evolve a liberal political structure.

A fourth school of thought, that of the pluralists, emphasizes the sociological configuration which underlies political structures. This view has its roots in the writings of Aristotle, Montesquieu, Jefferson, Mill, Acton, Adams, and, more contemporaneously, C. Wright Mills and David Riesman.*

* C. Wright Mills, for example, described American democracy before the Civil War in these terms: "Nineteenth-century America was a middle-class society, in which numerous small and relatively equally empowered organizations flourished. Within this balancing society there was an economy in which the small entrepreneur was central. . . . If at times it was not a world of small entrepreneurs, at least it was always a world in which small entrepreneurs had a real part to play in the equilibrium of power." [12] Mills looked back on this period with nostalgia, for he believed that a "power elite" had replaced pluralism in America. He agreed with E. H. Carr that the old picture of a

The pluralistic school believes, pristinely stated, that a liberal political structure grows only in a society characterized by multiple economic checks and balances, one in which no minority class has total economic dominance over the majority. It distrusts a society in which a single elite (whether a feudal aristocracy, a Brahmin caste, corporation executives, or the government) has unchallengeable economic power, for in this environment political absolutism finds its natural habitat. Such theorists agree with Demosthenes that "eternal vigilance is the price of liberty," but they add the realistic *caveat* that vigilance has to be backed by weapons, particularly by economic force. This conviction was classically stated by Aristotle many centuries ago:

> . . . *It is manifest that the best political community is formed by citizens of the middle class. . . . Great then is the good fortune of a state in which the citizens have a moderate and sufficient property; for where some possess much and others nothing, there may arise an extreme democracy, or a pure oligarchy; or a tyranny may develop out of either extreme . . . but it is not so likely to arise out of the middle constitutions and those akin to them.*[15]

Nineteenth-century European history offers substantial support for this pluralistic conception of democracy's foundations. Three instances of the successful evolution from an authoritarian to a liberal polity—Denmark, Holland, and Switzerland—illustrate how economic pluralism served as the midwife of democracy. While each of these countries differed from the others and from the better-known example of England, history suggests that they exhibited an underlying similarity: all these nations underwent a process of economic pluralization *before* the advent of liberal democracy and, after its birth, liberals and socialists accelerated the process.*

Denmark represents one of the greatest deviations from the usual

---

balanced society continues only as a slogan in industrially advanced nations, as ". . . an ingenious moral device invoked, in perfect sincerity, by privileged groups in order to justify and maintain their dominant positon."[13] In contrast, David Riesman contends that industrialization has brought about a dispersion of power to new "veto groups," and that the pluralistic basis of American democracy continues, although in a new form.[14] The weight of evidence—including the recent "thaw" in Russia, following in the wake of its industrialization—lends Riesman's view greater authority.

* I do not wish to imply that the social conditions in these nations were exactly similar or that their problems were equivalent to those of, say, India. In sheer size alone, the differences are obvious.

interpretations of nineteenth-century democracy, for the liberation of the political order took place in a basically rural society. Demands for liberalization came from a freed peasantry, rather than from an urban bourgeois or proletariat class (as in the more familiar English and French situations).

The roots of Danish democracy must be traced to the eighteenth century, particularly to the agricultural revolution which so radically altered Denmark. Early in the century, a war with Sweden and a consequent decline in exports forced Christian VI to sell crownland. He disposed of his extra land at cheap rates to an already powerful nobility. In return, the lords agreed to collect taxes from the peasants, thus ensuring the state's sustenance. A close alliance developed between the throne and the nobility, for both aimed at holding the peasants in economic servitude.

Angered by their degradation and, particularly, by the loss of traditional rights to common land, the peasants sporadically agitated against government policy. Their rebellion bore fruit, partly because Denmark had acquired colonies. The colonies gave the king new fiscal resources, partially freeing him from his marriage of convenience with the noblemen. Since the throne did not relish its economic dependence upon the aristocracy, it allowed a basic land reform in 1784.

In initiating this first land reform in European history, the Reventlow Commission gave the peasants land as well as credit resources to reinforce it. A new freeholding class of peasants made its appearance. The agricultural reform had profound repercussions in the political realm. The king did not foresee the future, but one conservative nobleman had the prescience to predict that "the yoke of the peasants cannot be removed without Denmark shaking and quivering in its foundation." [16] Later events confirmed this judgment, for the creation of an economically freed peasantry stirred desires for political liberty and provided the peasants with sufficient economic leverage to enforce their demands.

Denmark's alliance with Napoleon and its subsequent military defeat provided the immediate trigger for political change. The war's aftermath led to an agricultural crisis, inflation, and a bank collapse. Abetted and led by a small bourgeois class created by colonial trade, the free peasants united in anger against the monarchy's absolutism. Formed at the beginning of the nineteenth century, a Liberal party expressed the aspiration of the peasants and the urban middle class for economic reform and, especially, for democratization of the political order.

Between them, these two groups played a highly significant (perhaps dominating) role in the Danish economy. The monarchy and the aristocracy could oppose liberal programs only at the cost of endangering their own economic survival. They fought hard, however, and the battle for political control swayed uncertainly throughout the nineteenth century. But the trend of events favored the liberal coalition. In 1834, Frederik VI granted some constitutional protections for individual liberty. In 1848, goaded by revolutionary threats and the Holstein situation, the monarch (now Frederik VII) allowed the establishment of the *Rigsdag* and an extension of individual liberties. In 1866, the conservatives temporarily managed to restrict suffrage, but by the 1880's a full liberal democracy had been created.

Once in power, the Liberals catered to three economic groups: the peasantry, the urban bourgeoisie, and, by the 1890's, a growing industrial proletariat. For the peasants, the Liberals further extended land reform (by 1905, 94 per cent of all land had become freehold), and they passed legislation encouraging the growth of co-operatives, mechanized agriculture, and folkschools. To the middle class, the Liberals gave financial encouragement and protection to the growth of industry. For industrial workers, who pressed their desires at the end of the century through the Social Democratic party, the Liberal coalition offered recognition of trade unions, old-age pensions, and health insurance.

Thus, in contrast to the English experience (where industrialization killed off the independent farmer), Danish democracy drew its mass support from a freed peasantry. Their assumption of economic independence at the end of the eighteenth century created a plural social order, in which the nobility could no longer maintain its place of economic pre-eminence. After winning some political power, the Liberals (and later the Socialists)—unlike their fellows in Germany, Italy, or Russia—consistently carried out a program by which economic power was even more diffused.

The evolution of democracy in the Netherlands provides a second illustration of how a liberal polity can evolve. Unlike both Denmark and England, the stirrings of change came primarily from a merchant class, rather than from the peasantry or from new classes produced by the Industrial Revolution. Because of its long involvement in international trade, the nation gave birth to a sturdy, independent merchant class who built a republican, *stadtholder* tradition in the seventeenth century. Reverses in war and other factors led to a temporary decline of this tradition throughout the eighteenth century, as William III replaced it with absolute rule.

By the end of the century, Enlightenment ideas—as well as William's own ineptness in war and his disastrous handling of the economy—had eroded the king's popular support. The urban merchants found the Enlightenment credo most appealing. They formed the backbone of the Patriots, an informal party that urgently pressed for political liberalization. Napoleon's invasion signaled the temporary rout of absolutism and gave the Patriots a chance to seize the reigns of power. Napoleon's defeat allowed conservative forces (led by the nobility) to regroup, but agitation for a parliamentary regime continued.

The Liberals received their mass support not only from urban merchants but also from the Belgian minority who desired and eventually won their independence from Holland. Although traditional opponents of liberalism, Roman Catholics also joined with the Liberals, desirous of gaining recognition for their religious rights. The central fact about their rather curious, eventually unstable coalition was that it held the preponderance of economic power; political demands could be backed with economic threats.

During the early part of the nineteenth century, this alliance pressed for political reform (particularly for an elected, property-based legislature), but with little success. In 1848, however, in response to fears unleashed by revolution throughout Europe and by the danger that the merchants, Belgians, and Catholics might cripple the economy, the government gave in. The throne granted basic protection for civil liberties, recognized the right of Catholics to practice their religion, allowed direct elections, and gave major influence to an elected States-General. The monarchy tried to keep conservatives in control, but the overwhelming liberal vote of 1868 forced the throne's capitulation.

Although the Catholics split from the liberals in the middle of the century over the issue of religious education, the liberals discovered new allies in the urban proletariat. Like the Danish Liberals (and later, the English), the Dutch passed a number of the workers' demands into law. By the 1890's, the franchise had been considerably widened, and the new coalition had brought into being various forms of social legislation, including workmen's compensation laws and free public education.

Although in a quite different context, the Netherlands underwent a process of economic pluralization like Denmark's. Increased world trade created a merchant class of growing proportions and power; the advent of industrialism at the end of the nineteenth century produced an industrial working class. The alliance of these two groups (and the temporary Belgian and Catholic allegiance) laid a solid economic base for the liberals' plea for a more open society.

A third nineteenth-century case, Switzerland, deserves attention, for its experience clearly indicates that a liberal polity can mature in a society lacking cultural or national homogeneity. Until the nineteenth century, Switzerland rested largely on a military alliance between highly disparate cantons—disunited religiously, socially, linguistically, economically, and politically—though the exigencies of invasion sometimes forced an uneasy co-operation between them. As early as 1291, the Swiss had from time to time joined together in defense. By 1648, a diet had been established, but this was no more than a meeting of independent ambassadors, each representing the "national" interests of his canton.

By the eighteenth century, little progress had been made toward political unity. The cantons functioned as separate entities—some undergoing the first throes of industrialization, others held as feudal baronies by great landowners, and still others comprised of independent farmers ruling themselves. Political power usually rested in the hands of a landed aristocracy or sometimes with urban guilds, whose membership was often hereditarily restricted to a small number of families.

By any standard, eighteenth-century Switzerland represented the prime example of a pluralistic society. Its peoples spoke four different languages, adhered to different religions, and had reached diverse levels of economic achievement.

The spur for political integration arose fortuitously from the Napoleonic invasions. Napoleon forced unity upon the cantons, and in some conquered areas—most prominently Zurich, Lucerne, and Berne—he introduced liberalizing institutions. Napoleon's eventual defeat carried an aristocratic reaction in its wake, as traditional ruling classes reasserted their authority. Nevertheless, once having taken root in a receptive social environment, the seeds of revolutionary thought could not easily be eradicated.

Inspired by French ideals, the urban bourgeoisie revolted in 1830 and threatened rural conservative forces with a serious economic crisis. Their actions brought about the beginnings of truly representative government. The revolution of 1848 reinforced the earlier gains: the liberals passed a constitution modeled on America's, and in later years pushed through such reforms as recognition of Jewish citizenship, the referendum, and various pieces of social legislation.

Support for Switzerland's liberation came from three groups: an urban middle class, urban artisans, and—after the birth of industrialism at the end of the century—from an industrial working class. Although divided on many other issues, these three strata had sufficiently common economic interests so that they could present a united front against the more conservative rural areas. Increasingly, as they gained economic influence, they succeeded in winning political freedoms.

By 1900, Switzerland, Denmark, and the Netherlands had evolved comparable liberal political structures. In each nation, a rule of law, aimed at protecting individual liberty and at offering the person a wide scope for governing his own fate, had taken precedence over traditional absolutism.

Few generalizations about the origins of democracy hold true for all these countries. A liberal polity did not always evolve gradually and peacefully. It did not, in all cases, appear in an atmosphere characterized by unity, cultural homogeneity, or a consensus on basic values. And certainly, a liberal political order appeared in countries which could hardly be characterized as either industrialized or as economically abundant. Universally, educational sophistication of the masses followed democracy, rather than preceded it. All of this should give us hope concerning the future of contemporary areas, for it suggests that the development of democracy is not inevitably tied to various social prerequisites. In the nineteenth century, the English and the Swiss, the Danish and the Dutch decided their political fate in the same fashion, even though their cultures and social structures differed radically.

We can, however, make a few generalizations about the experiences of these successful nineteenth-century democracies. Several economic factors—an increase in world trade, the agricultural revolution, and eventually industrialization—created new social classes able to sway, if not control, certain economies in Europe. These groups desired political and legal privileges commensurate with their economic status. And, to their good fortune, they had sufficient economic independence to enforce their wishes. In northwestern Europe, a new socioeconomic order appeared, one in which power was divided among several sectors of the community. This pluralistic foundation replaced a traditional way of life where a small aristocracy had controlled the economic fate as well as the political destiny of peasant masses.

As the social structure changed, the old system of values gave way to an ethic which stressed individualism at the cost of hierarchical respect, the desirability of change at the expense of fatalism, the utility of individual reason over blind faith. As a plural social system emerged, so, increasingly, did a new system of political ethics. And, of course, the converse also held true: to the degree that a country's values already stressed tolerance, diversity, and pluralism (as in those nations with a large Protestant population), the transition to a liberal political order became more probable.

The Failure of Democracy in Nineteenth-Century Europe

> There is no liberty where there is hunger . . . the theory of
> liberty demands strong efforts to help the poor. Not merely for
> safety, for humanity, for religion, but for liberty . . . the danger
> is not that a particular class is unfit to govern; every class is unfit
> to govern.
>
> LORD ACTON

For those concerned with the fate of freedom in developing countries,
attention must be paid not only to the successful evolution of democracy in the past but also to its emasculation. During the nineteenth
century, liberal institutions more often went down in defeat than rose
in triumph. Germany in 1848, Italy from 1860 to 1890, and Russia in
1905 present illustrations of a liberal society's fragility.

Aside from many specific, highly important historical factors, one
can trace the failure of democracy in these countries to two general
deficiencies: first, they lacked a pluralized economic order, such as that
evolved by England, Denmark, Switzerland, and the Netherlands. Secondly, when liberal parties (primarily of middle-class origin) "prema-
turely" seized power, they looked only to their own class interests
rather than the general welfare of the masses.

Italy, for example, underwent a series of erratic triumphs and re-
versals of liberalism, culminating in Crispi's dictatorship (and later, in
Mussolini's). French domination in the early part of the nineteenth
century first introduced libertarian ideas to Italy, but autocratic reaction—aided by Austrian military domination and by the Papacy's moral
authority—quickly took over after the Napoleonic debacle. The Risor-
gimento kept alive liberal and nationalist sentiments, particularly in
the North. The 1848 revolutions, led by Charles Albert of Piedmont
and various republican movements, crystallized these longings but generally failed to overthrow autocratic rule.

A happier era for liberalism dawned in 1859. Cavour in the North
and Garibaldi in the South led most of the nation to unification. Inspired by Enlightenment ideals, new liberal governments assumed
power. But they foundered in the face of a variety of challenges: brig-
andage in the South, hostility from the popes, agricultural riots, and
industrial unrest. Ministries alternated with chaotic frequency, and
even imperialistic excursions into Abyssinia and Tunisia failed to calm

the people with the opiate of national pride. By the 1890's, the Crispi dictatorship had won power, promising to end govermental inefficiency and corruption.

One of the primary reasons for Italy's failure to evolve a stable liberal polity must be traced to the nation's social structure. Only part of the North had developed an economically plural society, in which the middle class and industrial workers balanced each other as well as the power of older classes. The South remained in the economic grip of feudal landholders and under the intellectual control of the Papacy. Italy entered the twentieth century dominated by the values of a Catholicism which had little patience with an open society's ideals and hindered by an economic order in which traditional classes still held the predominance of power.

Of equal importance, liberal leaders blinded themselves to the potential dangers of their situation. Northern liberals refused to initiate programs of land reform or campaigns for literacy—the only way in which the feudalism of the South could have been altered. Mistakenly believing that their ultimate interest lay in crushing the workers, liberals also refused to grant the moderate social demands of new working classes growing up in northern cities. Irretrievably, they alienated both the peasants and industrial workers—throwing one group into the arms of the Church and the other under Crispi's magnetism.

Russia in 1905 sadly resembled Italy. The Manchurian disaster, agricultural unrest, and the events of Bloody Sunday had clearly revealed the bankruptcy of the tsar's regime. Isolated from his people, the tsar could ally himself only with the nobility and the upper clergy. In opposition, he faced a series of divided groups, united only in their dislike for the old autocracy. The Octobrists drew their support from a small urban middle class. The Social Revolutionaries attempted (in theory) to defend the peasants' interests. And the Social Democratic Labor party stood for the concerns of industrial workers. If a vision of the future could have overcome factional disputes, these groups might have formed a formidable coalition. But, even in the face of disaster, they found themselves unable to forge an alliance.

The tsarist regime artfully played upon these divisions. After some minor concessions to liberal demands, the tsar diverted the nation's attention with Jewish pogroms. He paralyzed the urban bourgeoisie with fears of a workers' revolt. And the Orthodox Church called upon its persuasive powers to lull the peasantry into quiescence. Soon, the tsar and the nobility felt strong enough to withdraw their promises of establishing an effective Duma, extending the franchise, and institutionalizing constitutional protections. The end came, of course, in the convulsions of 1917.

There are several reasons why this brief flirtation with a liberal society ended so abruptly. Russia's intellectual tradition did not lend itself easily to the ideas of liberal democracy. The strongly traditional Church dominated peasants' minds. And the intellectual elite split itself between "Westernizers" and Slavophiles like Dostoevski who praised the unique genius of Mother Russia and demanded a unified community. Further, the Russian economy remained essentially under the monolithic control of the aristocracy. Although the peasants—by far the majority in the country—had technically received their freedom, they remained financially dependent upon the nobility. While capitalism had advanced rather rapidly in the 25 years preceding 1905, the middle and working classes still constituted only a tiny fraction of the population. The eventual failure of the October general strike illustrated that the economic power possessed by the urban classes was only peripheral to the nation's life.

Much of the blame, too, has to be assigned to middle-class liberals themselves. Foggy about the nature of revolution, they again and again missed opportunities to gain wide support throughout the country. Fearing that they and their property might be consumed in a social conflagration, a majority of liberals did not support requests for fundamental land reform, nor did they seek to assuage the grievances of urban workers. Like the Italian liberals, they lost whatever opportunity they had to form a united front against authoritarianism. The fault lay not only in their social situation but in themselves.

The experience of Germany in 1848 poignantly expressed the nature of the liberals' responsibility. The events of 1848 in Germany marked a startling failure of liberals, after an early, easy success, to establish a viable political order. Inspired by France's example and by the discontent created by a highly inflationary situation, liberal revolutions swept through the German states. Initially, Frederick William IV and the other rulers gave in to liberal agitation: legislatures were appointed, protections for individual freedom extended, and the formation of the famed Frankfurt Assembly allowed. Charged with drafting an all-German constitution, the assembly produced a remarkably liberal document—superseded later only by the equally ill-starred Weimar Constitution. Implementation of the Frankfurt Constitution hinged on a single decision: Frederick William's willingness to assume the crown of a new German Empire from commoners. When he refused, the liberals collapsed, royal troops dismissed a rump meeting of the assembly, and a return to autocracy set in.

The economic order of Germany during this crisis bore some resemblance to Russia and Italy. The nobility still held great economic power, for the peasants found themselves economically as well as traditionally linked to the aristocracy. In consequence, the peasants remained quiet throughout 1848. Although the urban middle class took leadership during the revolt, it did not possess the same degree of economic independence as its English, Danish, or Dutch counterparts. A high proportion of the bourgeois leaders had professional status (as doctors, lawyers, or civil servants). Their appointments often came directly from the various princes and kings. Thus, many of them were tied to the old regime and lacked the economic independence available to a merchant or industrial class. They could not dare to seek the total elimination of autocracy, for this would have lost them their economic livelihood.*

Intellectually, German culture exhibited strains of Lutheran authoritarianism, a longing for imperial unity, and a romanticism which could not easily be reconciled with the ideals of a pragmatic, compromising democracy.

While the land of Goethe and Kant may not have been ripe for the emergence of a liberal polity, the social order did not offer the same forbidding opposition as did Italy's and Russia's. The failure of 1848 must be traced, I believe, more specifically to the attitudes and actions of the liberals themselves. At every opportunity, the liberal leaders failed to extend the pluralistic base of their society. When the gauntlet was thrown down, they chose nationalism and the preservation of their class interests over the cause of freedom.

In Berlin, at the height of the revolution, middle-class leaders refused to issue guns to a workers' militia which begged for them. The leaders mistakenly feared that the guns might be turned on them and their property. In consequence, royal troops held the balance of military power.

At Frankfurt, the liberal leaders rejected repeated demands for universal manhood suffrage, again alienating the working class. In the end, the liberals called upon monarchical regiments to put down workers' riots. Rather than trusting industrial workers with political responsibility, they put themselves in the hands of their real enemies, the aristocracy.

During the fading days of the revolt, members of the Prussian parliament failed to use their last effective weapon: a refusal to pay taxes to

---

* This fact lends an ironic twist to the traditional German contempt for England as a "nation of shopkeepers." Germany's lack of "shopkeepers" may be among the most important reasons for the defeat of its democracy.

the king. They worried that such an action might destroy the old social order and their own private property with it.

In each case, the majority of liberals protected the traditional society by denying increased power to their only possible allies, the urban industrial groups. In addition, they felt torn between desires for a liberal polity and nationalistic pressures for a greater German Reich. The lure of a German Empire, finally united under the Prussian monarch, eventually stifled the urge for individual liberty. When the final tests came, the liberals chose nationalism, unity, and property over the cause of freedom. As one historian commented in 1849, "The Germans found that their thirst for freedom could only be satisfied by power."

The personal failure of the German, Italian, and Russian liberals cannot be excused on the basis that they were simply unconscious victims of a narrow "class consciousness." When the pendulum of history might have swung either way, individual leaders made crucial decisions which ensured the death or survival of autocracy. Too often, they exercised their freedom in the service of despotism.

Implications

> The nation which will not adopt an equilibrium of power must adopt a despotism. There is no other alternative.
>
> JOHN ADAMS

The record suggests that stable liberal polities have evolved in the past through a two-step process. First, the socioeconomic order underwent pluralization. In certain nations, new economic classes appeared—sometimes, an industrial middle and working class; at other times, a freed peasantry or an independent merchant group. Enmeshed in battle against traditionalism, these groups increasingly attached themselves to the idea of liberty, to the belief that they as well as the old rulers deserved to govern their destinies. This attraction to freedom came partially from the intrinsic appeal of the new ideals propounded during the Enlightenment, but more often it probably emerged from a simple desire of each group to ensure its own independence.

Because of the economic power of these classes—and especially since the economic survival of traditional groups became increasingly dependent upon the newly autonomous classes—the rulers of the traditional order felt compelled to grant demands for democratization. Danish landlords depended on the export income of freed peasants; the Dutch monarch required taxes from urban merchants; Swiss capitalists needed the skills of artisans. They could refuse requests for greater liberty only at the danger of their own economic survival. Liberty triumphed only when autonomous groups, mutually antagonistic toward each other, had sufficiently massive power to check one another. "Experience tells us that whoever has power, tends to abuse it; he will go as far as he is allowed," Montesquieu observed in the eighteenth century, "Virtue itself needs limitations." [17]

Economic pluralism by itself did not ensure the growth of a liberal polity. We should not ignore a second factor of great importance: the decisions and actions of liberals after they had taken power. In successful democracies, the liberals followed a consistent policy of diffusing economic and political power throughout the society. When they failed to do so—as in Germany, Russia, and Italy—the traditional autocracy retained its influence or gave way to another form of authoritarianism, clothed in modern garb. In this impersonal age, when we tend to overlook the role of the individual, it is important to recognize again the significance of individual choice as a determinant of history.

Perhaps the most important lesson of this first springtime of freedom is the very paucity of generalizations which can be drawn from it. Most importantly, the past indicates that many of the arguments condoning dictatorship in the newer nations cannot be historically justified. Hardy democratic regimes have sprung up in rural, relatively poor environments, characterized by a lack of mass education, national unity, or cultural homogeneity. Further, it would appear that some of the explanations of the growth of democracy that are currently most fashionable may have fitted the European situation but do not apply at all to presently developing societies.

Urbanization, for example, has often been cited as a force leading to individualism and eventually to political liberty. Certainly, in nineteenth century Europe, the spread of cities went hand in hand with the development of liberal democracy. Yet, as sociologist Reinhard Bendix has ably shown, urbanization in developing countries is not taking the same form nor having the same results as in Europe. After examining various studies of the Indian situation, Bendix concluded:

Recent observations in India suggest that the generalizations and expectations we associate with the term "urbanization" may be excessively culture-bound. . . . As an outsider examines the statistics of unemployment, housing conditions, and population with sympathy for

the human condition, he naturally wonders whether the resilience of
kinship- and caste-ties . . . represents the one remaining social secu-
rity for the individual. . . . If these impressions are near the mark, then
every increase in population, every further crowding of the cities will
militate against . . . individualism.[18]

Leaders of developing countries, then, cannot look to Europe or any
other area as a sure source of political guidance nor can the contemporary autocrat imposing his despotism on restive peoples vindicate his
actions by reference to history. The democrat who seeks to build a liberal polity can find very few sociological generalizations upon which
to base his decisions. Like the men of 1848, he must start anew on a
poorly lighted path.

For those who desire freedom, history can offer at best only a
very general outline of possible strategies. The pattern of the nineteenth century indicates that those who desire to preserve a democratic
regime must seek to diffuse economic power as widely as possible. They
must welcome, rather than fear, the pluralization of their societies.
What this means in specific terms differs drastically for each state. In
India, a pluralistic policy would involve encouragement of a capitalist
middle class, of village *panchayats* and rural co-operatives. In Ghana, it
would mean reversing a policy currently aimed at making trade unions,
co-operatives, and all formerly autonomous groups simply instruments
of a monolithic party. In Nigeria, pluralism would demand the continuation of a federation in which highly diverse peoples work out their
destiny as Switzerland once did.

Surely, it is not easy to maintain "balanced" societies of this type,
but it has been done in the past. From this fact, contemporary liberals
and democratic socialists can take comfort. At the same time, they
must realize the immense responsibility which rests on their shoulders,
for "history is not a web woven with innocent hands." [19] If developing
nations succumb to authoritarianism, it will not be because inevitable
forces pushed them down the abyss. It will be due to the fact that at
moments of crisis, the leaders lost their nerve and their vision—just as
did the Germans, Russians, and Italians one hundred years ago. Perhaps history will repeat itself, but if it does, mankind cannot look back
to the past for alibis.

As Chief O. Awolowo wisely remarked in 1961, ironically just before
his imprisonment by the Nigerian central government:

We must read history books, and do more than merely read them:
We must learn, mark, and inwardly digest what we have read. We

must do all this if we would avoid a repetition of the costly mistakes of the past and benefit from the accumulated wisdom of the ages. . . . Under existing conditions, latecomers have the singular advantage of benefitting from the experience and accomplishments of older nations.[20]

XII

BREAD AND FREEDOM: THE PLURALISTIC APPROACH

> Our century will be chiefly remembered by future generations not as an era of political conflicts or technical inventions, but as an age in which human society dared to think of the welfare of the whole human race as a practical objective.
>
> ARNOLD TOYNBEE

Over one hundred years ago, while deeply engaged in the battles of his own epoch, John Stuart Mill had the vision to foresee the issues confronting our generation. He observed that the basic dilemma of the future would be "how to unite the greatest individual liberty of action with common ownership in the raw materials of the globe, and an equal participation of all in the benefits of combined labor." [1] With an immensely greater store of resources at our disposal than there was in Mill's time, there is no technical reason why the problem cannot be solved. And, too, we have the advantage of historical perspective, for we know the results of the various social, political, and economic experiments which mankind has conducted during the last century.

It would be presumptuous to claim that this accumulated wisdom provides a map to utopia for leaders in emerging nations. The convulsions of modern times have outmoded the programs, plans, and prescriptions for progress which abounded in the nineteenth century. History does, however, offer certain broad guidelines—or perhaps, one might better say, warnings—to leaders in developing nations. Some appreciation of these general points may help in unweaving the skein of social, economic, and political problems which burden the "Third World."

Responding to the Social Challenge

> The paramount requirement for the modernization of any society
> is that the people themselves must change.
> MAX MILLIKAN and DONALD BLACKMER

Behind the abstractions with which we have dealt lie millions of hungry and often angry human beings, aware more than ever before of their misery. The social milieu of these *les miserables* of the globe has undergone profound alterations during the last decade. Colonialism, the impact of two world wars, the beginnings of a market economy, and the extension of transportation have, for good or ill, broken down the proud isolation of the traditional village community. The average man in developing societies has become aware, however dimly, of a larger world with its new horizons. Then, too, the usual hierarchical system of traditional societies—its respect for ancestors, or its caste ranks, or its reliance on the all-powerful patrons and priests—has haltingly given way to modern concepts of individuality and equality. Impelled by a belief in equality (sometimes conceived as the equal ranking of groups, sometimes as individual equality of opportunity), new political forces have been let loose which leaders everywhere find it difficult to trammel.

Perhaps of greatest significance, the fatalism characteristic of stagnant societies has been eroded by concepts of progress, by a vision that man's condition can be improved here and now, not in some hazy future. Platitudes and promises no longer serve to satisfy transitional men, nor do the usual metaphysical explanations continue to justify their lot in life. This emancipating, if often frustrating, belief in progress has worked its way down to even the most primitive villages. It has created a new type of man infected with "this-worldliness," as Barbara Ward has phrased it, an "immense interest in *this* world, in its processes, in its laws and construction, in the ways in which it can be set to work and made over according to human ends and purposes—in a word the world as an arena of work and effort where needs and dreams can be satisfied." [2]

To fulfill this hunger for progress requires that transitional men, already leavened with revolutionary ideas, need to undergo still further changes in their customs, habits, and values. By this, I do not mean that governments should set about dismantling the entire culture of their countries. Not only do such attempts usually fail, as Russia's early experiments indicate, but to mount an assault upon tradition *per se* unwarrantedly insults the past efforts of mankind. The old religions, social relationships, festivals and rites were built over centuries to give sense, dignity, and a measure of happiness to barren lives. It would take a foolhardy prophet to suggest that modernization, with all of its penalties as well as benefits, can repay a people for the conscious planned destruction of traditions which gave existence a meaning. Contrary to the gloomy, if currently fashionable, view, traditional cultures do not lack in entrepreneurs nor need they impede a thrust toward economic modernization. In periods such as those of Meiji Japan and nineteenth-century Denmark, a substantial part of the old society survived, or even gained in vigor, while a new economy emerged. Rational governments merged the ancient and the modern in a way which changed the economy but left the traditional culture with some integrity. This middle path should be the basic policy of governments today.[3]

Nonetheless, in almost every developing country, certain social reforms, sometimes of a far-reaching nature, will have to be enacted to produce the right climate for economic growth and individual liberty. In terms of specific policies, most emerging nations should envisage a social program embodying these elements:

The economic and political power of feudal ruling groups, firmly entrenched in the *status quo* and ideologically dedicated to its total preservation, has to be undermined.

In the economic realm, the need is obvious. The process of rural modernization, for example, must almost universally begin with land reform, and the old landlords will stringently oppose such change with any means available. The resistance of a feudal elite to progress may well extend into less obvious areas. It seems natural to suppose, as one instance, that everyone would favor the abolition of illiteracy and ignorance. Yet, in making this naïve assumption, as one American political scientist has correctly observed, "We forget that there are many countries in the world where the maintenance of illiteracy is one of the chief political weapons in defense of the status quo. . . . even if *we* don't know it, the oligarchies in those countries know that education, the enlightenment of these oppressed masses, represents an implicit challenge to the status quo." [4] In one fashion or another, the grip of these oligarchs upon their societies must be loosened.

Sometimes, the required change in a feudal structure will occur in an evolutionary fashion, as the natural growth of Indian trade unions, "scheduled caste" organizations, and business groups has begun to balance the power of landlords. More often, a change in the structure of power needs to be made swiftly, although not necessarily violently, as Egypt rid herself of landlords, Bolivia took over the tin barons' fiefs, and India expropriated the princes. Particularly in Latin America, one cannot conceive of equitable economic development as long as the present rigid and reactionary social structures prevail. The required "structural" changes can be made, *if* the ruling government is sufficiently dedicated to the improvement of its society and *if* the emerging nation receives moral and economic support from advanced regions, particularly the United States.

As the old social groupings—communities based on language, religion, or ethnic considerations—tend to disappear, a developing nation should consciously plan to replace them with newly articulated interest groups —unions, co-operatives, workers' or village councils. Without toleration of such interest groups, the elite can seldom gain accurate knowledge of the economic desires or negotiable interests that exist within their society; the people, on the other hand, do not possess agencies which would express their specific interests. The crushing of "modern" interest groups, as in Ghana and Indonesia, runs the risk of depriving the elite of information concerning the wants of the people and the degree to which they would tolerate a particular decision; the end result can be economic stagnation or retrogression.

India provides a prime example of a state which has not only allowed but encouraged the growth of interest groups. Thousands of voluntary agencies, caste groups, and unions have spontaneously emerged in India. Beyond this, however, the government has launched its boldly conceived Panchayat Raj program which will for the first time draw the mass of peasantry into the push and pull of politics. The new plan has two aspects: first, the government wishes to decentralize political power down to the village level, in the expectation that this will eventually give the numerically superior lower castes a genuine form of self-government; secondly, the new plan allots significantly greater power to village councils in allocating development funds— hopefully, this new economic influence will draw the peasant into the center of development, rather than treating him as a passive recipient of charity. The Panchayat Raj ambitions may well be frustrated in the foreseeable future: traditional elites will attempt to maintain their privileges and will, certainly for a time, win a majority of seats in the village councils.[5] Looking further ahead, however, one may expect that the peasantry will eventually exert their latent power and energies in the service of development.

In addition, new means of communication have to be opened between the elite who governs and the people who subsist and suffer. Somehow, the small governing class at the top of every developing nation must communicate its eventual goals, aspirations, and decisions to the people. By far the best manner in which to do this is through personal contact between the leaders and the governed. In this respect, certain nations could serve as models. China has poured millions of men into the rural areas in a more or less successful attempt to educate and indoctrinate the peasantry. India has hundreds of thousands of development officers at work in the often disappointing, but vitally necessary, task of convincing peasants to adopt new methods. An even more ambitious plan has been advanced by Asoka Mehta, head of India's Praja Socialists. He has argued for a draft system which would send perhaps two million university graduates into rural areas for two years of service. Such a corps could undertake projects of rural development, give the lead to modernization, help end the exodus to cities and allow "the dialogue of development . . . to reach the people." [6] Without such efforts, developing nations who now adhere to democratic methods of persuasion will have to fall back on coercion to achieve their aims.

Education must, of course, receive strong emphasis. While exact calculations are difficult, some experts attribute 60 per cent of economic growth in the West during the last fifty years to the effects of education and research.[7] And, as we have seen, much of the success of Russia and Japan in achieving their exceptional economic progress should be traced to their unusually large investments in education. Bespangled universities must not, however, become the fetish of new nations; too much as well as too little can be spent on education. Not one of the newer nations can long afford the luxury of a system of education which would immediately produce both universal literacy *and* squadrons of university-trained men. Because of budgetary rigors, the leadership in developing countries must draw a delicate balance between concentrating its resources in building an "elitist pyramid" of university graduates, doctors, skilled personnel, mechanics, technicians, and other types of people who are immediately needed—and simultaneously, using cheap, informal means of mass education.

The proper mixture will differ for each region. Clearly, unconventional techniques will be tried: television as in Colombia, solar radios in former French Africa, teaching machines in Ghana, or the each-child-teach-an-adult method as in Cuba. The folkschools of nineteenth-century Denmark also deserve emulation in many contemporary countries.

Only a balanced combination of formal and informal approaches to education can produce a skilled elite necessary for economic growth, an informed public required for political sophistication—and a national budget which does not stagger under the burdens of school building and teacher training. A slim volume of technical, high-level education, built on a foundation of unconventional methods of mass information, has to be the aim of educational advance in the newer nations.

Attitudes toward human reproduction must alter, if economic advance is to occur. As of now, the breeding of babies exceeds or matches expansion of economic production in Latin America, Asia, and the Middle East. Only a well-financed program of birth control can reverse the pattern and save future generations from starvation. We know that the most illiterate peasant can accept these facts of life and will welcome methods which will enhance the chance of survival for his offspring. Experiments throughout the world—in Puerto Rico and Ceylon, Japan and India—have demonstrated that mankind everywhere can comprehend the need for birth control and learn effective techniques. If advanced regions contribute their knowledge, assistance, and moral force to the furthering of this cause, there can be little doubt that the "human explosion" will be contained by the 1970's.

Most generally, the elite must look to the village as the foundation for its programs and must seek to reverse the flow of urbanization. There are many sound reasons why land reform, technical assistance, education, and other forms of aid to the peasantry should receive the highest priority: Planners in every nation must seek the modernization of village life in all its dimensions since, without a marked increase in rural productivity, no program of economic development can succeed; urbanization, at this point in history, has worsened the material welfare of city immigrants; in consequence, the anomic urbanite falls prey to extremist political appeals which threaten a democratic body politic; and after experiencing the city's frustrations, a majority of immigrants would choose voluntarily to return to their village, if they could be assured of economic opportunities. Even setting aside strictly economic concerns, a wise government should undertake measures to invigorate village life, decentralize industries in the countryside, transform agriculture, and avoid a concentration of industries in the already glutted cities. Egypt's experience and (until 1960) China's suggest that such an approach can achieve marked success. Well-planned programs can bring forth the immense constructive potentiality of the rural areas, where the great majority of transitional men live.

From the turmoil of the last decades, one clear, if obvious, lesson has appeared: social planning, based on persuasion rather than force, must go together with any move toward economic modernization or political liberation. If developing nations conceive sound attempts to alter the feudal structure, produce a skilled and literate population, control the birth rate, close the gap between the elite and the masses, and revolutionize village life, there can be a realistic hope that emerging peoples will build a world without want.

Responding to the Economic Challenge

> So long as freedom from hunger is only half achieved, so long as two-thirds of the nations of the world have food deficits—no citizen, no nation can afford to feel satisfied or secure. We have the ability, we have the means, and we have the capacity to eliminate hunger from the face of the earth. We need only the will. . . .
>
> JOHN F. KENNEDY

No battle on earth has greater importance than the striving to end poverty in all of its grim aspects. Yet while we possess the resources, as John F. Kennedy knew, we can have no certainty that victory will be won. The campaign to abolish poverty faces massive obstacles, for its path, to paraphrase economist Benjamin Higgins, is paved with vicious circles.

It is obvious, for example, that a change in one sector of an economy can precipitate motion in other sectors. An increase in rural productivity, for instance, issues a food surplus which can free men for industrial work; this, in turn, provides consumer goods which flow back to farmers. The obverse also holds true: stagnation in one critical area of an economy can retard development in other areas. Without an injection of capital, food production cannot improve; without a rural surplus, industrialization proceeds only fitfully, if at all; without industrialization, new sources of capital will not emerge—and, in consequence, agriculture will remain quiescent. Since progress seldom occurs simultaneously on every front, the essential problem which faces those who desire a more abundant life is how to enter this interlocking chain. It would be fruitless to try to pinpoint the exact place where continuous, self-sustaining growth can best be stimulated, for developing nations are at such different stages in their evolution. Only a specific and pragmatic evaluation of each country's potentialities can provide the answer to this problem. Any strategy of economic growth, however, has to take into consideration a few principles which apply with more or less validity throughout the "Third World":

The first commandment of development is that agriculture must be transformed. In every instance of "take-off," whether in the West, Russia, or Japan, an agricultural revolution preceded other forms of economic growth. Lacking virgin land and outlets for an expanding population, developing nations today must again look to the peasant for their economic salvation. Farm production has to increase, since the bulk of the emerging world's population lives on the land and provides the main source for capital accumulation. If a rural surplus can be obtained, some of it can be transferred to other parts of the economy—either in the form of food, raw commodities, or capital. Greater rural productivity is needed not only to feed urban industrial workers and to provide funds for development but simply to keep in step with an unprecedented population expansion. And clearly, if the countryside does not prosper, new industries will fail to find markets for their products.

That the transformation of farming presents a formidable challenge hardly requires restatement. Traditional landowners are not normally found in the front ranks of innovative entrepreneurs. And the peasant who lives within a step of starvation naturally hesitates to adopt new techniques or a market-oriented attitude. Further, the usual nostrums of the past do not apply today. The Soviet example (or the Chinese model after 1958) simply cannot be adopted by most emerging countries as a guide to rural development: unused land does not exist in most regions; mechanization could not solve the problem, since it would raise the demand for capital to an impossible level; the vast number of people thrown out of work by attempts at collectivization and mechanization could not be absorbed in an urban environment; and, above all, the attachment of peasants to their present holdings, however tiny, can be eradicated only by a violent suppression unmatched in history. "Such a terrific transformation would involve the destruction of many millions of men," a Socialist leader has commented about India, "and would raise such vast problems of adjustment that no dictatorship could solve them." [8]

While not susceptible to easy solutions, the cause of changing agriculture is by no means hopeless. Japan's experience in the cultivation of postage-stamp plots of land offers a great deal of promise to developing regions. And contemporary experiments in such diverse areas as Egypt, Kenya, Nigeria, and parts of India show that rural productivity can mount rapidly when certain conditions are met. Land reform, of one type or another, is almost always essential, and normally the government must take the initiative in changing the land-tenure pattern. The farmer must also receive guidance, tools, marketing outlets, and low-interest loans from an outside agency. In addition, the government has to assume responsibility for building the irrigation and transport systems to sustain rural advance. And most importantly, the peasants have to be taught the reasons for innovation, the methods to bring it about, and the rewards which they may expect. Taken together, these measures can modernize agriculture in developing nations and lay the base for all other forms of economic advance.

Clearly, the pace of saving and productive reinvestment has to be stepped up. Unless a society reaches a point where the people devote some 15 per cent of national income to capital formation, an economy cannot prosper. This simple, if crucial, fact places a major burden on poor countries, for it means that the propensity to consume has to be checked rather severely.

Domestically, only two sources of capital formation exist: the profits derived from private enterprise or the funds which come from government taxation. It is most difficult to provide a rule of thumb which would determine the proper balance between these two sources. Certainly, a private sector of some magnitude should be allowed to function, since the "self-correcting" mechanism of the profit motive can often work to a nation's advantage. By concentrating all major sources of capital in the government's hands, a country courts the economic disaster which has overtaken Indonesia. Such a policy scares away useful foreign enterprise; it can destroy the initiative and vigor which sometimes, as in India, characterizes the private sector; and it undermines the variegated economic foundation needed for political freedom. Nonetheless, governments must directly or indirectly play a much more prominent role in capital formation than they did in the West's early evolution. Only the government can undertake certain projects which confer indiscriminate benefits on the people; only the government can finance large-scale projects which would be unattractive to domestic investors; and only the government can promulgate measures which will persuade the private investor to place his funds in productive enterprises rather than luxury consumption.

Thus, much of the burden of capital accumulation in a developing country must fall on the state. Both to fill its own coffers and to stimulate useful private investment, a free state can venture a variety of policies: increased income taxes, taxes on unused land, restrictions on nonessential consumption, tax rebates for productive enterprises, the initiation of a moderate inflationary policy, and a reduction in consumer imports. At least some of these policies have to be implemented in every developing region for the nation to reach a point where capital formation exceeds the pace of population growth.

Light, decentralized, consumer-oriented industries should form the base of the industrial sector in most emerging nations. Japan has amply demonstrated that such small-scale enterprises, particularly when integrated with the development of complementary heavy industries, can set an economy solidly on the road of economic progress. Today, both the economic and the sociological reasons for giving preference to light industry are even more compelling than during the Meiji period: such a program conserves precious capital; it avoids the hidden costs which heavy industrialization and consequent urbanization entail; it draws upon the talents of idle labor; it provides the mass of people with the experience, attitudes, sense of self-sufficiency, and other motives necessary for modernization; it satisfies the immediate, limited demands of transitional man, thus relieving political tensions; and it allows the emerging nations to replace consumer imports with domestically produced items, thereby reducing the strain on foreign exchange reserves.

Unfortunately, developing countries have too often ignored these advantages.[9] The symbols of the 20th century have sometimes blinded them to their country's real needs for economic development. With his usual asperity, Hans Morgenthau has noted:

Many underdeveloped nations want not economic development in the liberal economic sense; what they want rather, are the symbols of power—the symbols of having arrived in the 20th century. I have always been impressed with the statement which Nehru made to Chou En-lai . . . when Chou En-lai visited India, and Nehru showed him a hydroelectric dam and said, "here is where I pray." And in a less noble fashion, perhaps, you find underdeveloped nations wanting to have an airline of their own which they cannot produce, which they cannot run, and which they cannot maintain. . . . In the 50's a steel mill performed the same function. . . . The steel mill is now in the process of being supplanted by the atomic reactor. This has nothing to do with genuine economic development. . . .[10]

It is a good omen that in the 1960's, India and some other countries have demonstrated a new, firmer commitment to the encouragement of light industries, for it is in this area that the most meaningful advances can be made. As the costs become apparent, a government's infatuation with the symbols of modernity tends to wither.

Leaders in the new nations have often followed another will-o'-the-wisp: the nationalist goal of economic self-sufficiency. For most of the developing countries, this is an unattainable aim even at some ultimate stage of development. Except for rare exceptions, the emerging areas have neither the resources nor large enough markets to try to detach themselves from the world economy. And even the exceptional cases, like China, will need to import industrial goods and some commodities (such as oil) from abroad for the foreseeable future. Any plan for national development, then, depends on finding viable ways to fit a new nation's products into the international economy.

While it is impossible for developing nations to extricate themselves from the world market, it should also be confessed that global economic operations often work to the detriment of an emerging economy, particularly when a country depends upon a single export for its foreign revenue. A sensible government can find its way out of this puzzle, although the process of moderating the world market's impact on an economy may take many years. To the best of its ability, any emerging country should attempt to diversify its exports and thus reduce its dependence on fluctuations in the world price for a particular item. Specifically, such a policy would aim at diversifying commodity production, since exports of manufactured goods have little chance of competing with products from industrially advanced countries. In some areas, it should prove possible for developing countries to establish common markets among themselves and to reach agreements with advanced nations whereby the prices for commodities can be kept at a more stable level. Foreign private enterprise, when properly held in check, can also serve a useful purpose in providing skills, capital, and new industries for the home market. These measures, when buttressed by co-operation from industrially advanced regions—ideally, by the type of co-ordination which once existed between Russia and China—would allow developing regions to merge equitably into the world market.

National development plans should be encouraged. Without an overall strategy and a sense of the critical links in the economy where an impetus to growth might best be started, enormous waste can occur. Burma, for example, built a steel rolling-mill when no one had surveyed the availability of resources, workers, or managers; at great cost, outside technicians came to rescue the plant from total confusion. Now it produces a small range of products. Some foresight would have avoided the unnecessary strain the experiment caused to Burma's economy. In every growing country, knowledge of available resources and co-ordination between various sectors of the economy, as well as ministries within the government, constitute essential ingredients in economic growth. The power to decide where a dam should be placed or whether a school will be built instead of a rural industry should be put in the hands of a public authority. Such economic planning, as in

India, must not be confused with government ownership or the use of force. All societies, including the United States, plan or "program" their economies. At the early stages of growth, such intelligent thinking ahead is particularly necessary for orderly and rapid economic growth.

These, then, constitute the necessary factors for breaking through the vicious circle of economic stagnation: encouragement of agriculture and small industries; higher taxes and higher savings; a sensible integration of a developing economy into the world market; economic planning for steady, efficient growth; and a set of social policies designed to encourage the development of attitudes and institutions receptive to modernization. Combined judiciously, these policies can ensure that the quest for bread will not end in a whimper.

Responding to the Political Challenge

> No, I shall not believe that this human race . . . has become a bastardized flock of sheep . . . and that nothing remains but to deliver it . . . to a small number of shepherds who, after all, are not better animals than are we, the human sheep, and who indeed are often worse.
>
> ALEXIS DE TOCQUEVILLE

In the drive for development, all signs point to the sovereignty of politics. At their core, attempts to change the wretched condition of transitional men rest on political choices. How to accumulate capital and yet resist the tempting path of compulsion? How to preserve traditional culture but still change a feudal social structure? How to build a growing economy and yet avoid the exploitation which accompanied the expansion of industry in the past? This is the apex of the problem, for political—or, if you will, ethical—decisions determine the answer to such questions.

In responding to the stresses which afflict their societies, leaders in developing countries have divided into two political camps. Ranged on one side stand the authoritarians who are willing to use any practical means, including force, to achieve their ends. Authoritarian ideologies, while presented in varied garbs, assert certain common goals:

The authoritarian wishes national independence, freedom for the State or People—but not for the individual. Sékou Touré of Guinea has stated this view with blunt openness, "We have chosen the freedom, the right, the power, the sovereignty of the people, and not of the individual." [11] The survival and power of the group comes first; no domain of the individual's life should remain—on principle or in fact—outside the purview of the state.

The authoritarian believes that only a single party can create a sense of nationhood and unity which he regards as necessary during a period of modernization. Autonomous organizations or political parties, each articulating its own goals, are dispensable. Through some mystic identification, the authoritarian contends, Leader, Party, and People can become one. The unified party supposedly serves as the vanguard of progress and discourages disunity, factionalism, and subversion during a time of great tensions.

The authoritarian demands that development should occur through "socialist" methods. He believes that only socialism, usually conceived as heavy industrialization, can eradicate the poverty, disease, and illiteracy characteristic of pauper nations.

For the authoritarian, all human resources must be mobilized in the service of Party and Productivity. While robed in new garments, the authoritarian of today can find ample, if unsavory, company in the past. His arguments have been advanced from the Pharaohs' epoch to that of Goebbels. Witness Frederick the Great, in his defense of a "modernizing" Germany: "At the moment when the State cries out that its very life is at stake, social selfishness must cease and party hatred be hushed. The individual must forget his egoism, and feel that he is a member of the whole body." [12]

The world has never lacked those who defend their own power, privileges, and perquisites in the name of a brave cause or those who have claimed that history will absolve them for any action they commit. The Cause, the Party, or God have almost always overridden the quiet cries of an unknown individual, caught in the movement of history.

Yet, with whatever effect—and sometimes it has been noble—a band of questioners have wondered whether the particular emperor wore any clothes. In the face of many temptations, these men still fight a battle for freedom in the developing countries. They can be found under a variety of labels: liberal, democratic socialist, even conservative. Yet, they share certain assumptions about the nature of man and society. This pluralistic political credo entails these commitments:

The pluralist affirms the potential creativity, rationality, and dignity of the individual. He rejects the supremacy of the State or People, as these abstractions are expressed in the arbitrary decisions of an uncontrollable leadership.

The pluralist views with suspicion any group which claims to have discovered "the true faith," for he believes that the road to progress is barred by dogma. He therefore rejects the pronouncements of those arrogant "shepherds" who assume that fate has elected them to herd the masses. He remembers Demosthenes' advice that "there is one safeguard known generally to the wise, which is an advantage and security to all, but especially to democrats as against despots. What is it? Distrust!"

The pluralist wishes to create political and judicial institutions which will assure freedom from arbitrary arrest, freedom to criticize authority, freedom of movement, and freedom to organize a representative opposition to those in power. He rejects the fashionable argument that the social context of new nations alters the essential nature of these liberties, for he contends that freedom's defense, in today's West Africa as in ancient Greece, requires a vigilant watchfulness expressed in a network of institutions reinforced by the rule of law.

The pluralist finds unconvincing the argument that a one-party bureaucracy can somehow be cleansed by the vigilance of the people. He recognizes that, regardless of the historical situation, the victim feels the same when he fears an informer, when he knows that his judge is a political stooge, when he is kept in ignorance by a muzzled press, or when he languishes in jail for political crimes. The pluralist believes that no discourse about "new" forms of freedom can convince a political prisoner in Ghana, China, or Indonesia that he really has his liberty.

The pluralist knows well that a society cannot release itself from fear until the curse of starvation has ended. He adheres to Lord Acton's dictum that "the theory of liberty demands strong efforts to help the poor. Not merely for safety, for humanity, for religion, but for liberty." [13] The pluralist, therefore, wishes to abolish privilege, end economic serfdom, and extend equality of opportunity to all. He does not, however, necessarily identify human happiness with a growth in national income or the spread of industrialization. He understands that industrialization has not always extended the scope of individual freedom, and he knows that the most wealthy nations have the highest rates of mental disorder, alcoholism, and suicide—unmistakable signs that even a cornucopia of material goods cannot make up for a loss of personal dignity and security. In consequence, the pluralist believes that economic growth should be measured in terms of the degree to which it ends suffering, enhances individual dignity, and widens the possibility of free choice.

It is of vital importance to assert once again these principles of liberty and to recognize that men live not by bread alone. But for the embattled leaders in emerging nations—faced with the anarchy of the Congo, or the irresponsible union movement in Bolivia, or the reactionary power of a caste system—mere expostulation does not go far enough. In building a better society, as Africanist Immanuel Wallerstein has commented, "the only useful question to ask, in the old-fashioned American pragmatic tradition, is how you get from here to there." [14]

Unlike the authoritarian, who has the propaganda advantage of claiming ready-made solutions to all problems, the pluralist has to content himself with accepting the uncertainties of responsibility. But the pluralist can depend on certain principles which history has validated:

The methods which leaders use affect them and their societies. If stampeded by cruel methods which destroy their dignity, self-reliance, and indigenous democratic institutions, the ruled lose their capacity for freedom and may, as in Indonesia, lose their prosperity, too. In particular, leaders must realize that an increase in wealth will not spontaneously produce a politically free society. History has yet to provide an example of a nation which, through the use of Draconian methods, achieved both literacy and prosperity, as well as liberty of conscience and a rule of law. As philosopher John Plamanetz has perceptively warned the new nations:

The recipe, first raise productivity and material well-being and abolish illiteracy, doing whatever needs to be done to these ends, and afterwards set about establishing freedom and democracy is bad . . . history gives us no example of a nation that first grew prosperous and acquired a strong centralized government and then afterwards became free and democratic. It is not true of the Greeks or the Romans or the Dutch or the English or the Swiss or the Americans; of any of the people who have cared most for freedom or democracy, or have enjoyed them the most securely. [15]

Those who desire both bread and freedom for their people should not be beguiled by the promise that authoritarian rule is merely a transitory stage.* From the beginning, leaders must use methods which are consonant with the goal of creating a free society.

* There are, of course, exceptional periods in history where a free society has put extraordinary limits on the individual's liberty and yet eventually recovered these freedoms. American history—with its record of Lincoln's suspension of

To create a politically open society, the leadership must work to maintain or build a plural social structure—depositories of power independent of the group which controls the government. A rule of law, the right to criticize, the right of privacy—all the majestic liberties first created in the West—depend upon a complex, interdependent social structure which no government thinking of its own survival would dare to attack. Only a balance of economic power between various segments of a community can serve to preserve liberty. In particular terms, this means that the government should give all possible encouragement to trade unions and entrepreneurs, to rural co-operatives and village councils, to small industries and a free landholding peasantry. These independent units should be nourished both because of the economic reasons which we have previously discussed and because they serve as the surest defense of liberty.

A corollary of this position is, of course, that the central state should, as far as possible, avoid any movement toward total collectivization of property. History has issued a clear warning concerning the relationship of state authority and economic collectivization. As political scientist Massimo Salvadori has observed:

> *Since the beginning of civilization there have been numerous collectivist societies. Not a single one has enjoyed free institutions. Miracles can happen; but it is wiser to believe in miracles (especially economic and political miracles) after they have happened and not before.*[16]

In a developing country the government must play a very wide role indeed, not only in maintaining justice and order but also in planning and co-ordinating the economy, building an infra-structure, and breaking up concentrations of power in feudal hands. Nevertheless the government should try most of all to plan consciously for a devolution, rather than a concentration, of economic power.

A paradox which confronts pluralists in almost all countries is that, while seeking to encourage a diversity of pressure groups, they must also imbue their peoples with a "public philosophy" and a sense of nationhood. The leadership must encourage interest groups within their society to listen, negotiate, and compromise with each other in the name of the "national good." It would seem that only the vehicle of nationalism can transform warring tribes, castes, regions, economic

---

habeas corpus, the Palmer raids, and McCarthyism—serves as a case in point. Fortunately, liberal forces in America were able to overcome these indignities. The general pattern is nonetheless clear: once a nation starts down an authoritarian path, it bcomes extremely difficult to retrace the steps.

or ethnic groups into united countries.[17] Yet, the dangers of narrowly
conceived nationalism are all-too-obvious. The nationalist credo has
served as an excuse for despotism, a hindrance to international economic co-operation, an incitement to wars large and small, and, in
this era of global history, it carries the ultimate threat of atomic
extermination.

The task is, therefore, a delicate one, calling for unusually talented
and enlightened leadership. Despite all its troubles, India has managed
an extraordinarily promising answer to this problem. While avoiding
the dangers of chauvinism, the Indian leadership has created a fragile
but still real sense of national identity in much of the population.
The symbolic images of Gandhi and Nehru, public investments to
strengthen national unity, institutional devices such as consultative
committees to the government and public hearings on basic issues have
been combined to make the people aware of themselves as Indians
rather than solely as members of a particular subgroup. Too often, in
viewing the give and take of Indian politics, observers see only the
weakness of disunity—which, as we have noted, is quite apparent—
while overlooking the achievements of the Indian leadership during
the past fifteen years. In commenting upon India's accomplishments,
Ambassador Chester Bowles has put the record in a more realistic
perspective:

> *If we should suddenly wake up to read that Europe had achieved
> unity comparable with that of India, with a single Prime Minister, a
> single Parliament, a single set of internal laws, with a common market
> and a common constitution, the event would be hailed as a modern
> political miracle. . . . Yet when the pessimists consider India they
> see not the remarkable unity of more than 450 million people in 15
> states under a common government that provides a basis for growing
> political and economic strength, but the* differences *which it is as-
> sumed will at some point fragment the whole.*[18]

While her problems are still vast, India's success—achieved with a
minimum of compulsion and without the destruction of competing
interest groups—gives reason to hope that unity amid diversity is not an
impossible goal for developing societies.

Leaders in emerging nations must accept the fact that the maintenance of a free society sometimes exacts a cost in economic efficiency.
Because of universal suffrage and the free play of political parties, a
developing nation may have to divert some of its resources from productive enterprises to the satisfaction of popular demands, to fulfilling

an increased wish for consumption, and to welfare services. Clearly, this has been the case in India: expenditures for consumption have been relatively high, and political considerations have sometimes forced the uneconomic placement of new industries. In Ghana, during the austerity budget crisis, a distinct choice had to be made between economic growth and political freedom. One observer commented at the time:

> The alternatives are clear-cut. The Government can revoke the system of compulsory savings; it can curtail less essential spending, spread the budget over a longer period of time, better prepare the people psychologically for new sacrifices, and be satisfied with a lower rate of economic development. Or the revolution can begin to consume its own children.[19]

In Ghana, the revolution "began to consume its own children," but even paying the devil's price did not bring the expected reward. Ghana has stagnated since 1960, while India, faced with similar alternatives, went a freer path and has maintained a steady, if modest, record of economic progress.

While admitting that freedom can carry a price tag, the leadership in developing nations must also come to understand a fact which it tends to ignore at this moment in history: that the imposition of an authoritarian regime can also levy a heavy economic cost. Authoritarianism can decrease the flow of information from the people to the elite; it can destroy the individual's belief that he can change things; it can waste a nation's resources with greater largess than in a democracy; it can transform the social conflicts which always attend economic change into fatally violent battles. Indonesia's record serves as ample evidence, as do China's and Ghana's between 1960 and 1963. At times, a dictatorship can stimulate the rate of production; at times, it can decisively retard it—a simple lesson, repeatedly taught throughout history, but as yet unlearned by many.

The task of those who desire to create a free and abundant society in the "Third World" is by no means easy: they must decentralize power but maintain stability and a sense of nationhood; they must create a basic consensus without suppressing dissent; they must maintain a pluralistic social structure but undermine the power of traditionalist groups who seek to hold back progress; they must put their faith in the villagers and respect the people's potentiality, while realizing that tutelage from above may long be required; they must comprehend that now, as in Europe of 1848, the decisions taken by individual leaders at points of crisis will critically affect their nation's destiny—and they cannot fall back on the comforting sense that history is on their side. They find themselves involved in a series of paradoxes which inspire fear, if not despair, in the stoutest of hearts.

But regard the authoritarian alternative: a single party controlling all aspects of life; an elite arbitrarily and often mistakenly directing the economy; detentions without trial; a *Gleichschaltung* program of ranging everything from unions to the family under the guidance of a party bureaucracy; a "Redeemer" who promises, but often fails to deliver, economic welfare; a regime which treats men as part of an experiment in animal husbandry. Is this the way to a good life for mankind? Is this some new constitutional form, or merely tyranny adorned with different slogans? Those of good will, those of historical perspective, those who respect individuals rather than abstract masses will, I am convinced, choose the more ambiguous but eventually more rewarding path of building a plural society.

"All Peoples of the Globe Together Sail"

> To create a more equal allotment of property and of rights throughout the world is the greatest task which confronts those who lead human affairs.
>
> ALEXIS DE TOCQUEVILLE

The fate of developing nations depends primarily on the courage and wisdom of their leaders—and on the responsiveness of the great peasant millions who are slowly awakening to the possibility of a better life. Yet, those of us lucky enough to have been born in an economically abundant region must also share the responsibility. For however Promethean the effort, it is clear that developing countries cannot bring the quest for bread and freedom to a successful ending without moral, economic, and political assistance from the rich nations.

On the economic level, the hard fact remains that only generous long-term aid from industrialized countries can provide the extra margin of capital and skills which emerging societies desperately need.

The world possesses abundant resources to fill the gap. War preparations alone gobble up $120 billion annually, a sum greater than two-thirds of the entire national income of all developing countries. If only a fraction of the capital now devoted to armaments were diverted to aiding developing nations, we would witness a real improvement in the material welfare of the majority of humanity. For example, to double the personal standard of living in the developing regions within the foreseeable future would use only 10 per cent of the capital saved from reducing armaments by one-half.

In those few instances where the rich nations have opened their purses to a poor country, the result has been an economic transformation of the region. Israel presents the best illustration. During the past fifteen years, the Israeli economy has grown enormously. While blessed with other fortunate attributes, Israel could not possibly have advanced so well without an unusually strong capital inflow. During her period of growth, Israel received the equivalent of some $2000 per person. Oscar Gass, an expert on the Israeli economy, has underlined the significance of this assistance:

> Israeli circumstances are somewhat special, the achievement in the case of Israel is greater than in other countries, the human material is different, the social situation is different. None of us working there, however, would have believed that anything remotely like what we achieved in Israel with a capital inflow of two thousand dollars per person could have been achieved with a capital inflow of five hundred dollars per person . . . we would probably have gone under, and the State of Israel would not have survived.[20]

In contrast to Israel's good fortune, Latin America—supposedly a major area of United States commitment—received an average of fifty cents per person between 1945 and 1960. Can one wonder, then, at the uneven performance of South American economies? The meager contribution in grants and loans from the United States could hardly have wrought an economic revolution even under the best conditions— and especially since the outflow of profits to North American companies greatly exceeded governmental aid.

In India, more substantial aid from the West, Japan, and Russia has led to steady progress, but this will continue only if advanced nations make a fully determined effort to aid India's experiment of combining economic development with freedom. In the third five-year plan, nearly 30 per cent of internal revenue will have to come from the equivalent of rupees from abroad. If this source of funds dried up, domestic austerities—already pushed to the boundary that persuasion allows—would have to be forcibly increased. But beyond this, India has to command an additional £2400 million in foreign funds to pay for vitally needed imports. Since exports cannot possibly rise enough to balance imports, at least £1950 million will be needed from abroad. If such aid is not forthcoming, the resulting chaos would doom India's attempt to create a prosperous, open, and plural society.

The facts are eminently clear: without massive sustained aid, there can be little, if any, economic progress in developing nations. And without such progress, the material welfare and even survival of the advanced nations themselves is endangered. On this issue, self-interest and morality dictate that advanced regions should have the vision to see beyond their own complacent horizons and accept the fact that they are members of the world family of man.

Politically, as Barbara Ward has rightly argued, "the need is to remove the work of world development from the subsidiary attention of the wealthy nations and to make it a central theme of their diplomacy, their international relations, their philosophy of world order. . . ." [21]

We must submerge nationalistic rivalries, as Russia and China did for a time, to establish a world common market which will give a margin of safety to the Third World's exports.

We must be willing to use our economic, moral, and, if necessary, military power to defend freely developing societies. This entails not only protecting India from further incursions by China but also the withdrawal of our support for petty dictatorships from Formosa to Saudi Arabia.

We must, of course, put our own house in order, for no society can proclaim its dedication to freedom while tolerating Little Rocks and *bidonvilles*, a Mississippi or a Notting Hill.

We must affirm, in words and actions, our belief that development can proceed without totally uprooting traditional culture; that a pluralistic society provides the surest defense of human dignity; and that totalitarian centralization offers no high road to abundance.

We must, when looking ahead to the grander sweep of history, press on for co-operation with Russia in the common task of consummating a world order. With a new philosophy of international relations and even a small degree of disarmament, the flow of aid to developing countries could be measurably increased.

All of this requires that we address ourselves with new seriousness to the encouragement of institutions which will protect freedom, feed the poor, and expand the scope of human dignity. To be sure, the task is grim and complicated. "But in such grave matters," Henry Kissinger has correctly observed, "the unforgivable sin is not to have failed but never to have tried." [22] If wisdom prevails, our grandchildren will live to see a world which fulfills Mill's prophecy: a more inhabitable planet, where the greatest sources of human degradation have been conquered by human care and effort.

hate, and indignity can be eradicated. As always, the intellectual has the further duty of delineating the complexity of the present, the indeterminacy of the future, and the consequent freedom and responsibility of those who decide society's fate.

I have written the book primarily for the thoughtful uncommitted person in developing regions. It is intended as a modest counterweight to the mass of literature which tells transitional man either that his fate is hopeless or that his salvation will come only at the hands of a dictator. In fact, I believe, little has been preordained about the future of developing nations; their rise or fall depends on the choices leaders make at this point of extreme crisis. My plea has been a simple one: that an authoritarian solution creates more social problems than it cures and that a pluralistic approach will, in the long stretch of history, go farthest toward satisfying man's longing for bread and freedom.

In preparing the book, I had the good fortune to visit various developing nations throughout the world in 1961, 1962 and 1964. Grants from Stanford's Public Affairs Committee (supported by the Ford Foundation), from the Stanford Graduate School, and from the Social Research Center, American University at Cairo, made possible these journeys. Everywhere I met with kindness, but I would like to thank the following individuals for their special thoughtfulness:

Dr. Zakir Hussain, Vice-President of India; S. K. Dey, Indian minister of Community Development; Asoka Mehta, R. Dave, Nath Pai, and M. Beharilal, all members of the Indian parliament; Raj Krishna of the Delhi Institute of Economic Growth; M. Ramakrishna of the Delhi section of U.S.I.S.; Kussum Nair, Indian author; M. Hutasoit, chairman of the Indonesian National Planning Council; Donald Toussaint and Kurt Nathan of the American mission to Indonesia; Dr. Alphonse Said of the Social Research Center, Cairo; M. Choynowski, Henrik Holland, Adam Sarapata, and Adam Schaff, all of the Polish Academy of Arts and Sciences; Julian Hochfeld, Maria Ossowska, Andrey Malewski, and Jan Szczepanski, professors of sociology in Poland; John Noon and Preston Valien of the American embassy in Nigeria; Ben Nzeribe, Kalu Ezera and A. Rosiji, members of the Nigerian parliament; Roy Hanley and Kevin Flannagan of the Nigerian Ministry of Education; Wolfgang Stopler, economic adviser to Nigeria; L. R. Abavana, Ghanaian Minister of Agriculture; A. J. Dowuona-Hammond, Ghanaian Minister of Education; Dr. Miller Craig, Principal Secretary for the Ministry of Economic Development, Ghana; Mr. J. E. Ababio, national organizer, Ghanaian Builder's Brigade; Dr. David Kimball, head of extra-mural studies, University of Ghana; David

Acquah, deputy director of the Ghanaian Department of Social Welfare; Dr. de Graft-Johnson, head of the Department of Sociology, University of Ghana; K. O. Thompson, Secretary of the Ghanian parliament; and Dr. Laila El-Hamasi, director of the Social Research Center, Cairo.

Karin Inge went through the laborious task of correcting and typing the book with her typical good humor. Several ex-students—Dale Johnson, Theodore Harwood, Sigrid von Keyserling, William Tuohy, and David Korten—encouraged and criticized the work.

In different form, various sections of this volume have appeared in *The New Leader, Dissent,* and *The New Sociology.* I appreciate the publishers' permission to reprint this material.

I am particularly grateful to some very good friends who not only read the manuscript, but extended aid, advice, and personal sustenance during its writing: Hans Kohn, professor emeritus of history, City College of New York; Dr. and Mrs. Charles Drekmeier, Stanford University; Dr. and Mrs. Richard Quandt, Princeton University; and Dr. Jan Howard, research associate in sociology, Stanford University.

NOTES

INTRODUCTION

1. Sidney Lens, "The Birth Pangs of the Revolution," *The Progressive*, Dec., 1961, p. 32.
2. Smith Hempstone, *The New Africa* (London: Faber & Faber, Ltd.), p. 641.
3. Robert Heilbroner, *The Future as History* (New York: Harper & Row, Publishers, 1959), p. 90.
4. *Ibid.*, p. 80.
5. Jacob Viner, "The Economics of Development," in *The Economics of Underdevelopment*, A. N. Agarwala and S. P. Singh eds. (Oxford University Press, 1958), p. 17.
6. Seymour Martin Lipset, *Political Man* (Garden City, N.Y.: Doubleday & Company, Inc., 1960), p. 77.
7. Alexis de Tocqueville, *Democracy in America*, Vol. I (New York: Alfred A. Knopf, Inc., Vintage ed., 1945), pp. 251-2.
8. Quoted in *Rich Lands and Poor* by Gunnar Myrdal (New York: Harper & Row, Publishers, 1957), p. 46.
9. Harrison Brown, *The Challenge of Man's Future* (New York: The Viking Press, Inc., 1956), pp. 228-9.
10. Carolina Maria de Jesus, *Child of the Dark* (New York: E. P. Dutton & Co., Inc., 1962), p. 11.
11. *Ibid.*, pp. 38, 47.
12. *Ibid.*, p. 38.
13. Robert Heilbroner, *The Great Ascent* (New York: Harper & Row, Publishers, 1963), p. 66.

CHAPTER I

1. Frank Tannenbaum, *Ten Keys to Latin America* (New York: Alfred A. Knopf, Inc., 1962), p. 22.
2. See John Gerassi, "What Is Castroism's Appeal?", *New Republic*, Jan. 12, 1963.
3. George Kimble, *Tropical Africa* (Garden City, N.Y.: Doubleday & Company, Inc., Anchor ed., 1962), Vol. II, p. 156.
4. Robert Redfield, *Peasant Society and Culture* (Chicago: University of Chicago Press, 1956).
5. *Report of the Select Committee of the House of Commons*, 1832, Vol. III, Appendix 84, p. 331.
6. Kussum Nair, *Blossoms in the Dust* (London: Gerald Duckworth & Co., Ltd., 1961), p. 125.
7. Colin Turnbull, *The Lonely African* (New York: Simon and Schuster, Inc., 1962), p. 82.
8. See Myron Weiner, *Politics of Scarcity* (Chicago: University of Chicago Press, 1962).
9. *Report of the Select Committee*, *op. cit.*
10. Max Millikan and Donald Blackmer, *The Emerging Nations* (Boston: Little, Brown & Co., 1961), p. 24.
11. Quoted in Turnbull, *op. cit.*, p. 78.
12. *Ibid.*
13. Colin Rosser, "A Hermit Village in Kulu," in *India's Villages*, M. N. Srinivas, ed. (Bombay: Asia Publishing House, 1960), p. 83.
14. H. O. Davies, *Nigeria: the Prospects for Democracy* (London: Weidenfeld and Nicolson, 1961).
15. Rosser, *op. cit.*
16. M. N. Srinivas, "The Social Structure of a Mysore Village," in *op. cit.*, p. 30.
17. Tannenbaum, *op. cit.*, p. 65.
18. David McClelland, *The Achieving Society* (Princeton, N.J.: D. Van Nostrand Co., Inc., 1961), pp. 395-6.
19. Nair, *op. cit.*, p. 195.
20. Paul Hoffman, *World Without Want* (New York: Harper & Row, Publishers, 1962).
21. Peter Bauer and Basil Yamey, *The Economics of Underdeveloped Countries* (Chicago: University of Chicago Press, 1957), p. 99.
22. Turnbull, *op. cit.*, p. 53.
23. *Ibid.*, pp. 83-4.

CHAPTER II

1. Kingsley Davis, "Urbanization in India," in *India's Urban Future*, Roy Turner, ed. (Berkeley: University of California Press, 1962), p. 7.
2. Arthur Lewis, "Economic Problems of Development," in *Restless Nations* (New York: Dodd, Mead & Co., 1962), p. 75.
3. *Ibid.*, p. 71.

4. Daniel Lerner, *The Passing of Traditional Society* (New York: Free Press of Glencoe, Inc., 1958).

5. Oscar Lewis, "Mexico Since Cardenas," *Social Research*, Spring, 1959, p. 26.

6. *Public Opinion Surveys* of the Indian Institute of Public Opinion, I, No. 3 (Oct. 1955), p. 10.

7. Unpublished poll conducted for the Institute for Sociological Research, Santiago, Chile, by Professor Eduardo Hamuy.

8. Colin Turnbull, *The Lonely African* (New York: Simon and Schuster, Inc., 1962).

9. Shanti Tangri, "Urbanization, Political Stability, and Economic Growth," in Turner, *op. cit.*

10. Nelly Xydias, *Social Implications of Industrialization and Organization in Africa South of the Sahara* (Paris: UNESCO, Tensions and Technology Series, 1956).

11. See: Oscar Lewis, *Five Families* (Holt, Rinehart, & Winston, New York: 1962); B. M. Spinley, *The Deprived and the Privileged* (London: Routledge & Kegan Paul, Ltd., 1953); and F. Zweig, *Labour, Life and Poverty* (London: Victor Gollancz, Ltd., 1949).

12. Cardina Maria de Jesus, *Child of the Dark* (New York: E. P. Dutton & Co., Inc., 1962).

13. Oliver La Farge, in Lewis, *Five Families, op. cit.*, pp. 9-10.

14. Turnbull, *op. cit.*, p. 42.

15. Thomas Hodgkin, *Nationalism in Colonial Africa* (New York: New York University Press, 1957).

16. D. N. Majundar, *Unemployment Among the University Educated* (Cambridge, Mass.: Center for International Studies, M.I.T., 1957), pp. 33-4.

17. Turnbull, *op. cit.*, p. 59.

18. *Public Opinion Surveys* of the Indian Institute of Public Opinion, II, No. 3 (Dec. 1956), p. 12.

19. E. T. Sherwood, quoted in "Self-Anchoring Scaling," by F. P. Kilpatrick and Hadley Cantril, *Journal of Individual Psychology*, XVI, No. 2 (Nov. 1960).

20. See *Public Opinion Surveys* of the Institute of the Indian Institute of Public Opinion, I, No. 3 (Oct. 1955), p. 10.

21. Kussum Nair, *Blossoms in the Dust* (London: Gerald Duckworth & Co., Ltd., 1961).

22. Paul Baran, *The Political Economy of Growth* (New York: Prometheus Paperback, 1960), p. 4.

23. Max Millikan and Donald Blackmer, *The Emerging Nations* (Boston: Little, Brown & Co., 1961).

24. These are, of course, extremely broad and intensely controversial generalizations about peasant cultures. Support for these opinions can, however, be found in such writings as Frank Tannenbaum, *Ten Keys to Latin America* (New York: Alfred A. Knopf, Inc., 1962); Turnbull, *op. cit.*; H. O. Davies, *Nigeria: The Prospects for Democracy* (London: Widenfeld and Nicolson, 1961); M. N. Srinivas, ed., *India's Villages* (Bombay: Asia Publishing House, 1960); and P. Bauer and Basil Yamey, *The Economics of Underdeveloped Countries* (Chicago: University of Chicago Press, 1957). For cogent argu-

ments in opposition to these generalizations, see David McClelland, *The Achieving Society* (Prniceton: D. Van Nostrand & Co., Inc., 1961); Paul Baran, *op. cit.*; and Robert Heilbroner, *The Great Ascent* (New York: Harper & Row, 1963).

25. Edward Banfeld, *The Moral Basis of a Backward Society* (New York: Free Press of Glencoe, Inc., 1958), p. 56.

26. For supporting evidence, see such writings as Michael Edwardes, *Asia in the Balance* (Baltimore: Penguin Books, 1962); *Africa: Continent of Change*, Peter Gould, ed. (Belmont, Calif.: Wadsworth, 1961); Barbara Ward, *Five Ideas that Change the World* (London: Hamish Hamilton, 1959); Jean and Simone Lacouture, *L'Égypte en mouvement* (Paris: Editions du Geuil, 1962); and the various Public Opinion Surveys published by the Indian Institute of Public Opinion.

CHAPTER III

1. Alec Nove, "The Soviet Model and Upper-Developed Countries," *International Affairs*, XXXVII, No. 1 (1961), pp. 29-38.

2. Eugene Staley, *The Future of Underdeveloped Countries* (New York: Harper & Row, Publishers, 1961), p. 80.

3. Joseph Schumpeter, *The Theory of Economic Development* (Cambridge, Mass.: Harvard University Press, 1959).

4. Paul Baran, *The Political Economy of Growth* (New York: Monthly Review Press, 1960), p. 145.

5. *Ibid.*

6. In his *Social Change and The Industrial Revolution* (Chicago: Univ. of Chicago Press, 1959), Neil Smelser has carefully traced the pattern of this greater differentiation.

7. Simon Kuznetz, *Proceedings of the World Population Conference* (New York: United Nations, 1954).

8. See Lilian Knowles, *Economic Development in the Nineteenth Century* (London: Routledge & Kegan Paul, Ltd., 1932), p. 186.

9. Oleg Hoeffding, "The Soviet Union: Model for Asia?" *Problems of Communism*, VIII, No. 6 (Nov.-Dec. 1959), pp. 38-46.

10. The divergence in estimates comes not from conscious falsehood on the Russian part, but rather from variations in the measures utilized. Calvin Hoover has ably elucidated the problem in his *The Economy, Liberty, and the State* (Garden City, N.Y.: Doubleday & Company, Inc., 1961).

11. For sophisticated, detailed discussion of the rates of growth, see *Soviet Economic Growth*, Abram Bergson, ed. (Evanston, Ill.: Row Peterson Co., 1953).

12. See Hoover, *op. cit.*

13. The government also employed a wide range of incentives, as well as the whip, to aid economic growth. Robert Campbell in his *Soviet Economic Power* (Boston: Houghton Mifflin Company, 1960) has dissected the nature of these incentives.

14. Both Robert Campbell (*ibid.*) and Alec Nove in *The Soviet Economy* (New York: Frederick A. Praeger, Inc., 1961) have traced the nature of these wastes in some detail.

15. Thomas Smith, *The Agarian Origins of Modern Japan* (Stanford, Calif.: Stanford University Press, 1959).
16. Robert Bellah, *Tokugawa Religion* (New York: Free Press of Glencoe, Inc., 1957), p. 184.
17. The entire process of capital accumulation has been closely analyzed by Henry Rosovsky in *Capital Formation in Japan* (New York: Free Press of Glencoe, Inc., 1961).
18. Baran, *op. cit.*, p. 155.
19. See Thomas O. Wilkinson, "Family Structure and Industrialization in Japan," *American Sociological Review*, Vol. 27, No. 5, Oct., 1962.
20. See James Abegglen, *The Japanese Factory* (New York: Free Press of Glencoe, Inc., 1958).
21. Max Millikan and Donald Blackmer, *The Emerging Nations* (Boston: Little, Brown & Co., 1961), p. 47.
22. Albert Hirschman, *The Strategy of Economic Development* (New Haven, Conn.: Yale University Press, 1958).
23. Robert Heilbroner, *The Great Ascent* (New York: Harper & Row, Publishers, 1963), pp. 98-9.
24. Kenneth Galbraith, *Economic Development in Perspective* (Cambridge, Mass.: Harvard University Press, 1962), p. 13.
25. Staley, *op. cit.*, pp. 82-3.

CHAPTER IV

1. Robert Heilbroner, *The Great Ascent* (New York: Harper & Row, Publishers, 1963), p. 27.
2. Following Allyn Young, "Capital," *Encyclopedia Britannica*, London, 14th ed.
3. Colin Clark, "Population Growth and Living Standards," in *The Economics of Underdevelopment*, A. N. Agarwala and S. P. Singh, eds. (London: Oxford University Press, 1958), p. 52.
4. See Harrison Brown, *The Challenge of Man's Future* (New York: The Viking Press, Inc., 1954).
5. Karl Marx, *Capital*, Vol. I (Chicago: 1906), p. 834.
6. I am indebted to Paul Baran's *The Political Economy of Growth* (New York: Monthly Review Press, 1960), p. 21, for this illustration (as well as for many other insights).
7. See *United Nations Economic Survey of Asia and the Far East* (1954), p. 63, and B. Datta, *The Economics of Industrialization* (Calcutta, 1952), p. 229.
8. Robert Alexander, *A Primer of Economic Development* (New York: The Macmillan Company, 1962), Chapter 6.
9. M. Bronfenbrenner, "The Appeal of Confiscation in Economic Development," *Economic Development and Cultural Change*, Vol. III, No. 3 (Apr. 1955).
10. Peter Bauer and Basil Yamey, *The Economics of Underdeveloped Countries* (Chicago: University of Chicago Press, 1957).
11. *Ibid.*, p. 151.
12. *Ibid.*, p. 201.

13. Henry C. Wallich, *The Cost of Freedom* (New York: The Crowell-Collier Publishing Co., 1962), pp. 48-9.

14. *Ibid.*, p. 49.

15. See Arthur Lewis, "Economic Problems of Development," *Restless Nations* (New York: Dodd, Mead & Co., 1962).

16. For penetrating discussions of how much a nation should spend on "social overhead," see Albert Hirschman, *The Strategy of Economic Development* (New Haven, Conn.: Yale University Press, 1958), and Arthur Lewis, *The Theory of Economic Growth* (Homewood, Ill.: Richard D. Irwin, Inc., 1955).

17. Lewis, *The Theory of Economic Growth, op. cit.*, Chapters 6 and 7.

18. Arthur Lewis, "Economic Problems of Development," *op. cit.*

19. See Ragnar Nurkse, *Problems of Capital Formation in Underdeveloped Countries* (New York: Oxford University Press, 1953); Benjamin Higgins, *Economic Development* (London: Constable & Co., Ltd., 1959), particularly Chapters 23 and 24; and Arthur Lewis, *The Theory of Economic Growth, op. cit.* For Indian proposals, see Nicholas Kaldor, *Indian Tax Reform* (Delhi: Ministry of Finance, 1956).

20. Simon Kuznets, *Proceedings of the World Population Conference* (New York: United Nations, 1954), Vol. V.

CHAPTER V

1. Elspeth Huxley, *A New Earth* (London: Chatto & Windus, Ltd., 1961), p. 188.

2. *Ibid.*, pp. 188-9.

3. *Ibid.*, p. 188.

4. See Josué de Castro, *The Geography of Hunger* (Boston: Little, Brown & Co., 1952).

5. See Arthur Lewis, *The Theory of Economic Growth* (Homewood, Ill.: Richard D. Irwin, Inc., 1955), p. 188.

6. See Jack Woddis, *Africa: The Roots of Revolt* (London: Lawrence and Wishart, 1960), p. 43.

7. *Borgo a Mozzano* (Genoa: Shell Italiana, 1961).

8. Guy Hunter, *The New Societies of Tropical Africa* (London: Oxford University Press, 1962), p. 65.

9. See Karl Sax, *The World's Exploding Population* (Boston: Beacon Press, 1960).

10. See Colin Clark, "Population Growth and Living Standards," in *The Economics of Underdevelopment*, A. N. Agarwala and S. P. Singh, eds. (London: Oxford University Press, 1958).

11. Chester Bowles, "The Key to Democratic Growth," *The Progressive*, Nov. 1962, p. 18 (italics added).

12. See Benjamin Higgins, *Economic Development* (London: Constable & Co., Ltd., 1959), Chapter 11 for a sophisticated discussion of this position and that of Neo-Malthusians.

13. For a brilliant defense of this view, see Henry Leibenstein, *Economic Backwardness and Economic Growth* (New York: John Wiley & Sons, 1957), as well as David McClelland, *The Achieving Society* (Princeton, N.J.: D. Van Nostrand Co., Inc., 1961).

14. Leibenstein, *op. cit.*, p. 263.

15. John Kenneth Galbraith, *Economic Development in Perspective* (Cambridge, Mass.: Harvard University Press, 1962), p. 9.

16. Kussum Nair, *Blossoms in the Dust* (London: Gerald Duckworth & Co., Ltd., 1961), p. 141.

17. Arthur Lewis in *Restless Nations*, Council on World Tensions (New York: Dodd, Mead & Co., 1962), pp. 80-1.

18. See John Johnson, ed., *The Role of the Military Underdeveloped Countries* (Princeton, N.J.: Princeton University Press, 1962).

19. Barbara Castle, "The Grass Roots of Egypt," *The New Statesman*, Feb. 22, 1963, p. 261.

20. *Ibid.*, p. 262.

21. Quoted in Frank Moraes, *India Today* (New York: Macmillan Company, 1960), p. 177.

22. *Ibid.*, pp. 176-7.

23. See *Third Five Year Plan*, Government of India, Planning Commission, (New Delhi: Govt. of India Press, 1961), particularly Chapters 1, 11, 20, 21, 22, 23, 25, 32.

24. See William O. Jones, "Food and Agricultural Economies of Tropical Africa," *Food Research Institute Studies*, Stanford University, Vol. 2, No. 1 (Feb. 1961), for evidence concerning the adaptability of African methods of cultivation to the climate.

25. Hunter, *op. cit.*, p. 96.

26. See *Miscellaneous Information*, 1960-61 (Accra, Ghana: Ministry of Agriculture, 1961).

27. V. D. Wickizer, "Some Aspects of Agricultural Development in the Tropics," *Tropical Agriculture*, Vol. 37 No. 3 (July 1960).

28. I. C. Jackson, *Advance in Africa* (London: Oxford University Press, Inc., 1956), p. 63.

29. *Ibid.*, p. 68.

30. Huxley, *op. cit.*, p. 191.

31. *Idem.*

32. *Ibid.*, p. 197.

33. *Ibid.*, p. 199.

34. See *Nature's Constant Gift* (Knoxville, Tenn.: Tennessee Valley Authority, 1963).

35. Hunter, *op. cit.* p. 110.

36. See Thomas F. Carroll, "The Land Reform Issue in Latin America" for a comprehensive discussion of the problem. (*In Latin American Issues*, ed., New York: The Twentieth Century Fund, 1961).

37. Quoted in *Gandhi*, by Louis Fischer (New York: Signet Key Book, 1954), p. 54.

CHAPTER VI

1. Quoted by Jawaharlal Nehru in *The Discovery of India*, reprinted in *The Ideologies of the Developing Nations*, Paul Sigmund, ed. (New York: Frederick A. Praeger, Inc., 1963), p. 92.

2. See Staley's discussion of this definition in "Development of Small Indus-

try Programmes," *Methods of Industrial Development* (Paris: Organization for Economic Co-operation and Development, 1962).

3. Nehru, *op. cit.*, p. 93.

4. *Ibid.*, p. 94.

5. Scarlett Epstein, "A Comparison of Social Change in a 'Dry' and in an 'Irrigated' Village in South India, 1957" (mimeographed), cited in Wilfred Malenbaum, *Prospects for Indian Development* (London: George Allen & Unwin, 1962), pp. 143-6.

6. *Ibid.*, p. 144.

7. *Ibid.*, p. 146.

8. See Ragnar Nurkse, *Problems of Capital Formation in Underdeveloped Countries* (New York: Oxford University Press, Inc., 1953), and *Patterns of Trade and Development* (Stockholm: Almgvist and Wicksell, 1959); Albert Hirschman, *The Strategy of Economic Development* (New Haven, Conn.: Yale University Press, 1958).

9. H. B. Chenery and T. Watanabe, "International Comparisons of the Structure of Production," 1956, cited in Albert Hirschman *The Strategy of Economic Development* (New Haven, Conn.: Yale University Press, 1961), p. 106.

10. *Ibid.*, p. 108.

11. Benjamin Higgins, *Economic Development* (London: Constable & Co., Ltd., 1959), p. 672.

12. Nehru, *op. cit.*, p. 93.

13. Hirschman, *op. cit.*

14. David McClelland, *The Achieving Society* (Princeton, N.J.: D. Van Nostrand Co., Inc., 1961).

15. Stuart Chase, *Mexico: a Study of Two Americas* (New York: The Macmillan Company, 1938), pp. 318-19.

16. McClelland, *op. cit.*, pp. 394-5.

17. Chou En-lai, *China and the Asian African Conference* (Peking: Foreign Languages Press, 1955), quoted in Sigmund, *op. cit.*, p. 53.

18. Raoul Prebisch in *The Economic Development of Latin America* (New York: U. N., 1949).

19. Paul Johnson, "The Plundered Continent," *The New Statesman*, Sept. 17, 1960, p. 382.

20. Barbara Ward, *The Rich Nations and the Poor Nations* (London: Hamish Hamilton, 1962), p. 96.

21. P. S. Lokanathan, "Cottage Industries and the Plan," *Eastern Economist*, New Delhi, July 23, 1943.

22. For supporting evidence, see William Brand, *The Struggle for a Higher Standard of Living* (New York: Free Press of Glencoe, Inc., 1958), especially pp. 85-93; and H. Belshaw, "Observations on Industrialization," *The Economic Journal*, LVII, No. 22 (Sept. 1947), pp. 379-87.

23. John Kenneth Galbraith, *Economic Development in Perspective* (Cambridge, Mass.: Harvard University Press, 1962), pp. 24-5.

24. See Staley, *op. cit.*

25. Arthur Lewis "Economic Problems of Development" in *Restless Nations* (New York: Dodd, Mead & Co., 1962), p. 74.

26. Johnson, *op. cit.*, p. 384.

27. Lewis, *op. cit.*, p. 70 (italics added).

28. Robert Heilbroner, *The Great Ascent* (New York: Harper & Row, Publishers, 1963), p. 120.
29. For supporting arguments, see B. F. Hoselitz, "Economic Growth and Rural Industrialization," *Economic Weekly*, New Delhi, Feb. 22, 1958, pp. 291-302, and Staley, *op. cit.*
30. For an excellent, objective discussion of Egyptian industrialization see *L'Égypte en Mouvement*, by Jean et Simone Lacouture (Paris: Editions du Geuil, 1962).
31. Elspeth Huxley, *A New Earth* (London: Chatto & Windus, Ltd., 1961), p. 202.
32. See Brand, *op. cit.*, p. 92.
33. Karl Meyer, "Mexico: the Frozen Revolution," *The Progressive*, May 1963, pp. 22-3.
34. See Staley, *op. cit.*, and Paul Hoffman, *World Without Want* (New York: Harper & Row, 1962), particularly pp. 72-4.
35. Ward, *op. cit.*, p. 96.

CHAPTER VII

1. Horace Miner, "Culture Change Under Pressure: A Hausa Case," reprinted in *Africa: Continent of Change*, Peter R. Gould, ed. (Belmont, Calif.: Wadsworth Publishing Co., 1961), p. 254.
2. John Kenneth Galbraith, *Economic Development in Perspective* (Cambridge, Mass.: Harvard University Press, 1962), p. 9.
3. Cited from "World Population Growth" by Harold F. Dorn in *The Population Dilemma* (New York: American Assembly, 1963), pp. 3-9. The figures are modified from the original source, *The Future Growth of World Population* (New York: United Nations, Department of Economic and Social Affairs, 1958) Table 5, p. 23.
4. *Ibid.*
5. Cited by Robert Cook in "Pitfalls of Progress," *The Nation*, Jan. 13, 1962.
6. See Ansley J. Coale, "Population and Economic Development" in *The Population Dilemma, op. cit.*
7. See Karl Sax, *The World's Exploding Population* (Boston, Beacon Press, 1960). pp. 140-42.
8. Paul Hoffman, *World Without Want* (New York: Harper and Row, Publishers, 1962), p. 63.
9. T. V. Ryabushkin in "Social Aspects of Population Structure and Movement," *United Nations World Population Conference*, 1954, Vol. 5, pp. 1032-3.
10. *Ibid.*
11. See "China's Birth Rate" by Robert Trumbull, *The New York Times*, June 20, 1963.
12. See "Issues of Population Policy" by Frank Lorimer in *The Population Dilemma, op. cit.*
13. *Ibid.* Also see Sax, *op. cit.*, Chapter 10, for further evidence.
14. Cook, *op. cit.*
15. Colin Clark, "Population Growth and Living Standards," in A. N. Agar-

wala and S. P. Singth, eds., *The Economics of Underdevelopment* (London: Oxford University Press, 1958), p. 33.

16. For information about these experiments, see "The Problem of Population Control" by Frank W. Notestein, Dudley Kirk and Sheldon Segal, in *The Population Dilemma, op. cit.*, and also Sax, *op. cit.*, particularly Chapter 7.

17. See Notestein et al., *op. cit.*

18. Sax, *op. cit.*, p. 192.

19. William J. Platt, *Economic and Comparative Education* (mimeographed) (Menlo Park, Calif.: Stanford Research Institute, 1962), p. 2.

20. See the presidential address by Theodore Schultz, *The American Economic Review*, Vol. LI, No. 1 (March 1961).

21. Galbraith, *op. cit.*, pp. 50-51.

22. Cited in Platt, *op. cit.*, p. 4.

23. Cited *ibid.*, p. 13.

24. For a description of this problem in Africa, see *Tropical Africa*, Vol. II, by George H. T. Kimble (Garden City, N.Y., Doubleday & Company, Inc., 1962); and *The New Nigerian Elite* by Hugh Smythe (Stanford Calif.: Stanford University Press, 1960).

25. For one side of the argument, see Platt, *op. cit.*, pp. 7-8; and Galbraith, *op. cit.*, Chapter 4. For the other side, see Arthur Lewis "Economic Problems of Development," in *Restless Nations* (New York: Dodd, Mead & Co., 1962); and Albert Hirschman, *The Strategy of Economic Development* (New Haven, Conn.: Yale University Press, 1958).

26. See as an example of some current empirical studies, *Research in Human Resources Development* by Paul Hanna (mimeographed) (Stanford, Calif.: Stanford University Press, 1963).

27. Platt, *op. cit.*, pp. 9-10.

28. *Ibid.*, p. 10.

29. P. N. Rosenstein-Rodan, "Problems of Industrialization of Eastern and South-Eastern Europe," in *The Economics of Underdevelopment, op. cit.*, p. 248 (italics added).

30. Hoffman, *op. cit.*, p. 53.

31. See *African Education Study* (mimeographed) (Accra: Primary Mathematics Program, 1962).

32. See D. S. Bushnell, *An Experimental Study of the Effectiveness of New Training Aids in the Training of Journeymen Electricians* (mimeographed) (Menlo Park, Calif.: (Stanford Research Institute, 1962).

33. See C. S. Coon, "Operation Bultiste—Promoting Industrial Development in Saudi Arabia," in *Hands Across Frontiers*, H. M. Teaf and P. G. Franck, eds. (Ithaca, N.Y.: Cornell University Press, 1955).

34. For information on some of these projects, see William J. Platt, summary remarks on *Seminar on Human Resources Development in Emerging Countries* (mimeographed) (Menlo Park, Calif.: Stanford Research Institute, 1962).

35. Schultz, *op. cit.*

36. See Joseph Stepanek, *Managers for Industry* (mimeographed) (Menlo Park, Calif.: Stanford Research Institute, 1960).

37. See Joseph Schumpeter, *Capitalism, Socialism, and Democracy* (New York: Harper & Row, Publishers, 1950).

38. See J. H. Boeke, lecture republished in *Indonesië*, Vol. VII, No. 4 (Apr. 1954). For an excellent exposition and criticism of Boerke's views, see *Economic Development*, by Benjamin Higgins (London: Constable & Co., Ltd., 1959), Chapter 12.

39. See *The Achieving Society* by David McClelland (Princeton, N.J.: D. Van Nostrand Co., 1961).

40. Everett Hagan, *On the Theory of Social Change* (Homewood, Ill.: The Dorsey Press, Inc., 1962), p. ix.

41. Lewis, *op. cit.*, p. 81. Also see "La Mentalité d'Entrepreneur aux Premières Phases du Développement" by Réne Clemens, in *Transactions of the Fifth World Congress of Sociology* (Louvain, Belgium: International Sociological Association, 1962). Vol. II.

42. Lewis, *op. cit.*, p. 83.

43. Higgins, *op. cit.*, p. 312.

44. McClelland, *op. cit.*, p. 406.

45. Wilbert E. Moore, "The Social Framework of Economic Development" in *Tradition, Values and Socio-Economic Development*, Ralph Braibanti and Joseph Spengler, eds. (N.C.: Duke University Press, Durham, 1961).

46. For examples, see Braibanti and Spengler, *op. cit.*; W. F. Wertheim, *Indonesian Society in Transition* (The Hague, Netherlands: N. V. Uitgevij W. van Hoeve, 1956); Arthur Lewis, *The Theory of Economic Growth* (Homewood, Ill.: Richard D. Irwin, 1955), Parts II and III; and Gould, *op. cit.*

47. Oscar Lewis, *Tepoztlán* (New York: Holt, Rinehart & Winston, Inc., 1960).

48. Alex Inkeles, "Social Change and Social Character: The Role of Parental Mediation" in *Personality and Social Systems*, Neil J. Smelser and William T. Smelser eds. (New York: John Wiley & Sons, Inc., 1963), p. 365.

49. Bert F. Hoselitz, "Tradition and Economic Growth" in Braibanti and Spengler, *op. cit.*

50. Max Millikan and Donald Blackmer, *The Emerging Nations* (Boston: Little, Brown & Co., 1961), p. 97.

51. *Ibid.*, p. 49.

CHAPTER VIII

1. See *The Great Fear* by John Gerassi (New York: The Macmillan Company, 1963), Part I.

2. See "New Perspectives" by Barbara Ward, in *Restless Nations* (New York: Dodd, Mead & Co., 1962).

3. See *The Prospects for Indian Development* by Wilfred Malenbaum (London: George Allen & Unwin, 1962), particularly pp. 305-8.

4. See *India and the West* by Barbara Ward (London: Hamish Hamilton, 1961), particularly Chapter 12.

5. See *World Without Want* by Paul Hoffman (New York: Harper & Row, Publishers, 1962), especially pp. 130-34.

6. See *The Attack on World Poverty* by Andrew Shonfield (London: Chatto & Windus, Ltd., 1961), particularly pp. 79-81.

7. P. N. Rosenstein-Rodan, "International Aid for Underdeveloped Countries," cited in the Appendix of *Restless Nations, op. cit.*

8. See *Quarterly Report,* "Foreign Grants and Credits by the United States Government" (Washington: U.S. Department of Commerce, Office of Business Economics, 1961).

9. See Hoffman, *op. cit.,* pp. 112-15.

10. See "Foreign Aid Re-examined" by J. B. Condliffe, *Journal* (Menlo Park, Calif.: Stanford Research Institute, 1963), p. 18.

11. See Shonfield, *op. cit.,* Chapter 2.

12. See Condliffe, *op. cit.*

13. See *The Nature of the Non-Western World* by Vera Michaeles Dean, (New York: New American Library, 1957), particularly Chapter 11.

14. U Nu, "Toward a Socialist State," reprinted in *The Ideologies of the Developing Nations,* Paul Sigmund, ed. (New York: Frederick A. Praeger, Inc., 1963), p. 64.

15. See Gerassi, *op. cit.,* pp. 142-3.

16. *Idem.*

17. *Ibid.,* p. 151.

18. See *Cuba: Anatomy of a Revolution* by Leo Huberman and Paul Sweezy (New York: Monthly Review Press, 1961), Chapter 3.

19. Robert Alexander, *A Primer of Economic Development* (New York: The Macmillan Company, 1962), p. 105.

20. See *Statistical and Economic Review,* United Africa Co., Mar. 1958.

21. See *Tropical Africa* by George H. T. Kimble (Garden City, N.Y.: Doubleday and Company, Inc., 1962), Vol. II, Chapter 8.

22. Sigmund, *op. cit.,* p. 19.

23. See "Multinational Companies," *Business Week,* Apr. 20, 1963.

24. Shonfield, *op. cit.,* pp. 89-90.

25. See Alexander, *op. cit.,* and Shonfield, *op. cit.,* for an elaboration of this view.

26. Condliffe, *op. cit.,* p. 14.

27. Cited in *Common Sense About a Starving World* by Ritchie Calder (New York: The Macmillan Company, 1962), pp. 11-12.

28. See *Giant Among Nations,* by Peter Kenan (New York: Harcourt, Brace and World, Inc., 1960).

29. "Network of Total International Trade, 1953-1960," *International Trade,* 1960 (Geneva: Gatt, 1961).

30. Condliffe, *op. cit.,* p. 9.

31. See "Latin America," *Business Week,* Sept. 22, 1962.

32. See Mario Rossi, *The Third World* (New York: Funk & Wagnalls Co., 1963), p. 124.

33. Robert Heilbroner, *The Great Ascent* (New York: Harper and Row, Publishers, 1963), p. 126.

34. See "Stabilization of Export Proceeds," by Henry Wallich in *Economic Development for Latin America,* Howard S. Ellis, ed. (London: Macmillan & Co., Ltd., 1961).

35. Theodore Schultz, "Prospects for Primary Production" in *ibid.*

36. Shonfield, *op. cit.,* p. 31.

37. Alexander, *op. cit.,* p. 38.

38. See "Problems of Industrialization of Eastern and South-Eastern Europe" by P. N. Rosenstein-Rodan, *The Economic Journal,* June-Sept. 1943.

39. See David Bell, letter to *The New York Times*, July 23, 1963.
40. "Report of Panel on Foreign Aid," *The New York Times*, Mar. 25, 1963.
41. Eric Sevareid, "A Realistic Look at Foreign Aid," Hall Syndicate, 1962.
42. Quoted in *Newsweek*, Aug. 7, 1962, p. 35.
43. *Ibid.*, p. 36.
44. See "Bread upon the Waters, The Problems and Promises of Development," in *Britannica Book of The Year* (Chicago: Encyclopedia Britannica, 1962), p. 8.
45. See *The Politics of Foreign Aid* by John D. Montgomery (New York: Frederick A. Praeger, Inc., 1962), pp. 48-51.
46. See "How Much Aid for India?" by N. Pattabhi Raman, *The New Leader*, June 10, 1963.
47. See Montgomery, *op. cit.*, pp. 38-40.
48. Edwin Lieuwen, *Arms and Politics in Latin America* (New York: Frederick A. Praeger, Inc., 1961), pp. 232-3.
49. Ward, *India and the West. op. cit.*, p. 239.

CHAPTER IX

1. Obafemi Awolowo, "Awo," reprinted in *The Ideologies of the Developing Nations*, Paul Sigmund, ed. (New York: Frederick A. Praeger, Inc., 1963), p. 224.
2. *Ibid.*, p. 225.
3. *Bhoodan*, July 3, 1957, p. 4.
4. See *India: The Most Dangerous Decades* by Selig Harrison (Princeton, N.J.: Princeton University Press, 1960), pp. 326-8.
5. See *Development for Free Asia* (Fairlawn, N.J., Essential Books, 1956).
6. Harrison, *op. cit.*, p. 5.
7. S. K. Chatters, *Report of the Official Language Commission* (Delhi: Government of India Press, 1957), p. 313.
8. A. L. Mudaliar, *Verbatim Record of the Educational Conference of 1948* (Delhi: Ministry of Education, Government of India Press, 1949), pp. 56, 59.
9. Harrison, *op. cit.*, p. 79.
10. Myron Weiner, *The Politics of Scarcity* (Chicago: University of Chicago Press, 1962), p. 37.
11. See *Kingship and Community in Early India* by Charles Drekmeier (Stanford, Calif.: Stanford University Press, 1962).
12. Harrison, *op. cit.*, p. 102.
13. *Ibid.*, p. 115.
14. N. V. Gadgil, *Proceedings*, House of the People, Dec. 17, 1952, col. 2612.
15. See "Order and Disorder in the Labour Force: the Jamshedpur Crisis of 1958," by Morris David Morris, *Economic Weekly*, X (Nov. 1, 1958), 1387-95.
16. See Weiner, *op. cit.*, Chapter 7 for a perceptive discussion of this problem; also see "The Culture of the Indian Intellectual" by Edward Shils, *Sewanee Review*, LXVII, No. 2 (Apr.-June 1959).
17. See Weiner, *ibid.*, Chapter 7 for a detailed analysis of these events.
18. See "A New Look at Nationalism," by Hans Kohn, *Virginia Quarterly Review*, Summer 1956.

19. Arnold J. Toynbee, *East and West* (New York: Oxford University Press. Inc., 1958), p. 101.

20. Subhas Chandra Bose, quoted in Harrison, *op. cit.*, p. 314.

21. *Idem.*

22. "Marx in India," *National Herald*, Jan. 5, 1954.

23. Nehru, *Hindu Weekly Review*, Apr. 12, 1954.

24. See Harrison, *op. cit.* p. 301.

25. *Ibid.*, p. 338.

26. John Gerassi, *The Great Fear* (New York: The Macmillan Company, 1963), p. 201.

27. Richard Patch, "Bolivia and U.S. Assistance," in *Social Change in Latin America Today* (New York: Random House, 1961), p. 115.

28. For an account of Bolivia's turmoil, see *The Bolivian National Revolution* by Robert Alexander (New Brunswick, N.J.: Rutgers University Press, 1958).

29. Gerassi, *op. cit.*, p. 203.

30. See "Showdown in Bolivia" by Juan de Onís, *The New York Times*, July 15, 1963.

31. See "Administration of U.S. Foreign Aid Programs in Bolivia," *Report No.* 1030 of the Senate Permanent Subcommittee on Investigations of the Committee on Government Operations, 86th Congress, 2nd session (Washington: U.S. Government Printing Office, 1960).

32. Patch, *op. cit.*, p. 131.

33. *Ibid.*, p. 157.

34. *Ibid.*, pp. 162-3.

35. Gerassi, *op. cit.*, p. 205.

36. Mario Rossi, *The Third World* (New York: Funk and Wagnalls Co., 1963), p. 41.

37. Edward Shils, "Old Societies and New States," in *Democracy in the New States, Rhodes Seminar Papers* (New Delhi: Congress for Cultural Freedom, 1959), p. 20.

38. Carlos Romulo quoted in Rossi, *op. cit.*, p. 67.

39. *Idem.*

40. See *Politics, Personality, and Nation Building: Burma's Search for Identity*, by Lucian Pye (New Haven, Conn.: Yale University Press, 1962).

41. Lionel Landry, "Book in the News," *Saturday Review of Literature*, Mar. 17, 1962, p. 22.

42. Asoka Mehta, "Opposition in the New States" in *Democracy in the New States, op. cit.*, p. 86.

43. Raghavan Iyer, "Strengthening Political Democracy" in *Ibid.*, p. 174.

44. Michael Edwardes, *Asia in the Balance* (Baltimore: Penguin Books, Inc., 1962), pp. 85, 86.

45. Nehru, *The Discovery of India*, excerpted in Sigmund, *op. cit.*, p. 102.

46. Nkrumah, quoted in "Africanism's Constitutional Malarkey" by Susan and Peter Ritner, *The New Leader*, June 10, 1963, p. 18.

47. Karim Kassem, "The Army and the Parties" in Sigmund, *op. cit.*, p. 118.

48. Sukarno, "Lecture to the Students of Hasanuddin University," in *ibid.*, p. 60.

49. Robert Heilbroner, *The Great Ascent* (New York: Harper and Row, Publishers, 1963), p. 158.

CHAPTER X

1. Michael Edwardes, *Asia in the Balance* (Baltimore: Penguin Books, Inc., 1962), pp. 78-80.
2. Richard Hughes, quoted in *Awakened China* by Felix Greene (Garden City, N.Y.: Doubleday & Company Inc., 1961), pp. 387-8.
3. A. J. Balfour, quoted in Edwardes, *op. cit.*, p. 79.
4. Susan and Peter Ritner, "Africanism's Constitutional Malarkey," *The New Leader*, June 10, 1963, p. 8.
5. Greene, *op. cit.*, p. 62.
6. See *Political Development in the New States* by Edward Shils (The Hague: Mouton and Co., 1962).
7. See *Mao Tse-tung* by George Paloczi-Horvath (Garden City, N.Y.: Doubleday and Company, Inc., 1963), for a detailed discussion of Mao's difficulties with Stalin and with various leaders of the Chinese Communist party.
8. Mao Tse-tung, *The Long March* (Peking: Foreign Language Press, 1958), p. 91.
9. Chang Po-chun, quoted in Paloczi-Horvath, *op. cit.*, p. 8.
10. *Current Affairs Handbook*, Peking, Feb. 25, 1952.
11. "The Chairman's Reports," *Current Background*, Hong Kong, No. 39, 1950.
12. "Report of the Free Trade Union Council of the A.F.L.," in Paloczi-Horvath, *op. cit.*, p. 241.
13. *Ibid.*, p. 254.
14. Sripati Chandra-Sekhar, *Red China* (New York: Frederick A. Praeger, Inc., 1961), p. 8.
15. *People's Daily*, Peking, Nov. 4, 1958.
16. Ko P'ei-ch'i, *People's Daily*, May 31, 1957.
17. Lo Lung-chi, New China News Agency release, Aug. 10, 1957.
18. Ke Yang, New China News Agency Release, July 26, 1957.
19. Hu Feng, *People's Daily*, Peking, May 13, 1955.
20. *Ibid.*
21. For a penetrating analysis of this issue, see C. K. Yang, *The Chinese Family in the Communist Revolution* (Cambridge, Mass.: Technology Press, 1959).
22. Quoted in Paloczi-Horvath, *op. cit.*, p. 4.
23. "General Report of the Peking Municipal People's Soviet," *Current Background*, Hong Kong, No. 72, p. 9.
24. New China News Agency release, Peking, July 26, 1955.
25. Amaury de Riencourt, *The Soul of China*, cited in Edwardes, *op. cit.*, p. 71.
26. Greene, *op. cit.*
27. Paloczi-Horvath, *op. cit.*, p. 294.
28. Chandra-Sekhar, *op. cit.*, pp. 6, 8.
29. *Ibid.*, p. 119.
30. Yuan-li Wu, *The Economic Development and Use of Energy Resources in Communist China* (Berkeley, Calif.: University of California Press, 1963).
31. Choh-Ming Li, *The Economic Development of Communist China* (Berkeley, Calif.: University of California Press, 1963).

32. Tibor Mende, *China and Her Shadow* (Bombay: Asia Publishing House, 1961), p. 261.

33. W. R. Geddes, *Peasant Life in Communist China*, The Society for Applied Anthropology, Monograph No. 6, 1963, Ithaca, New York.

34. Chandra-Sekhar, *op. cit.*, p. 119.

35. For the best comparisons of India and China see two articles: Wilfred Malenbaum, "India and China: Development Contrasts," *Journal of Political Economy*, LXIV, No. 1 (Feb. 1956); and Wilfred Malenbaum and Wolfgang Stopler, "Political Ideology and Economic Progress: the Basic Question," *World Politics*, Vol. XII, No. 3 (Apr., 1960).

36. Malenbaum and Stopler, *op. cit.*, cited in *Comparative Politics*, Roy Macridis and Bernard Brown, eds. (Homewood, Ill.: The Dorsey Press, 1961). p. 535.

37. See Mende, *op. cit.*, particularly pp. 260-3.

38. Greene, *op. cit.*, Appendix.

39. See Malenbaum and Stopler, *op. cit.*

40. Mende, *op. cit.*, p. 178.

41. Malenbaum and Stopler, *op. cit.*, pp. 537, 540.

42. Yuan Li Wu, *op. cit.*

43. Mende, *op. cit.*, p. 204.

44. Patrick O'Donovan, *The New Republic*, Dec., 1961.

45. Tawia Adamfio, "A Portrait of the Osagyefo, Dr. Kwame Nkrumah," quoted in *Ghana in Transition by David Apter* (New York: Atheneum Publishers, 1963), pp. 325-6.

46. *Ibid.*, p. 354.

47. Stanley Diamond, "Modern Africa: The Pains of Independence," *Dissent*, Spring, 1963.

48. Nkrumah, quoted in "Ghana: Background to Conflict," by Irving Markovitz, *Root and Branch*, No. 1 (1962), p. 63.

49. *Idem.*

50. Sidney Lens, "The Birth Pangs of Revolution," *The Progressive*, Dec. 1961, p. 35.

51. K. A. Gbedemah, *Economic Survey* (Accra: Government of Ghana, 1960), p. 16.

52. *West Africa*, Sept. 1, 1962, pp. 953-4. Also see "The Relation of Political Authority to Economic Development in Ghana: 1946-1962" by Bruce Ferguson (unpublished honors thesis, Stanford University).

53. Ferguson, *ibid.*

54. Lewis Coser, editorial, *Dissent*, Autumn, 1961, p. 162.

55. Guy Pauker, "The Military in Indonesia," in *The Role of the Military in Underdeveloped Countries*, John Johnson, ed. (Princeton, N.J.: Princeton University Press, 1962), p. 220.

56. Lucian Pye, "Southeast Asia" in *The Politics of the Developing Areas*, Gabriel A. Almond and James S. Coleman, eds. (Princeton, N.J.: Princeton University Press, 1960), p. 93.

57. See *Indonesia* by Jeanne Mintz (Princeton, N.J.: D. Van Nostrand Co., Inc., 1961), for a succinct summary of Indonesia's colonial history.

58. James Mossman, *Rebels in Paradise* (London: Jonathan Cape, Ltd., 1961), p. 35.

59. *Ibid.*, pp. 76, 77.
60. Guy Pauker, *op. cit.*, p. 185.
61. *Ibid.*, p. 220-21.
62. Susan and Peter Ritner, *op. cit.*, p. 19.
63. Edward Shils, "The Political Development of New States" in Johnson, *op. cit.*, p. 63.
64. Henry Kissinger, *The Necessity for Choice* (Garden City, N.Y.: Doubleday & Company, Inc., 1962), pp. 302, 303.

CHAPTER XI

1. Lord Acton, Introduction to the *Cambridge Modern History* (Cambridge: Cambridge University Press, 1898).
2. Hans Kohn, *The Age of Nationalism* (New York: Harper & Row, Publishers, 1962), p. 31.
3. See "The Value Patterns of Democracy: A Case Study in Comparative Analysis," by Seymour Lipset, *American Sociological Review*, Vol. XXVIII, No. 4 (Aug. 1963).
4. See *The Liberal Tradition in America* by Louis Hartz (New York: Harcourt, Brace & World, Inc., 1955).
5. David Potter, *People of Plenty* (Chicago: University of Chicago Press, 1955), Chapter 5.
6. Seymour Lipset, *Political Man* (Garden City, N.Y.: Doubleday & Company, Inc., 1960); see particularly Chapter 2.
7. Kalman Silvert, cited in *The Great Fear* by John Gerassi (New York: The Macmillan Company, 1963), p. 248.
8. Massimo Salvadori, *Liberal Democracy* (London: Pall Mall Press, 1958).
9. *Ibid.*, p. 64.
10. Lipset, "The Value Patterns of Democracy," *op. cit.*
11. See *Nationalism and Liberty: the Swiss Example* by Hans Kohn (London: George Allen & Unwin, 1956).
12. C. Wright Mills, *The Power Elite* (New York: Oxford University Press, Inc., 1956), pp. 259 and 260.
13. E. H. Carr, *The Twenty Years Crisis* (London: Macmillan & Co., Ltd., 1949), p. 80.
14. See *The Lonely Crowd* by David Reisman, Reoul Denny, and Nathan Glazer (New Haven, Conn.: Yale University Press, 1950).
15. Aristotle, "Politics" in *The Basic Works of Aristotle* (New York: Random House, 1941), pp. 1221-2.
16. See *Denmark* (Copenhagen: Royal Danish Ministry of Foreign Affairs, 1961), "History" by John Danstrup.
17. Montesquieu, *Spirit of Laws*, cited in Salvadori, *op. cit.*, p. 130.
18. Reinhard Bendix, "Concepts and Generalizations in Comparative Sociological Studies," *American Sociological Review*, Vol. XXVIII, No. 4 (Aug. 1963), pp. 534 and 535.
19. Lord Acton, manuscript notes, cited in Kohn, *op. cit.*, p. 45.
20. O. Awolowo, *Awo* (New York: Cambridge University Press, 1961), reprinted in *The Ideologies of the Developing Nations*, Paul Sigmund, ed. (New York: Frederick A. Praeger, Inc., 1962), p. 226.

CHAPTER XII

1. John Stuart Mill, quoted in *The Age of Nationalism* by Hans Kohn (New Yorker: Harper & Row, Publishers, 1962), p. 44.
2. Barbara Ward, *The Rich Nations and the Poor Nations* (London: Hamish Hamilton, 1962), p. 19.
3. For evidence that ancient traditions can coexist with economic change in today's developing countries, see Reinhard Bendix, "Concepts and Generalizations in Comparative Sociological Studies," *Transactions of the Fifth World Congress of Sociology* (Louvain: International Sociological Association, 1963).
4. Hans Morgenthau, "America and the World Revolution," *Commentary*, Oct. 1963.
5. See "Public Authority in a Developing Community: The Case of India," by Reinhard Bendix, *Archives Européenne de Sociologie*, Vol. IV (1963).
6. Asoka Mehta, "No Pre-ordained Path," *The Economic Weekly*, June 1960, pp. 855-9.
7. Ward, *op. cit.*, p. 136.
8. Asoka Mehta, "Can Asia Industrialize Democratically?" *Voices of Dissent* (New York: Grove Press, 1958), p. 256.
9. See *Prospects for Indian Development* by Wilfred Malenbaum (London: George Allen & Unwin, 1962).
10. Morgenthau, *op. cit.*
11. Sékou Touré, quoted in *West Africa*, July 22, 1961, p. 799.
12. Frederick the Great, quoted in "Africanism's Constitutional Malarkey," by Susan and Peter Ritner, *The New Leader*, June 10, 1963, p. 18.
13. Lord Acton, quoted in Kohn, *op. cit.*, p. 44.
14. Immanuel Wallerstein, "An Africanist's Reply," *The New Leader*, June 10, 1963, p. 22.
15. John Plamanetz, *On Alien Rule and Self-Government* (London: Longmans, Green & Company, Ltd., 1960), pp. 139-40.
16. Massimo Salvadori, *Liberal Democracy* (London: Pall Mall Press, 1958), p. 85.
17. See *Expectant Peoples*, K. H. Silvert, ed. (New York: Random House, 1963), pp. 19 and 428.
18. Chester Bowles, *The New York Times*, Nov. 16, 1963, p. 7.
19. Irving Markovitz, "Ghana: Background to Conflict," *Root and Branch* No. 1 (1962), p. 68.
20. Oscar Gass, "America and the World Revolution," *Commentary*, Oct. 1963.
21. Barbara Ward, *New Perspectives in Economic Development* (Oxford: Oxford Conference on Tensions in Development, 1961), p. 8.
22. Henry Kissinger, *The Necessity for Choice* (Garden City, N.Y.: Doubleday & Company, Inc., 1962), p. 329.

INTRODUCTORY BIBLIOGRAPHY

The flow of publications concerning developing countries has become so vast that no single listing can do justice to the literature. Indeed, some presses have published entire books which are simply bibliographies of writings on the problem of economic or political development. The following bibliography, then, is by no means exhaustive but includes only a selection of the more enlightening books.

JAMES ABEGGLEN, *The Japanese Factory* (New York: Free Press of Glencoe, Inc., 1958). Particularly valuable for its discussion of the social context of industrialization in Japan.

RICHARD ADAMS, *Social Change in Latin America Today* (New York: Random House, 1961). The best single collection of articles on South America.

A. N. AGARWALA and S. P. SINGH, *The Economics of Underdevelopment* (New York: Oxford University Press, Inc., 1958). A representative sample of some classical articles.

ROBERT ALEXANDER, *The Bolivian National Revolution* (New Brunswick, N.J.: Rutgers University Press, 1958). The best account of social change in Bolivia.

ROBERT ALEXANDER, *A Primer of Economic Development* (New York: The Macmillan Company, 1962). Perhaps the best introduction to the problem.

GABRIEL ALMOND and JAMES COLEMAN, *The Politics of Developing Areas* (Princeton, N.J.: Princeton University Press, 1960). An impressive attempt to put the politics of new nations in theoretical perspective.

DAVID APTER, *Ghana in Transition* (New York: Atheneum Publishers, 1963). An important work describing the processes of politics in Ghana.

OBAFEMI AWOLOWO, *Awo* (New York: Cambridge University Press, 1960). An autobiography by one of Africa's most important liberal leaders.

C. E. AYERS, *The Theory of Economic Progress* (New York: Shocken Books, 1962). A study of economic development and cultural change.

NNAMDI AZIKIWE, *Zik* (London: Cambridge University Press, 1961). Collected speeches of one of Africa's leading figures.

PAUL BARAN, *The Political Economy of Growth* (New York: Prometheus Paperback, Monthly Review Press, 1960). An eloquent defense of the Marxist view of economic development.

PETER BAUER and BASIL YAMEY, *The Economics of Underdeveloped Countries* (Chicago: University of Chicago Press, 1957). An incisive application of laissez-faire principles to the problems of development.

ROBERT BELLAH, *Tokugawa Religion* (New York: Free Press of Glencoe, Inc., 1957). Analyzes the basic values of ancient Japan.

MORROE BERGER, *The Arab World Today* (Garden City, N.Y.: Doubleday and Company, Inc., 1962). A comprehensive account of the contemporary situation.

ABRAM BERGSON, *Soviet Economic Growth* (Evanston, Ill.: Row Peterson Co., 1953). An authoritative discussion of the scope and reasons for Russia's industrial expansion.

JACQUES BERQUE, *Les Arabes d'hier à demain* (Paris: Editions du Seuil, 1960). Treats the problems of Middle Eastern states from the point of view of one of France's leading sociologists.

F. M. BOURRET, *Ghana: the Road to Independence* (Stanford, Calif.: Stanford University Press, 1960). An objective record of Ghana's political evolution.

WILLEM BRAND, *The Struggle for a Higher Standard of Living* (New York: Free Press of Glencoe, Inc., 1958). A standard work on economic development.

HENRY L. BRETTON, *Power and Stability in Nigeria* (New York: Frederick Praeger, Inc., 1962). An authoritative account of the strains of Nigeria's independence.

HARRISON BROWN, *The Challenge of Man's Future* (New York: The Viking Press, Inc., 1956). A distinguished biologist examines the technical potentialities for the globe's development.

NORMAN BUCHANAN and HOWARD ELLIS, *Approaches to Economic Development* (New York: The Twentieth Century Fund, 1955). A sober appraisal of economic history and the chances of achieving development in the contemporary world.

K. A. BUSIA, *The Challenge of Africa* (New York: Frederick A. Praeger, Inc., 1962). A discussion of Africa's past and future by the former leader of Ghana's opposition.

CLAUDE BUSS, *The Arc of Crisis* (Garden City, N.Y.: Doubleday & Company, Inc., 1961). A broad survey of contemporary Asia.

ROBERT CAMPBELL, *Soviet Economic Power* (Boston: Houghton Mifflin Company, 1960). A clearly written exposition of Russian economic growth.

GWENDOLYN CARTER, *African One-Party States* (Ithaca, N.Y.: Cornell University Press, 1962). A compilation of views concerning the evolution and nature of one-party systems.

GWENDOLYN CARTER, *Independence for Africa* (New York: Frederick A. Praeger, Inc., 1960). Delineates the forces behind Africa's drive for independence.

JESUÉ DE CASTRO, *The Geography of Hunger* (Boston: Little, Brown & Co., 1952). Explores the causes and consequences of starvation.

SRIPATI CHANDRA-SEKHAR, *Red China* (New York: Frederick A. Praeger, Inc., 1961). A recent appraisal of the Chinese situation by an Indian visitor.

CHOH-MING LI, *Economic Development of Communist China* (Berkeley, Calif.: University of California Press, 1958). One of the best descriptions of the early period of Chinese growth.

COLIN CLARK, *The Conditions of Economic Progress* (London: Macmillan & Co., Ltd., 1951). A major contribution to the theory of economic growth.

Congress for Cultural Freedom, Rhodes Seminar Papers, *Democracy in the New States* (New Delhi: 1959). A collection of important papers by Westerners and men from the developing countries.

Congress of Cultural Freedom, *Problems of Economic Growth* (New Delhi, 1958). Report of a conference of intellectuals and politicians on issues of economic development.

Council on World Tensions, *Restless Nations* (New York: Dodd, Mead & Co., 1962). An important report summarizing the views of world experts.

H. O. DAVIES, *Nigeria: The Prospects for Democracy* (London: Weidenfeld and Nicolson, 1961). A plea that Nigeria's culture provides a fertile base for democracy, if her leaders make sensible choices.

VERA MICHAELES DEAN, *The Nature of the Non-Western World* (New York: New American Library, 1957). A good introduction to the "revolution of rising expectations."

THEODORE DRAPER, *Castro's Revolution* (New York: Frederick A. Praeger, Inc., 1962). A critical account of shifts in Castro's policy.

CHARLES DREKMEIER, *Kingship and Community in Early India* (Stanford, Calif.: Stanford University Press, 1962). A brilliant discussion of the intellectual and cultural history of ancient India.

MICHAEL EDWARDES, *Asia in the Balance* (Baltimore: Penguin Books, Inc., 1962). A good introduction to Asian problems.

HOWARD ELLIS, *Economic Development for Latin America* (London: Macmillan & Co., Ltd., 1961). An excellent anthology of views about the prospects for Latin America.

GEORGE FOSTER, *Traditional Cultures and the Impact of Technological Change* (New York: Harper & Row, Publishers, 1962). Examines the cultural difficulties faced by those engaged in technical assistance work.

RAYMOND FROST, *The Backward Society* (London: Longmans, Green & Company, Ltd., 1961). A description of the requirements for economic progress, with special attention to problems of world trade.

KENNETH GALBRAITH, *Economic Development in Perspective* (Cambridge, Mass.: Harvard University Press, 1962). A lucidly written discussion of some problems of economic development by the former American ambassador to India.

WALTER GALENSON, *Labor in Developing Economies* (Berkeley, Calif.: University of California Press, 1962). A definitive analysis of labor in several developing countries.

JOHN GERASSI, *The Great Fear* (New York: The Macmillan Company, 1963). A biting analysis of South American problems and of the United States role in creating them.

PETER GOULD, *Africa: Continent of Change* (Belmont, Calif.: Wadsworth Publishing Co., 1961). An excellent anthology of articles.

FELIX GREENE, *Awakened China* (Garden City, N.Y.: Doubleday & Company, Inc., 1961). An eye-witness report on Communist China.

SIR PERCIVAL GRIFFITHS, *Modern India* (London: Ernest Benn, Ltd., 1957). A concise review of the history, current politics, and economic prospects of India.

EVERETT HAGAN, *On the Theory of Social Change* (Homewood, Ill.: The Dorsey Press, Inc., 1962). Presents an original theory of the way economic growth begins.

J. L. HAMMOND and BARBARA HAMMOND, *The Rise of Modern Industry* (New York: Harcourt, Brace & World, Inc., 1926). A descriptive account of the growth of industrialism.

SELIG HARRISON, *India: the Most Dangerous Decades* (Princeton, N.J.: Princeton University Press, 1960). An eloquently stated, if too pessimistic, view of political divisions within India.

LOUIS HARTZ, *The Liberal Tradition in America* (New York: Harcourt, Brace & World, Inc., 1955). A distinguished account of the origins of democracy in America.

ROBERT HEILBRONER, *The Future as History* (New York: Harper & Row, Publishers, 1959). A not too sanguine prophecy concerning the future of advanced and developing nations.

ROBERT HEILBRONER, *The Making of Economic Society* (Englewood Cliffs, N.J.: Prentice-Hall, Inc., 1962). Relates economic history to current problems of economic development.

SMITH HEMPSTONE, *The New Africa* (London: Faber & Faber, Ltd., 1961). A broad examination of the problems of tropical Africa.

BENJAMIN HIGGINS, *Economic Development* (London: Constable & Co., Ltd., 1959). A comprehensive source of information and guidance on the problem of economic development.

ALBERT HIRSCHMAN, *Latin American Issues* (New York: The Twentieth Century Fund, 1961). A series of essays on problems of economic development.

ALBERT HIRSCHMAN, *The Strategy of Economic Development* (New Haven, Conn.: Yale University Press, 1958). A hard-headed discussion of the merits of "unbalanced" economic growth.

PAUL HOFFMAN. *World Without Want* (New York: Harper & Row, Publishers, 1962). A helpful examination of the prospects for development by a distinguished U.N. expert.

CALVIN HOOVER, *The Economy, Liberty and the State* (Garden City, N.Y.: Doubleday & Company, Inc., 1961). A lucid analysis of the economic basis of freedom.

B. F. HOSELITZ and WILBERT MOORE, *Industrialization and Society* (Paris: UNESCO, 1963). Reports the results of a conference concerned with the social implications of technological change.

B. F. HOSELITZ, *Sociological Aspects of Economic Growth* (New York: Free

Press of Glencoe, Inc., 1960). A series of essays concerning the relation of social variables to the economy.

LEE HUBERMAN and PAUL SWEEZY, *Cuba: Anatomy of A Revolution* (New
York: Monthly Review Press, 1961). A good socialist defense of the Cuban
revolution.

GUY HUNTER, *The New Societies of Tropical Africa* (London: Oxford University Press, 1962). One of the very best summaries of the African situation.

ELSPETH HUXLEY, *A New Earth* (London: Chatto & Windus, Ltd., 1961).
A description of agricultural successes in Kenya and, in passing, a defense of
colonialism.

Indian Institute of Public Opinion, *Public Opinion Surveys*. One of the very
few sources of information on the specific attitudes of transitional men toward
public issues.

I. C. JACKSON, Advance in Africa (London: Oxford University Press, 1956).
A discussion of the advantages and mistakes of a community development
project in Nigeria.

CAROLINA MARIA DE JESUS, *Child of the Dark* (New York: E. P. Dutton &
Co., Inc., 1962). A poignant diary of the life of a Brazilian slum dweller.

JOHN JOHNSON, *Political Change in Latin America* (Stanford, Calif.: Stanford
University Press, 1958). A description of the emergence of middle-class politics.

JOHN JOHNSON, *The Role of the Military in Underdeveloped Countries*
(Princeton, N.J.: Princeton University Press, 1962). A symposium on the significant role of armed forces in the developing world.

GEORGE KIMBLE, *Tropical Africa* (Garden City, N.Y.: Doubleday & Company, Inc., 1962). An encyclopedia of information concerning Africa.

HENRY KISSINGER, *The Necessity for Choice* (Garden City, N.Y.: Doubleday
& Company, Inc., 1962). A critical essay on American foreign policy.

LILLIAN KNOWLES, *Economic Development in the Nineteenth Century* (London: Routledge & Kegan Paul, Ltd., 1932). A standard work on economic
change in several nations.

HANS KOHN, *The Age of Nationalism* (New York: Harper & Row, Publishers, 1962). A brilliant discussion of nationalism's past and its prospects in the
future.

HANS KOHN, *Nationalism and Liberty: the Swiss Example* (London: George
Allen & Unwin, 1956). A discussion of Switzerland, with great relevance to the
present world.

JEAN and SIMONE LACOUTURE, *L'Égypte en Mouvement* (Paris: Editions du
Geuil, 1962). The best book on the Egyptian revolution.

HARVEY LEIBENSTEIN, *Economic Backwardness and Economic Growth* (New
York: John Wiley & Sons, Inc., 1957). An important analysis of the conditions
of economic advance.

DANIEL LERNER, *The Passing of Traditional Society* (New York: Free Press of
Glencoe, Inc., 1958). Using empirical data from the Middle East, Lerner examines the relation of political development and such other variables as literacy, urbanization, and radio listening.

ARTHUR LEWIS, *The Theory of Economic Growth* (Homewood, Ill.: Richard
Irwin, 1955). A standard work by one of the world's experts on the issue.

OSCAR LEWIS, *Five Families* (New York: Science Editions, 1962). Records a
day in the life of five Mexican families drawn from different social classes.

OSCAR LEWIS, *Tepoztlán* (New York: Holt, Rinehart & Winston, Inc., 1960). An examination of social change in a Mexican village.

EDWIN LIEUWEN, *Arms and Politics in Latin America* (New York: Frederick A. Praeger, Inc., 1961). Lays bare the effect of American aid in building military dictatorships in South America.

SEYMOUR LIPSET, *Political Man* (Garden City, N.Y.: Doubleday & Company, Inc., 1960). A theoretical explanation of the social basis of democracy.

WILLIAM LOCKWOOD, *The Economic Development of Japan* (Princeton, N.J.: Princeton University Press, 1954). A good account of Japan's progress.

WILFRED MALENBAUM, *Prospects for Indian Development* (London: George Allen & Unwin, Ltd., 1962). A realistic evaluation of India's economic record and her future.

EDWARD MASON, *Economic Planning in Underdeveloped Areas* (New York: Fordham University Press, 1958). An examination of a crucial problem by an expert with wide practical experience.

DAVID McCLELLAND, *The Achieving Society* (Princeton, N.J.: D. Van Nostrand Co., Inc., 1961). An empirical, solid account of the relation between economic development and human motivation.

ASOKA MEHTA, *Democratic Socialism* (Bombay: Bhavan's Book University, 1959). An application of socialist principles to problems of development.

TIBER MENDE, *China and Her Shadow* (Bombay: Asia Publishing House. 1960). An objective evaluation of China.

MAX MILLIKAN and DONALD BLACKMER, *The Emerging Nations* (Boston: Little, Brown & Co., 1961). A group of M.I.T. experts come together to discuss American policy in relation to developing countries.

JEANNE MINTZ, *Indonesia* (Princeton, N.J.: D. Van Nostrand Co., Inc., 1961). A brief introduction to the history and current status of Indonesia.

LOIS MITCHISON, *Nigeria: Newest Nation* (London: Pall Mall Press, 1960). An introduction to the economy and polity of Nigeria.

JOHN D. MONTGOMERY, *The Politics of Foreign Aid* (New York: Frederick A. Praeger, Inc., 1962). Dissects foreign aid policy and its effects, real or imagined, on developing countries.

FRANK MORAES, *India Today* (New York: The Macmillan Company, 1960). An examination of India's history and current tensions by one of her leading journalists.

JAMES MOSSMAN, *Rebels in Paradise* (London: Jonathan Cape, Ltd., 1961). One of the few objective reports of rebellions against Sukarno.

GUNNAR MYRDAL, *Rich Lands and Poor* (New York: Harper & Row, Publishers, 1957). A scholarly discussion of the relation between industrialized and developing countries.

KUSSUM NAIR, *Blossoms in the Dust* (London: Gerald Duckworth & Co., Ltd., 1961). A brillian revelation of the problems confronting community development in India.

ALEC NOVE, *The Soviet Economy* (New York: Frederick A. Praeger, Inc., 1961). Traces the successes and wastes of Soviet economic policies.

RAGNAR NURKSE, *Problems of Capital Formation in Underdeveloped Countries* (New York: Oxford University Press, Inc., 1953). One of the first systematic treatments of the problem by the best-known exponent of "balanced growth."

NORMAN PALMER, *The Indian Political System* (Boston: Houghton Mifflin Company, 1961). A concise description of India's government and her experiment with democratic planning.

GEORGE PALOCZI-HORVATH, *Mao Tse-Tung* (Garden City, N.Y.: Doubleday & Company, Inc., 1963). An objective account of the personality and politics of China's leader.

K. M. PANIKKAR, *In Defense of Liberalism* (Bombay: Asia Publishing House, 1962). An account of liberal doctrines and their importance in Indian history.

JOHN PLAMENATZ, *On Alien Rule and Self-Government* (London: Longmans, Green & Company, Ltd., 1960). An eloquent essay on the problems of colonialization and decolonialization.

Proceedings of the World Population Conference (New York: United Nations, 1954). Informed discussions of population issues.

LUCIAN PYE, *Politics, Personality, and Nation-Building* (New Haven, Conn.: Yale University Press, 1962). An interesting discussion of the role of identity among national leaders, with special emphasis on Burma.

ROBERT REDFIELD, *Peasant Society and Culture* (Chicago: University of Chicago Press, 1956). A classic exposition of the basic values held by peasants.

HENRY ROSOVSKY, *Capital Formation in Japan* (New York: Free Press of Glencoe, Inc., 1961). A technical discussion of capital accumulation.

MARIO ROSSI, *The Third World* (New York: Funk and Wagnalls Co., 1963). A description of the attitudes of unaligned countries and a plea for world cooperation.

W. W. ROSTOW, *The Stages of Economic Growth* (London: Cambridge University Press, 1906). A provocative theory of the steps toward economic affluence.

NADAV SAFRAN, *Egypt in Search of Political Community* (Cambridge, Mass.: Harvard University Press, 1962). An analysis of the intellectual and political development of Egypt during the last 150 years.

MASSIMO SALVADORI, *Liberal Democracy* (London: Pall Mall Press, 1958). A defense of liberal principles in the tradition of John Stuart Mill.

KARL SAX, *The World's Exploding Population* (Boston: Beacon Press, 1960). An urgent plea for birth control.

JOSEPH SCHUMPETER, *The Theory of Economic Development* (Cambridge, Mass.: Harvard University Press, 1959). A classic analysis of the role of the entrepreneur in the development of capitalism.

ANDREW SHONFIELD, *The Attack on World Poverty* (London: Chatto and Windus, Ltd., 1961). Considers measures which would quicken the pace of economic development.

K. H. SILVERT, *Expectant Peoples* (New York: Random House, 1963). An examination of the role of nationalism in many new nations.

PAUL SIGMUND, *Ideologies of Developing Nations* (New York: Frederick A. Praeger, Inc., 1963). Collects the differing points of view of leaders in emerging countries.

NEIL SMELSER, *Social Change in the Industrial Revolution* (Chicago: University of Chicago Press, 1959). A sophisticated discussion of historical change.

THOMAS SMITH, *The Agrarian Origins of Modern Japan* (Stanford, Calif.: Stanford University Press, 1959). A scholarly analysis of agricultural change in Japan.

WILFRED CANTWELL SMITH, *Islam in Modern History* (New York: New American Library, 1957). An introduction to the development of the Moslem World.

HUGH SMYTHE and MABEL SMYTHE, *The New Nigerian Elite* (Stanford, Calif.: Stanford University Press, 1960). Exposes the attitudes and way of life of Nigeria's ruling class.

HERBERT SPIRO, *Politics in Africa* (Englewood Cliffs, N.J.: Prentice-Hall, Inc., 1962). An examination of new African political systems.

M. N. SRINIVAS, *India's Villages* (Bombay: Asia Publishing House, 1960). A number of anthropological experts on India examine village life.

EUGENE STALEY, *The Future of Underdeveloped Countries* (New York: Harper & Row Publishers, 1961). A warning that economic development will not bring democracy spontaneously in its wake.

FRANK TANNENBAUM, *Ten Keys to Latin America* (New York: Alfred A. Knopf, Inc., 1962). A general discussion of the major factors affecting Latin America.

ROBERT THEOBALD, *The Rich and the Poor* (New York: New American Library, 1961). A study of the economics of rising expectations.

COLIN TURNBULL, *The Lonely African* (New York: Simon and Schuster, Inc., 1962). Brilliantly written, the book captures the nostalgia of transitional men in the Congo.

ROY TURNER, *India's Urban Future* (Berkeley, Calif.: University of California Press, 1962). An important anthology concerned with the causes and effects of Indian urban growth.

UNITED NATIONS, *Processes and Problems of Industrialization in Underdeveloped Countries*, 1955. An objective report by a team of U.N. experts.

EGBERT DE VRIES, *Man in Rapid Social Change* (Garden City, N.Y.: Doubleday and Company, Inc., 1961). Presents the results of a World Council of Churches study of social change in developing countries.

IMMANUEL WALLERSTEIN, *Africa, the Politics of Independence* (New York: Vintage Books, 1961). An essay on the emergence of new nations in Africa.

HENRY WALLICH, *The Cost of Freedom* (New York: Collier Books, 1962). A study of the relation between economic efficiency and liberty.

BARBARA WARD, *India and the West* (London: Hamish Hamilton, 1961). Written with compassion and good sense, an analysis of India's economic situation and the obligations of the West.

BARBARA WARD, *Five Ideas that Change the World* (London: Hamish Hamilton, 1958). A discussion of the political themes dominant in today's world.

BARBARA WARD, *The Rich Nations and the Poor Nations* (London: Hamish Hamilton, 1962). A brilliant discussion of the prospects for democratic development.

DOUGLAS WARNER, *Ghana and the New Africa* (London: Frederick Muller, Ltd., 1960). A lively account of the vicissitudes of new nationhood.

ALBERT WATERSTON, *Planning in Yugoslavia* (Baltimore: Johns Hopkins University Press, 1962). An objective report on the organization and implementation of planning in one nation.

MAX WEBER, *The Protestant Ethic and the Spirit of Capitalism* (New York: Charles Scribner's Sons, 1956). A famous discussion of the relation between religion and economic change.

JACK WODDIS, *Africa: the Roots of the Revolt* (London: Lawrence and Wishart, 1960). A Marxist explanation of African problems.

MYRON WEINER, *Politics of Scarcity* (Chicago: University of Chicago Press, 1962). Examines the operation of interest groups in India and cautions Indian leaders not to seek unity at the cost of destroying these groups.

W. F. WERTHEIM, *Indonesian Society in Transition* (Bandung: Sumur Bandung, 1956). A study of social change.

RICHARD WRIGHT, *Black Power* (New York: Harper & Row, Publishers, 1954). A penetrating account of Ghana's move toward independence by an American Negro author.

NELLY XYDIAS, *Social Implications of Industrialization and Organization in Africa South of the Sahara* (Paris: UNESCO, 1956). An objective report on urbanization and industrialization in the Congo.

INDEX